# KINGS & QUEENS
## *of England & Great Britain*

# KINGS & QUEENS
## *of England & Great Britain*

*Eric R. Delderfield*

**David & Charles**

# ACKNOWLEDGEMENTS

The illustrations in this book are reproduced by kind permission of the following:
Hulton Picture Library (pages 114, 127, 132, 139, 143, 148, 152, 155), The Mansell
Collection (pages 129 and 137), The National Trust Photographic Library,
photographer Bryan S. Evans (page 83), The Telegraph Colour Library (pages 159,
162, 163, 166, 167, 170, 175, 178) and the Tim Graham Picture Library (pages 171,
178, 179, 183). All the remaining illustrations are reproduced by courtesy of the
National Portrait Gallery, London. The genealogical trees and maps (of Saxon England
and Modern Britain) were designed and drawn by Ethan Danielson, EDANART.

A catalogue record for this book
is available from the British Library

ISBN 0-7153-0265-5

KINGS AND QUEENS OF ENGLAND AND GREAT BRITAIN was published for the first time
in 1990 ; based on the work of Eric Delderfield and Anthony Lambert. Some text material was drawn from earlier
works by Eric Delderfield.

Typeset in Garamond ITC by
ABM Typographics Limited, Hull.
and printed in Germany
by Mohndruck Gmbh
for David & Charles plc
Brunel House  Newton Abbot  Devon

# CONTENTS

# LIST OF ILLUSTRATIONS

# THE DYNASTIES

There have been about sixty-six monarchs of England spread over a period of about 1,150 years. These men and women have represented the following dynasties:

Saxons
Normans
Plantagenets
House of Lancaster
House of York

Tudors
Stuarts
Hanoverians
Saxe-Coburgs
Windsors

# PART ONE

# SAXONS, NORMANS,

# PLANTAGENETS

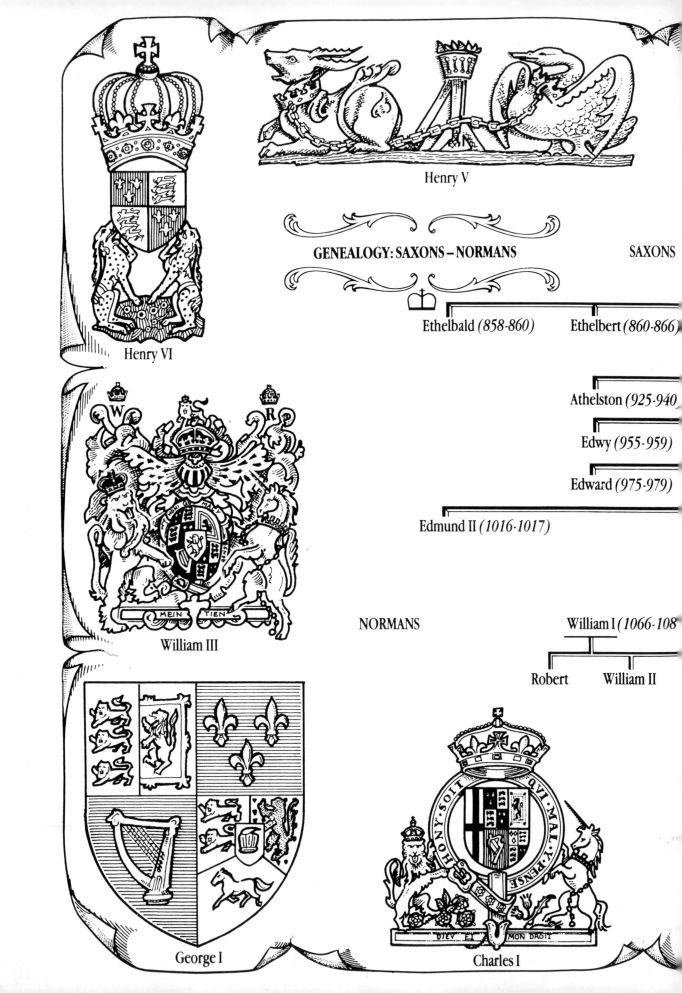

Henry V

**GENEALOGY: SAXONS – NORMANS**

SAXONS

Ethelbald *(858-860)*     Ethelbert *(860-866)*

Athelston *(925-940)*

Edwy *(955-959)*

Edward *(975-979)*

Edmund II *(1016-1017)*

Henry VI

William III

NORMANS     William I *(1066-108*

Robert     William II

George I

Charles I

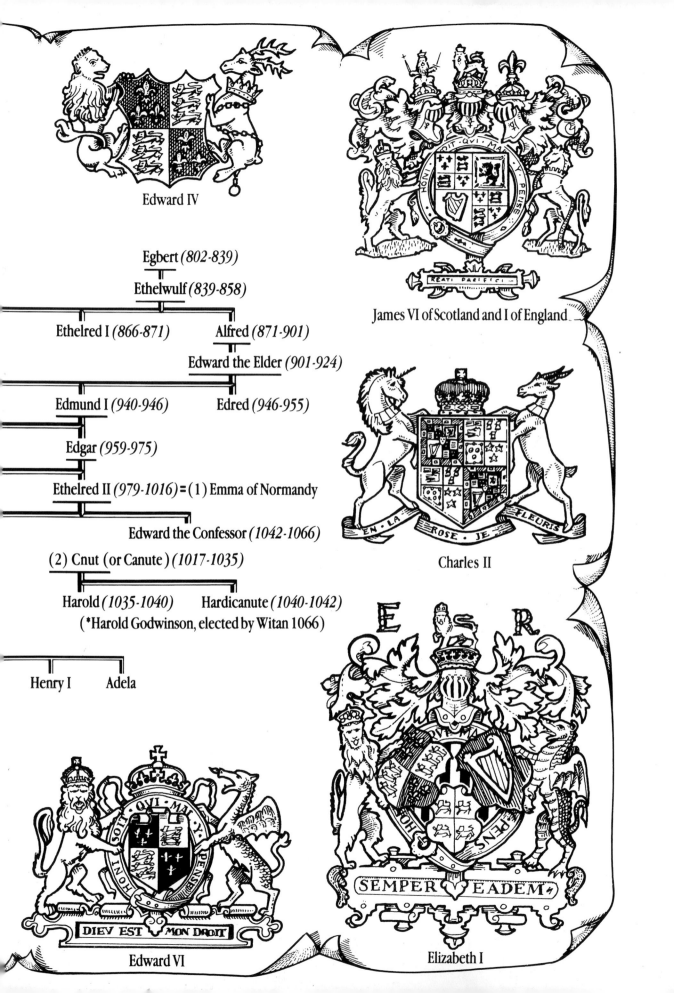

Edward IV

Egbert *(802-839)*

Ethelwulf *(839-858)*

Ethelred I *(866-871)*         Alfred *(871-901)*

Edward the Elder *(901-924)*

Edmund I *(940-946)*         Edred *(946-955)*

Edgar *(959-975)*

Ethelred II *(979-1016)* = (1) Emma of Normandy

Edward the Confessor *(1042-1066)*

(2) Cnut (or Canute) *(1017-1035)*

Harold *(1035-1040)*    Hardicanute *(1040-1042)*
(*Harold Godwinson, elected by Witan 1066)

Henry I    Adela

James VI of Scotland and I of England

Charles II

Edward VI

Elizabeth I

# PRE-CONQUEST KINGS

## Saxon Kings

**EGBERT:** ascended throne 802. Reigned 37 years. Died 839.

**ETHELWULF:** ascended throne 839. Reigned 19 years. (Son of Egbert.) Died 858. Buried Winchester.

**ETHELBALD:** ascended throne 858. Reigned 2 years. (2nd son of Ethelwulf. Married father's widow.) Died 860. Buried Sherborne.

**ETHELBERT:** ascended throne 860. Reigned 6 years. (3rd son of Ethelwulf.) Died 866. Buried Sherborne.

**ST ETHELRED I:** ascended throne 866. Reigned 5 years. (4th son of Ethelwulf.) Died 871. Buried Wimborne.

**ALFRED:** born c.848. Ascended throne 871. Reigned 28 years. (5th son of Ethelwulf.) Died 899, aged 51. Buried Winchester.

**EDWARD THE ELDER:** ascended throne 899. Reigned 26 years. (Son of Alfred.) Died 925. Buried Winchester.

**ATHELSTAN:** born 895. Ascended throne 925. Reigned 14 years. Died 939. Buried Malmesbury.

**EDMUND I:** born ?922. Ascended throne 939. Reigned 7 years. Died 946 (assassinated). Buried Glastonbury.

**EADRED:** ascended throne 946. Reigned 9 years. Died 955. Buried Winchester.

**EDWY:** born 940. Ascended throne 955. Reigned 4 years. Died 959, aged 19. Buried Winchester.

**EDGAR:** born 944. Ascended throne 959. Reigned 16 years. Died 975, aged 31. Buried Glastonbury.

**EDWARD THE MARTYR:** born c.962. Ascended throne 975. Reigned 4 years. Died 978, aged 16 (assassinated). Buried (i) Wareham (ii) Shaftesbury.

**ETHELRED II:** born ?968. Ascended throne 978. Reigned 38 years. Died 1016, aged 48. Buried St Paul's, London.

**EDMUND II:** born ?988. Ascended throne 1016. Reigned 6 months. Died 1016, aged 47. Buried St Paul's, London.

**EDWARD THE CONFESSOR:** born c.1002-1007. Ascended throne 1042. Reigned 24 years. Died 1066. Buried Westminster Abbey, London.

**HAROLD II:** born ?1022. Ascended throne 1066. (Brother-in-law of Edward the Confessor.) Reigned 10 months. Died 1066, aged ?44. Burial place unknown, possibly Waltham Abbey.

# Danish Kings

**CNUT** (or **CANUTE**): born c.995. Ascended throne 1016. Reigned 19 years. Died 1035, aged 40. Buried Winchester.

**HAROLD I:** born 1017. Ascended throne 1035. Reigned 5 years. Died 1040, aged 23. Buried St Clement Danes, London.

**HARTHACNUT:** born 1018. Ascended throne 1040. Reigned 2 years. Died 1042, aged 24. Buried Winchester.

# Saxon Kings

The Roman occupation of England left surprisingly little mark on the future. In France and Spain the effects of centuries of rule from Rome were of much greater significance: the very language of these countries is descended from the tongue of their conquerors. But in Britain most of what the Romans did perished or fell into disuse after they left. The Kingdom's language and institutions are Saxon. It is therefore with the Saxons that the continuous history of England begins.

The onset of invasion by Angles, Saxons and Jutes, sea-rovers from the shores of Germany and Frisia, began about the middle of the fourth century. The Saxon conquest of England was completed within the course of the next century and a half. As bands of Saxons settled in England, so 'Kings' became general. The word itself, 'Cyning', is probably connected with 'kin', indicating that the man stood at the head of his kindred or tribe. Kings were, then, mere tribal chieftains in origin.

By about AD 600 ten separate, but not necessarily independent kingdoms, had been established, the majority south of the Humber. The importance of seven of these kingdoms – Wessex, Sussex, Kent, Essex, East Anglia, Mercia and Northumbria – has given to the next two centuries the title of the Heptarchy.

Gradually three of the seven – Wessex, Mercia and Northumbria – began to establish some sort of domination over their smaller neighbours. Although the supremacy of individual kingdoms was usually short-lived, yet the very fact that from the late sixth century to the early ninth century they were at least subject to one common overlord, was an important influence in achieving the eventual unity of England.

Another vital factor making for unity was the appearance of Christianity in England in AD 597. Thereafter the spread of Christianity and changes of overlordship follow almost the same course. Following the death in 616 of the King of Kent, supremacy passed, along with Christianity, to Northumbria until about 685.

Mercia, which had also put aside heathen practices, filled the position left by the decline of Northumbria, almost until the end of the eighth century. But the death in 796 of Offa, perhaps the greatest of all Saxon kings save Alfred, was followed by another southerly shift of political power.

### First King of England

At the battle of Ellandun, thought to have been near Winchester, in 825, Mercia's supremacy was broken by **EGBERT,** 802–839, King of Wessex. Mercia was temporarily annexed in 828 and Egbert's lordship recognized by Northumbria, prompting some historians to claim that Egbert may be regarded as the first King of England, though he did not assume that style. But his hold over the vassal kingdoms was tentative: no garrisoned forts or standing armies secured his position in them, and it took only a year for Wiglaf, King of Mercia, 827–838, to reassert Mercian independence.

The lack of any developed institutions or structure made the personal qualities of the king of paramount importance. It was the threat from across the North Sea that was to test the leadership and resilience of Saxon kings; all but the West Saxon kings were to be found wanting. The first Viking raid occurred towards the end of the eighth century, landing on the coast of Wessex, though it was not until 866 that the Viking incursions began that would bring the kingdoms of Northumbria, East Anglia and Mercia to their knees. Only Wessex stood between the Vikings and the total conquest of England; it was due to the determination of Egbert's grandsons and successive kings of Wessex that they were foiled in this objective.

Previous efforts to unite England had failed because as soon as one kingdom became great it was in the interest of the rest to pull it down. England lacked the strongest possible motive towards union, namely the presence of a foreign foe. As the West Saxon kings evicted the Danes from the other Anglo-Saxon kingdoms, their extended power brought in prospect a single king ruling over a united England.

### West Saxon Kings

The outline story of the Saxon kings which follows is, then, the story of the West Saxon kings. The period from Egbert to Edgar, covering the best part of two centuries, was the golden age of the Saxon monarchy. But the next ninety years or so, to the time of the Norman Conquest, bring the story of one calamity after another: of the inability of the later Saxon kings to preserve England from Danish ravages; of the accession of weak kings like Ethelred and Edward the Confessor; and finally of the Norman Conquest itself.

Egbert died in 839, leaving a son **ETHELWULF,** 839–858. (His reign is chiefly known for the periods of bad weather connected with the name of his saintly advisor, Swithun.) He left behind him four sons: **ETHELBALD**, 858–860; **ETHELBERT**, 860–866; **ETHELRED I**, 866–871; and **ALFRED**, 871–899.

**ALFRED OF WESSEX,** perhaps the most famous of all England's kings, was born in 849 at Wantage in Berkshire and taken to Rome in 853. He came to the throne in 871.

The Danes had become settlers in eastern England during the middle of the ninth century, had conquered most of England and were pushing southwards into Wessex. In 871 the West Saxons fought nine battles against the Danes, at all of which Alfred was second-in-command. In the middle of the year his elder brother, Ethelred I, died. The twenty-two-year-old Alfred had won the confidence of the army and he was chosen king by the Witan (the council of the Anglo-Saxon kings). The victory at Ashdown, fought just before Alfred's accession, provided some respite from Viking incursions, but in 878 came the major crisis of his life. Guthrum, king of the Danes of East Anglia, burst into Wessex in mid-winter, compelling Alfred to seek refuge amidst the island fastnesses of the Somerset marshes. Having established a stronghold at Athelney, Alfred marshalled his forces, summoning the thegns of Wiltshire and Hampshire to rejoin his banner. It was while Alfred was at Athelney that he is said to have 'burned the cakes'. A Danish force landed at Alfred's rear and was defeated by the thegns of Devon, and in May 878 Alfred emerged to defeat the Danes at Edington in Wiltshire. In one of the pivotal battles in English history, Alfred prevented the Viking domination of England, winning such a victory that at the peace of Wedmore, Guthrum agreed to be christened.

For the next decade Alfred consolidated his hold over Wessex, created a navy and sent a fleet against the Danes of East Anglia in 884, taking London in 886. A treaty with Guthrum fixed Watling Street, the Great Ouse and the River Lea from its source as the southern boundary of Danelaw, leaving London to the English king. A period of respite enabled Alfred to turn his attention to the arts of peace, for which he showed as much aptitude as his martial skills. Alfred's varied accomplishments have led to the comparison with Charlemagne, whose scale of operation may have been larger but who never forged a united and permanent kingdom as did Alfred and his descendants.

Alfred created many fortified towns, some on old Roman sites, some on new ones; in all he founded some twenty-five towns, or about one-third the number founded by the Romans in three and a half centuries. Viking raids had destroyed libraries and even disrupted the passing on of religious knowledge and forms, leaving a clergy that no longer understood the meaning of the Latin mass they sang. He set aside a half of all revenue to be spent on educational needs; established schools where the sons of the nobility could be taught to read and write; brought in foreign scholars and craftsmen; restored monasteries and convents. He helped to design houses, invented a candle clock, mastered Latin and translated many books into Anglo-Saxon, including Boethius' *Consolation of Philosophy* and histories of Bede and Orosius. He ordered the compilation of the first English history book, the *Anglo-Saxon Chronicle*, which was continued for more than two centuries after his death. He published a collection of laws and enforced them, so that when troubles came after his death, 'men longed for the laws of King Alfred'. Had Alfred never fought a battle, he would still deserve a place among the greatest rulers of history.

Alfred the Great died in 899. The next three generations of kings were, with one exception, strong in the tradition of Alfred.

**EDWARD THE ELDER**, 899–925, son of Alfred, continued the work of his father and began the reconquest of Danelaw. In 910 he defeated the Danes of Northumbria at Tettenhall in Staffordshire, and spent much of the next decade struggling to clear them from Lincoln, Derby, Nottingham, Stamford and Leicester. Forts to secure the English frontier were built by Edward at Rhuddlan, Thelwall and Manchester. By the end of his reign he exercised authority over all Danish lands as far north as the Humber. A permanent union with Mercia was established in 918–19 and he developed an administrative framework for the kingdom of England. In this respect Edward the Elder is the first monarch who may be justly described as King of England. Though twice married, Edward's eldest son and successor was born of a mistress.

**ATHELSTAN**, 924–939, was crowned King of the West Saxons and Mercians at Kingston-upon-Thames in 924. He never lost a battle, conquering part of Cornwall, Wales and Northumbria and defeating an alliance of Welsh, Scots and Danes at Brunanburh in 937. He was the first king to have extensive contact with foreign monarchs, on religious and cultural matters as well as the negotiation of royal marriages. His religious devotion expressed itself in collecting quantities of relics and in neither marrying nor fathering any children. After a tireless life, he chose to be the first and last monarch to be buried at Malmesbury in Wiltshire, in preference to the usual mausoleum at Winchester.

Athelstan was succeeded by his half-brother, **EDMUND I**, 939–946, who further eroded Danelaw, reconquering Danish Mercia in 944. He also overran the kingdom of St Strathclyde and Cumbria before being killed by an outlaw at Pucklechurch in Gloucestershire. Edmund's brother **EADRED**, 946–955, succeeded him, and is best remembered for his defeat of a challenge to West Saxon supremacy from Eric Bloodaxe, King of York, who attempted to rid Northumbria of southern dominance. Expelled by Eadred in 948, Eric returned to fight for Northumbrian independence, but was again defeated, at Stainmore in 954. By the end of his reign Eadred was king of all England.

Eadred's nephew **EDWY** (or **EADWIG**), 955–959, accomplished little, being only fifteen when he ascended the throne. His reign was marked by his animosity towards his uncle's treasurer, Dunstan, whom he banished; Dunstan was later to become Archbishop of Canterbury during the reign of Edgar. A measure of the lack of confidence in which Edwy was held is given by the Northumbrians and Mercians renouncing their allegiance to him in favour of his brother **EDGAR**, 959–975. Known as 'The Peaceable', Edgar's reign was spared Viking invasions, and he even began to employ Danish subjects. His policy was shaped by Dunstan whose respected position helped Edgar's reputation amongst European rulers. New elements in monastic pageantry were introduced by him, his coronation at Bath emulating that of his kinsman, Otto the Great, as German

16

emperor. Edgar's Queen, Aelfthryth, was annointed at his side, recognizing the growing political role played by English queens. When seven British, Scottish and Welsh kings came to Chester to submit formally to Edgar, they purportedly rowed him on the River Dee. Though almost certainly apocryphal, the story reflects the dominance of the erstwhile West Saxon kings.

The story of Saxon downfall begins ominously with the murder of **EDWARD THE MARTYR**, 975–978. The son of Edgar, Edward encountered opposition to his claim to the throne from supporters of his younger half-brother Aethelred. It was while visiting Aethelred at Corfe Castle in Dorset that Edward was murdered; his step-mother, Aelfthryth, is suspected of having a hand in the affair so that her favoured son **AETHELRED II 'THE UNREADY'** ('devoid of foresight'), 978–1016, could become king. His reign was beset by a renewal of Viking raids, of a ferocity unknown since Alfred's time. Powerless to defeat the invaders, Aethelred resorted to buying off the Danes with silver (Danegeld) which only encouraged further raids. On St Brice's Day, 13 November 1002, he ordered the massacre of Danes resident in England, a treachery prompting a retaliatory invasion of 1003 under Sweyn, son of the Danish king. Sweyn's military successes so eroded support for Aethelred that he could no longer rely upon the nobility or the army, compelling him to flee to Normandy in 1013. (In 1002 he had established the first link with Normandy by marrying Duke Richard's daughter Emma.) Sweyn's death in 1014 enabled Aethelred to return, but he was deprived of half the kingdom by his son Edmund who made himself ruler in Danelaw.

On the death of his father in London in 1016, **EDMUND IRONSIDE**, 1016, was chosen king by the Londoners. The Witan in Southampton had other ideas and elected a Dane, Cnut, the son of Sweyn. After a series of battles, and despite the victory of Cnut at Ashingdon in Essex, a compromise was reached whereby Cnut would rule Mercia and Northumbria, while Edmund would hold Wessex; the survivor would succeed to the whole. Cnut did not have to wait long; within a few weeks Edmund was dead, and his sons had fled to Hungary.

After a brutal start to his reign, **CNUT** (or **CANUTE**), 1016–1035, developed into a temperate and devout ruler who adopted English ideas, gradually replaced Danish earls with native Englishmen and married Emma, the widow of Aethelred. His only military campaign was in Scotland where, despite a Scots' victory at Carham in 1018, he compelled the Scottish king to submit. His support for monasteries and churches was reflected in his pilgrimage to Rome in 1027-8, which strengthened ties with the Pope. The famous story related by Henry of Huntingdon about the king getting his feet wet was reputedly an aspect of his Christian humility, to demonstrate to his sycophantic nobles that even he could not halt the waves. Towards the end of his reign he alienated his links with Scandinavia, and his choice of Winchester as a final resting place confirmed his sense of identity with the country whose monarchy he had replaced.

The illegitimate elder son of Cnut, **HAROLD I**, 1035–1040, exploited the preoccupation of his half-brother, Harthacnut, with affairs in Denmark to seize the throne that Cnut had intended for his younger son. By the time **HARTHACNUT**, 1040–1042, returned to England, he found Harold dead and himself chosen king. None the less, the kingdom he inherited was already more fragmented than it had been under his father, and his short reign was marked by the persecution of Harold's supporters rather than attempting to further his father's policies.

The weakness of **EDWARD THE CONFESSOR**, 1042–1066, contributed to his failure to unite England, prompting Norman intervention and bringing to an end the old line of Anglo-Saxon kings. Though born at Islip in Oxfordshire, Edward spent much of his childhood in Normandy. At heart he was more a French monk than an English king and had little interest in secular affairs. Edward's accession was engineered largely by Godwin, Earl of Wessex, whose daughter Edward reluctantly married. It was to balance the power of Godwin that Edward introduced Normans into Church and State offices. Though Godwin was briefly banished, he returned with popular support for his stand against Norman influence, in a position to impose terms upon Edward. After Godwin's death in the following year, his influence passed to his son Harold, whose power in the south enabled him to exploit the uncertainty over the succession; that he did this despite an oath he made to Duke William of Normandy to support his claim to the throne, gave William the moral high ground in the eyes of many in Europe, notwithstanding the fact that the oath was extracted under duress. When Edward died at his new palace in Westminster, built so that he could be close to the abbey he had founded, Edmund Ironside's grandson, Edgar the Aetheling, was nearest heir. But he was only a boy, and fear of anarchy if a minor ascended the throne made the Witan choose Harold, who may have been named by Edward on his deathbed. However, Harold's weak claim to the throne encouraged both Norway and Normandy to attempt the conquest of England.

After his hasty coronation, **HAROLD II**, 1066, spent his brief reign largely sword in hand. Harold's own brother, Tostig, in alliance with Harald Hadrada, King of Norway, landed in the north. Marching south they camped at Stamford Bridge, to the east of York, where Harold surprised them and both were slain in the defeat of their army. Four days later William landed at Pevensey in Sussex. Harold and his mounted infantry headed south, reaching London in four days. Rather than wait for the unmounted infantry from the north and a force from the south west to join him, Harold decided to give battle at once. Fought 7 miles north west of Hastings, the battle* lasted all day and was close-run; only when a feint by the Normans induced the English to abandon their

*Our information about William's relations with Harold, his invasion preparations and the actual Battle of Hastings, is derived from the Bayeux Tapestry. This strip of canvas, many yards long and half a yard wide, is embroidered with detailed scenes – the first 'strip cartoon' – and is now in the Bayeux Museum, Normandy.

shield-ring and Harold was killed by an arrow through his eye did the invaders gain the upper hand. Harold's defeat ushered in an age that would leave none in doubt that England had become an occupied country.

# The Norman Conquest

It is not easy, if possible at all, to isolate and define the heritage of the Norman Conquest. For half a century before 1066 England and Normandy had been drawing closer together. Edward the Confessor himself was more Norman than English. Norman speech, habits and customs were prevalent at his court. But in the century after 1066 the followers and descendants of William the Conqueror diverted the main stream of national development and added a Latin strain to the mongrel blood of Englishmen.

Had the Conquest never happened, England would probably have become part of the northern Scandinavian world. For all its cruelty the Conquest united England to western Europe and opened the floodgates of European culture and institutions, theology, philosophy and science.

The Conquest effected a social revolution in England. The lands of the Saxon aristocracy were divided up amongst the Normans, who by c.1087 composed between 6,000 and 10,000 of a total population of about one and a half million. More important, each landowner had, in return for his land, to make an oath of allegiance to the king, and promise to provide him with mounted, armoured knights when required. The introduction of the 'feudal system', a system of land-holding in return for military obligations, provided the whole basis for medieval English society.

The Saxon machinery of government was, in large measure, retained and immensely reinforced, with a Norman monarch and the officials of his household as effective centralized controllers. Royal power was delegated in the provinces, so that government became less capricious: rebellion from Saxon or Norman was crushed with rough but equal justice. Royal justice was not only done but seen to be done. As well as giving the law a reputation for impartiality, the Normans brought with them their military arts – castle-building and fighting on horseback. They revolutionized English ecclesiastical architecture – witness Durham, Winchester, Ely and St Albans, with their rounded archways and doorways – introducing a standard plan for the great churches, and providing a point of departure for English medieval church architecture.

The Normans also transmitted large parts of the Saxon heritage – towns and villages, shires, traditions of monarchy, the basic structure of its language. They inherited a going, but run-down concern. They took over much that was indigenous and learnt from the conquered. They created a strong monarchy which, in medieval times, was gradually to complete the unification of England and obliterate the distinction between Saxons and conquering Normans, so that only Englishmen remained.

# THE NORMAN KINGS
## William I (The Conqueror)

*Born Falaise 1027. Ascended throne 1066. Reigned 21 years.*
*Illegitimate son of Duke Robert the Magnificent and a tanner's daughter.*
*Married Matilda of Flanders.*
*Four sons, five daughters.*
*Died Rouen 1087, aged 60 years. Buried St Stephen's, Caen, Normandy.*

William became Duke of Normandy at the age of seven. He married his second cousin Matilda, the daughter of the Count of Flanders, who transferred descent in the female line from the House of Wessex.

He was second cousin of Edward the Confessor. It is said that he was promised the throne by Edward (who stubbornly refused to give his wife a child, and England an heir) in 1051. In 1064, he extorted a promise along the same lines when the unfortunate Harold Godwinson, Edward's brother-in-law, was shipwrecked in Normandy.*

William's triumph over Harold (see p19) was the decisive event in the Conquest of England, but it was only a prelude to the country's subjugation. Even during his coronation at Westminster on Christmas Day 1066, a disturbance outside all but emptied the abbey. It took several years and a campaign of terror to subdue the whole country: after the south west was brought to heel, two rebellions in the north, led by earls Edwin and Morcar, were successfully defeated. The second revolt, attempted after both earls had been pardoned, provoked a savage response: between York and Durham not a house or human being visible to William's soldiers was spared. When the Domesday survey was carried out seventeen years later, many villages in the area were still without an inhabitant. The last assault on Norman hegemony came from East Anglia where Hereward, a Fenman with an aptitude for guerrilla warfare in that watery landscape, held out for some time on the Isle of Ely.

Once England was secure, William turned his attention to Scotland and Wales,

*The descent of the throne in Saxon times bore an hereditary aspect, but there was no principle of primogeniture, eg, in the tenth century only three out of eight kings immediately succeeded their fathers. The death of each king was followed by the election by the Witan (or council) of the most suitable candidate, royal birth being the prerequisite. After the Conquest the principle of primogeniture was gradually adopted.

invading the former in 1072 and compelling Malcolm III to do homage at Abernethy. Three years later he visited St David's, receiving submissions from the Welsh *en route*.

Physical evidence of the Conquest soon appeared throughout England: Saxon peasants were forced to build mounds of earth (mottes) on which fortresses of wood and later stone were erected. In London the domination of the White Tower reminded the independent Londoners of the new limitations on their freedom. From these bastions Normans enforced the confiscation of estates and their redistribution amongst those who had supported William's conquest. Feudal baronies were imposed as soon as each part of England was subjugated, resulting in some barons holding lands in different parts of the country. This had the added advantage for the monarch of preventing the consolidation of rival powers. To this end the great earldoms of late Saxon England were broken up and the shire, or county, became the principal unit of administration, superintended by sheriffs and special commissioners.

Even the French-speaking barons resented the restrictions imposed on their power by William's system of government, and as early as 1075 took up arms against him: the Norman Earl of Hereford joined Ralph the Breton, Earl of East Anglia, and the Englishman Waltheof. Their rebellion was easily contained, but it was only the first of many. Even William's eldest son, Robert, challenged his father in Normandy in 1079, and William was at war with France in 1087 when his horse stumbled in Mantes, giving him a fatal injury.

By his oath to observe the old Saxon laws and his imposition of Continental feudal customs, William effectively prevented the monarchy from exercising unlimited power, laying the ground for the development of English laws and liberties. The Church, too, stood between the king and the barons, helping to uphold a balance of power that did not infringe its own interests. Lanfranc, William's new Italian Archbishop, reorganized the English Church, and separate Church courts were established to deal with offences under canon law, an action which was to cause much trouble for the Plantagenet kings.

William the Conqueror, 'that stark man' as his subjects called him, was ruthless and cruel: although only one person was executed in his reign, thousands were mutilated, especially for breaches of the game laws – the 'New' Forest was created by him as a game park. 'He loved the tall, red deer, as if he were their father.' This penchant, however, was to sow the seed of trouble for centuries: in the eleventh century the Crown owned sixty-nine forests, almost a third of the whole acreage of the kingdom. Depriving those who lived in or near the forests of any rights in them caused great resentment, and the severe punishments for infringing forest law, enforced by Forest Courts, fed through into the draconian Game Laws of later centuries.

The *Anglo-Saxon Chronicle* gives a good impression of William's reign: 'He was mild to the good men that loved God, and beyond measure severe to the men that gainsaid his will . . . It is not to be forgotten that good peace he made in this land so that a man might go over his kingdom with his bosom full of gold . . . and no man durst slay another.'

William died at the Convent of St Gervais, near Rouen, on 9 September 1087.

# The Domesday Book

The Domesday survey, 1086, was the most comprehensive and detailed record of a country's physical resources produced in Europe during the Middle Ages. William conceived the idea while at Gloucester for Christmas in 1085, though it was not referred to as 'Domesday' until the twelfth century, intended to signify that, like the Day of Judgement, there was no appeal. Its primary purpose was to maximize tax revenues; its secondary use was to provide the necessary information for the efficient administration of the feudal system. The task of gathering the data fell to Commissioners using the shire courts and interviewing sworn juries, each made up of the priest, the reeve (the lord's manager) and six villeins. The survey covered the entire country except for Durham, Northumberland, Westmorland, Cumberland, northern Lancashire, London, Winchester and a few other towns. Its scope was exhaustive: as the Saxon chronicler recorded, 'so narrowly did he cause the survey to be made that there was not one single hide nor rood of land, nor – it is shameful to tell but he thought it no shame to do – was there an ox, cow or swine that was not set down in the writ.' The two volumes are kept in the Public Record Office at Kew, London.

# William II ('Rufus')

*Born c.1056–1060. Ascended throne 1087. Reigned 13 years.*
*Third son of the Conqueror.*
*Never married.*
*Died New Forest 1100 (? accidentally shot in the eye ? murdered). Buried in Winchester Cathedral.*

The Conqueror left Normandy to his eldest son, Robert, and England to his third son, William, his favourite. This arrangement was a great disappointment to Robert, a pleasure-loving knight with little control over his sparring barons. It was also a decision fraught with danger: enmity between the brothers was likely to lead to hostilities, and the division of his dominion split the loyalty of the leading Norman families, most of whom owned land on both sides of the Channel.

'Rufus', so-called because of his flaming red hair, was stern and avaricious, encouraging many Norman barons to take Robert's side. They preferred the idea of Normandy's anarchy under the easy-going Robert who made no attempt to restrict their freedoms in the way that William did in England. His admiration for a coarse chivalry and feats of arms attracted military adventurers from all over Europe, swelling his retinue with knights whose unbridled behaviour must have alienated further the Norman barons.

Rebellion came within a year of the coronation. Simultaneous uprisings by disaffected Norman barons might have been expected to triumph when William had little dependable Norman support; instead he appealed to the English, promising fair laws and taxes, and the restoration of the forests for hunting. They rallied to his call and defeated the rebels on land and Robert's invading force by sea. William kept none of his promises, and the death of Lanfranc took away the only man who attempted to mould William's moral conscience. The king's profligacy probably attracted him to the unctuous Ranulf, whose abilities at raising money were formidable. The see of Canterbury was left vacant after Lanfranc's death, and the revenues channelled into royal coffers. The practice was applied to other sees when their bishops died. Lay estates were also subject to Ranulf's skills at extracting money.

Repeated efforts by rebellious barons to overthrow William were thwarted by guile, false promises and military skill. Savage fines, mutilation or death were meted out to the plotters. William twice invaded Normandy, in 1090 and 1094. On the first occasion, after an initial defeat in the streets of Rouen, William returned in such force that Robert had no choice but to come to terms. The second was inconclusive and extremely costly. William completed the make-up of England by taking western Cumberland and Westmorland from Scotland in 1092 and building Carlisle Castle to defend his gains.

William briefly repented of his stand against the Church when illness brought him near death in 1093, prompting the appointment of an unwilling Anselm as Archbishop of Canterbury. On his recovery, conflict with Anselm was inevitable: when it came William tried to dismiss Anselm but he was deftly humiliated by a papal legate and had to be content with driving his troublesome archbishop into exile.

When Robert decided to go on a crusade, he entrusted Normandy to William by mortgaging it to him to help raise the money required for a rash but ultimately successful undertaking. William tried repeatedly to reconquer Maine, which Robert had lost, and intended to hold on to Normandy when Robert returned from the crusade. William never had the opportunity: on 1 August 1100 he was killed by an arrow while hunting in the New Forest; the site of his death is marked by the 'Rufus Stone'. The alacrity and precision with which Henry went through the motions to become king, the rewards he gave to the relatives of the suspected author of the arrow, even the fact that William's body was abandoned by the party and arrived in Winchester on a charcoal-burner's cart, make it hard to believe William's death was an accident.

# Henry I

*Born Selby (by tradition) 1068. Ascended throne 1100. Reigned 35 years.*
*Fourth son of William the Conqueror.*
*Married (i) Matilda of Scotland (ii) Adela of Louvain.*
*One daughter, one son.*
*Died near Rouen, 1135. Buried in Reading Abbey.*

The youngest and only English-born son of William the Conqueror, Henry had suffered at the hands of both his brothers by the time he took the throne of England (see above). Though the ablest of the three, he was capable of cruelty and deceit, and his avariciousness exceeded even that of William II. None the less he was a capable and efficient ruler, who like Rufus realized the value of English support against the barons and against his elder brother. To help secure their allegiance he wisely renounced the oppressive policies of his dead brother, issuing a charter of liberties that promised to restore the laws of his father and King Edward the Elder. Anselm was recalled and Ranulf imprisoned. And he astutely married Matilda, the daughter of Malcolm, king of Scotland, which made for peace with Scotland and pleased the English, Matilda being great grand-daughter of Edmund Ironside. Henry's promises proved as worthless as those of William II, the exigencies of his costly wars and growing bureaucracy taking precedence over the restoration of rights. Though the death penalty for crimes against property was restored and sentences were often savagely harsh, they were not arbitrary as they had been under William Rufus. All was done within the law.

The prospect of war with Normandy after Robert's return from the crusade was precipitated by the escape from prison of Ranulf, who persuaded Robert that the barons would support him if he invaded England. Robert landed at Portsmouth, and at Alton in Hampshire the Norman army met the local fyrd. Henry was able to prevent combat by a few promises, which he was not to keep, but Robert of Bellême, the most powerful baron in England, continued with his brothers to oppose the king and had to be defeated.

In exile in Normandy, Robert of Bellême formed the nucleus of a growing band of dispossessed and discontented barons whom Duke Robert was powerless to control, even if he had the inclination to do so. Henry used his brother's weakness as a pretext to invade Normandy in 1105, in order to destroy the external threat posed by the barons. After a slow start and unsuccessful negotiations to avoid combat, Henry routed the Norman forces at Tinchebrai, thereby uniting England and Normandy. Henry's brother spent the rest of his life imprisoned, first at Devizes and later at Cardiff. Surprisingly Henry did not imprison or constrain his nephew William the Clito whom many Normans regarded as Robert's rightful successor; for the rest of Henry's reign William provided the cause for further fighting between Normandy and rebellious barons in alliance with Louis VI, king of France. When Louis appealed to the Pope on behalf of William the Clito's claim, Henry's brilliant use of dynastic marriages paid off: the Pope was keen to make peace with the Holy Roman Emperor to whom Henry's daughter Matilda was married, so he was naturally reluctant to offend his father-in-law. William the Atheling, Henry's only legitimate son and heir to the English throne, was accepted as heir to Normandy too.

The conflict between king and Church continued under Henry, principally over the right to appoint bishops, which both claimed. The Pope had granted William I the right to invest his own bishops, but had no wish to extend the concession to his sons. After years of negotiations in a politer refrain than that between Anselm and William II, a compromise was reached that still left Henry with substantial influence and income from sees.

A major contribution to England's institutions was Henry's reorganization of the judicial system and the methods of raising taxes. He greatly extended the scope of the Curia Regis (King's Court), in future acting as an advisory body and as a court of law, as well as supervising taxation. Members of this court were sent out to bring even the remote districts into contact with royal taxation, as well as to make people familiar with royal justice. The extension of the Curia Regis's powers paved the way for its evolution into a Parliament, its inner members forming the Privy Council and the King's Bench. Henry's greatest agent was Roger, Bishop of Salisbury, who it is said commended himself to the king by the speed with which he could get through church services. Roger was once a poor Norman priest and an example of the way Henry appointed humble men of ability.

In 1120 Henry's legitimate son was drowned in the tragedy of the White Ship. It was expected that Henry would nominate his favourite nephew, Stephen of Blois, but instead, to English dismay, he chose as his successor his daughter Matilda who married as her second husband Geoffrey, Count of Anjou – Geoffrey Plantagenet. (Though Henry remarried, no children were born.) But when Henry died in 1135 of a surfeit of lampreys, the Council, considering a woman unfit to rule, offered the throne to Stephen.

# Stephen

*Born c.1097. Ascended throne 1135. Reigned 19 years.*
*Married Matilda of Boulogne.*
*One son, two daughters.*
*Died Dover 1154. Buried in Faversham Abbey.*

For seventy years after the Conquest, England had the benefits of strong government and the beginnings of rational justice. During the 'nineteen long winters' of Stephen's reign, England again knew what it was like to be governed by a weak king. Known as the anarchy, Stephen's years on the throne have been described as 'not a reign but a war of succession'.

There was a number of claimants to the throne, but the help of Stephen's brother Henry, Bishop of Winchester, in securing the support of the Church for Stephen's coronation was crucial. The barons' dislike of Henry's daughter Matilda, combined with Stephen's personal charm and wealth, gave him an advantage that he was soon to squander. His lack of resolve became manifest when David I, king of Scotland, invaded; in command of an army large enough to impose terms, Stephen weakly conceded Cumberland and Westmorland. His neglect to secure Normandy by thoroughly suppressing mutinous barons proved fatal to the peace in England: left in Normandy when Stephen returned to England, Henry's powerful illegitimate son, Earl Robert, renounced his allegiance to Stephen and transferred it to Matilda, prompting many in England to do the same. Stephen's ineptitude alienated other supporters, including Bishop Roger of Salisbury and others in the Church, just as Matilda and Earl Robert landed in Sussex in 1139, Robert making for the principal rebel castle, at Bristol, while Matilda installed herself at Arundel.

The nobility, during the decade of civil war that followed, threw in their lot with both sides, often to the highest bidder, and built castles from which they terrorized their areas. The countryside was ravaged, crops were destroyed, cattle were driven off and people starved. It was, as the chronicler put it, a time when 'Christ and his saints slept'.

At a critical battle outside Lincoln in 1141, Stephen was captured and taken to Bristol where he was imprisoned in chains. Only his queen and William of Ypres in command of Flemish mercenaries held out in Essex and parts of Kent. Matilda was on the point of being crowned when her arrogant rescission of grants made by Stephen alienated many barons. Her imposition of heavy taxes on Londoners induced them to take up arms, compelling Matilda to flee to Oxford. At another pivotal battle, at Winchester, Stephen's queen restored the balance by capturing Earl Robert. An exchange of Stephen and Earl Robert was arranged. The war dragged on in stalemate until in 1147, with the death of Earl Robert, Matilda gave up and left. But still the war dragged on, some in support of her son Henry Plantagenet, rather than Matilda. Stephen lost the Church's support over his demands that his son Eustace should be crowned, and his loyal queen died. When Eustace, too, died Stephen lost heart; the Treaty of Winchester ended the wretched war, confirming Henry Plantagenet as heir to the throne. Henry had only a year to wait for it.

# THE PLANTAGENET KINGS

Henry II was the first of a long line of fourteen Plantagenet kings. Their reigns stretched over more than three hundred years of English history, from the accession of Henry II in 1154 to the death of Richard III on Bosworth Field in 1485.

The name 'Plantagenet' was originally a nickname given to Count Geoffrey of Anjou, father of Henry II, because of the gay yellow broom flower (*Planta genista*) which he wore in his helmet. In time this emblem was embodied in the family arms.

For the sake of convenience the Plantagenets are usually divided up under the names of the three related families of Anjou, Lancaster and York, from amongst whose members the fourteen monarchs came. The next section presents the outline story of the Angevins, the Lancastrians and the Yorkists.

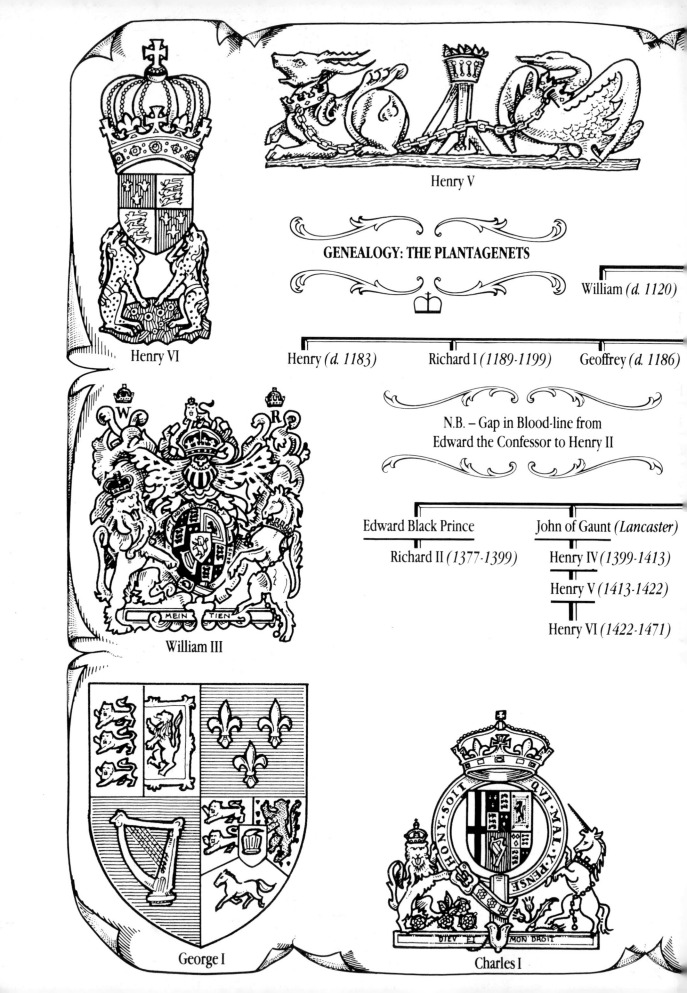

Henry V

Henry VI

**GENEALOGY: THE PLANTAGENETS**

William *(d. 1120)*

Henry *(d. 1183)*     Richard I *(1189-1199)*     Geoffrey *(d. 1186)*

N.B. – Gap in Blood-line from
Edward the Confessor to Henry II

Edward Black Prince          John of Gaunt *(Lancaster)*

Richard II *(1377-1399)*          Henry IV *(1399-1413)*

Henry V *(1413-1422)*

Henry VI *(1422-1471)*

William III

George I

Charles I

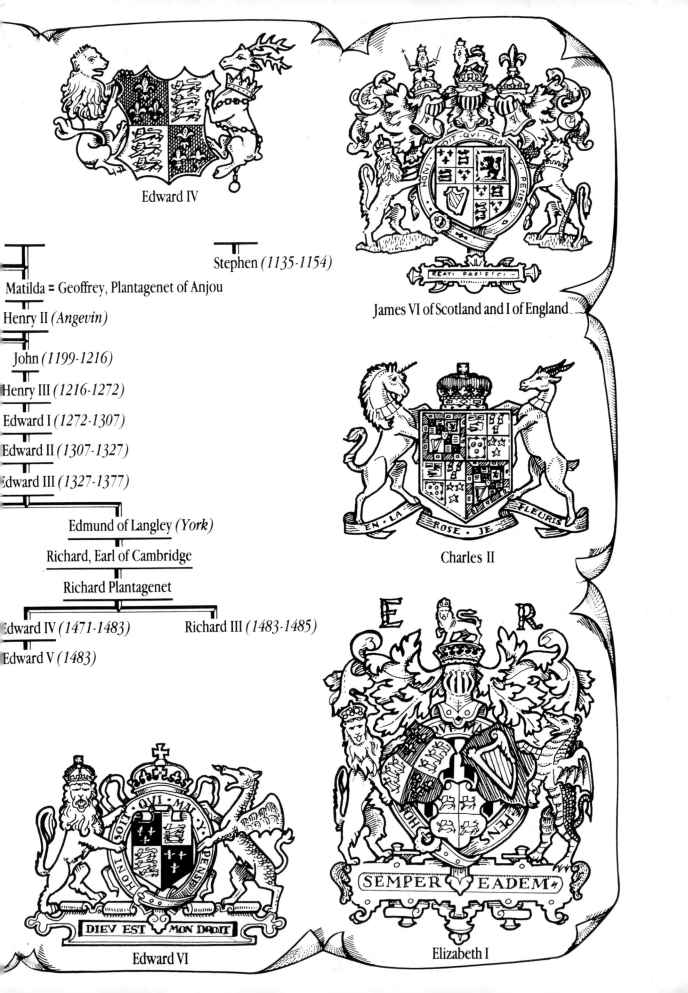

Edward IV

James VI of Scotland and I of England

Charles II

Stephen *(1135-1154)*

Matilda **=** Geoffrey, Plantagenet of Anjou

Henry II *(Angevin)*

John *(1199-1216)*

Henry III *(1216-1272)*

Edward I *(1272-1307)*

Edward II *(1307-1327)*

Edward III *(1327-1377)*

Edmund of Langley *(York)*

Richard, Earl of Cambridge

Richard Plantagenet

Edward IV *(1471-1483)*     Richard III *(1483-1485)*

Edward V *(1483)*

Edward VI

Elizabeth I

# Henry II

*Born Le Mans 1133. Ascended throne 1154. Reigned 35 years.*
*Eldest son of Matilda.*
*Married Eleanor of Aquitaine.*
*Five sons, three daughters.*
*Died Chinon 1189, aged 56. Buried at Fontevrault.*
*First of the Angevin kings.*

Henry II was a European ruler rather than an English king. His empire stretched from the Solway almost to the Mediterranean, and from the Somme to the Pyrenees. The size of Henry's inheritance was the result of two key marriages: his father's to Matilda who, as daughter of Henry I, was the probable heiress to England and Normandy; and his own to the vivacious Eleanor of Aquitaine. By the time he was crowned king at the age of twenty-one, Henry's wealth exceeded that of any other prince in Europe, even his nominal overlord, the king of France. To his inheritance he added Ireland, a mission entrusted to him by Pope Adrian IV (Nicholas Brakespear, the only Englishman ever to be Pope [1154–9]). And through diplomacy he forced Malcolm IV, the young king of Scotland, to return the counties of Westmorland, Cumberland and Northumberland which Stephen had lost.

The general aim of his policy in England was to undo all the harm caused by Stephen's reign. He triumphed brilliantly over the nobility, but he was, in turn, worsted by the Church.

His first concern was to restore order. Castles built by the rebellious nobles were demolished, royal castles were resumed, along with Crown lands. Henry was then able to plan for the future. He raised new taxes (scutage, or shield money) from the land-holders in lieu of their feudal military obligations. The old feudal limit of forty days' military service was of little use to a monarch who might need to take troops to Gascony. By a command of 1181 the basis of an English militia force was laid. Henry now had two armies: the mercenary army, paid for by the new taxes, and the militia; whilst his powerful subjects and their followers got less practice in the arts of war. As a result their attention turned to the lands they held and the techniques of agriculture, which were developed most skilfully by Cistercian monks on their estates. The stone castle gave way to the stone manor house, and the tournament became the only means for some to display their martial skills (Henry's son Geoffrey was killed at a tournament in Paris).

Royal justice was revived. Judges from the King's courts were again sent into the shires, where they now combined with twelve local men to administer the law; in this way Henry laid the foundations of Common Law (a law applicable to the whole country,

30

free of local customs), emanating from the Curia Regis, and of the modern English jury system. Gradually trial by judges, with the assistance of jurymen, replaced the barbarous trials by ordeal and trials by battle, in both criminal and civil cases. (For a trial by ordeal the accused was made to plunge his head into boiling water or carry a piece of red-hot metal. His guilt or innocence was decided by the speed with which the wounds healed.) The jury was not yet a group of 'outside' people brought in to hear and decide on a case, but witnesses to the fact.

These reforms were not inspired by Henry's high-mindedness but because the courts were his chosen instrument for enforcing and extorting payment of revenues. By the end of Henry's reign, the English had for the first time become accustomed to paying their taxes, to co-operating in government and to expecting fair play in the law courts. His system was so fundamentally efficient that it continued to work even under the weak rulers that followed him.

But, unjustly, it is probably for his quarrel with Thomas Becket that Henry is chiefly remembered. The Church of England was claiming more independence from lay control than Henry was prepared to allow. He wished to retain the right to nominate his own appointees to vacant bishoprics and to try in his own courts clerks* who had committed a crime, for the Church courts (introduced by William I) had no power of life and death – a cleric could only be downgraded. Any wrongdoer who could read a Latin text from the Bible passed the test of clerical status (the so-called 'neck verse'), and could claim 'benefit of clergy', or immunity from the king's justice. In the same way a criminal fleeing from justice could claim 'sanctuary' in the precincts of a church. The Constitutions of Clarendon ended the clergy's immunity from State prosecution by instigating a system whereby a clerk accused of a felony would appear first in a lay court, then be tried by a Church court and, if found guilty, be brought back to the lay court for sentence.

Becket, Henry's Chancellor and one-time convivial friend, turned ascetic and quarrelled bitterly with Henry over these questions, even rejecting the Constitutions of Clarendon. He was exiled from 1164 to 1170. In his stand against the king, Becket was not even supported by all the bishops, and lay opinion inclined to the king. Only Becket's murder gave him posthumous victory, thereby allowing anyone who could make a stab at reading to commit serious crimes without fear of heavy penalties. This only served to attract some dubious characters to holy orders in order to obtain protection from State law. But Henry stood firm over advowsons, and prevented them becoming the prerogative of the Roman Court, though this remained for centuries a cause for struggle between Pope and the patrons of English livings.

---

*A 'clerk' in the Middle Ages was anyone in orders, from the Archbishop of Canterbury to the humblest verger – about one in fifty of the population.

When Becket returned from exile he proceeded to anger Henry still further. The murder of Becket at Canterbury Cathedral on 29 December 1170, by men believing they were acting on Henry's orders, gave the Church a martyr and ultimately a saint, whilst Henry lost all. Not until the Reformation did royal power prevail over the Church. Chaucer's epic work reflected the popularity of the cult of St Thomas, giving to the language the word 'canter' as the pace at which pilgrims should ride.

The closing years of the reign were troublesome. Henry subjects on both sides of the Channel rebelled, and it was only with the aid of mercenaries and the militia that the realm was quietened at home and abroad. Much of the trouble was caused by the frustrations of Henry's sons, incited to rebellion by their mother, who were supported by the kings of France and Scotland. It was while Henry was fighting Philip of France in 1188 that his son Richard joined the French king. Military reverses compelled Henry to grant a peace treaty which granted a pardon to Richard's followers. Shortly before he died, Henry was devastated to find on the list the name of his favourite son John.

# Richard I (Coeur-de-Lion)

*Born Oxford 1157. Ascended throne 1189. Reigned 10 years.*
*Third son of Henry II.*
*Married Berengaria of Navarre.*
*No issue.*
*Died Châlus-Chabrol 1199, aged 42. Buried at Fontevrault; his heart at Rouen.*

Richard I had little English blood in him. He spent only ten months of his ten years' reign in England, and there is some doubt as to whether he could speak English (French remained the language of the upper classes until Edward III's time). He regarded his kingdom solely as a source of revenue for his crusading ventures: 'I would have sold London itself if I could have found a rich enough buyer,' he is reputed to have said. Many towns benefited by the Charters which they gained from Richard in return for financial assistance.

Henry II had promised to undertake a crusade against the Moslems to expiate the murder of Becket, a promise not altogether disinterested, as the Angevins acquired a title by marriage to the kingdom of Jerusalem. He bequeathed this promise to his successor and, though obedience to his father's wishes had not so far been his strong point, Richard took part in the best known of all the crusades, the third.

Its aim was to free the Holy Land from the Turks, who were Moslems. It failed to achieve this, but Jerusalem was made easier of access for Christian pilgrims. With Philip I, Richard left for Palestine in 1190, wintering in Sicily where Richard's sister Joanna lived as queen to King William. A second delay in reaching the coast of Outremer was caused by the insolent treatment of Richard's men by Isaac Commenus, ruler of Cyprus and pretender to the Byzantine throne. Richard was so enraged by Commenus's behaviour that, after marrying Berengaria of Navarre on the island, he conquered it before leaving to join the siege of Acre. The city fell in July 1191, after which the victors fell out amongst themselves, several deciding to return home, leaving Richard unquestioned leader of the crusade. There followed an example of his ruthlessness when, unjustly suspecting Saladin of breaking the terms of Acre's surrender, he slaughtered 2,500 men with their wives and children in full view of their fellow countrymen. But for his exploits in winning a total victory over Saladin's army at Arsuf and for taking Jaffa and other towns, Richard earned the admiration of all Christendom.

On his way home Richard was captured by the Duke of Austria, who sold him to the Emperor Henry VI. So a crusade begun for the rescue of the Holy Land ended with the sale of one Christian monarch to another. For fourteen months, until his ransom was paid, Richard was imprisoned in a secret imperial castle, where, legend tells us, he was found at last by his minstrel, Blondel. Never again did an English king leave his realm to go crusading.

Richard's absentee rule ushered in a period of some eighty years during which the Crown was weaker than in the previous century or so. The government of the country was fortunately in the hands of capable deputies, who successfully combated the ambitions of the king's brother, John, and the intrigues of the nobles, in addition to raising enormous sums of money for the expenses of the crusade and the King's ransom. The situation in Normandy, however, was such that Richard had to spend the last five years of his life fighting Philip, to whom his brother John had sworn homage in return for Richard's lands. It was while besieging a castle that he was killed.

# John

*Born Oxford 1167. Ascended throne 1199. Reigned 17 years.*
*Fourth son of Henry II.*
*Married (i) Isabel of Gloucester (ii) Isabella of Angoulême.*
*Two sons, three daughters by second wife.*
*Died Newark 1216, aged (?)49. Buried at Worcester.*

The archetype of the 'wicked king', John was the fourth son of Henry II, the child of his father's middle age. Not without some administrative ability, especially as regards the collection of money, he was yet cruel and avaricious.

He was nicknamed 'Lackland', because his brothers were given territory by their father when he received none until made King of Ireland in 1177. However, his campaign there in 1185-6 was disastrous and his brother recalled him for misconduct.

Though John had intrigued against Richard while his brother was on crusade, they were reconciled, and on his death-bed Richard made John his heir.

John continued to live up to his nickname, for in 1204 he lost Normandy and Anjou to the King of France, and by 1205 only a fragment remained of the vast Angevin empire. In the long run this enforced insularity fostered the growth of the English nation state.

In 1205 John quarrelled with the Church, because he refused to accept Stephen Langton, the Pope's nominee, as Archbishop of Canterbury. In 1207 England was laid under an interdict, and John was excommunicated two years later. The dispute ended with John's abject surrender to Innocent 111, one of the greatest of medieval popes.

The loss of England's French possessions, the ignominious failure of his quarrel with Rome, allied to misgovernment and the raising of extortionate taxes, united against John the articulate elements of society. John's conduct encouraged men of intellect to conceive of law as having an existence independent of and above the king. The gradual removal of feudal balances and responsibilities, begun by Henry II, required the substitution of other mechanisms to prevent despotism. It was John's extortions to finance incompetent expeditions to recover his Angevin inheritance that proved the final straw: during his absence on the Continent fighting against the French king, a project crowned with failure at the Battle of Bouvines in 1214, a party led by Langton came into existence. This is the first time in English history that a consensus of influential opinion enabled concerted action to be taken on such a scale against bad government. Londoners and the clergy supported the initiative of the Archbishop and the barons.

A demand was made for the confirmation of popular liberties. After the barons' forces had assembled at Stamford and marched to London, the king capitulated and on Monday 15 June 1215, on the small island of Runnymede in the Thames near Windsor, sealed the Magna Carta, the Great Charter, which restated the rights of the Church, the barons and all in the land. The three most important clauses laid down

1  That the Church was free to choose its own officials.
2  That no money, over and above certain payments, was to be paid by the king's feudal tenants without their previous consent.
3  That no freeman* was to be punished except according to the laws of the land.

Langton's key role was all the more remarkable for being contrary to the Pope's wishes; since John's agreement to hold England as a fief of the Papacy, Innocent III had supported him in the conflict. John soon reneged on his agreement with Langton and the barons, but after the barons invited the French Dauphin to lead them, the situation was reversed. John died at Newark, after eating peaches and beer, in the midst of an invasion, bequeathing enormous problems to his nine-year-old son.

*Medieval society distinguished, of course, between servile and free men.

# Henry III

*Born Winchester 1207. Ascended throne 1216. Reigned 56 years.*
*Married Eleanor of Provence.*
*Four sons, two daughters.*
*Died Westminster 1272, aged 65. Buried at Westminster.*

Henry III was born, and spent almost his entire life, in England. He was only nine years old when he came to the throne, but the government of the country was in the hands of capable deputies until he declared himself of age in 1227. During this period the French invaders were expelled and the few remaining adherents of John's party were crushed. Five years later Henry deprived the former Regent Hubert de Burgh of all his offices, and in 1234 took the administration into his own hands.

There followed a period of poor government, for in spite of some redeeming features Henry was a weak, untrustworthy character. He combated his poverty, a legacy from his father and uncle, by ruthless, extortionate taxation, yet engaged in costly, fruitless wars. He mounted three equally disastrous campaigns to France, which would have cost what Continental possessions remained from John's losses had it not been for the generosity of Louis IX. Moreover, Henry's spineless reluctance to oppose any decree from the Pope meant unsuitable appointments to benefices, the most flagrant example being the Pope's promise of rewarding the loyalty of Romans with the next 300 benefices that fell vacant in England. Without a bulwark to resist such arbitrary actions, anti-papal sentiments flourished, anticipating the growing resentment that would fuel the Reformation. But Henry's crowning folly was his agreement to finance papal wars in Sicily in return for the Sicilian crown for his son Edmund. The exorbitant sums Henry demanded, combined with the absence of any benefit for England, roused the barons to fury, leading to a period of civil war out of which would emerge an important development in the steps towards a Parliament.

Led by Henry's brother-in-law, Simon de Montfort, the barons compelled Henry to abide by the Provisions of Oxford, curtailing his power. When Henry repudiated them and Louis IX, to whom the matter had been referred, annulled them, de Montfort and the reformists fought and defeated the king at Lewes. But Henry's opponents were divided into two distinct interest groups: on the one hand the conservative barons and on the other the reforming barons and lesser gentry supported by many of the clergy, the students of Oxford University and the citizens of London. This split was cleverly exploited by Prince Edward, leading key barons to desert de Montfort and enabling the king to defeat him at the Battle of Evesham in 1265. De Montfort died on the battlefield, but his cause was not lost on Prince Edward who realized the need for the king to rule under the law and equally importantly that the Crown could be stronger for working through Parliament rather than in opposition to the nation. He appreciated the value of the consultative process set up by de Montfort when representatives from the shires and boroughs came to Parliament to discuss State and judicial affairs.

If he was a failure as a king, Henry III was probably the greatest of all patrons of medieval ecclesiastical architecture. During his reign the plain, massive style of the Normans gave way to the pointed arches, lancet windows, flying buttresses and elaborate decorations which are characteristic of the Early English and Gothic styles. The majority of English cathedrals had some portion of their fabric remodelled: Westminster Abbey was rebuilt; Salisbury Cathedral was built between 1220 and 1266.

During this long reign Franciscan and Dominican friars* set up establishments in England. This gave an impetus to works of charity and also to university teaching at Oxford and Cambridge.

By the time Henry died in 1272, he had all but relinquished government to his son.

# Edward I ('Longshanks')

*Born Westminster 1239. Ascended throne 1272. Reigned 35 years.*
*Married (i) Eleanor of Castille (ii) Margaret of France.*
*Three sons, five daughters by first wife; two sons, one daughter by second wife.*
*Died Burgh by Sands 1307, aged 68. Buried at Westminster.*

Edward I was an authoritarian statesman, a lawyer and a soldier. In these different capacities he modernized many aspects of English life. When he died at the beginning of the fourteenth century, much in English government, society and law had taken on a permanent form that in essentials was to survive the Hundred Years War and the Wars of the Roses.

Paradoxically, given his autocratic temperament, Edward has been called the father to the 'Mother of all Parliaments'. To his 'Model Parliament' in 1295 he summoned representatives from amongst the nobility, the greater and lesser clergy, the knights of the shires, the burgesses of the cities – thereby bringing Lords and Commons together for the first time. The growing demands on the government for justice and general administration meant that by now the feudal revenues were inadequate; Edward needed money from the new merchant class, and to summon national Parliaments was the only way to get it. In this way parliament became the established method of conducting public business. The need for finance was also behind the conflict with both the Church and the barons over taxation. Even a revival of anti-Semitism was used as an excuse to

---

*'Friar' Tuck, companion of Robin Hood, in John's reign is an anachronism.

expel the Jews in 1290 so that the Crown would benefit financially from forteitures.

Edward completed the judicial reforms begun by Henry II. The courts of King's Bench, Common Pleas and Exchequer were given separate staffs of judges and officials; and a Court of Equity, the Chancery Court, was set up to give redress where the other courts could provide no remedy. A whole series of Acts dealt with the position of the Church, the enforcement of public order, trade and the position of great landholders. 'Conservators of the Peace' were created, forerunners of the Justices of the Peace created by Edward III.

As usual the drain on royal finances was caused largely by costly wars. Edward possessed the necessary martial skills, learnt during the conflicts of his father's reign and on crusade in Egypt and Syria in 1270–4. For five years Edward had to fight Philip the Fair after the French king had invaded Gascony. Edward's ambition to rule over an undivided nation was checked by the independence of Wales and Scotland. The sustained opposition of Llywelyn ap Gruffudd from 1277 to his death in 1282 made the conquest of Wales a lengthy campaign, but English administration and law was extended to the Principality through the Statute of Rhuddlan (1284). Edward began the construction of fourteen new castles to secure his gains. The king's eldest son was created Prince of Wales in 1301, a title since borne by all male heirs to the throne.

Right until the day of his death Edward waged war unsuccessfully against the Scots, led first by Sir William Wallace and later by Robert Bruce. But the epitaph on his tomb at Westminster bears witness to the magnificence of his failure in Scotland: 'Here lies Edward the Hammer of the Scots'.

# Edward II

*Born Caernarfon 1284. Ascended throne 1307. Reigned 20 years (deposed).*
*Son of Edward I.*
*Married Isabella of France.*
*Two sons, two daughters.*
*Died Berkeley Castle 1327 (murdered), aged 43. Buried in Gloucester Cathedral.*

Edward II was Edward I's greatest failure. Feeble and perverted, he did nothing to carry on his father's work of consolidation. Yet by default, his laziness and incompetence strengthened the influence of Parliament, and the bureaucracy was improved by various reforms.

Addicted to worthless favourites, first Piers Gaveston, and later the Despensers (father and son), the king aroused the wrath of the nobles by leaving Gaveston as guardian of the kingdom when he left for France in 1308 to marry Isabella, daughter of

Philip IV. Besides Gaveston's status as a 'foreigner' (from Gascony) and the nature of his relationship with Edward, the barons were incensed by his habit of giving them nicknames. The barons forced Edward to banish Gaveston to Ireland in 1309, and his return led to the imposition of further limitations on royal power through the Ordinances of 1311, which again banished the king's favourite. Edward's attempts to circumvent the Ordinances and his recall of Gaveston led to armed revolt in which Gaveston was captured and beheaded.

The next fiasco was Edward's efforts to impose his rule on Scotland: despite invading with a large army, Edward was soundly defeated by Robert Bruce at the Battle of Bannockburn in 1314. This and Bruce's capture of Berwick four years later settled the question of Scottish independence until the Union of England and Scotland in 1707. Edward's standing was so low that he was forced to relinquish authority to his cousin Thomas, Earl of Lancaster, who had led opposition to the king – the first indication of the struggle that was to develop between the Angevins and the younger Lancastrian branch of the family. Earl Thomas's ineptitude allowed Edward, with the help of his new favourite Hugh le Despenser, to reassert his will by force, execute Thomas and annul the Ordinances.

Queen Isabella now headed the opposition to the husband she despised, taking Prince Edward with her to France, where she fell in love with a disaffected noble, Roger de Mortimer, Baron of Wigmore. Together they invaded England, landing in Suffolk. The Despensers were executed, and Edward, after being captured in South Wales, forced to abdicate. A rescue attempt on Berkeley Castle, where he was imprisoned, prompted his murder in September 1327.

# The Hundred Years War, 1337–1453

The struggle between England and France was carried on intermittently during the reigns of five English kings. The causes of the conflict included grievances over English territory and sovereignty in France, English commercial activity in Flanders, French support for Scottish independence, and the claim of Edward III, through his mother, Isabella, daughter of Philip IV, to the French crown.

Inevitably for a war carried on over a century, the fortunes of the two combatants fluctuated: until 1360 the advantage lay with England. The great naval victory of Sluys (1340) when the French fleet was surprised in the harbour, was followed by the famous English victories at Crécy (1346) and Poitiers (1356). At Crécy, the important role of the English bowmen and the exploits of the Black Prince in securing victory have become legendary. The English army at Poitiers was led by the Black Prince and won a decisive victory in which the French king was captured; King John was unable to raise the ransom demanded and died in London in 1364, The Treaty of Brétigny gave to England extensive land in return for giving up all claim to the French throne.

With the accession of the Black Prince in 1376, and the accession of Richard II (1377–99), English fortunes reached their lowest ebb with the defeat of the English fleet at La Rochelle (1372), though a Franco-Castilian invasion was thwarted off Margate in 1387. The reign of Henry IV (1399–1413) began a period of improvement, which was continued by Henry V (1413–22) at Harfleur and Agincourt (both 1415), marked by the Treaty of Troyes (1420) which allowed for the marriage of Henry to Catherine of Valois and made him heir to the French throne.

Henry's premature death did not end the run of English successes; it was only when Charles VII and Joan of Arc defeated the forces besieging Orléans (1429) that the tide turned. By 1453 Calais was all that remained of English possessions in France.

# Edward III

*Born Windsor Castle 1312. Ascended throne 1327. Reigned 50 years.*
*Son of Edward II.*
*Married Philippa of Hainault (the groom was aged 16, the bride 14).*
*Six sons, five daughters.*
*Died Sheen Palace 1377, aged 65. Buried at Westminster.*

Edward was hastily crowned king when his father was deposed by his mother and Roger de Mortimer. His marriage to Philippa of Hainault in 1328 was arranged before his coronation, and it was a further two years before he took control of the government, ordering the arrest of Mortimer at Nottingham and the imprisonment of his mother. Mortimer was hanged at Tyburn, and his mother was banished to Castle Rising in Norfolk where she spent the last twenty-eight years of her life.

The main interest of the long reign of Edward III lies in the opening stages of the Hundred Years War with France. Ostensibly the war began, in 1337, to support Edward's claim to the French throne,* a pretence marked by Edward's quartering of the lilies of France beside the leopards of England on his coat of arms. In reality the war was, in origin, an attempt to retain control of Gascony and the wine trade centred on Bordeaux; and to keep open the connections between the English wool traders and the woollen markets of Flanders.

Sluys (1340), a naval battle, gave England control of the Channel. Though spectacular victories, neither Crécy (1346) nor Poitiers (1356) achieved much in the longer term. Calais, after a twelve months' siege (1347), passed into English hands for the next hundred years. It was in this phase of the war that the king's eldest son, Edward

---

*A claim not finally surrendered until 1802.

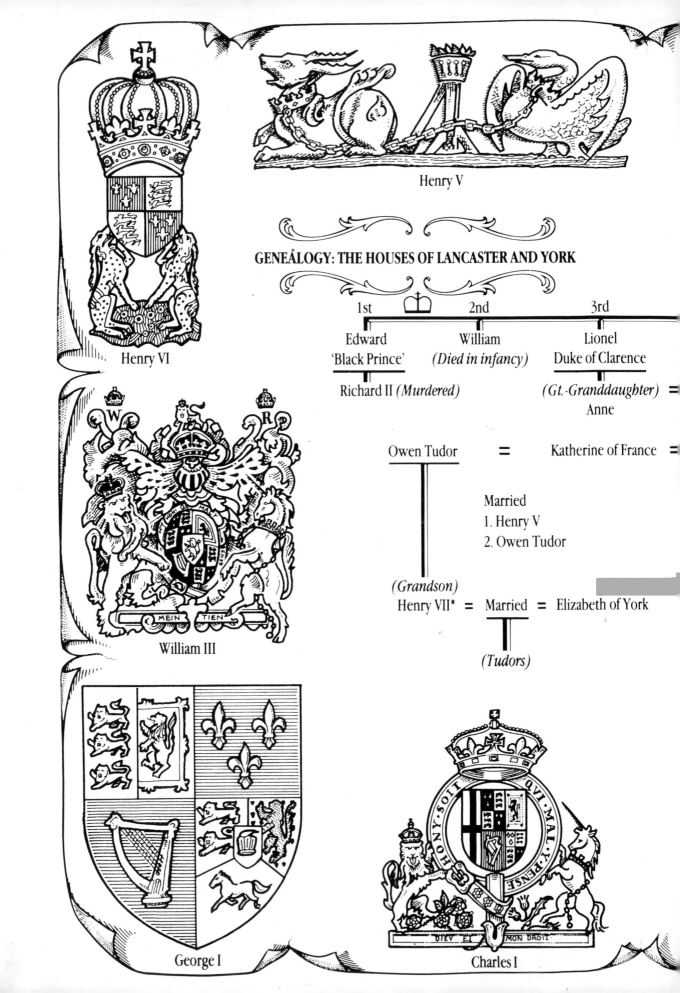

Henry V

## GENEALOGY: THE HOUSES OF LANCASTER AND YORK

| 1st | 2nd | 3rd |
|---|---|---|
| Edward 'Black Prince' | William *(Died in infancy)* | Lionel Duke of Clarence |
| Richard II *(Murdered)* | | *(Gt.-Granddaughter)* = Anne |

Owen Tudor = Katherine of France =

Married
1. Henry V
2. Owen Tudor

*(Grandson)*
Henry VII* = Married = Elizabeth of York

*(Tudors)*

Henry VI

William III

George I

Charles I

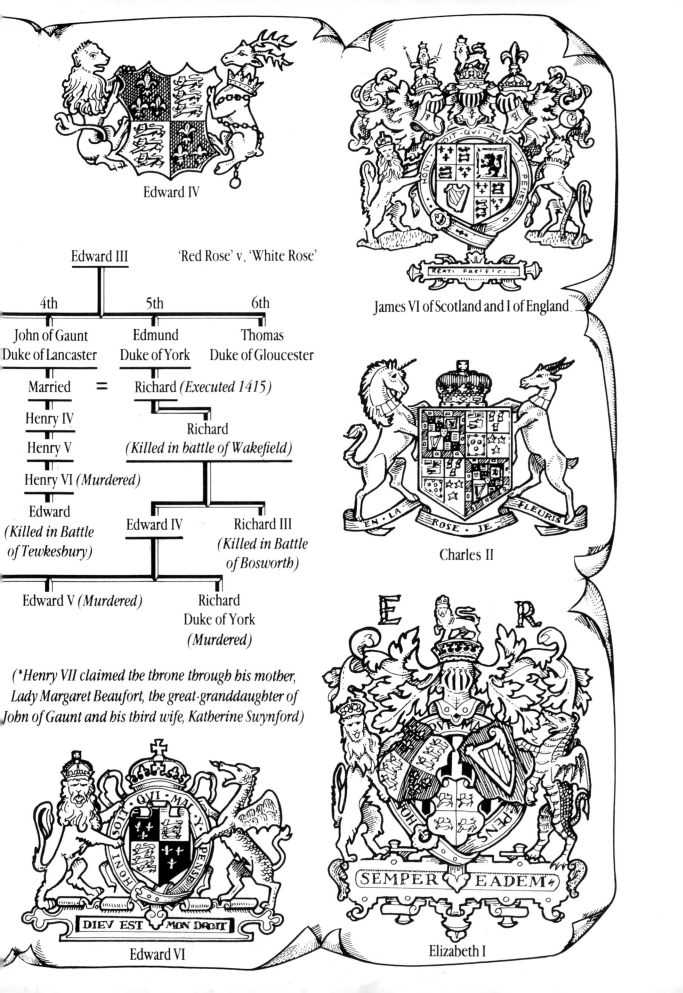

Edward IV

Edward III     'Red Rose' v. 'White Rose'

| 4th | 5th | 6th |
|---|---|---|
| John of Gaunt | Edmund | Thomas |
| Duke of Lancaster | Duke of York | Duke of Gloucester |

Married    =    Richard *(Executed 1415)*

Henry IV

Henry V      Richard
         *(Killed in battle of Wakefield)*

Henry VI *(Murdered)*

Edward    Edward IV      Richard III
*(Killed in Battle*             *(Killed in Battle*
*of Tewkesbury)*             *of Bosworth)*

Edward V *(Murdered)*      Richard
                            Duke of York
                            *(Murdered)*

*(*Henry VII claimed the throne through his mother,*
*Lady Margaret Beaufort, the great-granddaughter of*
*John of Gaunt and his third wife, Katherine Swynford)*

James VI of Scotland and I of England

Charles II

Edward VI

Elizabeth I

(1330–76), known to history as the 'Black Prince' (either because of the colour of his armour or, more likely, because of his foul Angevin temper), covered himself with glory.

The outbreak of bubonic plague, the 'Black Death', in 1348–50 removed a third of the population of England and undermined military strength. Originating in China and affecting the whole of Europe, the plague entered England through Melcombe Regis (now Weymouth) in 1348, and soon reached Bristol, Oxford and London. It inevitably raised the price of labour and weakened further the waning feudal system.

In 1360 the Treaty of Brétigny brought the war to a close. When Edward III died in 1377 all that was left of the English conquests were five fortified towns and the coastal lands around them.

Hostilities with Scotland were also resumed when Edward tried to bring an end to Scottish independence: supporting Edward Baliol's coronation in 1332, Edward invaded Scotland to defeat his rival, David II, at Halidon Hill near Berwick, but within five months Baliol had to flee. In 1346 David invaded England while Edward was fighting in France; Queen Philippa proved equal to the occasion by raising an army which defeated and captured David at Neville's Cross near Durham.

After Queen Philippa's death in 1369, Edward retreated to Windsor where he became increasingly senile. Public finances were in a parlous state, Edward's rapacious mistress Alice Perrers helped to erode the residual goodwill of the people and the sadness caused by the death of the Black Prince clouded his last years. He relinquished government to his fourth son, John of Gaunt, and reputedly died alone.

During Edward's long reign, many changes took place in England. Parliament, now divided into two Houses, met regularly to vote supplies for the conduct of the war. 'Treason' was defined by statute for the first time in 1352. The office of JP was created in 1361. In 1362 English replaced French as the official language of the law courts. Within twenty years John Wycliffe and the Lollards (the first 'protestants') were aiding their cause with the first 'English' translation of the Bible, and already Chaucer was writing 'English' masterpieces. The new merchant class and the spread of lay learning were building a national civilization.

# Richard II

*Born Bordeaux 1367. Ascended throne 1377. Reigned 22 years (deposed).*
*Son of the Black Prince and grandson of Edward III.*
*Married (i) Anne of Bohemia (ii) Isabella of France.*
*No issue.*
*Died Pontefract Castle 1400 (? murdered), aged 33. Buried (i) King's Langley*
*(ii) Westminster.*

Richard II: artist and date unknown *(The National Portrait Gallery, London)*.

Richard II succeeded his grandfather in 1377 at the age of ten, at a time of social unrest. Though government was entrusted to a council of twelve, it was dominated by John of Gaunt, Richard's uncle, until the fourteen-year-old king displayed a remarkable ability to defuse the dangerous threat posed by the Peasants' Revolt when 100,000 men from Essex and Kent marched on London. The Black Death had been followed by rapid increases in wages and prices; Parliament had passed legislation to restrain wages, but prices were not similarly regulated, and a series of poll taxes proved the last straw.

After seizing Rochester Castle, the men of Kent under Wat Tyler joined forces with the rebels from Essex and entered the city of London, destroying John of Gaunt's manor. Richard met the Essex men and persuaded them to return home by agreeing to meet their demands. The Kent rebels, meanwhile, burned Temple Bar, occupied the Tower of London and executed the Chancellor and Archbishop of Canterbury, Simon of Sudbury, before meeting the king at Smithfield. During negotiations the Mayor of London killed Wat Tyler, but Richard rode amongst the rebels and by granting their demands induced them to disperse. The other major uprising, in East Anglia, was ruthlessly put down by the Bishop of Norwich. By September the revolt had been suppressed and Richard's promises withdrawn.

After the Peasants' Revolt, John of Gaunt receded into the background, concentrating on winning his claim through his second wife of the crown of Castile.

Richard had only himself to blame for being 'the last of the Angevins'. He proved to be extravagant, unjust and faithless. His only good act was to terminate the struggle with France in 1396. His final undoing was to make plain his wish to abandon Parliamentary government, now an established part of national life. Richard never forgave Parliament or the lords who impeached his favourites in 1388, exacting vengeance a decade later when he had murdered, beheaded or banished those who had opposed him.

Richard's reign marked the beginning of the long struggle for the Crown between the descendants of Edward III, led first by John of Gaunt, Edward's fourth son, and then by Gaunt's son, Henry Bolingbroke. When Richard deprived Henry Bolingbroke of his father's estates on his death in 1399, he provoked his downfall: Henry landed at Ravenspur in Yorkshire while Richard was in Ireland. On his return, without an army he was obliged to submit to Henry at Flint. He resigned the Crown and was deposed by Parliament, which chose Henry as his successor. From the Tower, Richard was sent to Pontefract Castle where he was probably murdered to put a stop to risings in his favour. The conflicting claims that would lead to the Wars of the Roses had taken their first victim.

# The Wars of the Roses

The Wars of the Roses were a series of struggles for the Crown which lasted over a century and affected the reigns of seven English kings, from Richard II to Henry VII, though armed conflict formed a part only between 1455 and 1485. The name derived from the red and white roses of the houses of Lancaster and York, respectively.

The trouble started with Edward III's eleven children. He died leaving four surviving sons and some daughters, so that the succession could be disputed amongst too many. In addition, the marriages of royal children with the sons and daughters of powerful noble families created families which were semi-royal.

In 1399 Henry IV of Lancaster usurped the throne from the last Angevin king, Richard II. In 1461 the Yorkists in turn usurped the throne, when Edward IV deposed Henry VI. The usurpation of the Yorkist Richard III was terminated by Henry of Richmond, who was descended in the female line from an illicit union of John of Gaunt.

Henry VII's marriage to Elizabeth of York, the Yorkist heiress, united the claims of York and Lancaster, gave England the Tudor dynasty and removed the threat of further dynastic warfare.

# Henry IV

*Born Bolingbroke Castle 1367. Ascended throne 1399 (usurper).*
*Reigned 14 years.*
*Son of John of Gaunt.*
*Married (i) Mary de Bohun (ii) Joan of Brittany.*
*Four sons, two daughters.*
*Died Westminster 1413, aged 46. Buried in Canterbury Cathedral.*

'A scrambling and unquiet time' – so Shakespeare described the reign of the first Lancastrian king, Henry IV. The very nature of his accession; his usurpation of the throne when there were others with a better title, created problems for the future. From 1399 to about 1410 Henry was never free from rebellions.

Richard II's half brothers rose immediately on his behalf. The rising was put down severely, and in 1400 Richard's body was exhibited in London to disprove a rumour that he was still alive.

From 1401, Owain Glyndŵr kept up a continuous guerrilla warfare against the Marcher lords, capturing Lord Grey and Sir Edward Mortimer in the following year. Both married daughters of Glyndŵr and formed with him, the disaffected Harry Percy (Hotspur) and Douglas from Scotland, a league against Henry. At Shrewsbury in 1403 they were routed and Hotspur killed, but two years later the Earl of Northumberland, the Duke of York and the Archbishop of York attempted another rebellion. They were foiled and the Archbishop and other rebels executed. A third revolt by Northumberland was defeated in 1408 at Bramham Moor, near Tadcaster, when the Earl was killed. There was no further outbreak of civil war until 1455.

During the last years of his reign Henry was a sick man, suffering from epileptic fits which encouraged his son Prince Hal to take over the reins of government, ousting the king's Chancellor, Thomas Arundel, Archbishop of Canterbury. The king, who had dreamed of going on a Crusade, died in the 'Jerusalem' Chamber in the house of the Abbot of Westminster in 1413.

# Henry V

*Born Monmouth 1387. Ascended throne 1413. Reigned 9 years.*
*Son of Henry IV.*
*Married Catherine of Valois.*
*One son.*
*Died Vincennes 1422, aged 35. Buried at Westminster.*

Henry V, pious, stern and a skilful soldier after years spent fighting the Welsh, succeeded his father at the age of twenty-six. His magnanimity was immediately demonstrated by freeing the young Earl of March, a contender for the throne, and restoring to Hotspur's son his father's estates. Though he had to crush a conspiracy to further the Earl of March's claim and suppress Lollardy, Henry's reign was dominated by his renewal of the Hundred Years War. In doing so, he diverted England's attention away from possible internal discord: the nobles and their followers were anxious for war; Henry was equally anxious that they should not remain idle in England, and convinced himself that his cause was just, even pressing a claim to the French Crown through his great-grandfather, Edward III, whose mother was Philip IV's daughter. Despite some misgivings, Parliament voted money for the campaigns, and the Church was appeased by the king's continued persecution of the Lollards.

Henry was more successful in the French war than Edward III at his best, and succeeded in mastering northern France. In this he was assisted by an alliance with the Duke of Burgundy and the Emperor Sigismund, who visited England in 1416. Henry's army sailed from Southampton in 1415, using 1,500 ships to convey 8,000 troops and their equipment. Agincourt (1415), won in the face of tremendous odds and at a cost of 500 casualties to the French's 7,000, was only a stepping-stone to the Treaty of Troyes (1420). By the terms of this treaty – achieved with the aid of a disaffected group within

*Opposite:* Henry V: artist and date unknown *(The National Portrait Gallery, London)*.

France – Charles VI, the lunatic king of France, gave his daughter Catherine in marriage to Henry, and recognized him as his heir in preference to his own son, the Dauphin. Had he lived two months longer Henry V would, in theory, have been crowned King of France. In practice, however, the unconquered parts of France would never have accepted the treaty, and it is unlikely that Henry would have been able to assume the French crown without the complete conquest of the country. Given growing disquiet in England at his parlous financial position, it is doubtful whether he could have found the enormous sums required to fund such a campaign.

But Henry died suddenly of dysentery in 1422, leaving to his baby son a claim to the French throne that would be difficult to uphold, and a nobility in England that had gained practice in the business of warfare. The son was to reap the harvest of his father's policy.

# Henry VI

*Born Windsor Castle 1421. Ascended throne 1422. Reigned 1422–61 and 1470–1, 40 years.*
*Son of Henry V.*
*Married Margaret of Anjou.*
*One son.*
*Died London 1471 (murdered), aged 50. Buried (i) Chertsey Abbey (ii) Windsor (iii) ?Westminster.*

Henry VI came to the throne in 1422, aged nine months. Within two months, on the death of Charles VI, he was also nominally king of France, though the Dauphin assumed the title. For the first twenty years of Henry's reign the government of England and the conduct of the inevitable war with France were in the hands of his quarrelsome uncles and cousins.

At first the progress of the war continued the successes of Henry V: the able Duke of Bedford won a victory at Cravant in 1423 and the following year the Dauphin's army was almost annihilated at Verneuil. The lack of funds and leaders as capable as Bedford to prosecute the war helped Joan of Arc to reverse English fortunes in 1428, when she relieved the desultory siege of Orléans. Even when she was captured and handed over to the English in 1430, she had revived French morale sufficiently for others to continue the reconquest of English territories, particularly after Burgundy's change of sides. When the Hundred Years War at last ended in 1453, Calais was all that remained of Henry V's conquests. The French renaissance made Henry's coronation as French king in Paris in 1431 seem an absurd gesture. The loss of Normandy diminished still further the prestige of a government which was already noted for its incompetence. The Bishop of Chichester and the Duke of Suffolk were but two of the casualties of mob anger.

In England the reign of Henry VI witnessed the most acute phase of the Wars of the Roses. The weak government was unable to control the nobles, accustomed to fighting by the long French campaign. The two aristocratic factions represented by Edmund Beaufort, Duke of Somerset, and the heir presumptive, Richard, Duke of York, battled for supremacy but they left the mass of people unaffected. Peasants were gaining more freedom, and the merchant class more power.

In 1454 the king succumbed to the madness which was hereditary in his mother's family, and the Duke of York was appointed Regent. The king's recovery in 1455 was accompanied by the outbreak of open hostilities between the families of Lancaster and York at St Albans in 1458. The Yorkists triumphed and Somerset was killed, Henry VI was captured but treated with respect by York who resumed his Regency.

In 1459 a Lancastrian revival, directed by the queen, Margaret of Anjou, who was as vigorous as her husband was weak, saw the flight of York, and his chief supporter, Richard Neville, Earl of Salisbury, of the tremendously powerful Neville family. By 1460 the struggle had become so bitter that York had claimed the throne, but at the end of the year the Lancastrians routed the Yorkists at Wakefield. York and Neville were both slain. In the following year small firearms were used for the first time in English history at the second Battle of St Albans, where Margaret defeated the Earl of Warwick. It was the last real success for the Lancastrian cause. In 1461 Edward, the late Duke of York's eldest son, had himself crowned as Edward IV at Westminster Hall and hurried north to overtake the retreating Lancastrians; they met during a snowstorm at Towton, south west of York, where Margaret's forces were decisively defeated, compelling her to flee with Henry and their son to Scotland.

Neville's popular son, the Earl of Warwick and Salisbury (known as the 'kingmaker') continued the campaign against the indomitable Margaret in the north of England, terminating her struggle in 1464 and capturing Henry near Clitheroe, Yorkshire, in the following year. The most powerful noble in England, Warwick fell out with Edward when the king, in the midst of Warwick's negotiations with France for a suitable marriage, announced that he was already married to Elizabeth Woodville, a Lancastrian widow and a commoner at that. Warwick was further angered by the advancement of the Woodville relations. His influence lost, Warwick intrigued with the French king, Louis XI, and at his insistence with the exiled Margaret of Anjou. Having been at war with her for years, this was not an easy condition to meet, but ultimately Warwick's youngest daughter Anne was married to Margaret's only son, Edward, Prince of Wales. In 1470 an invasion led by Warwick succeeded in releasing the mad Henry VI from the Tower and restoring him to a puppet's throne.

Edward fled to Burgundy, only to return in 1471. In two battles in that year Edward regained the throne. Warwick paid the price for trying to perform the function of

Henry VI: artist and date unknown *(The National Portrait Gallery, London)*.

kingmaker to both sides, at Barnet. Henry VI's son, Prince Edward, was killed at Tewkesbury, extinguishing the hopes of the Lancastrians who lost many leaders in the battle or through subsequent execution. After Tewkesbury Henry VI was killed, probably by Edward IV's brother, Richard, Duke of Gloucester, of later and greater infamous memory.

# Edward IV

*Born Rouen 1442. Reigned 1461–70 and 1471–83, 21 years.*
*Son of Richard, Duke of York.*
*Married Elizabeth Woodville.*
*Two sons, five daughters.*
*Died Westminster 1483, aged 41. Buried at Windsor.*

Raised as the Earl of March, Edward proved to be a far more efficient statesman and soldier than the tragic Henry VI had been. But his morals were poor, disapproved of even by his not very particular contemporaries, and his greed was inordinate. His instruction to murder Henry VI's son Prince Edward and later his own brother Clarence while incarcerated in the Tower, together with his brutal treatment of captives, revealed his cruel ruthlessness. The nobles also took exception to his marriage to the daughter of Earl Rivers, compounded by the liberality with which Edward showered her family with favours.

After the death of Edward's father at the Battle of Wakefield in 1460, the Yorkist cause was revived by victory at Mortimer's Cross (1461), west of Ludlow. Although defeated at the second Battle of St Albans in the same year, Edward took advantage of Henry VI's plea to his victorious queen not to allow her wild levies to have the run of London, to enter the city and be crowned king. During the first part of his reign (see above), Edward's position on the throne was tenuous, having alienated his supporter Warwick and having to deal with rebellions fomented by Louis XI.

When Edward was compelled to flee to Flanders, he acquired an interest in literature and printing, encouraging him later to establish a book collection (now in the British Library) and to become patron to William Caxton who returned to England in 1476 after an absence of thirty-five years. Caxton established a printing-press at Westminster from which he issued a stream of books, many of them translated from Latin and French by himself.

The battles at Barnet and Tewkesbury put an end to the insecurity of the first part of his reign. He stimulated trade and strengthened control of the Welsh and Scottish borders, the last through his brother Richard whom he made 'King's Lieutenant in the North'. He also revived the old claim to the French throne and invaded France in alliance with his brother-in-law the Duke of Burgundy. At Picquigny in 1475 Louis XI paid 75,000 crowns and promised an annuity of 20,000 if Edward would return to England. Edward was able to live on this money and the proceeds from confiscated Lancastrian estates for the rest of his reign.

Edward's sudden death in 1483, worn out by a debauched life, was to lead to tragedy for his two sons, aged twelve and nine.

# Edward V

*Born Westminster 1470. Ascended throne 1483. Reigned 2 months.*
*Elder son of Edward IV.*
*Died London 1483 (?murdered). ?Buried at Westminster.*

Twelve-year-old Edward V succeeded his father in April 1483. At the time he was at Ludlow Castle, and was dispatched to London with a small retinue that included two Woodville uncles. His mother had wanted an armed escort, but was refused it. *En route,* they were intercepted at Northampton by Edward's uncle Richard, Duke of Gloucester, who arrested the Woodville uncles and had the king lodged in the palace part of the Tower. Elizabeth hurried her second son, the Duke of York, and all her daughters into the sanctuary of Westminster Abbey. Yet for reasons that will always remain a subject for conjecture, she released her second son, perhaps to keep her brother company now that the date of coronation had been fixed, perhaps because she had been persuaded that sanctuary could not apply to children incapable of crime. Both sons disappeared.

Basing his claim on the grounds that Edward's marriage to Elizabeth Woodville was invalid, and that his children were therefore illegitimate, Gloucester seized the throne as Richard III.

The story of Richard's probable murder of his nephews is well known. In 1674, the skeletons of two children were discovered during alterations in the Tower and subsequently interred in Westminster Abbey.

# Richard III

*Born Fotheringay Castle 1452. Ascended throne 1483 (usurper). Reigned 2 years.*
*Son of Richard, Duke of York, and brother of Edward IV.*
*Married Anne Neville. One son.*
*Died Bosworth 1485, aged 33. Buried at Greyfriars Church, Leicester.*

When he came to the throne in 1483 Richard was already credited with personal responsibility for the deaths of Henry VI, Henry's son and his own brother Clarence. Contemporaries, and posterity, were to saddle him with the murder of his two nephews, though his guilt is still questionable. Richard, Duke of Gloucester, had proved himself an able soldier and administrator, especially in the North. His nephew's youth, and the unpopularity of the Queen Mother's Woodville relations, might have seen England fall prey once again to internal wars. So Richard III's seizure of the throne in 1483 can be defended on the doubtful grounds of 'reasons of State'.

But the murder of his nephews and the ruthless extinction of anyone who opposed his will made his rule unpopular and set afoot many plots for vengeance. The first was led by his erstwhile collaborator, the Duke of Buckingham, who began treating with Henry Tudor, Earl of Richmond, and the focus of the Lancastrian cause. The rising collapsed and Buckingham was executed. It is thought that the princes in the Tower were executed shortly after this revolt, though Richard's complicity has never been proved. None the less his almost inevitable knowledge of the deed split the Yorkist party and lost Richard further support.

Richard tried to bribe the Duke of Burgundy to surrender Henry from his exile in Brittany, almost with success. Henry Tudor could trace his descent in the female line from John of Gaunt's illicit union with Katherine Swynford, making Henry's mother the great-great-granddaughter of Edward III. With such ancestry he was the 'nearest thing to royalty the Lancastrian party possessed'.

In France he gathered a small army, Lancastrian veterans and others anxious to see the end of Richard flocking to his support. Besides Richard's ruthlessness, his reliance on Northerners (understandable as he had spent much of his life in the North of England) antagonized people in the South. Henry landed at Milford Haven on 7 August 1485 and more men joined him. On 22 August at Market Bosworth in Leicestershire, the last important battle of the Wars of the Roses was fought. Richard III was killed in battle, and Richmond became king as Henry VII.

The marriage of Henry VII to the Yorkist heiress, Elizabeth of York, united the claims of Lancaster and York and gave England the Tudor line of monarchs. This remarkable woman was the daughter of Edward IV, sister of Edward V, niece of Richard III, wife of Henry VII, and mother of Henry VIII; she was also Queen of Scotland and of France.

*Above:* Edward IV: artist and date unknown *(The National Portrait Gallery, London)*.

*Opposite:* Richard III: artist and date unknown *(The National Portrait Gallery, London)*.

RICARDVS · III · ANG · REX ·

# PART TWO

# TUDORS

# AND STUARTS

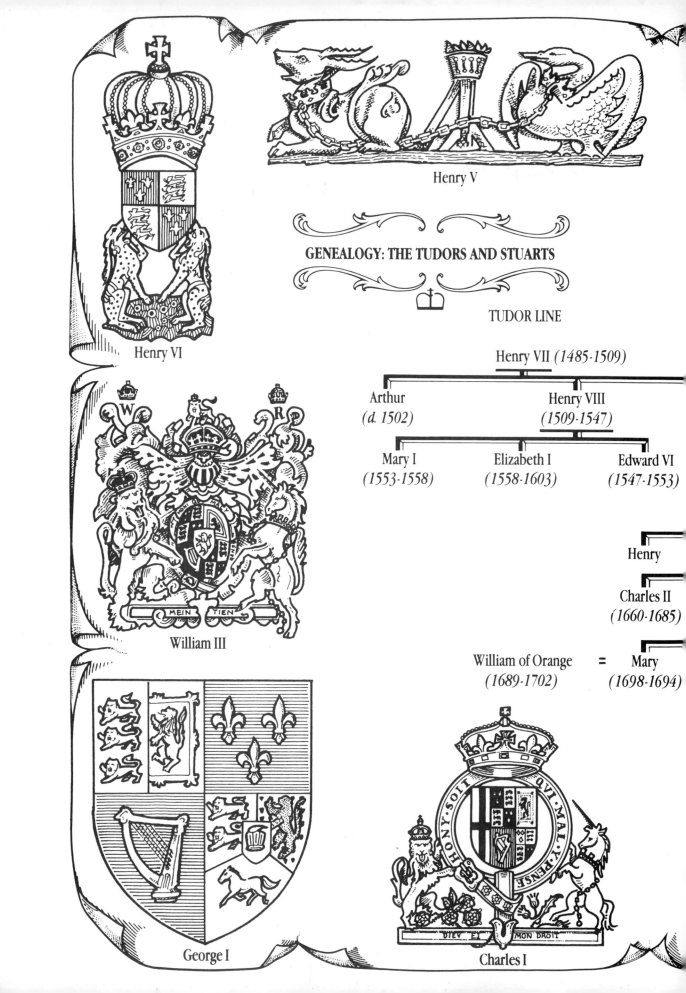

Henry V

## GENEALOGY: THE TUDORS AND STUARTS

Henry VI

TUDOR LINE

Henry VII *(1485-1509)*

Arthur
*(d. 1502)*

Henry VIII
*(1509-1547)*

Mary I
*(1553-1558)*

Elizabeth I
*(1558-1603)*

Edward VI
*(1547-1553)*

William III

Henry

Charles II
*(1660-1685)*

William of Orange
*(1689-1702)*

=

Mary
*(1698-1694)*

George I

Charles I

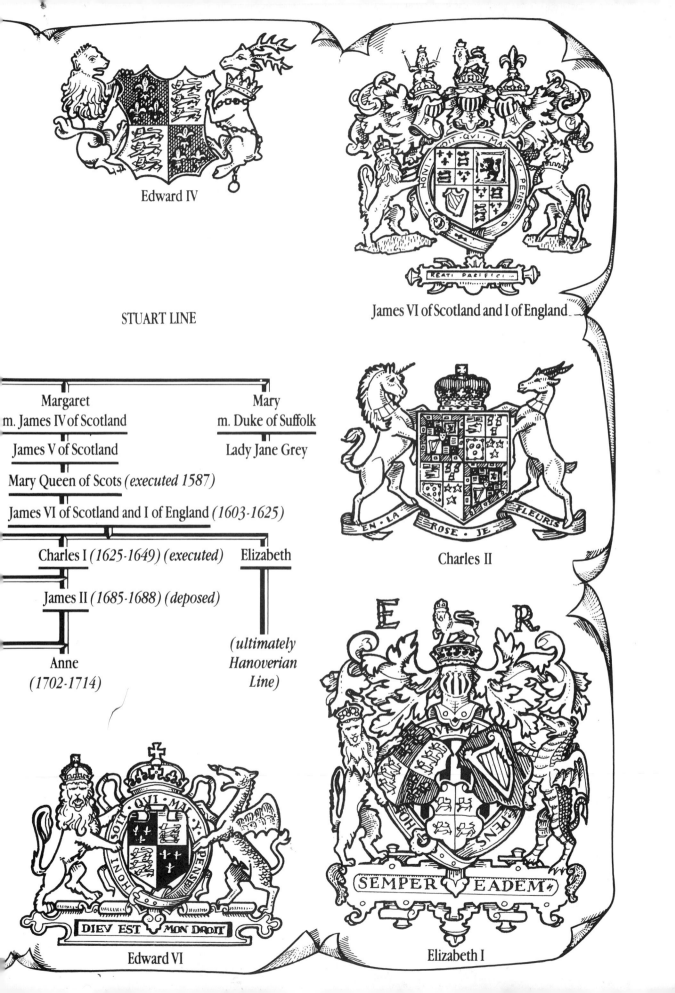

Edward IV

James VI of Scotland and I of England

STUART LINE

Margaret
m. James IV of Scotland

Mary
m. Duke of Suffolk

James V of Scotland

Lady Jane Grey

Mary Queen of Scots *(executed 1587)*

James VI of Scotland and I of England *(1603-1625)*

Charles I *(1625-1649) (executed)*

Elizabeth

James II *(1685-1688) (deposed)*

*(ultimately Hanoverian Line)*

Anne
*(1702-1714)*

Charles II

Edward VI

Elizabeth I

# THE TUDORS

## Henry VII

*Born Pembroke Castle 1457 (his mother was 14 years old).*
*Ascended throne 1485. Reigned 24 years.*
*Son of Edmund Tudor.*
*Married 1486, Elizabeth of York, eldest daughter of Edward IV.*
*Two sons, two daughters.*
*Died Richmond 1509, aged 52 years. Buried at Westminster Abbey.*

As victor at the Battle of Bosworth, where Richard III was killed, Henry Tudor ascended the throne in 1485. By his marriage in 1486 with the Yorkist heiress he finally ended the Wars of the Roses. Though the Tudor dynasty began in treason and bloodshed, it eventually brought a new, more peaceful era.

Henry was determined to restore order to the nation. By wise and firm – if sometimes avaricious – government, the old, fierce struggle between Crown and barons was ended. By heavy taxes and fines for misdemeanours, he impoverished the nobles and brought them to heel. The transitional period between the Middle Ages and Renaissance was bridged.

Henry's claim to the throne was weak, so it was not surprising that his position was challenged by pretenders and the disaffected. Lord Lovel in 1486 was followed by Lambert Simnel who was put forward as Clarence's son, Edward Plantagenet, the true Earl of Warwick; a baker's son, Simnel was crowned Edward VI in Dublin, but his forces met with little support in England and were crushed at Stoke, near Newark. The real Edward was released from prison by Henry to be paraded through the streets of London, and it was in Henry's kitchens that the captured Simnel was put to work.

More serious was the pretence by the Flemish Perkin Warbeck to be Richard, Duke of York, who was presumed murdered in the Tower: Warbeck was acknowledged as her nephew by Margaret, Edward VI's sister, and received by James IV of Scotland as the Duke of York. However, his invasion of the south west in 1498 was easily defeated and Warbeck executed after attempting to escape from the Tower. Another insurrection was prompted by the heavy taxation imposed by Henry; ill-armed Cornish miners and peasants marched on London and were within sight of the city before they were defeated.

To help counter threats arising from his poor claim to the throne, Henry sought to secure his position by dynastic marriages, though acceptance of his offers implied a tacit recognition of the likelihood of his holding the Crown: his eldest son Arthur was married to the Spanish princess Catherine of Aragon, and his daughter Margaret to King James IV of Scotland.

Henry sought peace in preference to pressing territorial claims in France, and after brief hostilities concluded the lucrative Treaty of Etaples with Charles VIII. Like the Treaty of Picquigny, it had a beneficial effect on commerce which was encouraged through trade agreements with Denmark, Florence and the Low Countries. In 1496 John Cabot was sent on the expedition which discovered Nova Scotia and Newfoundland; shipbuilding was encouraged with subsidies, and a start was made on establishing the navy.

Henry died exhausted by work. His attention to detail was legendary: he examined his accounts daily and bequeathed his personal fortune of £1½ million to his second son Henry who succeeded without opposition.

During Henry's reign, playing cards were first invented (1486): the portrait of his wife, Elizabeth of York, has appeared eight times on every deck of playing cards for over 500 years.

# Henry VIII

*Born Greenwich 1491. Ascended throne 1509. Reigned 38 years.*
*Second son of Henry VII.*
*Married six times.*
*One son, one daughter, by first wife; one daughter by second wife; one son by third wife.*
*Died Whitehall 1547, aged 56 years. Buried at Windsor.*

The best-known fact about Henry VIII is that he had six wives, which has often been presented as a reflection of his lust. In fact it had far more to do with his concern to produce as trouble-free a succession as he had enjoyed. The inability of successive wives to produce a male heir spurred him to dispose of wives by whatever means were necessary:

Catherine of Aragon (widow of Henry's brother Arthur) – divorced.
Anne Boleyn (mother of Elizabeth I) – beheaded.
Jane Seymour (mother of Edward VI) – died.
Anne of Cleves – divorced.
Catherine Howard – beheaded.
Catherine Parr – outlived the king.

*Above:* Henry VIII: after Holbein, c1536 *(The National Portrait Gallery, London)*.

*Opposite:* Henry VII: artist Michiel Sittow, painted in 1505 aged 48 *(The National Portrait Gallery, London)*.

Although Henry seems to have married Catherine of Aragon partly because he could not repay her dowry to Arthur, their marriage was happy, and only the death of their son after a few days, followed by a series of miscarriages and still births drove Henry to seek a more fruitful union. After giving birth to Princess Elizabeth and a miscarriage, Anne Boleyn was accused of incest and adultery, and beheaded along with the brother she is supposed to have bedded. Jane Seymour died giving birth to Prince Edward, and the marriage to the physically disappointing Anne of Cleves was annulled on the grounds of non-consummation. Catherine Howard's previous attachments were the pretext for an accusation of adultery that led to her death in the Tower. Catherine Parr had been married twice before, and her maturity and ability to get on with Henry's children doubtless helped her to survive Henry.

In his early manhood Henry was accounted the most handsome and accomplished prince of his time, skilled both in learning and athletics. Unlike his father, he was ambitious for military glory. Three years after becoming king, he invaded France in his capacity as a member of the Holy League; he commanded the English with Austrian mercenaries, and won a rather insignificant cavalry action that had to be dignified by the name 'Battle of the Spurs'. In his absence the Scots invaded England and were decisively beaten by Lord Surrey at Flodden Field. James IV, Henry's brother-in-law, was killed and the flower of the Scots nobility slain.

Like many monarchs before him, Henry was soon seduced away from the *minutiae* of State affairs by the attractions of hunting and jousting, for both of which he held a passion, and by his demanding relationships in and out of wedlock. The growing willingness to leave the burden of government to his ministers enabled the three principal advisers of his reign, Thomas Wolsey, Thomas More and Thomas Cromwell, to exercise exceptional powers. Wolsey, a butcher's son from Ipswich, became one of the most powerful ministers in English history, living on a grand scale and owning two palaces – York Palace and Hampton Court – that surpassed even the king's own houses; in 1515 Henry compelled him to hand over Hampton Court. State occasions were invested with the same extravagance: at an inconsequential meeting in 1520 between Henry and Francis I of France, known as the Field of the Cloth of Gold, Wolsey was attended by 300 servants and set up fountains filled with wine. It was Wolsey's failure to arrange for Henry's divorce from his first wife that led to his dismissal in 1529 and summons the following year to London on a charge of high treason; he died on the journey.

Cromwell inherited Wolsey's problems, and the obduracy of the Pope over the question of a divorce forced him to draw up ever more radical plans to achieve Henry's desires. Using the law of *praemunire* to accuse the clergy of treason, Cromwell extracted from them a recognition of Henry's position as Supreme Head of the Church of England. An attack on papal finances was followed by the declaration by the new

Archbishop of Canterbury, Thomas Cranmer, that Henry's marriage was invalid. Excommunication by the Pope led to a flurry of Parliamentary legislation that sealed the break with Rome: an act in restraint of appeals declared invalid any pronouncements from Rome, and Acts of Submission, Succession and Supremacy confirmed Henry's position as head of the Church.

Henry's anti-papal campaign did not end there. The Dissolution of the Monasteries began in 1536. Henry's costly foreign policy had already drained the resources inherited from his father, making attractive the idea of confiscating the extensive estates attached to the monasteries. Another reason for the spoliation was that, if left undisturbed, they would be hotbeds for Catholic propaganda against Henry's break with the Papacy. The monks were indeed vulnerable to attack at this time, far too many of them being idle and immoral. Wolsey had begun the work by closing 29 communities of less than 7 inmates, devoting the revenues to his educational foundations in Oxford and Ipswich. In dissolving the monasteries, Cromwell brought to an end a major element in English life that went back almost a thousand years, and in so doing wrought the most dramatic redistribution of land since William I. The wealth assumed by the Crown was partly frittered away on a futile expedition to France that required a massive army of 40,000 men for the single gain of Boulogne.

The break with Rome was not concerned with altering doctrine: the Statute of the Six Articles confirmed the fundamental tenets of the Church of Rome, and allowed for dire penalties if ignored; and in 1537 Henry ordered the publication of the *Bishops' Book* or the *Institution of a Christian Man,* a conservative and orthodox tract except on the issue of the supremacy of the Pope. Henry himself wrote a book on the Sacraments in reply to Luther, for which he had received the title of 'Defender of the Faith' from the Pope, a title since borne by all his successors.* His full title was By the Grace of God, King of England, France and Ireland; the Supreme Head and Sovereign of the Most Noble Order of the Garter.

Opposition to the suppression of the monasteries was compounded by the beginnings of the enclosure movement, which deprived peasants of residual feudal rights to common land and, in converting arable land to pasture, reduced employment. It was most strongly felt in the North, where the Pilgrimage of Grace of 1536–7 drew its main support. Neither papist nor anti-Henry, the rising was conservative in its inspiration and aimed at persuading Henry to dismiss the detested Cromwell and to save the monasteries as the main source of alms for the poor. With false promises the Duke of Norfolk pacified and disarmed the rebels before beginning his savage retribution which included hanging and quartering the ringleaders. Abbots who

---

*The title is still to be found on current British coinage, in the forms Fidei Defensor, Fidei Def., Fid. Def., or just F.D.

supported the Pilgrimage or denied the royal supremacy were hung or executed.

Henry carried on his father's work of creating an effective navy. He built the *Great Harry*, of 1,000 tons, then the largest ship ever known; the first dockyard was created at Portsmouth, in 1540, and the navy was separated from the army for the first time. At his death, Henry had added some eighty ships to naval strength and so began the challenge to the maritime supremacy of Spain. A constitutional monarch in name, Henry was in reality all but absolute, and the question of Tudor despotism has provided fertile ground for historical debate. But in spite of the almost summary execution of wives, ministers and clergy, Henry was popular with the people throughout his reign and was a brilliant statesman; at a time when Europe was in turmoil, he maintained order without an army.

# Edward VI

*Born Hampton Court 1537. Ascended throne 1547. Reigned 6 years.*
*Son of Henry VIII and his third wife, Jane Seymour.*
*Unmarried.*
*Died 1553, aged 15 years. Buried Westminster Abbey.*

Edward was nine years of age when he became king, and the reasons for Henry's anxiety about a weak succession became apparent: a weak child, he was never to exercise the authority of a king, dying of tuberculosis at fifteen. Edward's uncle, Edward Seymour, Earl of Hertford, was named Protector and virtually ruled the country, though with more humane methods than Henry.

He began by invading Scotland to enforce a marriage agreement between Edward and Mary, Queen of Scots, and defeated the Scots army at Pinkie. Soon created Duke of Somerset, Seymour with Archbishop Cranmer pushed further the religious revolution: John Knox, Ridley, Latimer and Hooper were appointed Court Preachers; Cranmer's beautifully written Book of Common Prayer (1549) was introduced to bring uniformity of worship and contributed to England's move towards becoming a Protestant state; the Six Articles (see page 65) were repealed along with Henry's heresy and treason laws. The debate over the Eucharist and the introduction of Cranmer's Prayer Book on Whit Sunday 1549 sparked a rebellion in parts of Devon and Cornwall, and in Norfolk, led by Robert Ket, resulting in bloody suppression and the fall of Somerset.

John Dudley, Earl of Warwick – a schemer with unbridled ambition – replaced Somerset as the leading noble in Council, and gradually introduced Edward into its affairs. The office of Protector was abolished, Warwick acting as Lord President of the Council. To help to restore order in the country, the office of Lord Lieutenant was created, charged with the preservation of peace in each shire. Soon made Duke of

Edward VI: after Holbein, c1542 *(The National Portrait Gallery, London)*.

Northumberland, Dudley hastened the pace of religious reform, introducing a second Book of Common Prayer. Northumberland mismanaged the country's already bad economy: prices were soaring, and hardship was keenly felt among the poor. He was more concerned, however, to secure the succession for his family, and to that end he married his fourth son, Lord Guildford Dudley, to Lady Jane Grey, who had a claim to be Edward's heir. Edward nominated in his will Lady Jane Grey as his successor, excluding his half-sisters, Mary and Elizabeth.

Edward died in the seventh year of his reign, leaving the country torn by opposing factions

# Lady Jane Grey

*Born Bradgate, Leicestershire 1537. Ascended throne 1553. Reigned 9 days.*
*Daughter of Henry Grey, Duke of Suffolk and Lady Frances Brandon.*
*Executed Tower Green 1554, aged 17 years.*

At Edward's death, the next in succession was his sister Mary. But Northumberland, anxious for his family's advancement, persuaded the dying Edward to exclude Mary from the throne on the grounds of religion – she was a staunch Catholic. Lady Jane's claim to the throne was through her mother, who was daughter of Princess Mary by Charles Brandon, Duke of Suffolk. By Jane's unwilling marriage to Northumberland's son, her fate was yoked to his father's ability to press her claim. His unpopularity sealed their fate.

Though Council recognized her claim and instructions for her proclamation were sent out, only two towns responded. When Mary raised her standard at Framlingham and called on all supporters of the Tudor dynasty to rally to her cause, she received many pledges of help. Northumberland's troops, at Cambridge *en route* to Framlingham to arrest Mary, melted away and the Councillors did a volte-face and proclaimed Mary queen.

Lady Jane, her husband and Northumberland were prisoners in the Tower by the time Mary entered London in triumph in August 1553. Lady Jane refused to foresake Protestantism and scorned Northumberland for his craven recantation, which failed to save his life. None the less Mary might have spared her but for Wyatt's rebellion in opposition to Mary's rule and her proposed marriage to Philip of Spain. Lady Jane was beheaded on Tower Green in February 1554.

# Mary I ('Bloody Mary')

*Born Greenwich Palace 1516. Ascended throne 1553. Reigned 5 years.*
*Daughter of Henry VIII and his first wife, Catherine of Aragon.*
*Married Philip II of Spain.*
*No issue.*
*Died St James's Palace 1558, aged 42. Buried at Westminster Abbey (no monument).*

Mary as the daughter of Catherine of Aragon had suffered an appalling childhood after her parents' divorce when she was ten. The subsequent neglect, persecution and ill-health obviously had their effect in the later days of her reign. In 1532 Mary and her mother parted, and Henry forbade Mary to see her mother even when Catherine was dying at Kimbolton. The following year Mary was declared illegitimate by Act of Parliament, and under great pressure she finally submitted to acknowledge Henry's supremacy and her own illegitimacy. After Edward's succession, a new kind of persecution began with attempts to make her abjure the mass. Like her mother she was to remain a devout Catholic. Her adherence to principle as the foremost guide to action helps to explain why her last years won her the appellation 'Bloody'.

She was thirty-seven years of age when she entered London as queen and exercised leniency towards Lady Jane and her husband. Only Northumberland and two accomplices were executed. Nor did she embark on a precipitate assault on all aspects of the Reformation in England. Rather she allowed Protestants who did not wish to live under a Catholic ruler to leave the country; they included four of Edward's bishops and some 800 who formed a Protestant Church of England in exile. Equally she was made well aware that the aristocracy and gentry would not tolerate an attempt to recover the monastic lands they had been given or bought. But the undoing of Cranmer's work was her priority and it began in 1553 when Parliament reluctantly passed the first Statute of Repeal. Priests who had taken wives were the first target. Catholic bishops, doctrines and practice were restored, and the papal legate, Mary's cousin Cardinal Pole, formally absolved the realm for its act of schism.

Her early marriage was considered essential and the Earl of Devon was the English candidate, but she chose instead her cousin, heir to the Spanish throne, the future Philip II who was already a widower and eleven years her junior. The Commons, realizing such a match would be the greatest threat to English independence since the days of Henry III, begged the queen to reconsider; but the consolidation of the Catholic religion in England was undoubtedly her aim, and she stood firm. Trouble broke out almost immediately with the rebellion led by Sir Thomas Wyatt who had hopes of simultaneous uprisings throughout England and the promise of French support. Neither materialized, though Wyatt reached Ludgate in the City of London, and only

*Above:* Mary I: artist, Master John, painted in 1544 aged 28 *(The National Portrait Gallery, London)*.

*Opposite:* Lady Jane Grey (Lady Dudley): attrib. Master John, c1545 *(The National Portrait Gallery, London)*.

Mary's personal plea in the Guildhall for the citizens of the capital to support her prevented the city falling to the rebels. Over a hundred executions followed, and Elizabeth was imprisoned on suspicion of complicity. The rising defeated, Philip came to England in 1554 and the marriage took place at Winchester the following year. Philip was to leave after only fourteen months, partly because of Mary's inability to conceive.

Mary surrounded herself with zealous Catholic advisers and then attempted to enforce the wholesale conversion of England. In the succeeding years she earned her title 'Bloody' Mary: Protestant bishops Latimer and Ridley and the sixty-seven-year-old Archbishop Cranmer were amongst those burnt at the stake. (The spot is marked by a bronze cross set into the roadway at Broad Street, Oxford.) The revival of the heresy laws led to the burning at the stake of almost 300 men and women, the overwhelming majority from the lower levels of English society. Few gentlemen who had been advocates of Protestantism under Edward VI were martyred, and it was this rather than the cruelty of burning that damaged the esteem in which the monarchy was held. The fires served only to rally more Englishmen to the Protestant faith.

Calais, which had been an English possession since 1347, was lost to France in 1558 after Mary had agreed to support the Emperor's struggle against France. Almost the only contribution to Elizabeth's inheritance was Mary's reform of finance and improvements to the roads, of which Elizabeth was to take full advantage.

Mary, after a life which had been one long tragedy, died in 1558.

# Elizabeth I

*Born Greenwich Palace 1533. Ascended throne 1558. Reigned 44 years.*
*Daughter of Henry VIII and his second wife, Anne Boleyn.*
*Unmarried.*
*Died Richmond 1603, aged 70. Buried at Westminster Abbey.*

Elizabeth, the last of the Tudors, found England in a sad state when she ascended the throne. It was torn by religious fears and differences; Calais, last foothold on the Continent, had been lost; the French king had one foot in Edinburgh. In addition, there were many who had doubts about her title to the throne, though her accession was uncontested: for Protestants it meant an end to persecution, and Catholics were aware that her religious beliefs were not held with the passion of Mary.

Elizabeth was a remarkable woman, noted for her learning, her reputed command of nine languages (which included Cornish, Irish and Welsh), sometimes wayward, often wise. She loved jewels and beautiful clothes, but had a hard, sceptical intellect, coupled with a total lack of fanaticism, which helped her steer a sensible and moderate course through the conflicts of her long reign.

From first to last she was undoubtedly popular with the people and received loyalty from her statesmen. She made progresses an art and an aspect of monarchy, spending several months each year visiting her noble subjects, who were sometimes brought near to ruin by the expense of entertaining the queen and her retinue. Many an extension to a country house was prompted by an impending visit. Apart from the ancillary purpose of giving the household at her palaces a chance to clean them thoroughly, their objective was to show the monarch to her subjects, and much ceremony attended her passage through towns.

Contributing to the lack of opposition to Elizabeth's accession was the fortunate predominance of women both in control of three important countries and as alternative claimants to the throne: Elizabeth, England; Mary, Queen of Scots, Scotland; and her mother-in-law, Catherine de Medici, was Regent for Charles IX of France.

From the outset Elizabeth showed moderately Protestant inclinations, undoing Mary's church legislation and reinstating her father's. In this her hand was forced by Pope Paul IV's insistence that she renounce all claim to the throne on account of her illegitimacy (the result of her father's marriage to Jane Seymour in 1536). As England was a fief of the Holy See (see page 34), the Pope claimed the right to dispose of the Crown. This compelled Elizabeth to establish the Anglican Church with its Thirty-nine Articles, Book of Common Prayer and the sovereign as its head.

Elizabeth did her utmost to avoid war, though her concern to maintain England's independence encouraged her to do anything she could to weaken any power that threatened it. But with the massacre of the Huguenots in France and the subsequent rise of the pro-Spanish and ultra-Catholic parties on the Continent, England felt insecure and an army went to the assistance of the French Protestants. After an initial reluctance to go to the support of rebels against a lawful sovereign, Elizabeth aided the Spanish Netherlands (present-day Belgium) in its struggle for independence from Spain. She also skilfully assisted the Protestant cause in Scotland when in the name of Protestantism the Scottish lords rebelled against the Catholic Regency of Mary of Guise, while her daughter Mary, Queen of Scots, lived in France with her husband the Dauphin. The Treaty of Edinburgh in 1560 enabled the Scottish Parliament to abolish the authority of the Pope in Scotland and to establish a Presbyterian form of Church.

It was an age of great adventurers and the queen undoubtedly had a genius for selecting capable advisers. Hawkins, Howard, Walsingham, the Cecils, Drake, Raleigh, Leicester, Essex, Burleigh, the Gilberts and many more made England both respected and feared. The disquiet caused by the massing of the Spanish Armada brought pressure on Elizabeth to allow Drake to attack Cadiz and in a brilliant action destroy the shipping ('singeing the King of Spain's beard', he called it). Catholic plots in support of Mary, Queen of Scots were repeatedly discovered, and after being beseeched by Parliament to execute her, Elizabeth acquiesced in 1587. When the Armada sailed in

1588 it was the largest expeditionary force known to history. Following on from Henry VIII's naval reforms, Sir John Hawkins had been equipping the navy with lighter and faster ships fitted with heavier, longer-range guns. Under the command of Lord Howard of Effingham, the English fleet harried the Armada up the Channel until Calais, where overnight Howard sent in eight fire-ships. They dispersed the Spanish and by a combination of fine captaincy by Drake, Hawkins and Frobisher, favourable weather patterns and superior navigational skills, a decisive victory was won, 44 of the 130 Spanish ships never returning to port.

Philip continued to attempt invasion with two further Armadas; both were defeated by the weather rather than English action, but it was in Ireland that he caused the greatest trouble with his support of Tyrone's rising in 1595. After inflicting a defeat on the English forces in 1597, Tyrone had an easy time of it in the face of the Earl of Essex's mixture of ineptitude and cowardice, which led to his downfall. Baron Mountjoy was sent to take over and defeated Tyrone and his 5,000 Spanish troops. Essex attempted a revolt in 1601, as ill-conceived as his Irish débâcle, and he was beheaded in the Tower.

During Elizabeth's reign England's progress in the field of discovery and colonization was tremendous. Raleigh's first Virginian colony was founded; Drake circumnavigated the globe, returning after a voyage of three years with £1½ million worth of treasure; the East India Company was founded, and English seamen left their mark in many parts of the world. Englishmen at this time were the lowest taxed in Europe.

Despite many suitors and offers of marriage, Elizabeth remained the only unmarried monarch of marriageable age since the Conquest. Part of her intention was not to diminish her authority or popularity, but also to prevent an alliance in support of the Counter-Reformation developing between France and Spain by protracting marriage negotiations with the French.

Elizabeth left the country secure, and religious troubles had largely disappeared. England was a first-class power. The queen proved herself particularly wise in statecraft, and though she held the Tudor view that the Crown had absolute supremacy over Parliament, she was tactful enough to avoid clashes between the two. The reign, too, was rich in learning: it was the age of Shakespeare, Sidney, Spenser, Bacon, Marlowe and many other famous names.

*Opposite:* Elizabeth I: artist unknown, c1575 *(The National Portrait Gallery, London).*

# THE STUART KINGS
## James I (VI of Scotland)

*Born Edinburgh Castle 1566. Ascended throne 1603. Reigned 22 years.*
*Son of Mary, Queen of Scots and Henry, Lord Darnley.*
*Crowned King of Scotland as James VI, after his mother's abdication in 1567.*
*Married Anne of Denmark.*
*Three sons, four daughters.*
*Died Theobalds 1625, aged 59. Buried at Westminster Abbey.*
*First of the Stuarts.*

James was born just three months after his mother's Court favourite had been butchered to death in an adjacent room. His whole childhood was pitiable, spent amid a turmoil of war, murder, plot and counter-plot, among as blood-thirsty a set of intriguers as could be found. His father was blown up when James was eight months old, and his mother married his murderer within a year, after which James was never to see her again. Within a few months of her remarriage, Mary was forced to abdicate and imprisoned at Lochleven.

James was crowned King of Scotland at Stirling, and though he made formal protests when his mother was executed in 1587 at Fotheringay, never showed any real feeling on the matter. In eleven years, four Regents exercised power, the first three coming to violent or suspicious ends. When sixteen, James was kidnapped by Lord Gowrie and held for eleven months. In 1589 he went to Christiania (now Oslo) to marry Anne of Denmark when he was twenty-three years of age and his bride fifteen. Though the marriage was somewhat lacklustre, it secured the succession with Prince Henry (1594) and Prince Charles (1600). During the 1590s, James gradually asserted control of the country, though there were repeated threats and the enigmatic Gowrie conspiracy, when an attempt was apparently made on James's life.

A Protestant, he was nevertheless engaged continually in intrigues with Rome up to the time of the death of Elizabeth, when he became James I of England and the first king to reign over both countries. Until then English and Scots had treated each other as foreigners, and James had a hard struggle to make the English take a milder attitude to Scotland. His journey south to assume the throne was something of a triumphal progress, during which he created over 300 knights and enjoyed the revels laid on for him at country houses *en route*.

James had a troubled reign. He ceaselessly preached 'the divine right of Kings', maintaining that the king was above the law; the House of Commons and the lawyers firmly opposed him, denying him money to pay his debts. He had high ideals, but he was no statesman, and his corrupt, ill-chosen favourites and extravagant Court aroused great animosity. So did his sale of titles which debased them and the Crown. Macaulay said of James: 'He was made up of two men – a witty, well-read scholar who wrote, disputed and harangued, and a nervous, drivelling idiot who acted.' Perhaps the most shameful episode of James's reign was his treatment of Sir Walter Raleigh, whom he offered to hand over to Philip III of Spain for execution after Raleigh's return from an ill-fated search for gold up the Orinoco River during which there had been a contretemps with the Spanish.

His first encounter with Parliament was an inept and tactless attempt to unify Scotland and England as Great Britain; it was coolly received by Parliament, so he introduced the name 'Britain'. It was the first of a series of conflicts that would lead ultimately to a king's execution, the Commons anticipating in the Apology of 1604 the deterioration into armed struggle: 'The privileges of the subject are for the most part at an everlasting stand . . . being once lost are not recovered but with much disquiet.'

In 1605 an attempt to blow up king and Parliament by Catholic sympathisers became known as the Gunpowder Plot. It failed, but brought a new wave of anti-Catholicism. The Puritans for their part were clamorous in their demands, challenging much of Elizabeth's Church settlement. Small religious groups found scant tolerance; in 1620 the Pilgrim Fathers sailed for America in their little ship *Mayflower*, seeking to found a community where their Calvinist tenets could flourish undisturbed. In 1611 the Authorised Version of the Bible was published, a landmark both for religion in England and for literature.

James's unproductive reign ended with the country close to war with Spain, partly due to the fiasco in which marriage negotiations for Charles ended. A cornerstone of James's foreign policy, such as it was, had been cordial relations with Spain; Charles and the royal favourite Buckingham had done much to undermine them in a madcap visit to Madrid in the expectation of securing the hand of the Infanta. They returned empty-handed and were urging the Commons into a bellicose position when James died. With the kingdom's finances in disarray and an antagonistic relationship between king and Commons, Charles inherited a delicate position.

*Above:* James I: after J. de Cutz the elder, date unknown *(The National Portrait Gallery, London)*.
*Opposite:* Charles I: artist, Daniel Mytens, painted in 1631 when aged 31 *(The National Portrait Gallery, London)*.

# Charles I

*Born Dunfermline 1600. Ascended throne 1625. Reigned 24 years.*
*Son of James I and Anne of Denmark.*
*Married Henrietta Maria of France.*
*Four sons, five daughters.*
*Died Whitehall 1649, aged 48 years (executed). Buried in Henry VIII vault, Windsor.*

Charles was a weak, rickety child, unable to walk until seven or talk until five, after which he had a slight stammer. Though he grew up to be courageous, he lacked judgement, and his strong prejudices accompanied by the tactlessness common to the Stuarts were to prove his undoing.

Several attempts were made when Charles was in his teens to arrange marriages that would form alliances, and to this end he was eventually married to the Catholic Henrietta Maria, daughter of Henry IV of France. Though it was eventually a happy union, it did not begin auspiciously. The terms of the marriage articles permitted Henrietta Maria to exercise her religion and to be responsible for the upbringing of any children until they were thirteen. As this contravened an undertaking Charles had given to Parliament, the terms had to be secret; none the less Parliament got wind of them, which helped to foment suspicion arising from the queen's strong devotion to Catholicism. Her huge entourage angered many at Court, and within a year Charles had sent packing a bishop, 29 priests and 410 attendants. The queen's advice and faction were later to play a crucial role in moulding Charles's opinions.

Early in his reign Charles encountered difficulties with Parliament, for he stubbornly refused to accept dictation. Three times it was summoned and three times dissolved, until from 1629 for eleven years he governed by personal rule, known as the 'Eleven Years' Tyranny'. Without Parliament there was no money, and the Commons' mistrust had been illustrated by granting Charles tonnage and poundage for only one year, instead of the customary sanction for life. He needed money for simultaneous war with Spain and France, but Parliament was reluctant to supply it, fearing its incompetent use by Buckingham, who continued to be the royal favourite. Their scepticism was justified by the catastrophic raid on Cadiz when an admiral who had never before put to sea vainly tried to emulate Drake's brilliant exploit (see page 73). Buckingham and Charles had hoped the raid might furnish booty on an Elizabethan scale; instead they were reduced to attempting to pawn the crown jewels, selling monopolies, exploiting royal forests and the extension of 'ship money' to inland towns and shires.

Buckingham's murder in Portsmouth *en route* to the relief of La Rochelle did not end the mistrust between king and Parliament. Though Buckingham had been described as 'the great author of our misfortunes', his views closely reflected Charles's and the first meeting of Parliament without him, in 1629, ended in violence and the arrest of three Members. Though there was a strong case for assisting Protestant countries fighting for survival under a Catholic onslaught, Parliament's suspicion over the uses to which an army might be put by Charles precluded such action.

The eleven years during which Charles governed without Parliament were dominated by religious issues, and particularly the work of Archbishop Laud in trying to rein in the drift towards Puritanism, both by control and improving the quality of candidates for ordination. Laud's reforms alienated not only Puritans but even landowners whose social position and property were threatened. It was the desire for uniformity in imposing a new Scottish prayer book based on the English one that was to trigger off a sequence of events leading to civil war. Charles would probably never have recalled Parliament had not the rioting that greeted the prayer book's introduction led to the situation in Scotland getting out of control. When Charles saw in York the rag-tag army that the Earl of Essex had assembled to impose order on the Scots, he realized the need to recall Parliament to obtain subsidies. In the Commons John Pym insisted that grievances should be heard before any subsidies were voted; Charles refused to concede or listen to the counsel of his principal adviser, Wentworth, Earl of Strafford, and dissolved this Short Parliament.

The Scots, meanwhile, advanced over the Tweed and occupied Newcastle. The Treaty of Ripon (1640) provided for the Scots to remain in Northumberland and Durham and receive £850 a day until a settlement was reached. Parliament was recalled and met in militant mood: Strafford and Laud were impeached and sent to the Tower, and other royal officials fled. Though proof of the charges against Strafford could not be found, he was sacrificed by Charles and executed, shortly followed by Laud. The Long Parliament dismantled the king's prerogative and began an assault on episcopacy when the Irish began butchering the Protestant English who had been settled in Ireland. Again, the question arose of who would command the troops raised to restore order. Amidst deliberately spread rumours that the queen might be impeached, in January 1642 Charles planned a coup in which five particularly troublesome Members would be seized; forewarned they had left the House by a back door. A gradual polarization of positions led to the Nineteen Propositions, in which Parliament claimed a major extension of its powers. Two months later Charles raised his standard at Nottingham.

The king's strength lay broadly in the north and west and amongst conservative elements and Catholics. The Scots Covenanters sided with Parliament which, besides its strength in the south and east, controlled London, Hull, Plymouth, Bristol, Gloucester and Portsmouth. It is estimated that the parts of country controlled by Parliament contained some two-thirds of the population and three-quarters of the country's wealth.

The first part of the war was indecisive, the major battle at Edgehill illustrating only the superiority of the royalist cavalry. After the battle, Charles entered Oxford in triumph, making the city his headquarters for his intended move on London. The help of the Scots and the creation of the New Model Army by Fairfax and Oliver Cromwell proved decisive. Although there were royalist victories even in early 1645, and Montrose's brilliant diversions in Scotland on behalf of the king raised morale amongst royalists, the scale of their defeats at Marston Moor (1644) and Naseby (1645), followed by Rupert's loss of Bristol (which had earlier been won from the Parliamentarians), meant the end of Charles's military hopes. He left Oxford in disguise and made his way to the Scottish camp outside Newark where he gave himself up. When Charles refused to accept the Covenant, he was handed over to Parliament. Eventually, in 1648, he was arraigned before a tribunal consisting of 135 judges, but he refused to recognize the authority of the court and so would not plead. Sentence was passed by sixty-eight votes to sixty-seven, and by one vote Charles lost his head, being executed in Whitehall.

# Oliver Cromwell

*Born Huntingdon 1599. Virtual dictator 1653–8.*
*Died 1658, aged 59 years. Buried initially Westminster and after Restoration at Tyburn.*

Oliver Cromwell was born into a moderately landed family with estates in Huntingdon and Cambridgeshire. Educated at Sidney Sussex College, Cambridge, where he imbibed Puritan thinking, he studied law in London before returning to farm the family lands.

When the troubles between Parliament and king began, Cromwell was an inconspicuous Member of Parliament. His puritanical fervour and passionate if clumsy oratory quickly led him to a position of eminence in the Commons. He had no military experience until his forty-fourth year at the first battle of the civil war where he was captain of a troop of horse. At Marston Moor his quick insight into the way the battle was developing and the strict training of his cavalry turned the course of the fighting and won the day.

Assuming the role of leader of the Independents (forerunners of today's Congregationalists), he pushed aside the more conservative generals like Manchester and created the New Model Army under Fairfax. After the victory at Naseby (1645), Cromwell negotiated with the king in the hope of reaching a settlement, but Charles's intrigues led Cromwell to denounce the king to the Commons as 'so great a dissembler and so false a man that he was not to be trusted'. Charles's machinations produced a Scots' invasion by Hamilton whose army Cromwell annihilated at Preston (1648).

In 1649, after Charles had been beheaded, Cromwell was given command in Ireland, where Royalist campaigns were still strong; he stormed Drogheda and Wexford,

Oliver Cromwell: after Robert Walker, date unknown *(The National Trust Photographic Library)*.

massacring the garrisons with a thoroughness that has left his name for ever notorious in Irish history; he alleged that the slaughter was 'the judgement of God' upon the people. The Puritans' Act of Settlement for Ireland showed a total absence of understanding of the country's needs.

Scotland, too, which was sheltering and supporting the young Prince Charles, had to be subdued. The battle against Leslie at Dunbar (1650) was at first close-run, but ended decisively. Cromwell occupied Edinburgh but illness laid him low for a year, during which time the Scots had reformed and moved south. Cromwell caught up with them at Worcester (1651) and ended royalist hopes, Charles II taking ship for France.

Cromwell became Lord General of the Commonwealth and then, in 1653, Lord Protector, a position which was a virtual dictatorship, even though in theory the nation was ruled by a Council of State, comprising seven army leaders and eight civilians. Cromwell lost patience with Parliament in much the same way as Charles had done, and used equally high-handed methods to obtain his objectives. England and Wales were divided into eleven districts with a Major-General over each. Scotland and Ireland were given representation in Parliament. Later Cromwell was offered the title of king, but republican sentiment in the army made him decline the suggestion.

Cromwell began a new foreign policy that restored the country's prestige and made the Commonwealth the head and protector of Protestant Europe. He made peace with Holland, concluded treaties with Denmark to reopen the Baltic to shipping and protect naval supplies, and hoped to expunge the humiliation of Cadiz (see page 80) by an alliance with France against Spain. Robert Blake took Jamaica, and after a blockade of the Spanish coast destroyed a Spanish treasure fleet in the bay of Santa Cruz. On land the Spanish were defeated at the Battle of the Dunes (1658) and Dunkirk was England's reward. Realizing the importance of the navy, Cromwell turned it into a full-time service with promotion structure and pay scales.

At home, Parliament was proving unable to cope with the country's chaotic condition. Its outlook was narrowly Puritan – far narrower than that of Cromwell himself in some ways; for instance severe penalties were laid down for travelling on Sunday or for profanity. The mass of the army, on whose support Parliament relied, disliked such measures; Cromwell was caught between the two, receiving much of the blame for the joyless, unsettled state of the country. A reaction set in against rule by the sword, and royalist plots and assassins threatened his life.

At his death he was buried with great pomp in Westminster Abbey, but at the Restoration his body was gibbeted at Tyburn and his head stuck on a pole outside Westminster Hall, remaining there for twenty years until it blew down in a gale. His body was buried at Tyburn and his head near the chapel at Sidney Sussex, Cambridge.

His son, Richard Cromwell, succeeded to his position, but was not a strong enough character to settle such a divided nation, nor to resolve the chronic financial problems bequeathed to him. Army and Parliament were unable to agree on a government, and the Restoration in 1660 was more or less a transaction between royalists and Puritans against the army – intended more as a Restoration of Parliament than of the king himself. Richard Cromwell had to go to France, but returned in 1680 and lived peaceably through four reigns, dying in 1712 at the age of eighty-six.

# Charles II

*Born St James's Palace 1630. Ascended throne 1660. Reigned 25 years.*
*Second son of Charles I and Henrietta Maria of France.*
*Married Catherine of Braganza.*
*No legitimate issue.*
*Died Whitehall 1685, aged 55 years. Buried at Westminster Abbey.*

As a lad of twelve, Charles was with his father at the Battle of Edgehill, and when the Civil War was nearing its end he escaped to France. Later, he moved on to Holland, and in 1650 landed in Scotland, where he agreed to terms stipulated by the Commissioners; having subscribed to the Covenant he was crowned King of Great Britain, France and Ireland at Scone. A year later he marched into England with 10,000 men; when battle was joined with Cromwell's troops at Worcester, the Scottish army was overwhelmingly defeated. Charles, with a price of £1,000 on his head, was a fugitive for six weeks before he made his escape to France on a coal-brig from Shoreham.

He roamed Europe for nine years, continuously plotting and hoping for a royalist uprising. Richard Cromwell's weakness led to the dominance of the army, the dismantling of the Protectorate and Cromwell's resignation. A timely letter from Charles reassured Parliament of his intentions, should he be made king. With General Monck's influence, Charles was invited to return; on 29 May 1660, his thirtieth birthday, he arrived in a joyful London. The Restoration had been remarkably quick, and without detailed discussion over the king's position. But as a result, certain issues remained unresolved. Charles was still bound by the Covenant, but Parliament ordered it to be burned in 1661, passing an Act of Uniformity the following year that imposed Anglican doctrine. The Restoration gave Scotland back its independence, and episcopacy was reintroduced into the Kirk.

It was said of Charles that 'he never said a foolish thing and never did a wise one' but this overlooks his acute handling of several crises. He was intelligent, tolerant and much interested in scientific developments; if he submitted to working through a Parliament that was becoming a two-party system, Whig and Tory, it was as much because he preferred the pursuits of racing, hunting and women than that he conceded the need for a limitation on monarchical power. But then following Charles I, only a

Charles II: studio of Joseph Michael Wright, date unknown *(The National Portrait Gallery, London)*.

James II: artist Sir Peter Lely, date unknown *(The National Portrait Gallery, London)*.

fool would have allowed a repetition of his dealings with Parliament. Charles II's busy social life gave Edward Hyde, Earl of Clarendon, a free hand as High Chancellor until his exile in 1667 after being impeached due to his unpopularity.

It was the war with Holland, declared in 1665, that proved Clarendon's final undoing. The plague that year claimed 70,000 lives in London alone, naval funds were so depleted that many ships were laid up and sailors' pay in arrears. The following years France and Denmark joined the coalition against England. In 1667 a Dutch squadron sailed up the Thames estuary, burned English warships and towed away the flagship, the *Royal Charles*. Following on the heels of the Great Fire of London, which destroyed 13,000 houses the previous year, a scapegoat for the spate of disasters was needed and found in Clarendon, whom Charles made no effort to save.

Charles's 'foreign policy' has been the subject of much debate: though the sale of recently acquired Dunkirk (see page 84) for £400,000 angered the nation, the town was of little value without Calais or other strongholds to support it. But it was Charles's secret treaties with France that aroused the most suspicion; by the Treaty of Dover he even undertook to declare his personal Catholicism, and many doubted the wisdom of any agreement that bolstered further France's growing power. The return to war with Holland was without benefit. The failure to produce an heir raised the fear that, with the conversion to Catholicism of James, Duke of York, in 1669, England would again be faced with religious strife. This helped the nonsensical accusations by Titus Oates in the Popish Plot of 1678, whereby Jesuit priests were to murder the king, to gain an undeserved credence. Neither the facts nor the logic of Jesuit priests killing a Catholic-inclined king stand up to a second's scrutiny, but it raised all manner of further allegations throughout the country. Oates's accusations led the Opposition to try to force Charles to alter the succession, putting forward the Protestant Duke of Monmouth or William of Orange as candidates. But Charles would not sign an Exclusion Bill to forbid James's succession, and after the real treason of the Rye House Plot, in which a number of Whigs planned to kill Charles and his brother on their way back from Newmarket, Charles won the upper hand. James's accession was assured, and Charles died a Catholic, the priest who had helped him to escape from Worcester in 1651 being smuggled into his room to receive him into the faith.

After years of war and exile, Charles had hoped for an easier life: he married the Portuguese Catherine of Braganza in 1662, glad of her dowry of £300,000 with the naval bases of Tangier and Bombay; but he also had thirteen known mistresses, including Lucy Walters (mother of James, Duke of Monmouth), Barbara Villiers (later Countess of Castlemaine) and the famous Nell Gwynne, all of whom he treated with consideration. In all there were fourteen acknowledged illegitimate offspring. Of twenty-six dukes in England today, five are direct descendants on the wrong side of the blanket of Charles II. This applies to several marquesses and earls.

# James II (VII of Scotland)

*Born St James's Palace 1633. Ascended throne 1685. Reigned 3 years.*
*Third son of Charles I and brother of Charles II.*
*Married (i) Anne Hyde (ii) Mary of Modena.*
*Four sons, two daughters by first wife. Two sons, five daughters by second wife.*
*Died St Germain, Paris 1701, aged 68 years. Buried at St Germain, Paris.*

Like his brother, James took part in the Civil War, and when exiled took service with the French and Spanish, respectively in Holland and Flanders, where he distinguished himself.

James developed a reverence for established institutions from his father-in-law, particularly for the Church but also for the law and the authority of Parliament. He expected advisers to have the same reverence for him, letting it be known that the way to his favour was 'to follow his wishes blindly, and to own an attachment to his interests that was without any qualification or reserve whatsoever'. Yet he saw concessions as a weakness, and significantly regarded the reason for Charles I's downfall not as obduracy but his giving any ground at all. James said he 'knew the English people and they could not be held to their duty by fair treatment'.

James had been converted to Catholicism in 1669 and admitted it openly when the Test Act was passed in 1673. The Act limited government offices to those who subscribed to the Anglican sacraments; James therefore had had to relinquish his position at the Admiralty. The violent anti-Catholic feeling which followed the Popish Plot in 1678 had made him very unpopular and he was persuaded by Charles II to go abroad; his brother, however, successfully thwarted attempts to exclude James from the succession. At the end of the following year, James returned, to be High Commissioner for Scotland.

Within six months of James's accession, another James, the Duke of Monmouth, illegitimate son of Charles II by Lucy Walters, landed at Lyme Regis, Dorset, and was proclaimed king by Protestant adherents at Taunton. A battle fought at Sedgemoor crushed the rebellion at a stroke. Monmouth was captured hiding in a ditch, the king refused a pardon and he was executed. The uprising was followed by the 'Bloody Assizes' of Judge Jeffreys (his 'campaign in the west' as James put it) when many hundreds of those who had taken part were transported for life. Some 230 were executed and many hundreds died in prison or were fined or flogged.

Religious persecution began on a large scale. James committed every stupid error that was possible: he heard mass in public, suspended the Test Act, bestowed ecclesiastical benefices on Roman Catholics, violated the rights of Oxford and Cambridge universities by imposing Catholic masters, intrigued with the French king

William III: after Sir Peter Lely, date unknown *(The National Portrait Gallery, London)*.

Mary II: after W. Wissing, date unknown *(The National Portrait Gallery, London)*.

(from whom, like his brother, he received a subsidy), packed Parliament with his supporters and crushed Protestantism. Ignoring even the advice of loyal Tories, he became a deeply loathed figure. Nor did the odd combination of piety and debauchery add to the regard in which he was held. By ignoring the lessons that could have been learned from his father's handling of Parliament, James lost the throne Charles had so tenaciously preserved for him.

In November 1688, William of Orange, who had married Mary, the daughter of James, landed at the head of 14,000 men at Brixham in Devon to start the 'Glorious Revolution'; he came at the invitation of seven aristocrats who assured William that the overwhelming majority of Englishmen would welcome him as a deliverer. At first the men of the west were slow to join William, having bitter memories of the Monmouth Rebellion, but as he neared the capital men of all parties rallied round simultaneous risings in Cheshire and Yorkshire, and even James's daughter Anne and her husband Prince George of Denmark went over to William's side.

James, in the months before William's landfall, tried to reverse some of his more disliked decisions, but to no avail; he had alienated all but a few Catholics and loyal Tories. Though James had plenty of warning of William's intentions and had made preparations to resist, James fled the country without a fight, leaving the throne vacant. Louis received James hospitably, lending him St Germain. He made an effort to regain the throne in 1689, but was heavily defeated at the Battle of the Boyne in Ireland and returned to France, where he died.

# William III and Mary II

*William:*
*Born The Hague 1650. Ascended throne 1689. Reigned 13 years.*
*Son of William II, Prince of Orange (of Holland) and Mary, eldest daughter of Charles I.*
*Died Kensington 1702, aged 52 years. Buried at Westminster Abbey.*

*Mary:*
*Born St James's Palace 1662.*
*Daughter of James II and Anne Hyde. No issue.*
*Died Kensington 1694, aged 32. Buried at Westminster Abbey.*

William of Orange was the champion of the Protestant cause in Europe. After the murder of the Dutch leader De Witt, William was chosen to be the Stathouder of the United Provinces, then at war with France. William's military and diplomatic skills brought the war to an end with a treaty advantageous to the Netherlanders. He married Mary in 1677.

Given the circumstances of the invitation to invade England (see page 92), it is not surprising that William was enthusiastically received in London, though it was far from clear how the constitutional position would be resolved. William was in a strong position with so large an army of mercenaries, and he made it clear that he would not be happy with a Regency; he would accept the Crown or nothing. For Mary's part, despite an ostensibly cool marriage, she was devoted to William and would not think of ruling without him. Accordingly Parliament had little alternative but to offer them the Crown jointly as king and queen regnant, which they accepted and were crowned in 1689. Princess Anne, Mary's younger sister, reluctantly surrendered her place in the succession to William, who would thus have the Crown for life if Mary died before him; Mary did in fact die all too soon, of smallpox, in 1694.

The importance of the Glorious Revolution was that the monarchy became constitutional and Parliamentary; the fundamental struggles between Crown and Parliament were largely resolved, and arguably spared Britain the turmoil that overtook many European countries during the nineteenth century. William had been declared king by Parliament; the theory of the king as divinely ordained and set apart was finally dead. To prevent a recurrence of the Catholic revival under James, a Bill of Rights decreed that no Catholic or person with a Catholic spouse could be eligible to hold the Crown. But one area that continued to cause friction between Crown and Parliament was finance; Parliament was determined to retain its supply as a lever, and was deliberately parsimonious. Moreover, the pragmatic nature of William's return and settlement left other issues unresolved; perhaps chief amongst them was what was to become the perennial question of how much influence or control the monarch's ministers should have over Parliament, and how much say Parliament should have in the ministers' selection.

William was a brave, unfanatical king, respected though not loved by his people; there were even examples of unnecessarily cruel restrictions on his household that reflect ingratitude for helping to relieve the country of James II. His heart lay always with the Dutch and the desire to diminish French power. His wife Mary was more in favour, and helped win English loyalty until her early death.

A convention held in Scotland extended the English offer of the throne to William and Mary, provided they agree to abolish the episcopacy and institute Presbyterianism. Though a Calvinist, William was impartial on religious matters, and he worked hard to settle Scotland, where politics and religion were combining to produce a violent upheaval. James still had his adherents in the country, and the clans led by Viscount Dundee defeated William's troops under General Mackay at Killiecrankie in 1689; however, Dundee died of his wounds after the battle, and with him died James's cause in Scotland. The one blot on William's name was the Massacre of Glencoe in 1692, when a Highland clan, late in making submission to him, was almost obliterated.

Though the man who issued the order, the Secretary of State for Scotland, Sir James Dalrymple, was dismissed after a later inquiry, William gave him an indemnity and had himself signed the order, though whether he realized its import no one knows.

Jacobite plans to restore James to the throne haunted William's reign, the more dangerous being those outside the country. In 1689 James, fortified with French men and money, landed in Ireland, which was still held by the Irish Jacobite leader, the Earl of Tyrconnel. William himself headed an army of 36,000 men and decisively won the Battle of the Boyne; James fled to France for ever.

William soon had Britain, as part of a coalition of ten powers, at war with France, a war which went on ingloriously until 1697, when financial stress and diplomacy forced the allies to come to terms with their enemy.

The War of Spanish Succession, caused by the death in 1700 of the childless Charles II of Spain, brought a further menace from France; Philip, grandson of Louis XIV of France, claimed the throne, prompting an alliance of powers to prevent him succeeding. The danger was made greater by James's exile in France and his role in continual plots. With the army under the command of John Churchill, Duke of Marlborough, England joined the coalition opposing Philip. Marlborough had wielded considerable influence earlier in the reign, though for some years he had lived under the shadow of suspected Jacobite sympathies. The son of an impoverished Devon royalist, he had helped to quell the Monmouth Rebellion in 1685, but on William's landing he had joined him, being given an earldom to his earlier barony for his services. Part of his success was due to the close friendship of his wife, Sarah Churchill, with Princess Anne.

But to William should go much of the credit for Marlborough's victories during the war with France: his control of and interest in the army resulted in impressive reforms of men and materials, giving Marlborough subordinate officers of ability and, through war during the 1690s, experience.

William died from a hunting accident at Hampton Court, when his horse put a foot in a mole-hole and threw him, which incident gave rise to the Jacobite toast 'to the little gentleman in black velvet'. Despite only breaking a collarbone, his weakened body could not withstand the shock.

William III was: William I of Ireland; William II of Scotland; William III of England; William IV of Normandy.

Queen Anne and the Duke of Gloucester: studio of George Kneller, date unknown *(The National Portrait Gallery, London)*.

# Anne

*Born St James's Palace 1665. Ascended throne 1702. Reigned 12 years.*
*Second daughter of James II and Anne Hyde.*
*Married George, Prince of Denmark.*
*Two sons, three daughters (twelve others died soon after birth).*
*Died Kensington Palace 1714, aged 49 years. Buried at Westminster Abbey.*

During the brief reign of James II, Anne had taken no part in politics; but on the landing of William of Orange she supported his accession to the throne. She was married to the dim but faithful Prince George of Denmark – of whom Charles II had commented unkindly if accurately: 'I have tried him drunk and tried him sober, and there is nothing in him.' An ordinary and at times vulgar woman, she had seventeen children, all of whom died, twelve of miscarriages, one was stillborn and five at an early age of hydrocephalus, better known as water on the brain.

Anne was thirty-seven years old when she succeeded, by which time her unrelenting pregnancies had so wrecked her health that she was a semi-invalid. She was closely bound to the Churchills, Lady Marlborough being a long-standing friend, and for most of her reign they exerted great influence over her and public affairs. Political strife between Whig and Tory rivals was keen, and was complicated by the question of who was to succeed Anne, an issue which was eventually to lead to a bitter quarrel with the Duke of Marlborough. Sarah Churchill lost her place as confidante due to her excessive demands and hectoring tone; it was taken by Abigail Hill, a cousin of the Duchess.

As Commander-in-Chief, Marlborough prosecuted the War of Spanish Succession with skill and vigour. His military genius dominated the scene: his popularity with the queen, his diplomacy and his victories, kept up the country's heart for war. For ten years he won every battle he fought and secured every town to which he laid siege, though the later stages of the war were difficult and some victories marginal.

The decisively won battles at Blenheim, Ramillies and Oudenarde gave England a position of influence in the world never previously attained. Peace came in 1713, with the signing of the Treaty of Utrecht, which laid the foundation of English colonial power in the eighteenth century. It also confirmed Louis's recognition of Anne's title, with the consequence that James Stuart, the Old Pretender, was ordered to leave France.

The queen, the last Stuart sovereign, was not in any way a clever woman; but the men surrounding her were exceptionally talented. This was a brilliant age: Swift and Pope, Addison and Steele were writing in verse and prose; Sir Christopher Wren was building St Paul's Cathedral; Locke and Newton were propounding new theories of philosophy and science.

The most important constitutional act of the reign was the sealing in 1707 of the Act of Union between England and Scotland, thereby forming Great Britain. It entailed the abolition of the Scottish Parliament in return for representation at Westminster and economic equality. The ecclesiastical settlement and laws in each country were not altered.

Anne was a staunch high-church Protestant. Her creation of 'Queen Anne's Bounty' for the increase of the incomes of the poorer clergy, restored to the Church a fund raised from tithes which Henry VIII had taken for his own use.

# Principal Battles, 1485–1709

Bosworth Field    1485

Flodden    1513

Spurs    1513

Civil War Battles

   Edgehill    1642

   Worcester    1642 and 1651

   Devizes    1643

   Newbury    1643 and 1644

   Marston Moore    1644

   Naseby    1645

Sedgemoor    1685

Killiecrankie    1689

Boyne    1690

Spanish Succession

   Blenheim    1704

   Ramillies    1706

   Oudenarde    1708

   Malplaquet    1709

**At Sea**

   Cadiz    1576

   Spanish Armada    1588

   Beachy Head    1690

# PART THREE

# HANOVER
# TO WINDSOR

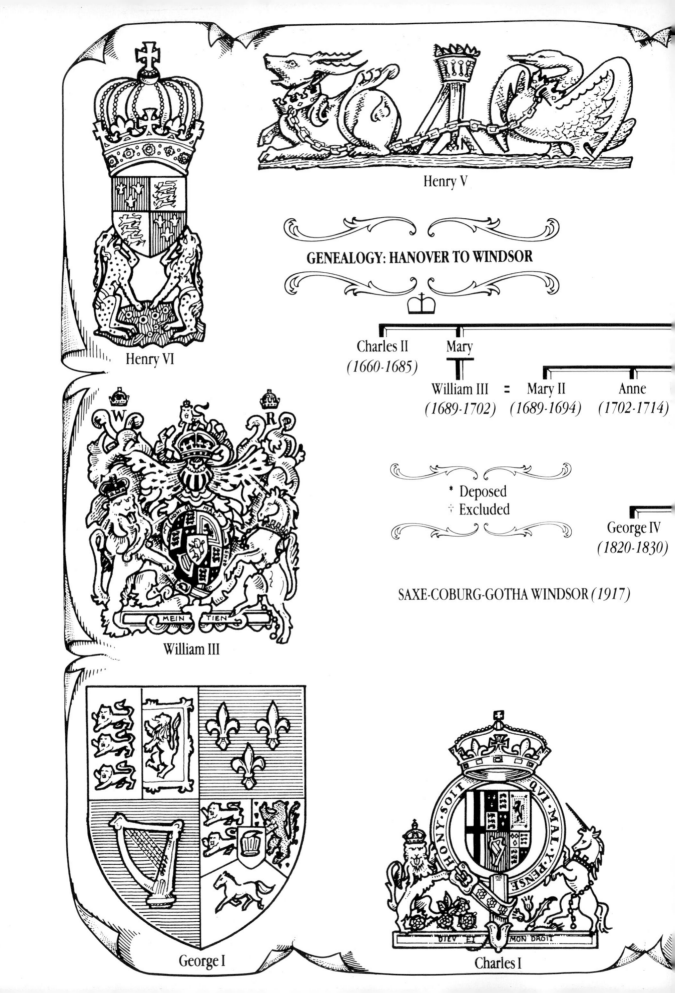

Henry V

# GENEALOGY: HANOVER TO WINDSOR

Charles II
*(1660-1685)*   Mary

William III   =   Mary II   Anne
*(1689-1702)*   *(1689-1694)*   *(1702-1714)*

* Deposed
÷ Excluded

George IV
*(1820-1830)*

SAXE-COBURG-GOTHA WINDSOR *(1917)*

Henry VI

William III

George I

Charles I

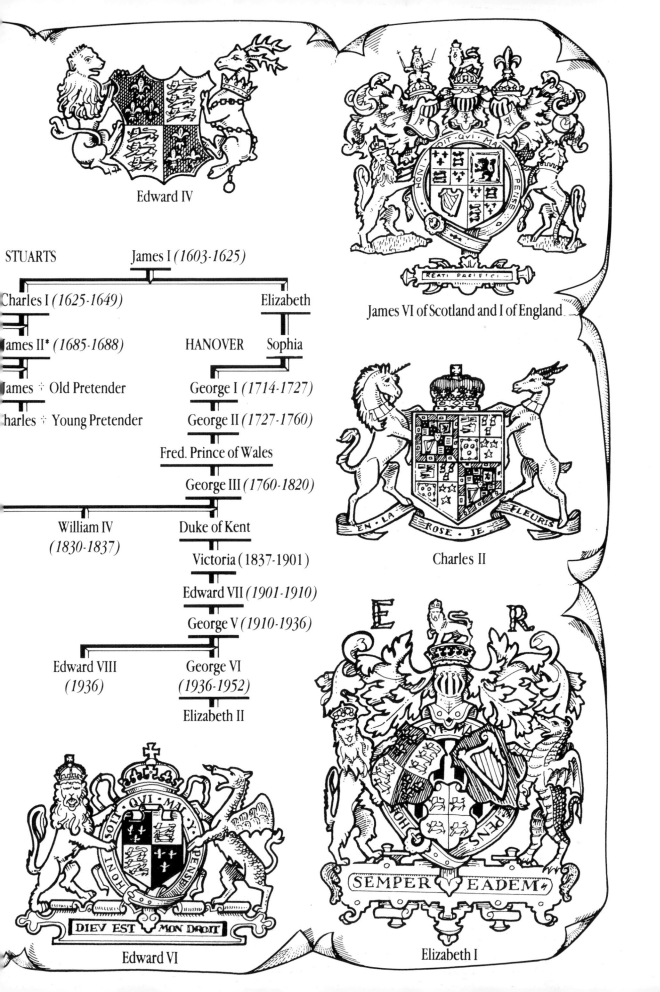

Edward IV

James VI of Scotland and I of England

STUARTS      James I *(1603-1625)*

Charles I *(1625-1649)*      Elizabeth

James II* *(1685-1688)*      HANOVER      Sophia

James † Old Pretender      George I *(1714-1727)*

Charles † Young Pretender      George II *(1727-1760)*

Fred. Prince of Wales

George III *(1760-1820)*

William IV      Duke of Kent
*(1830-1837)*

Victoria (1837-1901)

Edward VII *(1901-1910)*

George V *(1910-1936)*

Edward VIII      George VI
*(1936)*      *(1936-1952)*

Elizabeth II

Charles II

Edward VI

Elizabeth I

# HANOVER TO WINDSOR

During the latter part of the seventeenth century, the question which dominated all others was that of the royal succession. In 1689, the deposed James II (1685–8) and his infant son James (b. 1688), were effectively excluded from the throne by Act of Parliament. The Act said that henceforth no Catholic, nor anyone married to a Catholic, could be sovereign of England.

William III (1689–1702) and his wife Mary II (died 1694) had no children. When the last of Queen Anne's seventeen children, the Duke of Gloucester, died in July 1700 at the age of ten, provision for the succession had to be made. The Act of Succession, 1701, vested it in the nearest Protestant relatives of the Stuarts – Sophia, the wife of the Elector of Hanover, and her descendants. Sophia was the fifth, and only Protestant, daughter of Elizabeth of Bohemia – James I's only daughter (see the family tree). This Act deliberately passed over the superior hereditary rights of the Stuarts, represented by the Catholic James II and his son; the Hanoverian claim was purely statutory – on the score of heredity the family had no real right to the throne. (In 1910 it was estimated that there were over 1,000 descendants of Charles I who had hereditary precedence over Queen Victoria, her son and grandson.)

Sophia of Hanover died two months before Queen Anne (1702–14), and on 1 August 1714 Sophia's son George Ludwig became the first Hanoverian king of England as George I. Hanover was an offshoot of the Duchy of Brunswick-Lüneberg, which had been governed by the Guelph family since the twelfth century; hence the Hanoverian kings were referred to in England as Hanoverians, as Guelphs or as the House of Brunswick.

The joint rulers of England and Hanover were:

George I      (1714–1727)
George II     (1727–1760)
George III    (1760–1820)
George IV     (1820–1830)
William IV    (1830–1837)

*Opposite:* George I: artist, Sir George Kneller, 1716 (*The National Portrait Gallery, London*).

The accession of Queen Victoria in 1837 saw the separation of England from Hanover, which had become a kingdom in 1815. As the succession to the throne of Hanover was governed by Salic law and therefore could not pass to a woman, it passed to the nearest male relative, Ernest, Duke of Cumberland, fifth son of George III; and to mark the change the German arms were removed from the royal arms of England, leaving them as they are today. Hanover was later swallowed up in Bismarck's Germany.

Edward VII, the eldest child of Queen Victoria and the Prince Consort, took his father's family name – that of Saxe-Coburg-Gotha – but popularly the royal family was still known as the House of Hanover or Brunswick. In July 1917, during World War I, King George V announced that he had abandoned all German titles for himself and his family, who would be known henceforth as the House of Windsor.

# George I

*Born Hanover 28 March 1660. Ascended throne 1714. Reigned 13 years.*
*Son of Ernest Augustus, Elector of Hanover.*
*Married Sophia Dorothea, Princess of Brunswick-Zell (1682).*
*One son, one daughter.*
*Died Osnabrück 11 June 1727, aged 67. Buried in Hanover.*

Under the terms of the Act of Settlement, 1701, George Louis of Brunswick–Lüneberg, who had become Elector of Hanover in 1698, became king of England when Queen Anne died.

George I saw clearly that the Hanoverians had been brought in by the Whigs,* in preference to the Catholic Stuarts, merely as the lesser of two evils. Any line of action he initiated was likely to offend at least half the country. In fact George, aged fifty-four when he became king, had only a limited command of the English language and spent more time in Hanover than in England. His character was in any case ill-suited to the position.

The Court, always the centre of government, virtually ceased to exist except, at first, as a lively social forum. This was partly because George, with reason, mistrusted many of the noblemen around him; some had dabbled in treason and it was not surprising, therefore, that he preferred to rely on Hanoverians. George brought to England two mistresses but no wife: he had married his cousin Sophia in 1682, but dissolved the marriage in 1694. After George had taken a mistress following their marriage, Sophia had an affair with the Swedish Count Königsmarck; in 1694 the couple were surprised

---

*The terms Whig and Tory were both originally terms of contempt coined in the late seventeenth century. Whigs were Scottish 'whiggamores' or horse-drovers; Tories 'Irish robbers'.

and the Count killed. Sophia was confined to the castle of Ahlden where she died in 1726. The two children of the marriage were the future George II and Sophia Dorothea, who was to be the mother of Frederick the Great of Prussia.

Between George I and his son began the hostility between sovereign and heir-apparent which was to become traditional in the House of Hanover. It was reflected in the king's refusal to grant the Prince the status of Regent while the king returned to Hanover to attend to State matters. The Prince was denied any influence or responsibilities by his father, so it was readily assumed that while the king was away, the mice would play and intrigue against the king. Suspicion over the visits of the Secretary of State, Lord Townshend, to the Prince at Hampton Court while the king was away led to Townshend's dismissal. This kind of conflict was recurrent for much of the century.

Of George's mistresses, Horace Walpole left a vivid picture of Charlotte Sophia Kielmannsegge, later Countess of Darlington: 'I remember being terrified by her enormous figure . . . Two fierce black eyes, large and rolling beneath two lofty arched eyebrows, two acres of cheeks spread with crimson, an ocean of neck that overflowed and was not distinguished from the lower parts of her body, and no part restrained by stays – no wonder that a child dreaded such an ogress, and that the mob of London were highly diverted at the importation of so uncommon a seraglio!'

In common with other Hanoverians, George was rather stupid and as a lazy man only too content to leave the conduct of affairs in the hands of ministers, thereby transferring to their shoulders the responsibility for national policy. In choosing his ministers from among the Whigs, George laid the foundations of the Whig oligarchy which ruled England for the next fifty years. Cabinet government began in this reign, and Sir Robert Walpole (1676–1745), the chief minister of the majority party in the House of Commons, became England's first Prime Minister. His great chance came when the 'South Sea Bubble' burst in 1720: the South Sea Company, a highly speculative venture, had persuaded the government that it could redeem part of the national debt (see below); even the king was involved as investor and Governor of the Company. Walpole had strongly advised against it, and as First Lord of the Treasury he was able to salvage something from the wreakage that caused the death and loss of office of several ministers.

In 1715 the Jacobites, still supporting the Catholic Stuart line, attempted to supplant George I by James Edward Stuart, the 'Old Pretender', the son of James II. Led by the Earl of Mar, the rebels dispersed after the inconclusive Battle of Sheriffmuir, though another force reached Preston before surrendering. The rebellion failed miserably: the Pretender did not arrive in Britain for his one and only visit until it was over, and help promised by France never materialized because of the death of the French king, Louis XIV. A small Spanish force provided by Philip V landed in the Western Isles in 1719, but with little local support laid down its arms at Glenshiel.

One of George's first appointments was to restore Marlborough's command of the army. Though the Act of Settlement released Britain from any obligation to participate in hostilities involving George's Hanover, the use of an English fleet in the Baltic raised controversy. Part of the fear was a further increase in the national debt, which after the War of Spanish Succession stood at £54 million. The interest absorbed almost a third of all annual revenue. The country remained at peace until the prospect of an alliance of Spain and Austria created a diplomatic crisis, leading to war with Spain until 1726. After an abortive expedition against Spain's American possessions, Walpole, who had detested the necessary tax increase to pay for the war, negotiated the treaty of Seville in 1729.

By then, George was dead, having suffered a stroke at Osnabrück on 11 June 1727 while on his way to Hanover.

# George II

*Born Hanover 10 November 1683. Ascended throne 1727. Reigned 33 years.*
*Only son of George I.*
*Married Caroline of Ansbach-Bayreuth (1705).*
*Three sons, five daughters.*
*Died Kensington Palace 25 October 1760, aged 76. The last English king to be buried at Westminster Abbey.*

George II, like his father before him, was first and foremost a German prince; but at least he knew English before he was too old to learn. Not much brighter than his father, George was short, unpredictable, impatient, meddlesome, courageous, a stickler for punctuality and routine, fond of music but none of the other arts. Importantly, he was capable of being bullied, and Queen Caroline of Ansbach was to exploit that fact in her support of Sir Robert Walpole whom George as Prince of Wales had disliked.

Unlike most Hanoverian kings, and despite a series of mistresses, George was devoted to his wife, who unfortunately died in 1737. There was, however, the usual Hanoverian friction between father and son, ending abruptly in 1751 with the death at Cliveden of Frederick, Prince of Wales. A contemporary wrote the epitaph:

Here lies poor Fred who was alive and is dead,
Had it been his father I had much rather,
Had it been his sister nobody would have missed her,
Had it been his brother, still better than another,
Had it been the whole generation, so much the better for the nation,
But since it is Fred who was alive and is dead,
There is no more to be said.

George II: artist, Thomas Hudson, 1744 *(The National Portrait Gallery, London)*.

George, like his father, had to rely on the Whigs, led at first by Walpole to whom the queen was a loyal and clever adviser. Walpole's methods and manners were crude, but his efficiency and desire for peace gave Britain a welcome respite and helped to establish the system of government through a Cabinet responsible to Parliament, which was in turn responsible to the electorate. Also, during the reigns of both George I and George II the Tories were suspect because of their associations with Jacobitism; as a consequence the custom was established that the Cabinet should consist of men of only one political party. This limited George's options for ministers, and no doubt contributed to his own sense of powerlessness.

Walpole's seeming impregnability led to a number of alliances against him, even amongst Whigs – it was then normal for a Whig or Tory ministry to have in opposition Members of the same allegiance. Walpole's opponents created an orgy of ministry-baiting, involving broadsheets, newspapers, ballads and libellous plays in the theatres. Walpole reacted badly to the insinuations. The opposition grew steadily, gradually eroding the regard in which he was held at Court. It was the extraordinary degree of ill-feeling between the Prince of Wales and his parents that heralded Walpole's fall. The king regarded his son as 'a monster and the greatest villain that ever was born'. The public felt much sympathy for the Prince's rejection, and his identification with the Opposition lifted their standing. The queen's death exacerbated Walpole's difficulties.

Against Walpole's wish, Britain drifted into war over the pragmatic sanction by which Maria Theresa had been guaranteed inheritance of her father's personal dominions. It was the beginning of a series of wars which was to last intermittently until 1815. In 1742 Walpole had to resign, dying three years later. The war extended, becoming the War of the Austrian Succession, aimed largely against France. Fighting began before war had been formally declared, and at Dettingen, in 1743, George II achieved the distinction of being the last reigning monarch to lead his subjects in the field. War against Spain followed an incident in which Captain Jenkins lost his ear, but which was more a pretext to challenge the Spanish monopoly of trade with South America than outrage at such treatment.

In 1745 the Jacobites tried once more to restore the Stuarts to the throne. Prince Charles Edward Stuart, the 'young Pretender', grandson of James II, landed at Eriskay in Scotland. At first he was much more successful than the protagonists of the 1715 uprising: Perth and Edinburgh were taken, Sir John Cope was defeated at Prestonpans, Carlisle fell and the Prince's army marched into Lancashire and on to Derby. But few rallied to his call, and a council of war in Derby determined on retreat. In April 1746 Charles was routed at Culloden Moor by the royal army under the king's second son, the Duke of Cumberland – 'Butcher Cumberland'.* Bonnie Prince Charlie escaped,

*The flower 'Sweet William' was named after him; in Scotland it is called 'Stinking Billie'.

lurking for six months in the Western Isles under the care of such loyal followers as Flora Macdonald; no one betrayed him, though a price of £30,000 was on his head. He moved later to France, dying a drunkard's death in Rome.

In 1756 the Seven Years War with France began, initially because of clashes in North America, though rivalries were also fierce in India where Clive's victory at Plassey (1757) paved the way for British rule. Wolfe's brilliant capture of Quebec by scaling the Heights of Abraham led to Canada becoming part of the British empire, and rich sugar islands like Martinique and Guadeloupe were taken. The British suffered severe reverses, and the government broke up. Against the king's wishes, William Pitt the Elder (1708–78), later Earl of Chatham, emerged as leader to meet the crisis.

George II died at Kensington on 25 October 1760, before the Seven Years War reached its successful conclusion.

# The Change of Calendar, 1752

Juilius Ceasar in 46 BC fixed the length of the year at 365 days, and 366 days every fourth year. The months had thirty and thirty-one days alternately, with the exception of February (then the last month of the year), which had twenty-nine in ordinary years, and thirty in leap years. To mark this change of calendar July was named after its originator.

The Emperor Augustus upset this arrangement by naming August after himself, and in order that it should have the same number of days as July (thirty-one), took one day from February in both ordinary and leap years.

The *Julian* Calendar made a slight error in the length of the year, a mere eleven minutes and fourteen seconds; but by the sixteenth century the cumulative error was about ten days. This was rectified by Pope Gregory XIII who, in 1582, decreed that 5 October should become the fifteenth. In order to prevent a recurrence of the fault, it was ordained that the centurial years (1600, 1700, etc) should not be leap years unless divisible by 400.

England did not accept this *Gregorian* calendar until 1752, thereby causing much confusion between English and Continental dates, whilst the disparity between the Julian and Gregorian calendars was now eleven days. An Act of Parliament in 1750 made 3 September 1752 into 14 September and moved the first day of the year from 25 March (still reckoned as the beginning of the financial year) to 1 January. In this way England was brought into line with the rest of Europe. Russia did not adopt the Gregorian calendar until the Revolution of 1917.

# George III

*Born Norfolk House, St James's Square June 1738. Ascended throne 1760.*
*Reigned 59 years.*
*Son of Frederick Louis, Prince of Wales; Grandson of George II.*
*Married Charlotte of Mecklenburg-Strelitz (1761).*
*Nine sons, six daughters.*
*Died Windsor, 29 January 1820, aged 81. Buried at Windsor.*

The first Hanoverian to be born in Britain, George was twenty-two when he ascended the throne, determined to rule as well as reign. He wished to recover the power of the Crown from the Prime Minister, and he temporarily succeeded in doing so. Parliament had no great popular support in the country, as too many MPs sat merely at the bidding of an individual patron. William Pitt, elected Prime Minister to meet a war crisis, which he did brilliantly, was unpopular afterwards with the Whigs in power.

During the first two decades of his reign, George worked methodically to break the power of the Whigs which had lasted since 1714. The Tories were able to shed their association with Jacobitism, now that the cause was well and truly dead. George was also determined to bring his tutor, Lord Bute, into the administration, which raised the thorny issue of the king's right to appoint ministers. In keeping with customary political methods, he used bribery to create his own party, the 'King's friends', and changed the composition of his ministries with extraordinary frequency and little obvious sense of purpose. Lord Bute, with little experience of government, could not stand the heat and, to George's disappointment, quit after less than a year. The king finally made a wise choice with the appointment of Lord North as first minister.

On his accession, George wanted an immediate end to the war with France, but before peace was negotiated, Britain was also at war with France's new ally, Spain. The Treaty of Paris (1763) confirmed Britain's position as the leading colonial power.

George III and Lord North must bear the responsibility for the loss of England's North American colonies. The colonists were exasperated by repeated attempts by the British government to impose taxes on them. Higher taxes were needed to pay for the mounting costs of military and naval forces protecting the colonists and to offset the huge loss in tax revenues caused by smuggling; an estimate of 1763 suggested that only one-tenth of imported tea was subjected to the statutory duty. The colonists' anger found outlets in incidents like the 'Boston Tea Party' (1773), and in 1775 war finally broke out.

The colonists unrealistically tried to use the king as an intermediary, petitioning him for protection against his ministers. The king's role became more active, hiring five battalions of troops in Hanover and supporting North. When France and Spain came

George III: studio of A. Ramsay, c.1767 *(The National Portrait Gallery, London)*.

into the war on the side of the colonists, and the Opposition clamoured for peace, the outcome was inevitable. The colonists proclaimed their independence on 4 July 1776, and achieved it at the Peace of Versailles signed in 1783. George's obstinacy in dealing with people whom he believed to be rebels had much to do with the causes of the war and its needless protraction. The Whigs in general had no clear ideas on colonial policy; they still thought of colonies merely as markets for British goods. But they soon saw that the recovery of the American colonies was impossible, particularly after the British surrender at Yorktown, and refused to support the king in continuing the war.

This brought to an end George III's period of personal rule. In 1783 he resigned much ministerial power to the twenty-four-year-old William Pitt the Younger (1759–1806), famous son of a famous father; a Tory, he was to be Prime Minister with only one break (1801–4) until his death in 1806.

George III had married Charlotte of Mecklenburg-Strelitz, who was brought over to England by a squadron of yachts under the command of Lord Anson, the Admiral who captained the second circumnavigation of the globe by an English ship. George was devoted to her, and at first to their fifteen children (nine sons and six daughters), but the tradition of hostility between reigning monarch and the heir-apparent later developed strongly. However, George broke the family tradition in being a model of domestic virtues, eschewing the open womanizing of his ancestors.

The king was highly neurotic with a flair for music, furniture and gardens; he liked making buttons and putting watches together (his grandfather had enjoyed an eccentric passion for cutting out paper figures). He was keenly interested in the agricultural improvements which took place during his reign; the creation of model farms on his estate at Windsor earned him the nickname of 'Farmer George'. He was a patron of the sciences and the arts, and his collection of books laid the foundation for the future British Museum Library.

During the closing years of his reign, he had little influence on English affairs. His mind had always been weak and vindictive, and after 1811 he was at times both blind and insane, exacerbated by the critical illness of his favourite child, Princess Amelia. His violent outbursts had to be restrained by the use of a straitjacket. His eldest son, George, ruled for him as Prince Regent.

England was guided through the long French Revolutionary and Napoleonic Wars (1793–1815) by Pitt and the military and naval genius of such men as the Duke of Wellington (1769–1852) and Lord Nelson (1758–1805).

Significant changes were made under George in Ireland: violence extracted the concessions of legislative independence in 1782 and the Catholic vote in 1793, but Pitt the Elder fell over the issue of full emancipation, which George refused. None the less the Act of Union in 1801 joined the two countries until home rule was established in 1920–1. Catholic emancipation was finally granted under George IV in 1829.

Other radical reforms included the introduction of income tax by Pitt in 1799, intended to be temporary and to help to finance the war against France. In 1807 the slave trade was abolished in lands under British control, but slavery continued in British possessions until 1833.

Besides great statesmen like Pitt and Fox, and great captains like Wellington and Nelson, George III's long reign was graced by some of the greatest names in English literature: Johnson, Gibbon, Cowper, Crabbe, Scott, Jane Austen, Byron, Coleridge, Wordsworth, Southey, Shelley and Keats. Artists like Reynolds (the first President of the Royal Academy, founded in 1768), Gainsborough and Romney founded a school of English painters.

The pace of change in England during the eighteenth century accelerated as the century neared its close. The population more than doubled, stimulating far-reaching changes in agriculture and industry in order to keep pace with the growing demands for food and manufactured goods. During George III's reign, despite the growth in output, higher tax revenues and a fourfold increase in foreign trade, the national debt rose from £138 million to £800 million, largely as a result of costly wars. Transport was revolutionized, with new roads, tramways and the first canals. (George, however, took little advantage of the new turnpike roads, never venturing further than an annual holiday in Weymouth during the 1790s.)

George III died on 29 January 1820, having spent the last nine years of his reign in seclusion. He was succeeded by his eldest son George, the Prince Regent, as George IV.

# The American War of Independence, 1775–83

The train of events that was to lead to the independence of the American colonies began with the Seven Years War and the difficult task of dislodging the French from their chain of redoubts stretching from Pennsylvania, along the Ohio River and down to the Mississippi. The French had intended them to mark the boundaries of their 'interior' empire west of the Appalachians. With some Indian tribes as allies, the French succeeded in fending off, first the Virginians, and later much larger numbers of troops sent from Britain and the colonies, even when heavily outnumbered. Six years' fighting were required to win control of Canada and the French lands beyond the Appalachians.

The question for the British government was how to organize this huge area. Clearly the lax control of previous years had to be replaced by something more formal – and costly – as was the case in India after the Mutiny. It was the ham-fisted way in which unimaginative and ill-informed ministers in London tried to resolve this problem, combined with the experience of colonists fighting together against the French, that created a unity amongst states that had previously had little common ground but language. This unity was forged by the colonists' response to a series of measures

The American War of Independence 1775–82: Signing the Declaration of Independence: engraved after Trumbull *(Hulton–Deutsch Collection)*

designed by the British government to raise money to pay for the defence and administration of the colonies.

Laws restricting American trade and increasing export taxes on European goods sold to America inevitably irritated the colonists, as did the declaration that all land west of the Appalachians was Crown property closed to settlers. But it was not until the Stamp Act of 1765 that feelings boiled over; those responsible for selling the stamps which were to be affixed to just about everything had a rough time, and within a year the Act was repealed. Jubilation soon ended when George III and his compliant minister Lord North imposed a further catalogue of taxes and restrictions, the most infamous being that on tea. Precisely who started what at Boston in 1770 no one can say, but a fight outside the Customs House caused the death of five people. From the protest meetings sprang articulate argument and propaganda against what were seen as unwarrantable interferences with the Colonists' freedoms. The celebrated Boston Tea Party (1773) is only the best known of the acts of sabotage directed against North's taxes.

The knee-jerk response of the British government was to send troops to impose order, as well as closing the port of Boston to all trade. From here on, the movement amongst colonists appears in retrospect to have developed a momentum of its own. Groups sprang up to express grievances, and the Virginians led the way in the treasonable act of setting up a Provincial Convention, an independent legislature. The

Declaration of Independence (1776), largely written by Thomas Jefferson, was agreed on all but two points by a vote of twelve of the colonies/states, and formed the manifesto of the justices for which the colonists were prepared to fight. With the expectation of help from France and Spain, the colonists took up arms. The first clash, at Concord, Massachusetts, went to the colonists and inspired others. The superiority of the colonists' rifled barrels over the British smooth-bore muskets for the kind of scrappy engagements that characterized much of the war, was a significant factor in helping untrained colonists from all walks of life to defeat a professional army.

With George Washington in command of the colonists' forces, the war at first went badly for them: Philadelphia was lost and the first winter saw Washington's troops decimated by illness, only saved by the timely arrival of French *matériel* and soldiers. Washington's dogged determination won the war, creating a legend barely diminished by his peacetime shortcomings.

George III and many in Britain were dumbfounded that the American colonies could have been lost. But in defeat he displayed a regal magnanimity; he greeted America's first Minister to the Court of St James's, John Adams, with the gallant words: 'I will be very frank with you. I was the last to consent to the separation: but the separation having been made, and having become inevitable, I have always said, as I say now, that I would be the first to meet the friendship of the United States as an independent power.'

# French Revolutionary and Napoleonic Wars, 1793–1815

In 1793 England and a coalition of other European powers went to war against the French revolutionaries who, having seized power and overthrown the monarchy in France, seemed bent on conquering Europe. The invasion by France of the Austrian Netherlands, with its threat to Britain's maritime interests, was the deciding factor. France's declaration of war in 1793, much to George's delight, was followed by an ignominious campaign in Flanders under the Duke of York that ended in a retreat through Germany and evacuation in 1795. However, the Duke's reforms of the corruption and barbaric conditions in the army were vital for Britain's ability to withstand the French onslaught.

But at sea the war began more auspiciously: conquests of French territories were made in the West Indies, followed by the capture of Corsica, Pondicherry, Trincomalee and Ceylon. A French invasion of Ireland in 1796 was only aborted due to bad weather, and plans to invade England frustrated by naval victories that helped to make 1797 the turning point of the war, despite the fact that Britain now stood alone. Nelson and Jervis inflicted substantial damage on the Spanish fleet at Cape St Vincent (William, Duke of

Clarence, later William IV, fought in this battle). At Camperdown Duncan won a decisive engagement against the Dutch fleet that eliminated its ability to act as a spearhead for the invasion of England. Britain's naval supremacy was consolidated by Nelson's total victories at Aboukir Bay (1798), which nullified Napoleon's gains on land in Egypt, and at Copenhagen (1801). In 1798 the second coalition of Britain, Russia, Turkey, Naples, Portugal and Austria was formed, but fell apart in 1801. Peace was made at Amiens in 1802.

Napoleon Bonaparte (1769–1821) who seized supreme power in France in 1801 and who was to become Emperor in 1804, used the next few months to reorganize the French fighting forces prior to launching an attack against England. War was renewed in 1803. For two years Napoleon tried to invade England, but his schemes were hampered by a third coalition between Britain, Russia, Austria, Sweden and Naples and ruined by Nelson's defeat of the combined French and Spanish fleets off Cape Trafalgar in 1805. However, in Europe Napoleon won a series of victories against the Austrians, Russians and Prussians.

Napoleon then resorted to economic warfare in an attempt to bankrupt the 'nation of shopkeepers' by the Continental System, excluding British trade from European countries or colonies, but Britain's navy frustrated his plans. Moreover, the subject nations grew increasingly tired of French tyranny. Napoleon's use of Spain, both as part of the Continental System and to help partition Portugal, backfired when the Spanish people rose up in May 1808 and, after slaughtering any Frenchmen they could find, appealed to Britain for help. With the landing of British forces under Arthur Wellesley, later Duke of Wellington, and the ensuing Peninsular War (1808–13), British troops were to remain on the Continent until after Waterloo.

With Napoleon's invasion of Russia in 1812, it became evident that Napoleon had overreached himself: he had had to commit 30,000 troops to hold the Iberian peninsula, and was compelled to withdraw many for his disastrous campaign in Russia, allowing Wellesley to drive the French forces back into France by the end of 1813. At Leipzig (1813) the combined armies of the fourth coalition decisively defeated the French. The English blockade of Europe at this time caused much trouble with neutral countries, and the Anglo-American War, which broke out in 1812, lasted until 1814.

Peace negotiations with the French were opened in 1814. Napoleon was exiled to Elba from where he escaped, returned to France, and began his 'Hundred Days Campaign' which ended with 25,000 French dead on the field of Waterloo in 1815. Napoleon was exiled to St Helena, where he died in 1821.

# George IV

*Born St James's Palace 12 August 1762. Ascended throne 1820.*
*Reigned 9 years.*
*Eldest son of George III.*
*Married (i) Mrs Maria Fitzherbert (1785); (ii) Caroline of Brunswick-Wolfenbuttell (1795)*
*One daughter.*
*Died Windsor 26 June 1830, aged 67 years. Buried at Windsor.*

'He will be either the most polished gentleman, or the most accomplished blackguard in Europe – possibly both', said the tutor of the future George IV when he was fifteen.

From Carlton House, where he set up his own establishment in 1783, 'the first gentleman of Europe' became the leader of fashionable London society, setting the pattern in dress and patronizing the arts and architecture. He 'discovered' Brighton and had the Pavilion built in 1784. Regent Street and Regent's Park were laid out and named after him for the encouragement he gave to the architect John Nash; the term 'Regency style' passed into the English language. No monarch has done more for the artistic and architectural wealth of the country.

Both before and during his reign, George IV did much harm to the cause of monarchy. Subjects who had grown accustomed to the irreproachable family affairs of George III were exasperated by his immorality. His reckless extravagance was the more conspicuous at a time when the after-effects of the Napoleonic Wars and the upheaval of the Industrial Revolution were causing much social distress and misery. As a result he was probably the most despised of all monarchs, the subject of astonishingly vicious attacks by caricaturists and columnists. As Prince of Wales, his coach was hissed and pelted in the streets of London. He was a great embarrassment to Lord Liverpool's government which, though committed to *laissez-faire* economics and far from reform-minded, was concerned to reduce costs and ease poverty.

George had a steady flow of mistresses while he was Prince Regent; this was stemmed in 1785 when he married secretly a twice-married young Catholic widow, Mrs Maria Fitzherbert. Since he married without the king's consent, the union was invalid under the Royal Marriage Act of 1772; in any case a prince married to a Catholic would not be allowed to succeed to the throne. The Prince of Wales was dishonest enough to later deny that any marriage to Mrs Fitzherbert had taken place.

So in 1795, in order to placate his father who refused to settle his debts on any other terms, George married his cousin, Caroline of Brunswick. He treated her abominably throughout their married life together, which barely survived the birth of their only child early in 1796. Between 1814 and 1820 she lived with an Italian abroad, but to

George IV: artist Thomas Lawrence, date unknown *(The National Portrait Gallery, London)*.

George's annoyance returned when he became king to assert her place as queen. Her popularity amongst the populace was in marked contrast to feelings about George, and his attempts to divorce Caroline disgusted the country.

From 1811, as Prince Regent, he was king in all but name. The death of George III in 1820 gave him the title of king without altering in any way the situation which had existed since 1811. George IV's first act at his accession was to attempt to exclude his wife's name from the traditional prayers offered for the royal family; and he succeeded in having her excluded from his coronation in July 1821.

That George while Prince of Wales had befriended the Whigs to annoy his father rather from conviction, was borne out by his continuing his father's appointment of Tory ministers. His reign saw a further contraction of the monarch's powers, due to the straitened financial position of the monarch, the growing complexity of government and the reduction of perquisites, pensions and places with which monarchs had been accustomed to buy support and power. George failed in his attempts to oppose some of the major changes of his reign, such as Catholic emancipation (1829) or the recognition of the newly independent South American republics. The difficulty of governments working with George IV, particularly when he was in a tantrum or prone to incoherent and interminable arguments, convinced the Whigs that when power was theirs, they would impose Charles James Fox's dictum that a monarch should reign but not rule.

This coincided with popular demands for Parliamentary reform, which was seen as the key to improving the lot of the working- and middle-classes. During George's Regency, there were many demonstrations in favour of reform, and many thought the country on the verge of revolution. Mass meetings often ended in violence, most notably in Manchester where the Peterloo massacre (1819) left eleven dead, but dragoons were to be seen on the streets of many towns, particularly in the north. Troops had to be used, since the metropolitan police force was not established by Sir Robert Peel until 1829, and throughout the rest of the country until the middle of the century. In 1820 a plot to assassinate the cabinet was discovered and the protagonists arrested in a hayloft at Marylebone; the five ringleaders were hung. The government response was suppression, and the Six Acts of 1819 were designed to prohibit public meetings and curb the radical press.

But George IV was not without either intelligence or aptitudes: his faults were the result of indolence and lack of application. He had a sensitive appreciation of literature; he was a fervent admirer of Jane Austen and kept a set of her novels in each of his residences. 'I shall always reflect with pleasure', he said, 'on Sir Walter Scott's having been the first creation of my reign.' When George visited Scotland in 1822, Scott organised a magnificent reception for him. George gave his father's library to form the basis of the British Museum Library, and persuaded the government to buy the

Angerstein collection of pictures which formed the basis of the National Gallery. George was, in addition, probably the wittiest of all monarchs, Charles II excepted.

After his father's reclusiveness, he revived royal travels, journeying to Hanover, Scotland and Ireland, where he was the first visiting monarch since Richard II. Having a sense of theatre, George was well suited to public appearances, which did something to diminish the hostility his Regency had aroused. 'He was the most extraordinary compound of talent, wit, buffoonery, obstinacy and good feelings, in short, a medley of the most opposite qualities, with a great preponderance of good – that I ever saw in any character in my life,' was the Duke of Wellington's summation of him.

His earlier energy sapped by corpulence, George IV died on 26 June 1830, an event hailed with relief. The report in *The Times* reveals, besides its low opinion of the man, how outspoken the press of the day was about the monarchy:

> There never was an individual less regretted by his fellow creatures than this deceased king . . . What eye has wept for him? What heart has heaved one throb of unmercenary sorrow . . . for that Leviathan of the *haut ton* George IV . . . Nothing more remains to be said about George IV but to pay, as we must, for his profusion; and to turn his bad conduct to some account by tying up the hands of those who come after him in what concerns the public money.

George IV was succeeded by his brother, the Duke of Clarence, as William IV, because his only legitimate child, Princess Charlotte, had died in 1817.

# William IV

*Born Buckingham Palace 21 August 1765. Ascended throne 1830.*
*Reigned 6 years.*
*Third son of George III.*
*Married Adelaide of Saxe-Coburg and Meiningen (1818).*
*Two daughters.*
*Died Windsor 20 June 1837, aged 71. Buried at Windsor.*

Following the death in childbirth of Princess Charlotte in 1817, William, Duke of Clarence, and his brothers, the Dukes of York, Kent and Cambridge, were prevailed upon to quit their middle-aged semi-retirement in order to secure the succession. When the elder brother, the Duke of York,* died in 1827, William became heir to the throne.

---

*The 'Noble Duke of York' of the nursery rhyme, Commander-in-Chief of the British Army between 1798 and 1827. He was no military general but a very able administrator.

Known as the 'sailor king', William IV had entered the navy in 1779 at the age of thirteen and saw service in America and the West Indies, becoming an Admiral of the Fleet in 1811 and a violent and difficult Lord High Admiral for a year from 1827. On his accession, William was popular: his unassuming character, exemplary private life (at least since his marriage – from 1790 to 1811 he had lived at Bushey Park with the actress Mrs Jordan, by whom he had had ten children) and his known hatred of pomp and ceremonial (he even wanted to dispense with the coronation) rendered him an agreeable contrast to George IV. William had lived in relative poverty, the press speculating who kept who at Bushey Park (Mrs Jordan continued her career in the theatre).

The great question in 1830 was Parliamentary reform. George IV had been resolutely opposed to any and every reform. In 1830 Wellington's Tory administration lost the general election despite the king's support, the first time this had happened. Lord Grey won on a ticket of Parliamentary reform, to which William was inevitably opposed, meaning as it would a further decline in the monarch's power. After a difficult passage a reform bill was piloted through the lower chamber in 1831, but its continual rejection by the Lords brought England close to revolution again. The new, articulate middle-class insisted that no longer could the hereditary landowners remain solely responsible for a nation so urgently needing financial, economic and social overhaul. William refused to create the peers demanded by the Whigs to enable the bill to pass through the Lords. Grey resigned, but when the Tories proved unable to form an administration, William relented and though still against the reform conceded that 'as a sovereign it was his duty to put those feelings and prejudices aside'. To such *realpolitik,* William probably owed his throne, for during a period of revolutions that threw other European countries into turmoil, he was the only European monarch of his day to survive the advent of democracy.

The Reform Act was passed in 1832. It extended the franchise to the middle-class on the basis of property qualifications; it left the working-classes bitterly disappointed, and encouraged the development of the Chartist movement to persuade the government to introduce universal male suffrage* and effect other reforms that are now taken for granted, such as voting by ballot and payment of MPs. None the less the Reform Act did mean that the landowning class had at last decided to share government with the more prosperous tenant farmers, skilled artisans and industrialists. As for the monarchy, the history of the Reform Bill's passage meant that yet another weapon in the monarch's arsenal had been appropriated by party politics – the control of peerages. It also marked a new ascendancy of Commons over Lords.

*Subsequent Acts of 1867, 1884, 1918, 1928 and 1969 gradually extended the franchise, until by 1969 all men and women over the age of eighteen had a vote.

*Above:* William IV: artist M. A. Shee, date unknown *(The National Portrait Gallery, London)*.
*Opposite:* Queen Victoria: artist, Sir George Hayter 1863, after a portrait of 1838 *(The National Portrait Gallery, London)*.

A few months after William's accession, the Liverpool & Manchester Railway was opened to great acclaim. The forerunner of the modern railway, it was the world's first public railway to be entirely operated by steam locomotives from the outset over its own tracks. Its success in lowering prices of raw materials, finished goods and food, because of the huge savings railways offered in transport costs, brought about the railway age. The adoption of Greenwich time (or Railway time) as standard throughout the country was only made possible by the railway, reflecting the way that accelerated journeys helped to impose a uniformity of products, ideas and manners over the country. Queen Victoria was the first monarch to travel by train.

In 1833 slavery was abolished in British colonies, thereby completing the work begun in 1807; the government set aside £20 million as compensation for the slave owners. The Poor Law was reformed in 1834, for the first time since 1601 – although this measure created the workhouse system, so graphically depicted by Dickens in the pages of *Oliver Twist.* In 1834 the Houses of Parliament burned down, to be replaced by the present buildings, which were designed by Barry and Pugin. Local government was reformed in 1835.

When William died on 20 June 1837, the press was no more complimentary or less forthright than for George IV: the *Spectator* commented that 'though at times jovial and, for a king, an honest man, [William] was a weak, ignorant, commonplace sort of person . . . Notwithstanding his feebleness of purpose and littleness of mind, his ignorance and his prejudices, William IV was to the last a popular sovereign, but his very popularity was acquired at the price of something like public contempt.'

# Victoria

*Born Kensington Palace 24 May 1819. Ascended throne 1837. Reigned 63 years.*
*Daughter of Edward, Duke of Kent, and Victoria Maria Louisa of Saxe-Coburg;*
*granddaughter of George III.*
*Married Prince Albert of Saxe-Coburg (1840).*
*Four sons, five daughters.*
*Died Osborne 22 January 1901, aged 81. Buried Frogmore, Windsor.\**

> I sing of Georges four.
> Since Providence could stand no more
> Some say that far the worst
> Of all was George the First.
> But yet by some 'tis reckoned
> That worse still was George the Second.
> And what mortal ever heard,
> Any good of George the Third?
> When George the Fourth from the earth descended,
> Thank God the line of Georges ended.
>
> (Walter Savage Landor, 1775–1864)

Landor's bitter lines give some indication of eighteen-year-old Queen Victoria's heritage in 1837. William IV had been a great improvement on his brother, but he was not an impressive figure. The throne which Queen Victoria inherited was weak and unpopular and it took her a long time to live down the irreverence with which the nation had treated her Hanoverian uncles.

Victoria's coronation was something of a fiasco, with a Lord rolling down the steps of the Abbey, the altar at St Edward's Chapel being covered with plates of sandwiches and bottles of wine, and the Archbishop putting the ring on the wrong finger. There was some question of a Regency, despite her age, on account of her inexperience, but this was part of a typically disagreeable intrigue by Sir John Conroy to paint Victoria incapable of assuming the responsibilities of a queen in the hope that he would be appointed Regent. It was soon realized that Victoria was perfectly capable of performing her duties.

Victoria was the only child of the second marriage of Princess Victoria of Saxe-Coburg to Edward, Duke of Kent, fourth son of George III. Her father died when she was eight months old, and his place was filled by her uncle Leopold of Saxe-Coburg (later King of the Belgians). He was responsible for the general character of her early

---

\*The queen did not wish to be buried amongst her Hanoverian uncles.

125

education, and remained a faithful correspondent. Victoria had a sheltered childhood, seldom mixing with girls her own age, which made for the maturity and firmness she displayed in the early years of her reign. Despite spending her childhood largely at Kensington Palace (then less a part of London than now), she saw little of the royal family due to William's dislike of the Duchess of Kent. He was barely able to conceal his feelings about her, and was furious over her royal progresses round the Isle of Wight with her daughter when, under the prompting of the unpleasant Sir John Conroy, she exacted royal salutes from the king's batteries and ships. 'The popping must stop,' ordered the king.

An early example of her independence was her refusal to change her ladies-in-waiting after the fall of Melbourne's government. Many of the ladies-in-waiting were related to Whig ministers and it had been the custom to change them when a new administration came to power. For this expression of personal will, the London mob shouted 'Mrs Melbourne' after her during what was called the 'Bedchamber crisis', another indication of public disrespect for the monarchy at the beginning of her reign.

In February 1840 the Saxe-Coburg influence upon her life was strengthened by her marriage to her cousin, Albert of Saxe-Coburg-Gotha (1819–61). Tactless, serious, intelligent, conscientious and very German, Albert never endeared himself to the English people. There was no precedent, maintained the Archbishop of Canterbury, for his being included in the customary prayers for the royal family; he was excluded from any official position in the political life of the country; although he was made a British citizen, he was never granted the titular dignity of an English peer; nor, until he and Queen Victoria had been married for seventeen years (1857), was he made Prince Consort. Prince Albert, however, did quietly exert tremendous influence over the queen, a fact which became fully apparent only after his death.

He proved to be a devoted husband and father, and helped to raise the monarchy to the lofty pinnacle of respectability where it has since remained. He left two permanent legacies to England: one was the Christmas tree, which he introduced from his native Germany; the other grew out of the Crystal Palace Exhibition of 1851, behind which Albert was the driving force. Six million people visited the Exhibition, which showed a profit of £186,000. With the money, thirty acres of land were purchased in Kensington, to be developed as a shrine to science and art. This land now bears, amongst similar institutions, the Victoria and Albert Museum, the Science Museum, the Imperial College of Science and Technology, the Royal College of Music and the Royal Albert Hall.

The death of the Prince Consort from typhoid on 14 December 1861 was followed by the queen's withdrawal to the seclusion of Osborne, Balmoral, Windsor or the Riviera, for a period of mourning which, despite mounting public criticism, lasted until the Golden Jubilee celebrations in 1887. It allowed people to ask what value the country was deriving from the monarchy, fuelling republican sentiments. Parliament expressed

Queen Victoria opening The Great Exhibition of 1851 *(Hulton–Deutsch Collection)*.

its displeasure by growing reluctance to grant money for the civil list. Fortunately for Victoria, imperial developments distracted the country's attention.

During her seclusion the queen was not inactive. Her husband had taught her to be a conscientious public servant, and she gave close attention to daily routine business and administration, at a time when great political and social reforms were transforming Britain. None the less her continual absence from the seat of government meant that much of her work was a formality and entailed little exercise of real power, except in the choice of ministers. As late as 1892 she put her foot down over having Henry Labouchere in the Cabinet unless he gave up the radical paper *Truth* which he had founded, and in 1895 stopped Henry Mathews' reappointment as Home Secretary. The only legislation that can be ascribed to Victoria was the Public Worship Bill of 1874, doing away with Popish trappings from the Anglican Church.

The chief advances through legislation were the Mines Act (1842) forbidding the employment of women and children underground; the repeal of the Corn Laws in 1846; various factory acts which eventually established a ten-hour day; several Public Health acts from 1848; the Education Act of 1870, which introduced universal elementary education in England and Wales; the Artisans' Dwelling Act (1875); Trades Union Acts (1871 and 1876) and the Reform Acts of 1867 and 1884 which widened the franchise. A measure of the way society was transformed during Victoria's reign and took on many of the elements of today's world is that in 1868, for example, flogging in the army during peacetime and the transportation of criminals were abolished, and the Trades Union Congress was formed.

These Acts were implemented by the ten Prime Ministers of Victoria's reign: Lord Melbourne, Sir Robert Peel, Lord John Russell, Lord Derby, Lord Aberdeen, Viscount Palmerston, Benjamin Disraeli, William Ewart Gladstone, Lord Rosebery and Lord Salisbury. Melbourne and Disraeli had the greatest influence over the queen, Melbourne acting as her colourful tutor on English history, a subject inevitably seldom touched upon by her Uncle Leopold. Victoria was particularly well disposed towards Disraeli; after his death in 1881, the queen returned to Disraeli's house, Hughenden Manor in Buckinghamshire, which she had visited in 1877, just so that she could sit in his study and recall the man whose career she regarded as 'one of the most remarkable in the annals of the Empire'. She would never have written anything complimentary ɐbout Gladstone whom she disliked intensely; she once complained that he addressed her as if she were a public meeting. It was to Gladstone that she sent perhaps her most stinging telegram; she was staying at Holker Hall when Khartoum fell and General Gordon was killed, whereupon she cabled the Prime Minister: 'To think that all this might have been prevented and many precious lives saved by earlier action is too frightful.' Its truth did not help Gladstone to forgive the rebuke.

During Victoria's reign the British Empire doubled in size, principally with additions in Africa and India. New Zealand became a part in 1840. The status of some older colonies changed: Canada became a Dominion in 1867 and the six colonies of Australia made into a Commonwealth in 1900. The Empire was consolidated and expanded, though with much more difficulty, in Burma, the Pacific, Egypt, southern Africa and India. Wars were fought in Afghanistan, Zululand, Egypt, the Sudan and South Africa (Boer Wars in 1881 and 1899–1902), and a mutiny suppressed in India (1857), before English rule was finally established in those countries. In India the change was fundamental: the Mutiny made inevitable the full assumption of formal sovereignty over British India, taking over many of the former responsibilities of the East India Company.

Victoria took particular pleasure from her title of Queen-Empress of India, bestowed upon her by Disraeli in 1876. (She even acquired an Indian servant after the 1877 Jubilee celebrations when Indian princes and a cavalry escort were present to pay their respects.) In 1875 Disraeli purchased the controlling interest in the Suez Canal. Apart from participation in the Crimean War (1853–6), during which the queen introduced the Victoria Cross, England was involved in no major European entanglements between 1815 and 1914.

The queen's unique position at the head of one large European family was probably a contributory factor in keeping her country at peace. She was related, either directly or by marriage, to the royal houses of Germany, Russia, Greece, Romania, Sweden,

Queen Victoria wearing the small Imperial Crown and photographed for her 66th birthday in 1855 *(The Mansell Collection)*.

Denmark, Norway and Belgium. The Tsar of All the Russias was her 'dear Nicky', and the Emperor of Germany, the dreaded Kaiser Wilhelm II, was 'Willy' her own grandson. Queen Victoria ruled her own, and this wider European family, despotically.

The queen's tastes, her virtues and her limitations, reflected those of the middle-class generally. She disliked all 'modern' music ('You couldn't drink a cup of tea to that,' she remarked of a drinking-song by Rubenstein); she found 'modern' paintings odd. Perhaps partly due to the strong sense of duty imbibed from Prince Albert, Victoria had little time for 'the society of fashionable and fast people', as she phrased it, the very people whose company Edward, Prince of Wales relished. The obverse of this distaste for the indulgent and dissolute preoccupations of some of the aristocracy was a rejection of class divisions and a warm regard for the lower orders. Her friendship with the forthright John Brown was, for many, an uncomfortable expression of her preferences. On women's suffrage and extensions of the democratic process, however, Victoria had a reactionary view, though she thought of herself as a liberal. Until Victoria's reign few people would have had any accurate visual knowledge of the royal family; the invention of photography and the millions of *cartes-de-visite* sold of her portrait changed that.

The advent of railways enabled Victoria to travel as no monarch before her. At first Victoria and Albert used the Royal Pavilion at Brighton as an escape from London, but the insatiable curiosity of the people meant that they were mobbed on arrival at Brighton station. A remote house was wanted and found in 1845 at Osborne on the Isle of Wight, the Italianate house becoming their principal country refuge in England. For longer periods away from the capital, the purchase of Balmoral in 1842 provided a Scottish baronial retreat. Victoria developed a particular attachment to the Highlands, which offered her the peace and solitude her retiring nature craved. Even Balmoral was too busy, and she spent much of her time on the estate at the small villa she built in the late 1860s beside Loch Muick. After the death of Albert, Buckingham Palace was hardly used for forty years (Edward referred to it as 'the Sepulchre'), Victoria preferring to stay at Windsor. Victoria was the first British sovereign to visit France officially (1855) since the coronation in Paris of Henry VI in 1431.

Queen Victoria died in the sixty-fourth year of her reign* on 22 January 1901; it was not just the end of a reign but the end of an era. She had reigned three years longer, and was three days older at the time of her death, than George III. During that time France had known two dynasties and become a republic; Spain had seen three monarchs and Italy four. She was succeeded by her eldest son as Edward VII.

*Longest reigns: Louis XIV of France, born 1638, reigned for seventy-two years, 1643–1715; Francis Joseph, Austrian Emperor, born 1830, died in 1916 after a reign of sixty-eight years, 1848–1916.

Queen Victoria with John Brown: photographed by Wilson, Whitlock and Downey, date unknown *(The National Portrait Gallery, London)*.

Queen Victoria was survived by six children, forty grandchildren and thirty-seven great-grandchildren – including four future sovereigns: Edward VII, George V, Edward VIII and George VI.

*The Family of Queen Victoria and the Prince Consort*

1 Princess Victoria (1840–1901) married Frederick, later Crown Prince of Prussia and Frederick III. Their son became Wilhelm II. A daughter married the King of Greece.

2 Edward VII (1841–1910) married the daughter of the King of Denmark. A daughter married the King of Norway.

3 Princess Alice (1843–78) married the Duke of Hesse-Darmstadt, and was the first of Victoria's children to die, of diphtheria. A daughter, Alix, married the ill-fated Tsar Nicholas II of Russia, and was assassinated with him and other members of the Russian royal family at Ekaterinburg (Sverdlovsk) in 1918. A granddaughter of Princess Alice married a future King of Sweden; the late Lord Louis Mountbatten was her grandson and HRH Prince Philip, Duke of Edinburgh, is her great-grandson.

4 Prince Alfred, Duke of Edinburgh (1844–1900), married Marie, daughter of Tsar Alexander II. A daughter married the King of Romania. A granddaughter married the King of Yugoslavia.

Queen Victoria and members of the royal family, c.1872 *(Hulton–Deutsch Collection)*.

5 Princess Helena (1846–1923) married Prince Christian of Schleswig-Holstein (German principality).

6 Princess Louise (1848–1939) married Lord Lorne, heir to the Duke of Argyll.

7 Prince Arthur, Duke of Connaught (1850–1942) married Princess Louise of Prussia.

8 Prince Leopold, Duke of Albany (1853–84), married Princess Helena of Waldeck (German principality), and died of haemophilia.

9 Princess Beatrice (1857–1944) married Prince Henry of Battenburg. A daughter married Alfonso XIII, the last king of Spain.

# Edward VII

*Born Buckingham Palace 9 November 1841. Ascended throne 1901. Reigned 9 years. Eldest son of Queen Victoria.*
*Married Alexandra of Denmark (1863).*
*Three sons, three daughters.*
*Died Buckingham Palace 6 May 1910, aged 68. Buried at Windsor.*

Edward was the first heir born to a reigning monarch since 1762. He was educated privately, and at the universities of Edinburgh, Christ Church, Oxford, and Trinity, Cambridge. Attempts to reduce the isolation that was inevitable in a royal upbringing by asking over boys from Eton had to be abandoned because of Edward's brutal behaviour to them. Later in life he would still take sadistic pleasure from stubbing out a cigar butt on the hand of an unsuspecting guest. It was probably his unpredictability that led Sir Frederick Ponsonby to write that 'there can be no doubt that even his most intimate friends were all terrified of him'.

Even after the death of his father in 1861 he was consistently denied any share in government, for his mother continued in the attitude of suspicion towards the heir-apparent which had marked all the rulers of Hanover. However, there was evidence enough of Edward's indiscretion, and Victoria's strong sense of duty was not reflected in any actions of Edward's. Victoria remained frozen in the grief and resentment she felt towards Edward when Albert died in 1861, deeply troubled on his deathbed by the liaison of Edward and an Irish actress while a guest of the cavalry on the Curragh in Ireland. It must have been hurtful to the Prince to see his mother instead take his sisters into her confidence. The Prince, denied an outlet for his energies, dissipated his great and growing powers in petty and unsuitable pursuits; after his marriage, he continued to have affairs which were public knowledge, the actress Lily Langtry, Lady Brooke and Mrs Keppel being amongst the best known of his mistresses; and he was involved in the Tranby Croft scandal, when a friend with whom the Prince was playing baccarat was accused of cheating, and the Mordaunt divorce case.

At the age of fifty-nine Edward VII, by then a grandfather, came to the throne. Many had shared Victoria's reservations about her son, largely due to his evident distaste for hard work and the intellectual pursuits that might have provided him with some knowledge of the empire whose sovereign he would become. It was soon apparent that Queen Victoria's usually sound judgement had been seriously at fault for, as king, Edward VII soon displayed skill in dealing with his ministers and with foreign rulers. Yet Edward's attempts to assert his influence, or at least the right to be consulted, were often rebuffed. particularly by Balfour who refused to discuss with him questions to be put to the Cabinet. But Edward continued the tradition of some predecessors in taking a particular interest in the armed services: he supported reforms, opposed cuts, backed Admiral Fisher's campaign for Dreadnoughts and played a prominent role in the creation of the Territorials, even summoning all the Lords-Lieutenant to Buckingham Palace to press them to make the force effective in their counties.

The field of foreign affairs was Edward's *forte*; what he lacked in knowledge from reading or questioning of ministers, he compensated for through his world-wide travels, made as Prince of Wales to Italy, Spain. America, Canada, India, Egypt and the Holy Land, Ireland, Denmark, France, Germany, Belgium and Russia. Speaking French and German fluently and Spanish and Italian adequately helped Edward to forge many useful links abroad. However, his visits were primarily useful for cementing personal relations and creating goodwill rather than having an impact on policy. If within two years of his accession he had become known as 'Edward the Peacemaker', this tribute to his constant attempts to foster international friendship was somewhat fanciful. Edward was still capable of the indiscretion and naivety that had discouraged Victoria from entrusting him with responsibilities: in 1901 he handed to the Kaiser the briefing notes Edward had been given for the meeting.

However, his genial disposition, active social life and popularity gave the monarchy a higher profile after the reclusiveness of so much of Victoria's reign. Even his extra-marital affairs were viewed tolerantly. Edward revived the custom of opening Parliament in person, which Victoria had given up, and restored some of the pageantry for which the British monarchy is admired.

Edward's involvement in domestic issues included being a member of the Housing Commission appointed by the Liberals in 1884. His questioning of witnesses illustrated that he was well aware of the difficulties faced by many men and women, and it was on the subject of housing that he made his only full speech to the Lords. Though his lifestyle suggested detachment from the poverty and squalor endured by many Britons, he was troubled by the extremes of wealth and poverty. Nor did his patriotism blind him to the injustices produced by the supercilious attitude of some privileged officials: when

*Opposite:* Edward VII: artist Sir Luke Fildes, date unknown *(The National Portrait Gallery, London)*.

visiting India in the 1870s he expressed strong disapproval of such conduct.

The reign of Edward VII saw important changes in England. During the last two decades of Queen Victoria's reign there had been a dearth of social legislation (successive Liberal and Conservative governments had been wrestling with the problem of Ireland, and Lord Salisbury did not believe in social improvement by legislation) and there was much headway to be made up. In 1902, an Education Act provided secondary education at the State's expense. The Liberal government after 1906 passed a series of reforms to benefit children, introduced old-age pensions (1908) and Labour Exchanges (1909), and laid the basis for the National Insurance scheme which was to be enacted early in the next reign. The money for these schemes was budgeted for in 1909, and the Lords' rejection of the Budget in that year sparked off a constitutional crisis.

The Chancellor responsible for the budget was Lloyd George, disliked by Edward since he had compared the costs of keeping a Duke and a Dreadnought (the battleship was cheaper). The Prime Minister, Asquith, demanded and got a dissolution of Parliament because of the Lords' veto, the first confrontation between the two houses over money for over two hundred years. Asquith asked Edward whether, if the Lords again rejected the Budget, he would create enough peers in the Lords to push through a Parliament Bill that would end the exercise of such power by the Lords. Recalling Victoria's belief that 'to threaten the House of Lords is, in fact, to threaten the monarchy itself', Edward agreed with great reluctance, provided that the issue was put to the country at a general election. The crisis was at its head when Edward died, leaving George V the unenviable task of resolving it.

During Edward's reign, the first Nobel prizes were awarded (1901), the world's first concentration camps were set up by Britain during the Boer War (1901), the Japanese routed the Russian navy and defeated the army through sheer weight of numbers during a two-year war (1904–5), signifying the emergence of a new power that threatened traditional empires, and the first buses driven by internal-combustion engines began operating in the streets of London.

A Saxe-Coburg by birth, upbringing and in appearance, Edward VII was really a Hanoverian. He possessed the social graces, shrewdness and care for personal appearance which had characterized that family; he set the fashions of the day. But he also had tact, kindness and warmth, qualities in which the Hanoverians had been markedly deficient. His affability and dandyism made him a popular figure with the majority of his subjects. Edward's sporting interests and activities had much to do with his popularity. His racing yacht *Britannia* was one of the most successful of her day, and the king had many wins on the turf. He became the first reigning monarch to win the Derby, with *Persimmon* in 1896, and won both the Derby and Grand National in 1900.

After Edward's accession, Edward's annual round was Christmas at Sandringham,

Edward VII: date unknown *(The Mansell Collection)*.

three or four weeks at Buckingham Palace, an avoidance of February or March weather in England by a spell in Biarritz; Easter at Windsor, the summer at Buckingham Palace broken up by breaks for Ascot and Goodwood and perhaps an official tour abroad; Cowes week would be followed by country-house visits for grouse-shooting, three weeks at a foreign spa in September, Balmoral for October and Buckingham Palace for the rest of the year, with a break at Sandringham for his birthday in November. Edward particularly enjoyed his time at Sandringham, the Norfolk house and estate bought for him in 1860. The house is architecturally unremarkable, but Edward was less interested in aesthetics than its potential for shooting, which was excellent.

Edward VII married Alexandra, eldest daughter of Christian IX of Denmark, in 1863. There were six children of the marriage: his eldest son, the Duke of Clarence, who died in 1892; the Duke of York, who succeeded his father as George V in 1910; the Princess Royal, who married the Duke of Fife; Princess Victoria; Princess Maud, who married King Haakon VII of Norway; and Alexander who was born and died in 1871.

King Edward died on 6 May 1910. Nine crowned heads of Europe followed him to his grave: the kings of England, Norway, Spain, Portugal, Belgium, Sweden and Denmark, the Tsar of Bulgaria and the Emperor of Germany. In addition, there were five heirs-apparent (including the ill-fated Archduke Franz Ferdinand of Austria*), seven queens and a host of minor royalty and foreign ambassadors, representing more than seventy different countries.

*See section on World War I, page 186.

# George V

*Born Marlborough House 3 June 1865. Ascended throne 1910. Reigned 25 years.*
*Second son of Edward VII.*
*Married Princess Mary of Teck (1893).*
*Five sons, one daughter.*
*Died Sandringham 20 January 1936, aged 70. Buried at Windsor.*

The new king was the second son of Edward VII. Without expectation of succeeding to the throne, he was educated as a professional naval officer and saw service throughout the world. The death of his elder brother, the Duke of Clarence and Avondale, in 1892, forced him to relinquish his active naval career and assume the duties of heir-apparent.

In 1893, the Duke of York, as he now was, married his cousin, Princess Mary of Teck (1867–1953). The Princess, better known at this time as Princess May, was the daughter of Francis, Duke of Teck, a minor penurious German prince, and Mary Adelaide, the daughter of the Duke of Cambridge, seventh son of George III. She had been engaged to George's elder brother, but two months after the engagement he caught influenza and pneumonia and died at Sandringham. Her marriage to George proved felicitous. Throughout George's reign and after his death, Queen Mary was noted for her dedication to the interests of women and children, and for her general philanthropic work.

As a wedding present Edward VII gave them York Cottage, formerly known as Bachelor's Cottage and built as an annexe for male guests at Sandringham. Too small for the entertaining George V so disliked, he was particularly attached to its low-key domesticity, Mary less so, but they continued to live there until 1925. Harold Nicolson remarked that 'the rooms inside . . . are indistinguishable from those of any Surbiton or Upper Norwood home'. George's recreations were shooting (he was an excellent shot) and stamp collecting, and he dreaded public ceremonies. Allowed access to State papers by Edward VII that Edward himself that he had been denied as Prince of Wales, George acquired a fuller knowledge of the nation's affairs, augmented by his extensive travels, though he spoke no foreign language.

George V succeeded to the throne in the middle of a constitutional crisis. The Lords, containing a preponderance of Tory peers, had rejected the radical Liberal budget of 1909, the 'People's Budget'. This was an unprecedented act and the Liberals were seeking to restrict the powers of the Lords by Act of Parliament. After two elections in 1910 (the only year this has occurred in British history), George V was induced to agree to create sufficient Liberal peers to ensure the passage of the Parliament Bill in the House of Lords, should it be necessary. He strongly resented the pressure that he had been put under, not helped by contradictory opinions from his advisers.

George V: Coronation Portrait *(Hulton–Deutsch Collection)*.

Rather than be swamped by new Liberal peers, sufficient Conservatives stayed away or voted with the Liberals for the Bill to become law. The Parliament Bill prevented the Lords' rejection of any money bill, limited their power to block a bill to three successive occasions, after which it would automatically become law, and reduced the length of a Parliament from seven to five years.

Having become in the second election dependent upon the Irish members for a working majority, the Liberals opened up the prospect of Irish Home Rule. Both sides began armed preparation in Ireland, as there was no longer any possibility of the Lords blocking it for any length of time. The new Conservative leader, Bonar Law, suggested to George V that the royal veto might be used, but as one Liberal minister sagely advised, royal interference of that kind might 'reduce the throne to a hopeless ruin'. Talks in 1914 between Asquith and Bonar Law achieved nothing; a conference hosted by Buckingham Palace, which was resented by Radicals and Irish nationalists, collapsed over the issue of the borders of a separate Ulster. The outbreak of World War I only postponed the agony.

During World War I the king made several visits to the front line in France and Belgium. He was a war casualty himself: during a visit to France in 1915, his horse rolled on him and he received serious internal injuries from which he never fully recovered. The war enabled the king and queen to come into close contact with the mass of their people, to an extent unknown since the seventeenth century. Given the strong anti-German feelings in Britain, expressed arbitrarily to anyone with a foreign-sounding name, it was considered a propitious moment for the royal family to change its surname from Guelph (or Welf) and the House of Saxe-Coburg-Gotha to Windsor.

The survival, even the enhanced prestige, of the monarchy as a result of World War I occasions no comment by many historians, but of all wars it marked the end of monarchy as a feature of the hierarchy in most countries. This was partly because the royal family was closely identified with the war effort, but also because the nature of the monarchy's constitutional position was radical in comparison with the autocracies of Europe. The refusal of the British monarchy to be tarred with the brush of unreformed autocrats was reflected in the denial of asylum to the Russian royal family, despite Nicholas II being a cousin of George V; few could have anticipated their execution. A measure of the wide regard for the royal family, even after the shock waves of the Bolshevik Revolution, was that a Labour Party Conference motion that the royal family was no longer a necessary part of the constitution was defeated by a ratio of 10 votes to 1. Of course, part of the affection for the monarchy may be said to stem precisely from the turbulence and rapidity of change in so many areas of modern life, making it a symbol of continuity. Also the spread of the cinema made George V better known to the people of Britain than any previous monarch.

When the war ended the king was fifty-three, with another seventeen years of his reign left and innumerable crises and problems to overcome. The post-war years saw much social unrest and trouble in Ireland. The 'Sinn Fein' ('Ourselves Alone') Easter Rising of 1916, when the Irish Republican Army tried to create an independent state by force, was followed by a general election in 1918 at which Sinn Fein won seventy-three seats. They would not take them up at Westminster, forming instead a provisional government. British troops tried to suppress it, but negotiations between Lloyd George and Irish leaders produced the Government of Ireland Act, 1920, allowing for assemblies in Dublin and Belfast, divided on religious lines. In 1921 the king and queen visited Belfast to inaugurate the Northern Ireland Parliament. Following further armed resistance to achieve fuller independence than provided for by the 1920 Act, an agreement was reached the following year to set up the Irish Free State in the south, having Dominion status.

Social and industrial unrest resulted in the formation of the first Socialist government, which held office for a brief period, although in a minority in the Commons, in 1924. The Prime Minister was Ramsay Macdonald. In 1926, the General Strike took place: a sympathetic strike by the transport trade unions in support of the Miners' Federation brought the country to a halt. The strike lasted from 4 to 13 May, caused the loss of about 160 million working days and involved over 2 million employees. During the strike broadcast news bulletins, which replaced newspapers, proved the importance that radio was to have. The BBC had been established in 1926, and in 1937 the famous Christmas Day broadcast by the monarch was inaugurated.

The world economic crisis of 1929–31 had a drastic effect on Britain; there was a phenomenal rise in the number of unemployed and the finances of the country were on the verge of collapse. George V was instrumental in persuading the leaders of the three political parties – Ramsay Macdonald (Labour), Stanley Baldwin (Conservative) and Sir Herbert Samuel (Liberal) – to form a National Coalition government in August 1931, under the premiership of Macdonald. This was an extension of George's desire to act as mediator between the parties and the strongly divergent views of the time; as Harold Nicolson put it, 'unfalteringly and assiduously he sought to create a good blood'.

Not the least important feature of George V's reign was the change in the relationship between Britain and the other members of the Empire. This grew from a demand for self-government in New Zealand and the newly formed South Africa. (Following the two Boer Wars, in part over the refusal of the Boers to grant political rights to foreigners in the Transvaal and the Orange Free State, the Union of South Africa was established in the first month of George's reign, comprising the two Boer states and the previously British provinces of the Cape of Good Hope and Natal.)

Prior to 1914, the foreign policy of the Empire was determined by the British government, but after the war Dominion ministers began to express their determination that the imperial system must undergo radical change, so as to allow the whole Empire

George V: artist Lance Calkin, c1914 *(The National Portrait Gallery, London)*.

George V: military bust, 1914 *(Hulton–Deutsch Collection)*.

some voice in policies which affected the whole. The principle of Dominion independence was gradually accepted, and it received statutory definition in 1931, when the Statute of Westminster created the British Commonwealth of Nations. The Dominions were now no longer a group of colonies subordinated to England, but a Commonwealth of free nations. Outside the Commonwealth were still the Colonies, as distinct from the Dominions, and India. The last was accorded a measure of self-government in the Government of India Act, 1935, as the beginning of a transitional period which ended with the granting of India's independence in 1947. George V was, incidentally, the first reigning sovereign to visit India, when he attended a Durbar at Delhi in 1911, followed by a fortnight's big game shooting in Nepal.

George V and Queen Mary's six children were Prince Edward (Edward VIII); Prince Albert (George VI); Princess Mary, the Princess Royal (died 1965); Prince Henry (the Duke of Gloucester); Prince George (the Duke of Kent, killed in an air crash in 1942); and Prince John (died 1919).

George V celebrated his Silver Jubilee amidst vast crowds around the Palace in May 1935 and died of influenza on 20 January 1936. He was succeeded by his eldest son as Edward VIII.

# Edward VIII

*Born White Lodge, Richmond 23 June 1894. Ascended throne 20 January 1936.*
*Abdicated 11 December 1936. He was never crowned.*
*Eldest son of George V.*
*Married Mrs Wallis Simpson (1937).*
*No issue.*
*Died Paris 28 May 1972, aged 77. Buried at Windsor.*

Edward VIII became king on 20 January 1936, and was to have the shortest reign in the country's history, with the exception of that of his namesake, Edward V.

Called David by his family, Prince Edward later regarded his childhood at York Cottage on the Sandringham estate as having been unhappy; the evidence points to a delightfully carefree time until dispatched to the Royal Naval Colleges at Osborne and Dartmouth. Yet after eight terms at Oxford, the Prince went into the Grenadier Guards, serving on the Western Front where he was kept well out of harm's way. After a period in the navy, Edward travelled extensively, making successful official visits to Canada, the United States, New Zealand, Australia and India; Lloyd George called the Prince 'our greatest ambassador', though the Prince's predeliction for unofficial nocturnal companions caused concern. Always under the scrutiny of his father, whose letters sometimes upbraided him for a minor sartorial solecism, the Prince was cast in the mould of his grandfather, preferring the life of the smart set at nightclubs to anything that might be regarded as preparation for becoming king. Though his physical appearance and charm won praise, he was never able to conceal boredom, and would sometimes start chatting about racing or other subjects congenial to him in the middle of an important meeting. He disliked the ceremonial aspects of monarchy, and tried to reduce such commitments.

Before the death of George V, rumours were circulating of an attachment which the Prince of Wales had formed, and after the accession as king these grew in volume, particularly in American and Continental newspapers; the British press had agreed between themselves to ignore the subject. The details of this relationship with Mrs Wallis Simpson were kept from the British public for a remarkably long time.

Mrs Simpson, born Wallis Warfield, was the daughter of a Baltimore family with old and aristocratic connections in Maryland and Virginia. She had divorced her first husband, Lt Winfield Spencer of the US navy, in 1927, and married in the same year Mr Ernest Simpson, a London stockbroker of Anglo-American parentage. The Prince had met Mrs Simpson in 1930, and she first visited his house within Windsor Great Park, Fort Belvedere, in 1932. By 1934 his former consorts, Lady Furness and Mrs Dudley Ward, had been dropped to devote more time to Mrs Simpson. Though the king and Mrs Simpson went on holiday together to the Balkans in the summer of 1936 and they were much photographed by press photographers, the newspapers still maintained a silence. It was only when Bishop Blunt of Bradford hinted in a sermon that the king might be neglecting his spiritual responsibilities and the *Yorkshire Post* looked for a reason behind Dr Blunt's comments that the story broke.

With the news that Mrs Simpson was filing a divorce petition the crisis was at hand. Stanley Baldwin tried to defuse it during an audience when he warned the king of the possible hazards and the feeling that the relationship was engendering in the country. The leaders of the Liberal and Labour parties concurred with Baldwin's view that Mrs Simpson would be unacceptable as queen. On 27 October 1936 she was granted a decree nisi, and it became clear that the king intended to marry her. Constitutionally the king could marry whom he wished; but if he did so against the advice of his Cabinet, and the Cabinet resigned over the issue, there would be a general election which would be damaging to the concept of constitutional monarchy.

Edward was not without support, though some of it came from quarters that were not likely to encourage others or do the king's cause much good; others supported him for reasons that had little to do with the fundamental issues. The newspaper barons Lords Rothermere and Beaverbrook supported a morganatic settlement, and Churchill pleaded in the Commons for a delay. There were demonstrations outside Buckingham Palace that united Communists and Fascists, and it was reported that about sixty MPs were willing to support a king's government.

There were in theory four courses open to the king: he could marry Mrs Simpson and make her queen; he could contract a morganatic marriage – that is, neither Mrs Simpson nor any issue of the marriage would share in the royal status or property; he could abdicate and then marry; he could abandon Mrs Simpson.

The national objection to Mrs Simpson was not that she was an American, nor that she was a commoner. Both Edward IV and Henry VIII had married commoners, as had the king's own brother, the future George VI. But Mrs Simpson had divorced two husbands, both of whom were still alive; and although there was a royal precedent for a king's marriage to a divorced person – that of Henry II to Eleanor of Aquitaine – the idea was disliked. Marriage to a divorced person would raise in acute form the question of the king's relationship to the established Church, whose official doctrine censured the whole concept of divorce. Moreover, it still carried a stigma that could end public careers of lesser mortals than a king. English law did not recognize any such thing as a morganatic marriage, so Edward VIII's choice was between abandonment of the throne or of the woman he loved.

Relations between the king and Mrs Simpson formed the only topic of conversation throughout the British Isles, despite the plight of 2 million unemployed, Mosley and the Fascists, the Spanish Civil War and the threat of Hitler on the Continent. It was well said at the time that Hitler might have seized Austria without the British public either knowing or caring.

Denied the possibility of a morganatic marriage by the Cabinet, Edward informed Baldwin that he wished to make a broadcast that would effectively have complained of his treatment by the government. When this was refused, the king conceded the inevitability of abdication and made a broadcast announcing his decision and the reasons for it on 11 December 1936. He asked the country to support his brother Albert, and left England from Portsmouth aboard the destroyer HMS *Fury*. On the previous day, by the Declaration of Abdication Act, Edward VIII formally renounced his throne and was succeeded by his brother, the Duke of York, as George VI; one of the first new king's acts was to create the ex-king Duke of Windsor.

The Duke of Windsor and Mrs Simpson were married in 1937, but Mrs Simpson was refused the title of Royal Highness. It was a denial that was to rankle Edward for the rest of his life, referring to it as 'a kind of Berlin Wall alienating us from my family'. Given a handsome annuity by George VI in return for relinquishing his life interest in Balmoral and Sandringham and their contents, the Duke led a somewhat resentful and self-indulgent exile in comfortable circumstances. They lived mostly in Paris, where the City provided an elegant house in the Bois de Boulogne, though during World War II Edward was Governor of the Bahamas after a short period with the British Military

*Opposite:* Edward VIII: artist P. G. Eves *(The National Portrait Gallery, London).*

Mission in France and six weeks in Spain, where he indiscreetly forecast Britain's defeat. His pre-war expressions of admiration for Germany did not endear him to those who could foresee the makings of catastrophe. Post-war life in France was filled with golf, gardening and cairn terriers. The Duchess of Windsor was not received by the royal family until Elizabeth II relented on the occasion of the dedication of a memorial to Queen Mary. Mrs Simpson died in 1986 and is buried beside her husband at Frogmore.

Edward VIII: photographed when he was Prince of Wales *(Hulton–Deutsch Collection)*.

# George VI

*Born Sandringham 14 December 1895. Ascended throne 1936.*
*Reigned 15 years.*
*Second son of George V.*
*Married Lady Elizabeth Bowes-Lyon (1923).*
*Two daughters.*
*Died Sandringham 6 February 1952, aged 56. Buried at Windsor.*

Like his father George VI had not expected to become king. Known as 'Bertie' to the family – he was christened Albert Frederick Arthur George – Prince Albert's childhood was clouded by illness and a stammer he developed at eight. Educated at Dartmouth Naval College and Trinity College, Cambridge, Prince Albert served during World War I aboard HMS *Collingwood,* seeing action during the Battle of Jutland (1916). Invalided out, he became an air cadet at Cranwell and was a talented tennis player, winning the Royal Air Force doubles and in 1926 playing at Wimbledon in the All-England Championships. After the war he became closely involved with the problems of human relations in industry, giving his patronage to the Industrial Welfare Society and becoming president of the Boys' Welfare Association, establishing the Duke of York's boys camps for public school and working-class boys.

George's marriage in 1923, described as the wisest decision of his life, was made possible by his father's relaxation of the policy on royal marriages, for his wife, the Lady Elizabeth Bowes-Lyon, though a direct descendant of the kings of Scotland, was a commoner; George had been the first prince (but not princess) of royal blood to marry a commoner since the reign of George III. As George VI's official biographer wrote, 'the Duchess was not only to be the partner of his happiness but his inspiration and encouragement in the face of adversity, his enduring source of strength in joy and sadness. Hers was the ability to sustain or reward him by a single smile or gesture in the public battles he waged with his stammer; hers the capacity to calm with a word that passionate temper which every now and again would burst its bounds.' In 1927 the Duke and Duchess went on a long tour of Australia and New Zealand.

The new king needed all the support he could get. The prestige of the throne was lower than at any time since the accession of Queen Victoria. Soon after his accession, George wrote that he hoped he would be allowed sufficient time 'to make amends for what has happened'. The abdication crisis would have figured more prominently in British history had it not been over so quickly as far as the public was concerned and because it was so soon overshadowed by the outbreak of World War II. However, it was soon apparent that George VI had inherited the steady virtues which had distinguished his father and endeared him to the English people.

George VI: artist P. G. Eves, 1924 *(The National Portrait Gallery, London)*.

Elizabeth (Queen Mother): artist Sir Gerald Kelly, c1938 *(The National Portrait Gallery, London).*

George VI had hoped to hold a durbar following his coronation, but it never proved politically expedient. However, in 1938 the king and queen visited France, and in the summer of 1939 Canada and the United States. Shortly after the coronation, Neville Chamberlain took over from Stanley Baldwin as Prime Minister; George favoured Chamberlain's policy of appeasement, as did many at the time, and even suggested personal appeals to Hitler, the Italian king and Japanese emperor, an idea not endorsed by the Cabinet. With the outbreak of war, Chamberlain's shortcomings as a wartime leader became apparent and he was compelled to resign after the failure of the Norway expedition. The king at first favoured the Foreign Secretary Lord Halifax as Chamberlain's successor, but being in the Lords, Halifax felt that he would be at arm's

George VI and family: Royal Lodge, Windsor 1940 *(Hulton–Deutsch Collection)*.

length from the Commons. The king later wrote: 'Then I knew that there was only one person I could send for to form a Government who had the confidence of the country, and that was Winston.' At first the relationship between the King and Winston Churchill was cool, but formal meetings soon gave way to a weekly lunch at the Palace to discuss the latest developments in the war, and Churchill entrusted the king with the most guarded secrets. He was one of only four people to know the detailed plans for the use of the atom bomb.

The war enhanced the importance of the throne, as it had done in George V's time. When it began, King George VI and Queen Elizabeth were little more than constitutional abstractions; by the time it had finished they were firmly entrenched in the nation's affections. The king and queen set an example of fortitude, raising morale by visiting troops, munitions factories, docks and bomb-damaged areas, freely showing their concern for people under stress. It was these peregrinations through bomb-scarred streets that gave the king the idea for the George Cross and the George Medal. They refused to leave Buckingham Palace, even though it was directly hit by a bomb while they were in the building, thereby expressing their willingness to share with Londoners the nightly terror of the Blitz. The king also visited the front line in North Africa, Malta and Italy.

After the war the emergency coalition, led by Winston Churchill, was replaced by Britain's third Socialist government under the leadership of Clement Attlee. The king was deeply disappointed by the country's rejection of the man who had done so much to secure victory, but he was not averse to the Labour manifesto on principle, supporting Attlee's intention of giving independence to India. However, he did think the nationalization of the Bank of England, the mines, railways, road transport, gas and electricity, the health services, and iron and steel too much for the country to assimilate in a single Parliament. But there were few problems with Attlee's administration, and the king was gratified by the Prime Minister's agreement that the three senior orders of chivalry (the Garter, the Thistle and St Patrick) should no longer be political rewards but the prerogative of the monarch.

In 1947 the king and queen toured South Africa and neighbouring Protectorates, the programme being so taxing that the king lost 17lb (7.6kg). Arteriosclerosis and lung cancer took their toll on the king's health, and he died in his sleep in February 1952 while Princess Elizabeth and Prince Philip were on the first leg of a visit to East Africa, Australia and New Zealand.

Like his father, George VI had a strong sense of duty, a great respect for tradition and continuity and was a stickler for dress. Before the annual trooping the colour, he would wear the Brigade of Guards bearskin cap while gardening to accustom himself to its weight.

George VI was succeeded by his eldest daughter as Elizabeth II.

# Elizabeth II

*Born 17 Bruton Street, London WI, 21 April 1926. Ascended throne 1952.*
*Elder daughter of George VI.*
*Married Philip Mountbatten, RN, formerly Prince Philip of*
*Schleswig-Holstein-Sonderburg-Glucksburg (1947)*
*Three sons, one daughter.*

When Princess Elizabeth was born at the London home of the Duchess of York's parents, there was little expectation that she would become queen; the Prince of Wales was then only thirty-one and there was every possibility that her parents would have a son who would take precedence. Edward VIII's abdication made her heir presumptive. As a child she captivated those around her with her quick intelligence and relaxed formality; during a visit to Balmoral when Princess Elizabeth was two, Sir Winston Churchill wrote that 'she has an air of authority and reflectiveness astonishing in an infant'. Later, when Princess Elizabeth was sixteen, Lady Airlie noted that 'there was about her that indescribable something which Queen Victoria had'.

Educated privately, Princess Elizabeth spent much of the war at Windsor Castle, and became a subaltern in the ATS. Given the very changed prospects for her future, courses in constitutional history and the French language, literature and history were added to the curriculum. After the war she accompanied her parents on their 1947 tour of South Africa, and it was in Cape Town that she celebrated her twenty-first birthday, making a broadcast speech of dedication to the Commonwealth.

On their return from South Africa, the engagement was announced of Princess Elizabeth to her third cousin Lieutenant Philip Mountbatten (see p 157) whom the Princess had first met at Dartmouth Naval College in July 1939 and corresponded with throughout the war. The wedding in November 1947 was a relaxation from the post-war austerity, providing a day of pageantry and colour; Princess Elizabeth had been given an extra 100 clothing coupons for her satin dress. The honeymoon was at Broadlands, the Hampshire home of Lord and Lady Mountbatten, and at Birkhall on the Balmoral estate. There are four children of the marriage: Prince Charles, born 14 November 1948; Princess Anne, born 15 August 1950; Prince Andrew, born 19 February 1960; and Prince Edward, born 10 March 1964.

Princess Elizabeth was only twenty-five when she and Prince Philip were recalled from their royal tour in Kenya on the death of King George VI. Her independence was asserted in the preparations for the coronation on 2 June 1953 when she insisted against the advice of the Prime Minister Sir Winston Churchill, the Cabinet and the Archbishop of Canterbury that the ceremony be televised. It was watched by 20 million and heard by 12 million people.

George VI and Princess Elizabeth: Royal Lodge, Windsor 1942 *(Hulton–Deutsch Collection)*.

Queen Elizabeth's accession was accompanied by a constitutional innovation: she was proclaimed in each of the self-governing countries of what used to be called the British Empire as Queen of that particular country. The formal abandonment of the principle of the indivisibility of the Crown was confirmed by statute in 1953, and a new description, 'Head of the Commonwealth', was inserted amongst the royal titles to allow for the inclusion of republics like India and Pakistan. A feature of the reign has been the number of independent states which have come into being, the Commonwealth in 1986 comprising forty-nine states.

The Queen's role as Head of the Commonwealth has taken her on numerous tours of member states, one of the most notable being the 56,000 mile tour of Commonwealth countries in 1977, the year of the Queen's Silver Jubilee. She is also responsible for the appointment of Governors-General on the advice of the particular country's prime minister. The Queen's concern for the Commonwealth and her position as its head is reflected in her ire over the cavalier invasion of Grenada, of which she is head of state, by the United States in 1983; as a close ally, the least that might have been expected was notification of its intentions. The strains imposed upon relations within the Commonwealth by Prime Minister Thatcher's refusal to agree to economic sanctions against South Africa has also been a source of concern to the Queen.

Elizabeth II, and the royal family as a whole, has played a much more strenuous role in the life of the nation and Commonwealth. The continual round of state visits, overseas tours, attendance at all manner of events within Britain, and entertaining of guests from all walks of life has placed a much greater burden on the monarch than on her predecessors. The strain of being forever in the public eye and the focus of countless press and television cameras has meant that those times when it has been possible to relax with her family are rarer and more precious than for previous monarchs. Resentment of the *papparazzi*'s intrusion on such moments has fuelled debate over the role of the tabloid press in depriving the royal family of what little privacy they enjoy.

Though the theoretical powers of the monarch remain considerable – Bagehot cited examples such as disbanding the army and navy, creating a universal peerage in the kingdom and dismissing the civil service – Queen Elizabeth's exercise of them is limited to that of a constitutional sovereign who has to abide by the advice of ministers on government policy. But the resignation of two Conservative prime ministers has placed the Queen in the position of choosing a successor. When Anthony Eden resigned in 1957, Harold Macmillan was appointed by the Queen in preference to R. A. Butler, who had deputized for Eden's absences due to ill-health. This occasioned surprise amongst the public but not amongst the Cabinet and others whose opinions were canvassed, such as Churchill. The resignation of Macmillan in 1963, again on the grounds of ill-health, produced a greater choice of candidates; the Queen followed the advice of

Macmillan in sending for Lord Home as the most acceptable choice for the whole party. This awkward situation cannot arise again, as the Conservative Party has followed the Labour Party in establishing a system for choosing their leaders.

The royal family have of course been affected by the post-war change in social outlook and habits; their frequent travels, with Prince Philip's cheerful informality and hard work for good causes, have done much to identify them with the everyday life of the nation. Some of the anachronisms of court life have been done away with, such as the presentation of debutantes and the refusal of admission into the royal enclosure at Ascot even of innocent parties to a divorce case. At the same time, in an age of recurrent international crises and economic problems, the monarchy's stability and the pageantry still surrounding it have remained a valuable focal point for the nation's self-respect and sense of identity.

The Queen's principal recreation has been horses, attending race meetings, often to watch her own horses compete; but the aspect that interests her most is breeding and training, and she has been on private visits to the United States to look at stud farms.

In 1965 Sir Winston Churchill died, one of Britain's greatest statesmen; he was given what will probably be the last lavish state funeral. He had served six monarchs and held a variety of high offices from 1905 to 1955, when he retired as Prime Minister, but he will be remembered most for his brilliant leadership during World War II.

# Prince Philip, Duke of Edinburgh

Prince Philip was born in Corfu, Greece, on 10 June 1921. He was the fifth child and only son of Princess Alice of Battenburg (a great-granddaughter of Queen Victoria) and Prince Andrew of Greece. Prince Andrew owed his life to British intervention. In 1922, after the Greek disaster in Asia Minor at the hands of the Turks, the Greek ministers in office were executed; Prince Andrew, who had commanded the right wing of the Greek army, was awaiting trial with the certainty of the death sentence following. An unofficial ambassador was sent to Athens and succeeded in securing his release. Prince Andrew's eighteen-month-old son Philip is said to have been brought on board in an orange box.

From 1923 to 1935, the Greek royal family was in exile in England. Prince Philip was educated at Cheam School, Gordonstoun and the Royal Naval College, Dartmouth, and spent much of his childhood in England under the guardianship of his maternal uncle, the 2nd Marquess of Milford Haven. During World War II he saw active service with the Royal Navy and he served on the battleship HMS *Valiant* at the battle of Cape Matapan (1941). He later took part in the Sicily landings and was aboard the American battleship *Missouri* when the Japanese surrendered in Tokyo Bay.

He became a British subject in February 1947, renouncing his Greek titles and membership of the Greek Orthodox Church, and adopted the name of Mountbatten, the

*Above:* Elizabeth II: artist Pietro Annigoni, 1969 *(The National Portrait Gallery, London)*.

Elizabeth II taking the salute at the Trooping the Colour *(Daily Telegraph Colour Library)*.

anglicized form of his mother's family name of Battenburg. The day before he married Princess Elizabeth, George VI conferred on him the title of Duke of Edinburgh and the qualification of 'His Royal Highness'. In 1957, the Duke was granted the titular dignity of Prince of the United Kingdom.

After his marriage, the Duke of Edinburgh returned to his naval career, becoming commander of the frigate HMS *Magpie*. He has continued his interest in the Services and holds numerous important appointments, including Admiral of the Fleet and Marshal of the Royal Air Force. He has continued George VI's interest and work in industrial relations and developments, being Patron of the Industrial Society and the sponsor of six international study conferences on the human problems of industrial societies. The Duke of Edinburgh awards scheme reflects his interest in the capacity of young people to play a role in community service, develop their appreciation of outdoor recreation and test their self-reliance.

Prince Philip is well known for his concern for the environment; he has spoken out strongly on the threats posed by man to the world's fragile ecology and the dangers of ignoring the mounting evidence of serious environmental damage. He has been closely involved with the World Wildlife Fund since 1961, and is President of the renamed World Wide Fund for Nature. His recreations include four-in-hand driving and polo, and he is a qualified pilot, regularly taking the controls of aircraft in the Queen's Flight.

# The Prince of Wales

*Prince Charles Philip Arthur George, Prince of Wales and Earl of Chester,*
*Duke of Cornwall, Duke of Rothesay, Earl of Carrick and Baron Renfrew.*
*Lord of the Isles and Great Steward of Scotland.*
*Born 14 November 1948 at Buckingham Palace, the eldest son of Queen Elizabeth II*
*and HRH Prince Philip.*
*Married Lady Diana Spencer.*
*Two sons.*

HRH Prince Charles was created Prince of Wales and Earl of Chester on 26 July 1958. His investiture as Prince of Wales took place on 1 July 1969 at Caernarfon Castle. He is the twenty-first holder of the title.

Many radical decisions were made by his parents with regard to education and upbringing to fit him for a supposedly egalitarian society. He was the first heir to the throne to be educated outside the royal homes. After preparatory school he went on to the school his father had attended, at Gordonstoun, Scotland, where he learned to adapt himself to the rigorous conditions which were to fit him for his chosen Royal Navy career. However, Prince Charles is believed to have disliked the spartan regime with its emphasis on character building at the expense of more intellectual pursuits. He also spent a period in Australia at Timbertop, an outpost in the Victorian Alps of the Geelong Church of England Grammar School, the Australian equivalent of Eton, afterwards travelling extensively round the country, including spending a week in the Snowy Mountains with the Queen Mother. He was at Trinity College, Cambridge, from 1967 to 1969 and later at the University College of Wales before graduating as BA (Cantab) in June 1970. He is the first Prince of Wales to have gained a university degree.

Prince Charles is a well-qualified pilot and helicopter pilot. He served with the RAF in 1971 and later transferred to the navy, eventually commanding the coastal mine-hunter HMS *Bronington* based at Rosyth, Scotland. His service career continued until December 1976 when he left the Royal Navy, having served in the West Indies, Singapore and the Arctic, interrupted by other visits.

He has represented the Queen on many occasions, the first being in 1967 at the memorial service of Harold Holt, Prime Minister of Australia. With a dedication and professionalism which impresses all who meet him, not least the ever-critical Press with whom he has established an excellent relationship based on mutual respect, he has enjoyed a breadth of experience unrivalled by any previous Prince of Wales. His thirst for excitement and adventure is apparent from the list of pursuits he has followed, including training as a frogman and commando, parachute jumping, hang-gliding and diving under icecaps. He has climbed the foothills of the Himalayas, dived for sunken treasure, and has ridden in many steeplechases. In addition he is an expert rifle shot and an excellent swimmer.

On the polo field – one of his particular pleasures – he is first class and like other members of the royal family loves horses and riding. Whilst obviously an outdoor man, he has many other interests such as music and painting. He has been an entertaining and forceful critic of architectural ill-manners and unimaginative commercial developments that give pleasure to no one but those who profit by them. He has also championed aspects of conservation that his father has not encompassed, such as the use of chemicals in farming and food production.

His sensibilities are reflected in the choice of Laurens van der Post as godfather to one of his sons. Prince Charles's obvious concern about the quality of life in Britain has won him admiration and respect from all quarters; it has resulted in his involvement with many organizations designed to improve opportunities for the underprivileged, such as The Prince's Youth Business Trust, The Prince's Trust, The Prince of Wales' Community Venture and The Prince of Wales' Advisory Group on Disability.

Prince Charles has no income from the State. He heads the organization which administers the estates of the Duchy of Cornwall. Comprising some 130,000 acres, it makes him one of the largest landowners in the country. His home outside London is Highgrove House in Gloucestershire, bought from the late son of Harold Macmillan.

Prince Philip enjoying one of his favourite sports – carriage driving *(Daily Telegraph Colour Library)*.

*Above:* HRH The Duke of Edinburgh *(Daily Telegraph Colour Library)*.

*Below:* HRH The Prince of Wales, heir to the throne *(Daily Telegraph Colour Library)*.

# The Princess of Wales

*Diana Frances Spencer.*
*Born 1 July 1961 at Park House on her father's property on the Sandringham estate.*
*Daughter of 8th Earl Spencer and the Hon Mrs Peter Shand Kydd.*
*Two sons.*

The Earl Spencer, educated at Eton and Sandhurst and a Guard's officer, served as equerry to King George VI and the present Queen. His home is the 15,000 acre estate at Althorp, Northamptonshire, a family seat for more than 450 years. The Earl can trace his ancestry back to the fifteenth century. Lady Diana and Prince Charles are 11th cousins once removed.

Lady Diana captured the hearts of the British public immediately the possibility of a royal engagement became known. Her natural dignity, when the Press and other media brought her under the spotlight of intense publicity which must have made her life unbearable, was greatly admired and she received the sympathy of the nation.

Though Lady Diana was brought up at her father's house on the Sandringham estate, it was probably not until 1977, when Prince Charles attended a shooting party at Althorp, that they met. Lady Diana was educated at private schools where she played tennis and lacrosse and was described as average academically. She left school at sixteen and attended Swiss finishing school for six months before arriving in London to start working with obvious enjoyment as an assistant at a private kindergarten in Pimlico – a role she was quietly pursuing until the outburst of publicity over her relationship with the Prince.

# The Royal Wedding

*The Engagement*
The announcement of the engagement was made at 11am on Tuesday 24 February 1981, in the following style:

*It is with the greatest pleasure that the Queen and the Duke of Edinburgh announce the betrothal of their beloved son, the Prince of Wales, to the Lady Diana Spencer, daughter of the Earl Spencer and the Honourable Mrs Shand Kydd.*

History plays an important part in the marriage of a royal heir. When the announcement had been made by the Palace, the Queen had to give her formal assent to the marriage. This she must do under the Royal Marriage Act that was passed in 1772 by George III who disapproved of the marriages made by his two brothers.

The Queen assented to the marriage of her son and Lady Diana at a meeting of the

Privy Council, following which a document, or instrument, was drawn up for the Queen's signature. The instrument was sealed with the Great Seal of England – the mark of authenticity on all important government documents. Dating from late Anglo–Saxon times, the Great Seal, which weighs over 8lb (3.6kg) and is recast for each reign, was taken to Buckingham Palace from its home in the House of Lords. Only when the sovereign's formal assent had been given could the marriage take place.

Overall responsibility for the organization of royal weddings rests with the Lord Chamberlain, Lord Maclean, who was appointed to the office in 1972, and organized the wedding of Prince Charles's sister, Princess Anne, to Captain Mark Phillips at Westminster Abbey.

The marriage of Lady Diana to Prince Charles was the first time for more than 300 years that the heir to the throne of England has married a British subject. The last time this happened was in 1659, when Charles II's brother James, later James II, married Lady Anne Hyde, elder daughter of the 1st Earl of Clarendon. The same situation nearly arose in 1785 when the then Prince of Wales, who later became George IV, secretly married his great love, a widow – Mary Anne Fitzherbert; but because in law, marriage to a Catholic entailed the heir's forfeiting his right of succession to the throne, the marriage was declared invalid, and George subsequently married Caroline of Brunswick.

On her marriage Lady Diana became Princess of Wales. Her predecessor in this rank was the wife of George V, who became Queen Mary in 1910.

## The Wedding

The wedding took place on 29 July 1981. Britain had suffered a dismal summer with very few sunny and warm days but fortune smiled on the happy couple and produced a beautiful day.

Never before in history had there been such a 'public' wedding; so great was the interest all over the world that it is estimated that including those of the Commonwealth a total of fifty countries, from Poland to Indonesia, watched and listened for hours on end. The audience totalled some thousand million people.

In London some people began camping out along the wedding route more than forty-eight hours before to secure vantage points for the pageantry which only Britain with its long tradition can mount with such expertise. It was a day of colour and warmth that was perfect in every way. The streets of London were thronged with an estimated million people and never were there such good-humoured crowds. Full of fun they turned out to line the processional routes to laugh, sing and cheer.

They were well rewarded for there were three processions travelling from Buckingham Palace to St Paul's Cathedral, all in the full panoply of state with beautiful horses, historic carriages and the shining breastplates and plumed helmets of the

*Above:* HRH The Prince of Wales at the Trooping the Colour *(Daily Telegraph Colour Library)*.
*Opposite:* Prince Charles off duty after a game of polo *(Daily Telegraph Colour Library)*.

Household Cavalry. The streets were lined with men of the three services and more than 5,000 police were on duty.

From Clarence House came a fourth procession – that of the bride accompanied by her father – which was escorted only by mounted police for she was then still a commoner.

The wedding dress had been kept a complete secret and was first seen fully when she stepped from her coach at St Paul's to be greeted by a roar of welcome from the assembled crowds. It was indeed a fairytale dress, with a boned and fitted bodice of ivory silk paper taffeta and antique lace, hand-embroidered with tiny mother-of-pearls; a deep, gently curved neckline and billowing sleeves, both trimmed with bows and elaborately embroidered lace flounces to match the centre panel. The veil made from ivory silk tulle was spangled with ten thousand mother-of-pearl sequins and held in place by the magnificent Spencer family diamond tiara. The sweeping train, trimmed and edged with sparkling lace, was twenty-five feet long.

The bride was attended by five bridesmaids who, as is so often the case, almost stole the show. They were: Lady Sarah Armstrong-Jones aged seventeen; India Hicks, granddaughter of the late Lord Mountbatten; Sarah Jane Gaselee; Catherine Cameron; and Clementine Hambro, aged five, great granddaughter of Sir Winston Churchill to whom the Princess of Wales is related. There were two pages, Lord Nicholas Windsor, son of the Duke and Duchess of Kent, and Edward van Cutsem. The groom had previously arrived with his two brothers as supporters. By tradition, there was no best man.

The couple themselves chose St Paul's Cathedral as the venue, and to set the scene inside there was a red carpet stretching from the pavement to the High Altar, a distance of 652 feet. Inside the building there was a galaxy of colour, accentuated by the Yeomen of the Guard in their Tudor uniforms, the members of Her Majesty's Body Guard of the Honourable Corps of Gentlemen at Arms and the dresses and headgear of the 3,500 invited guests from many parts of the world. Placed in the Cathedral to relay every part of the service were twenty-two television cameras.

Many of the invited guests arrived some two hours before the ceremony was to begin. Apart from all the members of the British royal family, foreign guests included the Princess of Monaco, the Prince and Princess of Liechtenstein, the Grand Duke and Duchess of Luxembourg, the Queen and Prince Claus of the Netherlands, the King and Queen of Sweden, the Queen and Prince of Denmark, the King of Norway (Edward VII's last grandson), the Crown Prince and Princess of Norway and the King and Queen of the Belgians. Other heads of state included the President of the French Republic, M. Mitterrand, the first lady of America, Mrs Nancy Reagan, and the King of Tonga. The Ministers of the government were headed by Mrs Margaret Thatcher, Harold Macmillan, Sir Alec Douglas-Home, Sir Harold Wilson, Edward Heath and James Callaghan. Guests also included the three former flatmates of the bride and 200 workers from the royal estates who sat side by side with the famous of many lands.

In addition to the state trumpeters, three orchestras and the Bach choir took part in the service. The Prince of Wales, himself a keen musician, had paid special attention to the choice of music and it was indeed beautiful.

The service was conducted by the Archbishop of Canterbury, Primate of all England, assisted by the Dean of St Paul's, the Cardinal Archbishop of Westminster and the Moderator of the General Assembly of the Church of Scotland. The Right Honourable George Thomas, Speaker of the House of Commons, read the lesson.

On her return journey to the Palace, the bride, now Princess of Wales, ranked as the third lady of the land to whom all others except the Queen, Prince Philip and the Queen Mother must bow or curtsey. The carriages, all of them open, made their way through the hundreds of thousands of wildly cheering spectators.

When all had arrived at the Palace, the police, with superb organization and masterly control, allowed the vast crowd to filter into the Mall until it seemed as if every inch of space was filled, from the railings of the Palace back to Admiralty Arch. The crowd was in good humour and exuberant spirit and kept up a chant for the royal family to make their appearance on the balcony. Never before had a Prince kissed his bride publicly – a spontaneous gesture which was noted with wild delight by the crowd.

# Married 29 July 1981;
# Separated 9 December 1992

After little more than a decade, the fairytale has ended in tears. Patrick Lichfield's wedding portrait captures the shining hopes of a couple – and of a nation – which have now been cruelly disappointed.

In the 1990s more than one in three British marriages are ending in failure. But not since the eighteenth century has the heir to the British throne parted from his wife.

Charles and Diana are separating on 'amicable terms' and both will continue their public work. There is no reason, according to the Prime Minister, why one day they should not reign as King and Queen.

On behalf of the Church of England, of which Charles will one day be Supreme Governor, the Archbishop of Canterbury has added his support. This is a public tragedy, but also an intensely private one.

As the British people, too, feel sorrow, they will hope the couple can now be left in peace to rebuild their lives and support their children through the toughest crisis any family can face.

Prince William was born in June 1982 and Prince Harry in September 1984.

HRH The Princess of Wales: Sandhurst 1987 *(The Telegraph Colour Library)*.

# Marriage of The Princess Anne

In 1993 the Princess Royal was married to Commander Tim Lawrence RN at a quiet family service held at Crathie church in Scotland. Earlier that year the Princess's marriage to Captain Mark Phillips had been dissolved. They had announced their separation in 1989. Their two children, Peter (born 1977) and Zara (born 1981), continued to live with their mother at the family home at Gatcombe Park in Gloucestershire.

The work of the Princess Royal on behalf of the Save the Children Fund has brought her much acclaim, and it is a work that takes her all over the world, besides undertaking many public duties. Commander Lawrence remains in the Royal Navy.

# Marriage of The Prince Andrew

In 1993 it was announced that Prince Andrew, Duke of York, and his wife Sarah had agreed to separate on amicable terms.

The two children of the marriage, Beatrice (born 1988) and Eugenie (born 1990), will live with their mother, Prince Andrew continuing to serve in the Royal Navy.

They were married on 23 July 1986. Miss Sarah Ferguson was the daughter of Major Ronald Ferguson and his former wife Mrs Hector Barrantes.

The engagement of Prince Charles and Lady Diana Spencer *(Tim Graham Picture Library)*.

# The Queen's 'Annus Horribilis'

First came the divorce of Princess Anne the Princess Royal from Captain Mark Phillips, who were married in November 1973. There are two children, Peter, born 1977 and Zara, born 1981. The divorce took place in 1993. Princess Anne then married Commander Tim Lawrence.

In 1993 the Duke of York (Prince Andrew) and the Duchess agreed to separate. There are two children of the marriage, Beatrice, born 1988 and Eugenie, born 1990.

Then came the disastrous fire at Windsor Castle which broke out on 20 November 1992. Fire brigades fought the blaze for hours but the damage was estimated at £40 million.

The Queen in an unprecedented move immediately came forward with the idea of opening eighteen of the grand rooms of Buckingham Palace to the public on 6 August in order to raise money towards the restoration, which was put in hand immediately. The Palace closed on 30 September 1993.

On the bright side was the engagement of the Queen's nephew, Viscount Linley aged thirty-three, son of Princess Margaret, now twelfth in line to the throne who planned to marry Miss Serena Stanhope. The marriage took place at St Margaret's Church, Westminster on 8 October 1993. The twenty-three-year-old bride's father, Viscount Petersham, heir to the 11th Earl of Harrington, led her to the altar. After the ceremony the six hundred guests left for the reception at St James's Palace.

# The Civil List

In an historic move the Queen responded to the feeling of the nation on 26 November 1992, by surrendering her tax-free status.

With her ability to divine the public mood undimmed by a year of personal turmoil her consent to pay income tax eased the growing disenchantment with the royal family. In answering the criticism that the House of Windsor is insensitive, she also agreed to carry the cost of most of the royal family.

The revolutionary change to the taxation of the Queen and Prince Charles took MPs by surprise when it was announced in the Commons by the Prime Minister.

From the spring of 1994 the Queen will pay the Inland Revenue tax on her private portfolio of investments. At the same time she will take over responsibility for financing most of her family, saving the taxpayer more than £1,000,000 annually from the £10,000,000 paid in the Civil List.

The Queen's action reversed a trend established by George VI in 1937 when income tax for the royal family was formally abolished.

This decision will not affect the royal yacht *Britannia*, The Queen's Flight or the royal train. The Queen, however, will be charged Council Tax on her private residences of Balmoral and Sandringham.

# Removed from the Civil List

| | No of public engagements carried out in 1992 |
|---|---|
| The Queen removed eight royals from the Civil List in 1993 as follows: | |
| The Duke of York (age 33) received £250,000 | 107 |
| Prince Edward (age 29) received £100,000 | 251 |
| Princess Royal (age 43) received £230,000 | 745 |
| Princess Alexandra (age 56) shared a sum of £630,000 with the Duke of Gloucester and Duke of Kent. The sum was refunded by the Queen to the Treasury. | 148 |
| Princess Margaret (age 63) received £220,000 | 102 |
| Princess Alice (age 91), dowager Duchess of Gloucester received £90,000 | 51 |
| Duke of Gloucester (age 49) | 144 |
| Duke of Kent (age 58) | 109 |

The £7.9 million the Queen receives from the Civil List to maintain the royal household will be maintained, as will the £643,000 paid to the Queen Mother and the £359,000 received by Prince Philip.

# Royal Line of Succession

1. The Prince of Wales (1948)
2. Prince William of Wales (1982)
3. Prince Henry of Wales (1984)
4. The Duke of York (1960)
5. Princess Beatrice of York (1988)
6. Princess Eugenie of York (1990)
7. The Prince Edward (1964)
8. The Princess Royal (1950)
9. Peter Phillips (1977)
10. Zara Phillips (1981)
11. The Princess Margaret, Countess of Snowdon (1930)
12. Viscount Linley (1961)
13. Lady Sarah Armstrong-Jones (1963)
14. The Duke of Gloucester (1944)
15. The Earl of Ulster (1974)
16. Lady Davina Windsor (1977)
17. Lady Rose Windsor (1980)
18. The Duke of Kent (1935)
19. Lord Downpatrick (1962)
20. Lord Nicholas Windsor (1970)
21. Lady Helen Windsor (1964)
22. Lord Frederick Windsor (1979)
23. Lady Gabriella Windsor (1981)
24. Princess Alexandra, The Hon Lady Ogilvy (1936)
25. James Ogilvy (1964)

*Notes overleaf*

*Notes*

(1) The succession is governed by the Act of Settlement 1701 (12 and 13 Will 3 c 2) which limits the succession to the Throne to the heirs, being Protestants, of Princess Sophia of Hanover, granddaughter of King James I. Section 6(4) of the Legitimacy Act of 1959 ('Nothing in this Act affects the succession to the Throne') is also relevant.

(2) Prince Michael of Kent and the Earl of St Andrews were excluded from the succession to the Throne on marriage to Roman Catholics.

# Royal Residences

*Audley End, Essex*    Purchased by Charles II in 1669. The house had been built in 1603 to the designs of Bernard Johnson. After Charles's death, it was conveyed back to the Earl of Suffolk, as the original purchase price had never been paid in full to his ancestor. The present house is an eighteenth- and nineteenth-century remodelling of the palace.

*Balmoral, Grampian*    Following two visits to the Highlands, Queen Victoria and Prince Albert rented a small turreted granite castle called Balmoral, near Ballater, from 1848. In 1852 they completed the purchase of the estate. The castle was replaced by a much larger square white granite building designed by Prince Albert with assistance from William Smith of Aberdeen, son of John Smith who had designed the first castle for Sir Robert Gordon. An idea of Victoria's delight in the castle and its surroundings is conveyed by her book *Leaves from the Journal of our Life in the Highlands.* The house remains a favourite holiday residence.

*Brighton Pavilion, Sussex*    George IV first visited Brighton in 1783 and on land leased to him by his Clerk of the Kitchen had Henry Holland build an elegant villa similar to Holland's London house in Sloane Square. Its transformation into an Oriental fantasy was carried out by John Nash between 1815 and 1822, after which the king spent much of his time there. William IV and Queen Adelaide also used it frequently, but Victoria disliked the close contact with the *hoi polloi* that visits to Brighton entailed. It was sold to the Town Commissioners in 1850 and is now open to the public.

*Buckingham Palace, London*    Built between 1702 and 1705 for John Sheffield, Duke of Buckingham, the house that took his name was designed by Captain William Winde in association with William Talman. The result, the *New View of London* reported in 1708, was 'a graceful palace . . . not to be contemned by the greatest monarch'. It was sold by Buckingham's heir in 1761 to George III who, with Queen Charlotte, took up residence in May 1762. Though royal birthdays continued to be celebrated at St James's Palace, Queen Charlotte had all but the first of her fifteen children at Buckingham Palace. After George III's death, the house's future hung in the balance as George IV lavished money

The sight the crowd had been waiting for – the bride and groom returning to the Palace
(*The Telegraph Colour Library*).

on Windsor. In 1825 John Nash was summoned to rebuild and extend the Palace. He chose to recast it in York stone, and improved its setting by remodelling St James's Park, creating the lake and winding walks. William IV disliked Buckingham Palace but ordered the work to continue. The rebuilding was almost finished when he died at Windsor, making Queen Victoria the first monarch to live in the new Palace. After Prince Albert's death, the house was seldom used until the twentieth century, during which it has been the London residence of the sovereign.

*Carlton House, London*    A red-brick house with wings, Carlton House was built in 1709 for Henry Boyle, Lord Carlton and bought by Frederick, Prince of Wales in 1727. Little was done to the house between the death of his widow in 1772 and the decision of the future George IV when Prince of Wales to make it his home in 1783. Henry Holland enlarged it and created some outstanding interiors. A fan-vaulted Gothic conservatory was later added by Thomas Hopper. The house was the setting for the first state visit of modern times when Tsar Alexander I was received after signing the Treaty of Paris in 1814. The house was demolished in 1827 and replaced by Carlton House Terrace overlooking St James's Park.

*Clarence House, London*    An extension to St James's Palace which was built for the future William IV when Duke of Clarence, Clarence House was the home of Princess Elizabeth and Prince Philip until her accession in 1952. It is now the London home of the Queen Mother.

*Edinburgh Castle, Lothian*    In use as a royal residence between the twelfth and late fifteenth centuries, Edinburgh Castle has been much altered over the years, only St Margaret's Chapel remaining of the earliest structures. None the less, it symbolizes the Scottish monarchy and contains the honours (regalia) of Scotland.

*Eltham Palace, Kent*    Many kings were familiar with Eltham Palace before it became royal property c1311 when the moated house was given to Isabella, Edward II's queen. Edward III and IV made extensive additions and it was a favoured residence during the fourteenth and fifteenth centuries. After Henry VIII met Erasmus at the Palace, it was seldom used, and by the seventeenth century was in disrepair. Little but the great hall survives.

*Greenwich Palace, London*    Queen Margaret, Henry VI's wife, extensively altered the earlier manor beside the Thames, and Henry VII used it as a major residence. Anne Boleyn's daughter, the future Elizabeth I, was born there, and Henry VIII enjoyed the place for its proximity to the dockyards creating the navy of which he was so proud.

He also made it the home of the Royal Armouries. Tradition has it that it was at Greenwich where Sir Walter Raleigh laid his cloak on the ground for Elizabeth I. The Queen's House at Greenwich, built by Inigo Jones for Queen Anne, wife of James I, is the oldest surviving Palladian villa in England. With Anne's death in 1619 work ceased; it was not resumed until 1630, being completed for Charles I's queen, Henrietta Maria. It was at Greenwich that she had her first child; being ten weeks premature, it died within a few hours. Greenwich was nearly sold by order of the House of Commons in 1652, but it was left to Charles II to demolish the old palace and commission John Webb to build a new one. All that was built was the eastern part of the present King Charles Block of the Royal Naval Hospital. Mary II ordered Wren to adapt what had been built into the Royal Naval Hospital. When the Royal Hospital School was moved to Holbrook in Suffolk, the National Maritime Museum was opened in the building in 1937.

*Hampton Court, Middlesex*   Wolsey reputedly built this enormous palace on a site selected by eminent physicians as having the best air within 20 miles of London. Besides the house, he created gardens and a park in the surrounding 2,000 acres. Wolsey did not have long to enjoy it. Building work began only in 1515 and Wolsey had to give it to Henry VIII in 1525 in a vain bid to retain the monarch's favour. Henry enlarged it still further. The future Edward VI was born here to Jane Seymour. When James I spent Christmas at the Palace in 1601, the 1,200 rooms were not enough and tents had to be erected in the park. Charles I, Charles II and William III all spent much time at Hampton Court. Wren rebuilt the royal apartments in the late seventeenth century. George II was the last monarch to live at Hampton since George III disliked the place, partly because of the violence done to him there by his grandfather, who boxed the boy's ears. After 1760 it ceased to rank as a royal residence, and though occasional receptions are held there, many apartments are now grace and favour residences.

*Hatfield House, Hertfordshire*   Once the residence of the bishops of Ely and confiscated at the Reformation, Hatfield was given to Anne Boleyn's daughter Elizabeth who was reputedly sitting under an oak tree in the park when told of her accession. James I disposed of Hatfield in 1607 by exchanging it for Theobalds in Essex with Robert Cecil, Earl of Salisbury.

*Holyroodhouse, Edinburgh, Lothian*   Originally an abbey founded by David I, the building was converted into a royal residence by James IV. After the Earl of Surrey burned it down in 1543, it was rebuilt by James V. Charles II had it completely rebuilt, leaving only the tower house, and Prince Charles Edward Stuart gave a ball there after his victory at nearby Prestonpans (1745). It remains a royal residence for ceremonial occasions.

*Above:* The famous balcony kiss *(The Telegraph Colour Library)*.

*Below:* Prince Edward, Tim Lawrence, Princess Anne, Zara and Peter Phillips at Sandringham *(Tim Graham Picture Library)*.

Prince Harry and Prince William: third and second in the royal line of succession after their father the Prince of Wales *(Tim Graham Picture Library)*.

179

*Kensington Palace, London*   The original house was built c1605 by Sir George Coppins, Clerk of the Crown. Because ministers and ambassadors grumbled about having to trek out to Hampton Court to see William and Mary, a London house proved desirable. William disliked Whitehall, so Mary's fondness for the 2nd Earl of Nottingham's house at Kensington encouraged its purchase. Wren was called upon to enlarge it, and William's provision of oil lamps along nearby Rotten Row was the first example of street lighting in England. William and Mary both died there. Queen Anne liked it as did George I who knocked down the last part of the old Nottingham House and replaced it with rooms decorated by William Kent. Work on the Serpentine to improve the house's setting was begun in the reign of George II who liked the Palace; his successor did not, allowing his brother the Duke of Kent to live there. Princess Victoria was born and grew up at Kensington Palace, and it became the residence of Princess May of Teck and currently of Princess Margaret. Kensington Palace stands at the western edge of Kensington Gardens.

*Kew Palace, London*   A compact red-brick mansion built in 1631 by a merchant, Samuel Fortrey. George III and Queen Charlotte made what was then known as the Dutch House their residence while James Wyatt was working on a nearby Gothic palace that was never to be completed. The almost unaltered house still stands today in Kew Gardens.

*Marlborough House, London*   Begun in 1709 and finished in 1711, the Duchess of Marlborough's red-brick £44,000 house was designed by Wren. It was the London home of the dukes of Marlborough until 1817 when it became the home for George IV's daughter, Princess Charlotte. It was later home to Edward, Prince of Wales, and Princess Alexandra and to George, Prince of Wales, and Princess Mary. As a widow Queen Mary returned to the house and died there in 1953. In 1959 it was transferred by the Queen to the government for use as the Commonwealth Centre, Holland Park, Kensington.

*Nonsuch, Surrey*   Construction of Henry VIII's vast palace of two adjoining squares began in 1538. It was granted by Mary I to the 12th Earl of Arundel in 1556. It became Elizabeth's favourite palace after she had acquired it some time between 1572 and 1592. It was there that the mud-bespattered Robert, Earl of Essex made his excuses to an unamused Elizabeth for his failure to carry out her orders in Ireland (see page 74). During the Civil War the Palace fell into disrepair, but repairs were put in hand before Charles II gave it to his celebrated mistress, the spendthrift Barbara Villiers. Always short of money, she sold it off like a twentieth-century asset stripper; by the mid-eighteenth century only the foundations were visible.

*Osborne House, Isle of Wight*    After purchasing the estate in 1845, Victoria and Albert erected a new house to an Italianate design by the Prince Consort. It was finished by 1851. Edward VII disliked the house and gave it to the nation in 1902, after which it became a convalescent home for officers. The House is open to the public.

*Richmond Palace, Surrey*    A manor house at Sheen used by Edward II and extended by Edward III, who died there, was partly demolished by Richard II. Henry V restored what was left, Henry VI enlarged it and Edward IV gave it to Elizabeth Woodville from whom Henry VII confiscated it. In 1497 fire totally destroyed it, giving Henry VII the chance to rebuild it on a grand scale, after which it was called Richmond Palace. It remained an important royal residence until the Commonwealth, after which it was stripped and sold off. Only Richmond Lodge survived, becoming home to George II as Prince of Wales and Princess Caroline, and to George III and Queen Charlotte before they moved to Kew.

*St James's Palace, London*    Amidst a desolate swamp beside the road from Charing Cross to Westminster stood a hospital for female lepers called the Sisters of St James in the Field. As there were only four inmates in 1532, Henry VIII felt able to give them an annuity, close the hospital and build a red-brick house with blue diaper work. He enclosed the surrounding area to form St James's Park, and took over the forest of Hyde Park, which had belonged to Westminster Abbey, enclosed it and stocked it with deer. As the principal palace for Court ceremonial, St James's was extended and embellished by Wren for James II. Critics continued to accuse it of being too unprepossessing for Court ceremonies, though even they conceded that its exterior gave no hint of the elegant interiors. After the birth of George IV, it ceased to be a royal home, though remaining the seat of sovereignty; a new monarch is proclaimed from a balcony in Friary Court, and ambassadors are still accredited to the Court of St James.

*Sandringham, Norfolk*    Purchased in 1861 for Edward, Prince of Wales, who enlarged the house and developed the estate for shooting. York Cottage in the grounds was the much-loved home of George V as Prince of Wales and as monarch. Now open to the public, the house is the residence favoured by the royal family for Christmas.

*Somerset House, London*    Built by Jane Seymour's ill-fated brother, Edward, Duke of Somerset, the House was conveyed to Princess Elizabeth (later Elizabeth I) in exchange for Durham House in the Strand. Standing on the site of the present Somerset House, the courtyard mansion was the first major building in England to reflect the influence of the Renaissance. Elizabeth briefly took up residence here after her coronation. After the House was granted to Queen Anne (wife of James I), she largely rebuilt it and named it Denmark House after her brother, King Christian IV, stayed there in 1606. Charles I built a chapel on the tennis court for his queen, and the House was not in the list of royal houses for disposal by the Commonwealth. Oliver Cromwell's body lay in state at the House, but its fabric was in a poor state at the Restoration. It was rebuilt to plans drawn up by Wren before he died at Somerset House. Thereafter it was frequently the royal dower-house. In 1775 Somerset House was handed over to the government in exchange for Buckingham Palace; Sir William Chambers rebuilt it for government use in the form that can be seen today.

*Stirling Castle, Central*   A fort of kinds stood on the impregnable volcanic outcrop at Stirling from the eleventh century. It became a royal residence in the following century, Alexander I staying there. What remains dates from the fifteenth century and later, of which the magnificent great hall built by Robert Cochrane is noteworthy. Involved in the recurrent warfare between England and Scotland, the Castle was a garrison until 1964.

*Theobalds, Hertfordshire*   James I acquired Theobalds by exchanging it for Hatfield House with Robert Cecil, Earl of Salisbury, in 1607. It became his favourite residence and he died there in 1625. Parliament ordered its sale in 1650 and it was gradually dismantled.

*Tower of London*   William I incorporated Roman walls in his castle to hold the capital. Successive rulers strengthened its fortifications, particularly the addition of the White Tower, completed c1100, to protect the armoury, mint, royal Treasury and wardrobe, where the Crown jewels are kept. Henry VIII was the last king to use it as a chief residence.

*Palace of Westminster, London*   The building history of the principal residence of English kings from Edward the Confessor to Henry VIII is complex. Much has been lost through fires and insensitive demolition during Victorian times, particularly the thirteenth-century Painted Chamber which was destroyed to make way for Barry's present Houses of Parliament. Since Henry's move to Whitehall, it has gradually become the meeting place for parliament and the site of government offices.

*Whitehall Palace, London*   Originally known as York Palace and handed over by Wolsey to Henry VIII, along with Hampton Court, Whitehall's change of name is referred to in Shakespeare's *Henry VIII*. Henry enlarged it with materials from Kensington Palace and Esher Palace, and James I built a Banqueting Hall which was destroyed by fire through the carelessness of workmen setting fire to 'oily clothes' used in a masque. Inigo Jones replaced it with the present Hall, decorated by Rubens for Charles I and the only part of

Members of the royal family watching the Trooping the Colour from the balcony of Buckingham Palace *(Tim Graham Picture Library)*.

the old Palace to survive following a devastating fire in 1798. Government offices were built on the site.

*Winchester Palace, Hampshire*    Winchester was the principal royal residence and seat of government of both the Anglo-Saxon and Norman kings, and the site of the Anglo-Saxon kings' mausoleum. The Domesday Book was kept in the Castle. In Henry II's reign the Exchequer and Treasury were transferred to Westminster. The various stages of building were repeatedly damaged by fire or siege (1141), and after the royal chambers were destroyed in 1302, they were never fully rebuilt. The Bishop's Palace became the residence for kings staying in the city. The great hall of Henry III – with its Arthurian associations through the great round table – remains, but the Castle was dismantled in 1651. A palace designed by Wren for Charles II was never completed and was adapted to become a barracks.

*Windsor Castle, Berkshire*    Originally a motte and two baileys built by William I in 1067, Windsor was developed by successive monarchs to become the main royal residence. Henry I first used stone and is thought to have built the shell keep on the motte, and

Henry II made extensive additions. By the end of Edward III's reign, the Castle had ceased to be primarily a military stronghold (it had been besieged unsuccessfully in 1194 and 1216) and became first and foremost a residence. Edward III created St George's Hall and founded the Order of the Garter. Edward IV began the Garter chapel of St George, and the most significant improvements and additions were thereafter made by Charles II, George III and George IV, who rebuilt much of the Castle.

*Woodstock, Oxfordshire*    Set in a royal forest, Woodstock was a pre-Conquest retreat for English kings. Henry I created a royal menagerie there, and for Henry II it competed with Clarendon (Wiltshire) as his favourite country residence, associated with his mistress Rosamund. Henry III was nearly murdered there, after which security at all royal palaces was tightened. By the sixteenth century the Palace was dilapidated, though it held out for twenty days during a Civil War siege. In 1705 the estate was given to the Duke of Marlborough for his service during the War of Spanish Succession and the last fragments of the old Palace were removed c1718.

# FACTS AND DATES
## European Monarchy in the Twentieth Century

When Queen Victoria died in 1901, England was one of about twenty European monarchies. In the second half of the twentieth century, only ten remain: Britain (Windsor); Denmark and Norway (with the common surname Schleswig-Holstein-Sonderburg-Glücksburg); Sweden (Bernadotte); Belgium (Saxe-Coburg-Gotha); Holland (Orange); Luxembourg (Orange); Monaco (Grimaldi); Liechtenstein (Brandis); and Spain (monarchy reinstituted on the death of General Franco in 1975).

Portugal was the first country to lose its dynasty, the Braganzas, in 1910. During and immediately after World War I the Romanovs (Russia), the Hohenzollerns (Germany), the Habsburgs (Austria), and the ruling house of Montenegro were overthrown.

Between the world wars Turkey (Ottoman) and Spain (Bourbon) became republics, as did Greece from 1923 to 1935, and again from 1973. The monarchies of Romania, Yugoslavia and Bulgaria disappeared during World War II. Italy (Savoy) and Albania became republics in 1946.

## Commonwealth Countries

There are 50 member countries of the Commonwealth. Queen Elizabeth is Head of State of 16; there are 29 republics and 5 are monarchies with other sovereigns. The Queen is symbolic Head of the Commonwealth.

*The Queen's Realm*   Antigua and Barbuda, Australia, Bahamas, Barbados, Belize, Britain, Canada, Grenada, Jamaica, New Zealand, Papua New Guinea, St Christopher and Nevis, St Lucia, St Vincent and the Grenadines, Solomon Islands and Tuvalu.

*Republics*   Bangladesh, Botswana, Cyprus, Dominica, The Gambia, Ghana, Guyana, India, Kenya, Kiribati, Malawi, Maldives, Malta, Mauritius, Namibia, Nauru, Nigeria, Pakistan, Seychelles, Sierra Leone, Singapore, Sri Lanka, Tanzania, Trinidad and Tobago, Uganda, Vanuatu, Western Samoa, Zambia, Zimbabwe.

*Other Monarchies*   Brunei, Lesotho, Malaysia, Swaziland, Tonga.

# Prime Ministers 1830–1990

1830 Earl Grey (Lib)
1834 Lord Melbourne (Lib)
1834 Sir Robert Peel (Con)
1835 Lord Melbourne (Lib)
1841 Sir Robert Peel (Con)
1846 Lord John Russell (Lib)
1852 Earl of Derby (Con)
1852 Earl of Aberdeen (Lib-Coalition)
1855 Lord Palmerston (Lib)
1865 Earl Russell (Lib)
1866 Earl of Derby (Con)
1868 Benjamin Disraeli (Con)
1868 William Gladstone (Lib)
1874 Benjamin Disraeli (Con)
1880 William Gladstone (Lib)
1885 Marquess of Salisbury (Con)
1886 William Gladstone (Lib)
1886 Marquess of Salisbury (Con-Unionist)
1892 William Gladstone (Lib)
1894 Earl of Rosebery (Lib)
1895 Marquess of Salisbury (Con-Unionist)
1902 A. J. Balfour (Con-Unionist)
1905 Sir Henry Campbell-Bannerman (Lib)
1908 H. H. Asquith (Lib)

1915 H. H. Asquith (Coalition)
1916 D. Lloyd George (Coalition)
1922 A. Bonar Law (Con)
1923 Stanley Baldwin (Con)
1924 J. Ramsay Macdonald (Lab)
1924 Stanley Baldwin (Con)
1929 J. Ramsay Macdonald (Lab)
1931 J. Ramsay Macdonald (National)
1935 Stanley Baldwin (National)
1937 Neville Chamberlain (National)
1940 Winston Churchill (Coalition)
1945 C. R. Atlee (Lab)
1951 Winston Churchill (Con)
1955 Sir Anthony Eden (Con)
1957 Harold Macmillan (Con)
1963 Sir Alec Douglas-Home (Con)
1964, 1966 Harold Wilson (Lab)
1970 Edward Heath (Con)
1974 Harold Wilson (Lab)
1976 James Callaghan (Lab)
1979, 1983, 1987 Margaret Thatcher (Con)
1990 John Major (Con)

Palmerston became Prime Minister at the age of 71. Disraeli was aged 69 in his second term of office. Gladstone formed governments when aged 71, 75 and 83. Campbell-Bannerman formed his first government when he was 69. Churchill was 75 when he led the Conservatives to victory in 1951, and was Prime Minister again in his 80th year.

# British Wars and Campaigns 1775–1990

With U.S.A. 1775–1782
With France 1778–1783
With Spain 1780–1783
With Netherlands 1780–1782
With France 1793–1802
With Napoleon 1803–1815
With U.S.A. 1812–1814
With Russia (Crimean War) 1854–1856
Indian Mutiny 1857–1858
With Abyssinia 1868
With Ashanti 1873–1874

With Afghanistan 1878–1880
With Zulus 1879
With Egypt 1882
With Sudanese 1881–1898
First Boer War 1880–1882
Boxer Rising 1896–1900
Second Boer War 1899–1902
First World War 1914–1918
Second World War 1939–1945
Falklands War 1982
Gulf War 1990

# Major British Army Operational Deployments 1945–1990

Palestine 1945–1948
Aden 1947, 1958, 1964–1967
Malaya 1948–1960
Korean War 1950–1958
Kenya 1952–1956
Suez 1956

Brunei 1962
Borneo 1963–1966
Northern Ireland 1969–
Falklands War 1982
Beirut (UN) 1983
Namibia (UN) 1989

# World War I 1914–1918

By 1907, Europe was divided into two armed camps: the Triple Alliance of Germany, Austria and Italy versus the Triple Entente of Britain, France and Russia. Between 1908 and 1913, a series of events in the Balkans and North Africa, reflecting nascent nationalism and international rivalries, brought Europe to the verge of war.

On 28 June 1914 the heir to the throne of Austria-Hungary, Archduke Franz Ferdinand, was assassinated at Sarajevo. Very soon only Italy and Britain remained aloof from the general European War. Britain strove to confine the war to the Balkans, but after German violation of Belgian neutrality was brought into the struggle on

4 August 1914. Italy joined in on the side of the Allies in 1915.

Britain's main contribution was on the Western Front, in France and Belgium. In 1914, and throughout 1915, the BEF, under the command of Sir John French, stabilized the Allied line southwards from the Channel ports with heavy losses, particularly at Ypres and Loos. At this stage Sir Douglas Haig replaced French. An attempt to distract attention from the Western Front by making a landing on the Gallipoli peninsula in the Dardanelles, was a disastrous and costly failure (1915). An Allied offensive along the Somme in 1916 gained a mere seven miles at a cost to Britain alone of 420,000 casualties.

There were few naval actions. A minor German success at Coronel, off Chile, in 1914 was quickly avenged at the battle of the Falkland Islands. In May 1916 a major fleet action took place at the Battle of Jutland. It ended indecisively and was followed by a German submarine offensive against Allied and neutral shipping.

In April 1917 the United States entered the war. This addition of manpower, and the Allied blockade of Germany, meant that the end was in sight. The German High Command withdrew twenty-five miles to the Siegfried, or Hindenburg, line to make Allied offensives more difficult – the Passchendaele offensive (1917) cost 300,000 British lives.

In 1918 the Germans threw all their resources into attacks which seriously undermined their already weak position. From September onwards the German army was on the point of defeat, whilst the civilian population was on the verge of starvation. The Armistice was signed on the morning of 11 November 1918, and ended the war in which three-quarters of a million British soldiers had died.

The peace treaty with Germany was concluded at Versailles (1919). The Allied signatories were Lloyd George (Britain); Clemenceau (France); Woodrow Wilson (America); and Orlando (Italy). Germany, which had not been a party to the negotiations, was saddled with an astronomical war indemnity, deprived of most of her coal, iron and steel, and separated from her possessions in Eastern Europe. The seeds of World War II were sown by the peacemakers after World War I.

# World War II 1939–1945

The principal cause of the war was Hitler's aggressive and expansionist policy, typified by the seizure of Austria, Czechoslovakia and Poland. Britain and France declared war on Germany on 3 September 1939, after German entry into Poland on 1 September. The Commonwealth countries followed Great Britain's example.

Germany invaded Norway, Denmark, Belgium and Holland; and Russia (bound to Germany in 1939) invaded Finland. The British Expeditionary Force in France found itself cut off and surrounded, and withdrew to Dunkirk, where evacuation took place in

May 1940. Italy now entered the war on Germany's behalf; the Germans entered Paris, and Britain was left alone against the Axis Powers.

In the late summer and autumn of 1940, the Battle of Britain was fought in the air and Britain saved from invasion. In 1941, Hitler invaded Russia and turned an ally into an enemy. Japan attacked Pearl Harbour and brought the United States into the war, which now became world-wide.

The year 1942 was the turning point. On land, at sea and in the air, the initiative gradually passed to the Allies. Montgomery and Eisenhower cleared the Germans out of North Africa, the prelude to the invasion of Sicily in 1943. At sea, radar and carrier-based planes were effectively combating the menace of German U-boats. Allied bombing raids ruined the productive capacity of the Ruhr.

The Allied invasion of Sicily in 1943 caused the downfall of Mussolini (July) and led to the Italian Armistice on 3 September. The conquest of German-occupied Italy began. In the Far East (1943), naval battles stemmed the Japanese advance in the Pacific and were followed by American landings on Pacific islands. British and Commonwealth forces halted the Japanese advance in Burma.

Allied landings in Normandy in 1944 resulted in the liberation of France and Belgium. The Allies entered Rome in June 1944. The Russians resumed the offensive on the Eastern Front, in Poland, the Baltic and the Balkans.

In March 1945, the Allies crossed the Rhine. Hitler's death was announced in May, shortly before the Russians entered Berlin. On 9 May the Germans agreed to unconditional surrender. On 12 September, following atom-bomb attacks on Hiroshima and Nagasaki, the Japanese surrendered.

# The Falklands War – 1982

In December 1981, a new government in Argentina led by General Galtieri and his Junta increased diplomatic pressure on Britain to negotiate the sovereignty issue of the Falkland Islands which had been under discussion for 150 years. He also began to consider military action.

An initial lack of information regarding the invasion of the Falklands paralysed government decision and when Mrs Thatcher, the Prime Minister, announced to an emergency session of Parliament that a task force was being prepared it led to an emotional debate, hostile to the government. A British resolution calling for withdrawal of Argentinian forces was supported by the United Nations who instructed both governments to look for a diplomatic long-term solution.

On 5 April 1982 the main Task Force set sail from Portsmouth. Commanded by Rear Admiral Sandy Woodward it comprised HMS *Invincible* and HMS *Hermes* with Sea Harrier planes and Sea King helicopters. No 3 Commando Brigade, an amphibious landing force of 3,500 men was also despatched.

Eighteen Royal Navy ships which had been on exercise off Gibraltar were to rendezvous with the ships from Britain at Ascension Island. Britain's difficulty was the immense distance involved.

On 12 April the British had imposed a 320km maritime exclusion zone round the Falklands banning all Argentine vessels. In great secrecy at the beginning of May the first real hostilities commenced, and at 4am on Sunday 1 May an RAF Vulcan bomber dropped twenty 1,000lb bombs on the Stanley airstrip. Attacks by Sea Harriers followed and the warships closed in to bombard the airfield.

On 2 May the most controversial episode of the campaign occurred when the Argentine cruiser *General Belgrano* was hit by two or three torpedoes. She sank with a loss of 368 lives. Argentina soon took revenge, HMS *Sheffield* was hit and sunk by an exocet missile with a loss of twenty-one men.

Peace talks proved unsuccessful and the British War Cabinet decided to order the Commando Brigade from Ascension Island where they had been waiting. At 4am on 20 May a landing took place at San Carlos on the opposite side of the island to Stanley where some ten thousand Argentinian troops were concentrated. Diversionary attacks were made at Darwin and other places.

Of the naval and merchant ships at anchor in San Carlos Bay, HMS *Ardent* was sunk and four other ships damaged, three helicopters and an RAF Harrier were lost and also a number of Argentine aircraft were shot down.

Preparations by the British forces for the advance on Stanley were consolidated. This was over difficult terrain with mine fields in the hills. Despite poor leadership and low morale the Argentinians were well equipped and held good defensive positions.

Finally on 13 June the outer defences were overcome and the men from 5 Brigade entered Stanley and at 9pm the Argentinians surrendered – the war was over. The Junta fell and a new regime replaced that of General Galtieri.

Returning home, the British forces received an overwhelming welcome. HRH Prince Andrew in his capacity as a helicopter pilot attached to one of the carriers was in action throughout the encounter.

# The Gulf War
# Operation Desert Storm – 1990

Iraq's invasion of Kuwait on 2 August 1990 followed a claim by Iraq that Kuwait had stolen $2.4 billion worth of Iraqi oil. Saddam Hussein, the Iraqi leader, had for some time been covetous of better access to the Gulf; he was also disputing the ownership of an oilfield and seeking a way to wipe out his debts to Kuwait.

It was widely believed that he would achieve these aims by threats rather than by military confrontation, so that despite increasing numbers of Iraqi troops on the Kuwait border the invasion was completely unexpected and found the Kuwaiti troops ill prepared and outnumbered. The initial engagement was short and sharp, the Iraqi troops and armour overwhelmed the border guards and a squadron of T-72 tanks were on their way to Kuwait City.

The Guard units leading the invasion had a prime objective: the capture of the ruling family of al-Sabah. Modern communications, however, spread the warning and the members of the Emir's family who were in Kuwait fled to Saudi Arabia.

The UN Security Council immediately demanded withdrawal of the troops and within a few days had imposed economic and trade sanctions on Iraq.

On 7 August US President George Bush ordered combat troops to Kuwait, and British aircraft were moved to Saudi Arabia. For the next few months, despite sanctions and mounting world-wide condemnation, Hussein remained defiant, and reports that Kuwait was being systematically plundered and its people brutally treated led the UN Security Council to authorize the use of force against Iraq if it did not withdraw by 15 January 1991. Whilst talks and negotiations proceeded the Allies were preparing for war and by the beginning of 1991 there were more than 300,000 US forces in the region.

On 12 January the US Congress voted for war and the UN deadline expired on 15 January. Almost immediately the Allies started an air war, which was to see thousands of raids on Iraqi targets. Saddam retaliated with Scud missile attacks on Israel and Saudi Arabia and by pumping oil into the Gulf. As an Allied land assault became inevitable, 600 Kuwaiti oil wells were set on fire.

All the lethal high-tech fire power of the Allies' 'new age' weaponry was mounted against Iraq. Tomahawk cruise missiles fired by warships on a pre-planned flight path, Stealth F117 fighter bombers with laser-guided bombs, together with Tornado and Jaguar fighters with their sophisticated weapons systems played a major part.

Continuing peace talks were still unsuccessful and on 24 February under the command of US General Norman Schwarzkopf the land battle was launched, advancing swiftly on all fronts. Within four days 70,000 Iraqi troops had surrendered and Saddam's elite Republican Guard was broken.

On 26 February Iraq announced its withdrawal from Kuwait, and Saddam in a radio address declared that Kuwait was no longer a part of Iraq.

President Bush declared victory ordering Allied operations to cease at 05 00 local time.

The war was an amazing historical event. The Coalition decided to right a wrong and transported hundreds of thousands of men and a vast amount of equipment half way round the world.

The Iraqi people were the chief victims and they continue to suffer.

# INDEX

*Page numbers in italics denote illustrations*

# INDEX

The BRITISH ISLES

N

Western Isles

Highland

Grampian

SCOTLAND

Tayside

Fife

Central

Lothian

Strathclyde

Borders

Northumberland

Tyne and Wear

Dumfries
and
Galloway

Northern Ireland

Londonderry

# The Dirty Secrets Club

MEG GARDINER

# The Dirty Secrets Club

HODDER &
STOUGHTON

First published in Great Britain in 2008 by Hodder & Stoughton
An Hachette Livre UK company

1

A CIP catalogue record for this title is available from the British Library

Hardback ISBN 978 0 340 89937 3
Trade Paperback ISBN 978 0 340 89938 0

Typeset in Plantin by Hewer Text UK Ltd, Edinburgh
Printed and bound by Clays Ltd, St Ives plc

Hodder & Stoughton policy is to use papers that are natural, renewable
and recyclable products and made from wood grown in sustainable forests.
The logging and manufacturing processes are expected to conform
to the environmental regulations of the country of origin.

Hodder & Stoughton Ltd
338 Euston Road
London NW1 3BH

www.hodder.co.uk

For Ann Aubrey Hanson

# ACKNOWLEDGEMENTS

For their help with this novel, I thank the AWS Writers' Group (experts on everything from grammar to leaping out of helicopters); Nancy Fraser; John Chamberlain, MD; Sara Gardiner, MD; and John Plombon, PhD. Special thanks go to my tenacious literary agents, Jonathan Pegg and Britt Carlson, and to my terrific editors on either side of the Atlantic, Sue Fletcher at Hodder & Stoughton and Ben Sevier at Dutton.

For his wholehearted support of my work, my deepest gratitude goes to Stephen King.

# I

Fire alarms sang through the skyscraper, piercing and relentless. Under the din, people poured across the marble lobby toward the doors, dodging fallen ceiling plaster and broken glass. Outside, Montgomery Street crackled with the lights of emergency vehicles. A police officer fought upstream to get inside. The blonde was ten feet behind, struggling through the crowd.

The man in the corner paced, head down, needing her to hurry.

People rushed by him, jumpy. 'Everything crashed off the bookshelves. I thought for sure it was the Big One.'

The man turned, shoulders shifting. The Big One? Hardly. This earthquake had just been San Francisco's regular kick in the butt. But it was bad enough. On the street, steam geysered from man-holes. And he could smell gas. Pipes had ruptured under the building. The quake was Hell saying *Don't forget I'm down here – you fall, I'm waiting for you.*

He checked his watch. Come on, girl, faster. They had ten minutes before this building shut down.

A fire captain glanced at him. He was tall and young and moved like the athlete he was, but nothing clicked in the fire captain's eyes, no suspicion, no *Is that who I think it is?* Out of uniform he looked ordinary, a plain vanilla All-American.

The blonde neared the doors. She stood out from the crowd: platinum-sleek, hair cinched into a tight French twist, body cinched into a tighter black suit. A cop stuck out an arm like he was going to clothesline her. She flashed an ID and slid around him.

He smiled. Right under their noses.

She pushed through the doors and walked up, giving him a hard blue stare. 'Here? Now?'

'It's the ultimate test. Secrets are hardest to keep in broad daylight.'

'I smell gas, and that steam pipe sounds like a volcano erupting. If a valve blows and causes a spark—'

'You dared me. Do it in public, and get proof.' He wiped his palms on his jeans. 'This is as public as it gets. You'll supply my proof.'

Her hands clenched, but her eyes shone. 'Where?'

His heart beat faster. 'Top floor. My lawyer's office.'

Upstairs, they strode out of the express elevator to find the law firm abandoned. The fire alarm was shrieking. At the receptionist's desk, a computer was streaming a television news feed.

'—minor damage, but we're getting reports of a ruptured gas line in the financial district . . .'

The blonde looked around. 'Security cameras?'

'Only in the stairwells. It's bad business for a law firm to videotape its clients.'

She nodded at a wall of windows. The October sunset was fading to dusk, downtown ablaze with light. 'You plan to do this stunt against the glass?'

He crossed the lobby. 'This way. The building's going to shut down in—' He looked at a red digital clock on the wall '—six minutes.'

'What?'

'Emergency procedure. If there's a gas leak the building evacuates, they shut down the elevators and seal the fire doors. We have to be out by then.'

'You're joking.'

The wall clock counted down to 5:59. He started a timer on his watch.

'Yeah. I was meeting with my lawyers when the quake hit. It limits damage from any gas explosion.' He pulled her toward a hallway. 'I can't believe you're scared of getting caught with me. Not Hardgirl.'

'What part of *secret* do you not understand?'

'If we're caught, they'll ask what we're doing here, not what we're hiding in our pasts.'

'Fair point.' She hurried alongside him, eyes bright. 'Were you waiting for an earthquake before you did this?'

Good guess – this was the third minor quake in the past month. 'I got lucky. I've been looking for the perfect opportunity for weeks. Chaos, downtown – it was karma. I figured seize the day.'

He rounded a corner. A glass-fronted display case along the wall had cracked, spilling sports memorabilia on the floor.

She rushed past. 'Is that a Joe Montana jersey?'

His stopwatch beeped. 'Five minutes.'

He opened a mahogany door. Across a conference room the red embers of sunset caught them in the eyes. The hills of San Francisco rose in front of him, electric with light and packed to the rafters, like a stadium.

He shrugged off his coat, took a camera from the pocket and handed it to her. 'When I tell you, point and click.'

He crossed the room and opened the doors to a rooftop terrace. Kicking off his shoes, he strode outside.

'You complained I was using the club as a confessional. You told me I was seeking expiation for my sins, but said you couldn't give me absolution,' he said.

Deep below them, the building groaned. She walked outside, breathing hard.

'Damn, Scott, this is dangerous—'

'Your dare was – and I quote – for me "to offer a public display of penitence, and for christsake get proof".'

He pulled his polo shirt over his head. Her gaze seared its way down his chest.

*Now*, he thought. Before his courage and exhilaration evaporated. He unzipped and dropped his jeans.

She gaped.

He backed toward the waist-high brick wall at the edge of the terrace. 'Turn on the camera.'

'You came commando-style to a meeting with your lawyers?'

Naked, he climbed onto the brick ledge and stood up, facing her. Her lips parted. Thrilled to his fingertips, he turned to face Montgomery Street.

A salt breeze licked his bare skin. Two hundred feet below, fire and police lights flickered through steam boiling from the ruptured pipe, turning the scene an eerie red.

He spread his arms. 'Shoot.'

'You have got to be kidding me.'

'Take the photo. Hurry.'

'That's not penitent.'

He glanced over his shoulder. She was shaking her head.

'*Bad?* You tattooed *bad* on your tailbone?'

His watch beeped. 'Four minutes. Do it.'

'You're a bad ass?' She put her fists on her hips. 'You get all torn up about a nasty thing you did in college, and want to unload it on us – fine. But you can't tattoo some preening jock statement on your butt and call it repentance. That's not remorse. Hell, it's not even close to being dirty.'

Frowning, she stormed inside.

He turned around. 'Hey!'

Was she leaving? No, everything depended on her getting the photo –

She ran back out, holding a piece of sports memorabilia from the display case. It was a jockey's riding crop. He swallowed.

She whipped it against a potted plant with a wicked crack. 'Somebody needs to take you down a notch.'

He nearly whimpered. She wanted points, too. This was even better.

Snapping the crop against her thigh, she crossed the terrace. Evaluating the ledge, she unzipped her ass-hugging skirt, wriggled it down and stepped out of it.

'It's time to make your act of contrition,' she said.

In the tight-fitting black jacket, she looked martial. The stilettos could have put out his eyes. The black stockings ran all the way to the top of her thighs. All the way to –

'What's that garter belt made from?'

'Iguana hide.'

'Jesus, help me.'

'I have a drawer full. I got them in the divorce.' She held out her hand. 'Don't let me fall.'

'I won't. I have perfect balance.' He felt crazed and desperate and *God*, he needed to get her up here, now. 'I get paid four million dollars a year to catch things and never let them drop.'

A wisp of her blonde hair had escaped. It softened her. He wanted her to put it back in place. He wanted her to put on leather gloves and maybe an eye patch. He pulled her up on the ledge beside him.

She gripped his hand. Her smooth stocking brushed his leg.

He could barely speak. 'This is penance?'

'Pain is just one step from paradise.'

She looked down. Her voice dropped. 'Christ. This is asking for a heart attack.'

'Don't joke.'

She looked up. 'No – I didn't mean it as a crack about David.'

But if David hadn't dropped face down with a coronary, they wouldn't be here. The doctor's death had created an opening, and Scott wanted to fill it. This was his chance to prove himself and gain admission to the top level of the club.

The breeze kicked up. In the lighted windows of the skyscraper across the street, people gazed down at the fire trucks. Nobody was looking at them.

'Right under their noses,' he said. 'Bonus points for both of us.'

'Not yet.' She handed him the camera. 'Set it so we're both in the frame.'

He set the auto-timer to take a five-shot series and posed the camera on the ledge. His stopwatch beeped. Three minutes.

She planted her feet wide for balance. 'What happens to guilty people?'

Blinking, he turned around and carefully knelt down on all fours. 'I've been bad. Spank me.'

She slapped the crop against her palm. 'What's the magic word?'

Relief and desire rushed through him. 'Hard.'

The camera flashed. She brought the crop down.

The pain was a stripe of fire along his backside. He gasped and grabbed the ledge.

'Harder,' he said.

She whipped the crop down. The camera flashed.

He clawed the bricks. '*Mea culpa*. I've been very, very bad. *More*.'

She didn't hit him. He looked up. Her chest was heaving, her hair spilling from the French twist.

'My God, you actually want to be punished, don't you?' she said.

'Do it.'

She swung the crop. It slashed him so hard he shouted in pain. She wanted to dish out punishment, all right, but not to him. She would use this to send a message to somebody else. The watch beeped.

'Christ, two minutes,' she said. 'Let's get the hell out of here.'

His eyes were watering. 'Not yet. Nobody's looking.'

'*Looking?* You're nuts. If there's an aftershock I'll lose my balance. We—'

A thumping sound echoed off skyscraper walls. A helicopter swooped over the top of the building.

It turned and hovered above Montgomery Street, rotors blaring. Everything on the terrace blew into the air. Dust, leaves, their clothes. The camera tipped over. Scott grabbed for it but it fell off the ledge.

She yelled, 'No, the evidence—'

The camera dropped, hit the building and sprang apart. He let out a cry. His penance, his memories –

The terrace was lit with a blinding white searchlight.

'Oh, no – it's a news chopper,' she said.

She leapt from the ledge to the terrace. Landed like a gazelle on her stilettos. He scrambled after her, buttocks stinging. They grabbed their clothes and ran for the door. The chopper rotated in the air, searchlight sweeping after them.

She looked back, her eyes brimming with joy and fury. The searchlight lit her hair like a halo.

'Turn around,' he shouted. 'You want them to get a close-up?'

'The city knows your face, not mine.'

'But it's about to know your glorious ass.'

He ran into the conference room, stopped and wrangled his left leg into his jeans. The spotlight caught them. He bumbled for the door.

Fumbling her way into her skirt, she sprinted into the hallway. 'It's chasing us like those things from the damned *War of the Worlds*.'

He urged her forward. 'Take the service elevator. The lobby downstairs is full of cops.'

She ran beside him, agile in the heels. His watch beeped.

'Oh, crap. No time.'

In the lobby, the fire alarm wailed a high-pitched tone. The digital clock flashed red. :58. :57. The TV news was showing pictures from the chopper's camera.

'Two people are trapped on the roof,' shouted the reporter. 'A woman was signaling for help. If we swing around . . .'

The alarm rose in pitch.

'How long to get down?' she said.

They ran to the service elevator and she pounded on the button. The searchlight panned along the windows. Like a white flare, it caught them in the eyes.

'I see them. They're attempting to escape from this deadly tower . . .'

She whacked the elevator button with the riding crop. '*Open.*'

With a *ping*, the elevator arrived. She dropped the crop and they lunged inside.

On the ground floor they burst out a back exit into an alley. The asphalt was wet and steaming. Scott clicked his stopwatch.

'Seven seconds. Time to spare.'

'Maniac,' she said.

They dashed through puddles toward the end of the alley. On the street a police car blew past, lights flashing. The helicopter thumped overhead, searchlight pinned on the roof.

Scott nodded at it. 'They got it on tape. You have evidence.'

'You're reckless. I think you actually want to get caught.'

'I carried out the dare. Did I make the cut?'

She fought with her zipper. 'We'll put it to a vote. No promises.'

They rushed out of the alley. The street, lined with banks and swanky stores, was being cleared by the police. They slowed to a walk, trying to look normal. He buttoned his jacket. She smoothed down her hair.

Elation flooded him.

'Admit it – that was awesome.'

'It was outrageous.' She pointed at him. 'And do not tell me it ended with a flourish.'

'Really?' He reached into his coat pocket and withdrew a baseball.

'What's that?'

He tossed it to her. She caught it.

'A Willie Mays autographed ball?' She looked up, surprised. 'From the law firm's memorabilia collection? You stole it?'

'On our way out. And it's not just any baseball. It's *the* ball – from the 1954 World Series. The greatest catch of all time.'

She gawped. 'It's got to be worth—'

'Hundred thousand.' He smiled broadly. 'Right under *your* nose.'

Anger flashed across her face. She shoved the ball back into his hands. 'Okay, bonus points for chutzpah.'

He laughed and tossed the baseball in his hand. 'Fear not, it'll be returned. That's the next challenge.'

'How? The building's locked down. And your fingerprints are all over it.'

'So? I'm a star client. My lawyer let me hold it. It doesn't matter that my fingerprints are on it.' He glanced at the police car down the block, and back at her. 'How will you explain that yours are?'

She stopped dead on the sidewalk.

He held the ball up. 'Return it without getting prosecuted. I dare you.'

He turned, faced the jewelry store they were passing and hurled the ball straight through its front window. Glass crashed. An alarm shrieked. He spun around.

'Have fun, Hardgirl.'

He took off down the street.

# 2

Headlights, that's the first thing Pablo Cruz saw, high beams that flared in his rearview mirror. Tail lights followed a fingersnap later as the car veered around him, streak, boom, gone. He made it a BMW, screaming through the intersection at Van Ness and California. He made the speed ninety plus. He made the infraction Driving While Stupid, because the traffic lights were cherry red, and his police car was black and white. Cruz lit up his light bar and rolled.

Grabbing the radio, he raised the dispatcher. 'In pursuit. Late model BMW, dark blue or black.'

One a.m., empty street. The BMW was already a block ahead. Cruz laid on the power. His Crown Vic accelerated to keep it in sight, lapping up the asphalt.

Why did the driver do it, blow straight past a police cruiser? Maybe high. Maybe throwing down a challenge. Maybe getting the hell out of town before another quake hit, like the one a few days back. Maybe fleeing the scene of a crime.

California Street ran bone straight between darkened businesses and Victorian apartment buildings. Cruz held tight to the wheel, trying to make out the shape of the BMW, keeping the side streets peripherally in his vision. Tail lights, low profile – it was an M5, and it was not slowing down. He gave the siren a yowl. No response.

The BMW skied up Nob Hill, slick as a hockey puck. Cruz roared after it, lifted over a ridge in the road at Leavenworth Street and went high against the straps of his seatbelt. Ahead, the M5 crested the rise and raced past Grace Cathedral at the top of Nob Hill. Cruz still had eighty yards to close on it.

The M5 blew past the Mark Hopkins hotel and reached the far side of the hilltop. For a second it looked airborne, before dropping out of sight for the long descent toward the financial district. Cruz followed. At the cusp of the hill the city lights accosted him. Downtown spread out below, glitter-gold, a spill of lights that stopped at the dark shore of San Francisco Bay.

Downhill the M5 slammed against the road, bottoming out. Sparks wheeled behind it. It raced toward another red light, ready to power straight through. From a side street a Volkswagen rolled into the intersection. The M5 slid into a left-hand turn, veered around the VW and took the corner in a skid, brake lights tapping on and off, the driver keeping control and powering up again. Damn, the guy knew how to handle that car.

Cruz had himself a full-blown car chase. His first ever.

He turned on the siren and let it sing. He tightened his hands on the wheel. Ahead, the BMW swung wide, onto the left side of the street past the cable car tracks, and its brake lights flashed. He was getting ready to turn right.

The passenger door swung open. Oh boy, Cruz thought, here we go.

What was he going to toss out – the cocaine or the slim jim he'd used to boost the car? Cruz kept the pedal down, eating up ground between them, teeth tight, breathing through his mouth. Hoping that what emerged from the M5 wasn't the barrel of a sawed-off.

Hand on the door, a woman leaned out.

Her arm was pale and slim. Her blonde hair batted in the wind. She stared at the pavement that fled beneath her.

'Jesus,' Cruz said.

She was trying to jump.

Like yanking a chain, the driver jerked her back inside the car. The BMW skated around another corner, back end sliding out, driver handling the oversteer. The momentum of the turn slammed the passenger's door shut. Cruz's pulse kicked up another notch. That BMW was quick and agile, but head down these streets and the blocks got narrow; drive into Chinatown and the restaurants would be emptying out. Lots of traffic, lots of obstacles to slow it down.

Like pedestrians.

He skidded around the corner, manhandling the patrol car, and saw the BMW swerve to the right. *Bam*, it racketed along cars parked at the curb, shredding against them like a can opener. Losing control, losing speed— no. Preventing the passenger from leaping out, if she wanted to keep her arms and legs from getting mangled. He felt how dry his mouth had become. The Crown Vic's headlights caught the rear window of the M5. Inside the vehicle Cruz saw a flurry of motion. The passenger was punching the driver.

And the driver kept the pedal flat. The car roared through narrowing streets rimmed in neon, red and gold, with people flowing along the sidewalks. Cruz's siren boomed. Pedestrians stopped, stepped back, but he knew the odds were miserable. This was heading for disaster.

In his headlights, he saw the BMW's license plate. It was a vanity tag, and he was finally close enough to read it. HARDGRL.

Hard girl. Holy Mother, a woman was at the wheel, handling that big car like Jeff Gordon?

With a burst of power the BMW roared away from him. She rounded another corner in a power skid. He followed seventy yards behind, in time to see her line up again, turn east on Stockton and race out of sight.

Goddamn. Stockton dead-ended a couple blocks that direction, directly above the tunnel. No way, Cruz thought – accelerating like that, the M5 would never make the turn onto Bush. He lined up to round the corner and follow it, thinking: downhill, dead end, bridge railing. Beyond that was a 50-foot drop to the street below. Even at this time of night, the cross street would be busy.

'Slow down,' Cruz willed her.

He muscled the patrol car around the corner onto Stockton Street, and saw his wish granted. Oh, fuck.

Dead ahead the BMW had stopped in the middle of the street. He slammed on the brakes.

He saw her backup lights flash white as she put it in reverse. She floored it. Through plumes of tire smoke the BMW bore at him like a black missile.

He had time, barely, to remember. Home. The baby. Shelly, asleep in their bed.

Ten seconds later it was all over.

# 3

Blue lights dazzled the night. From a block away, they told Jo
Beckett she was headed into trouble.

Dancing against the red lights of the fire trucks and the spotlight
Caltrans had erected, they erased the stars, turned the buildings
and road and onlookers ice-blue, threw Jo's shadow starkly behind
her as she walked toward the scene. On the overpass above the
tunnel, police officers milled near the bridge railing. A six-foot
stretch was blown out of it. Even in the Halloween light she could
see where the car had plowed through. A news helicopter circled
overhead, grotesque MC to the party. Two a.m., Bush Street at the
Stockton Tunnel, tune in and feast your eyes, people. Last dance
at the festival of carnage.

Jo nudged between a television news crew and a clot of bystanders, and approached the yellow police tape. Her breath
frosted the air. It was bitter for October, and diamond-clear.
The fog had shriveled away. Even the weather declined to lay
its veil over this scene. This was bad, and she had a feeling it was
going to the big.

She called to a uniformed officer standing inside the police tape.
'Excuse me. I'm looking for Lieutenant Tang.'

'Amy Tang?'

'She didn't give me her first name.' Just a curt phone call, asking
Jo to come to the scene.

'You the doc?'

Jo nodded. Though she focused on the cop, the scene behind
him expanded to fill her horizon. Brightly lit, the tunnel was a
shining maw that shrank like a snake to the far end. Noise echoed
through it, horns and traffic. And dead-center in front of it sat the

wreck. Though she knew it had crashed down from the road above, for all the world it looked like a metal gob the tunnel had hawked up.

She was right: bad, and big.

Car wrecks are either-or. Few are in between. It's either a Band-Aid on the elbow, or mutilation and death. And nobody here could be helped by a Band-Aid.

Jo exhaled. There was litter everywhere – the dirt, mess and stink of every crash site. She saw bandages and ripped packaging, caps from disposable syringes, an IV line that had fallen to the ground. This chaos had been created by rescuers' frenzy to save lives. Somebody had survived the collision, at least long enough for the paramedics to arrive.

'How many?' she said.

'Four dead, five injured.'

The BMW had hammered down onto another vehicle. She couldn't identify the make, but painted on a door the firefighters had pried open was *Golden Gate Shuttle*. The BMW had speared through the roof of an airport shuttle minivan.

A forensic team was collecting evidence. The Medical Examiner was bent over his equipment case. A police photographer snapped photos. Each flash of the camera was like a silent shriek.

The deformations of wrecked machinery always shocked her. Once-gleaming metal had shredded, collapsed, been strewn across the road like bomblets. Like the lives of the people inside. Fragmented into shards of remembrance that cut like shrapnel. Firefighting foam lingered on the street, though there had been no fire. She saw no charring; smelled the residual stink of gasoline, not burnt rubber. Not, thank God, burnt flesh.

Two police officers unfurled a blue plastic tarp to cover the worst of whatever could be seen from the bridge.

The cop cleared his throat. 'Medics had to amputate one guy's arm to get him out.'

The officers slid the tarp across the top of the minivan. God, Jo thought, what a lousy job they had. You had to admire these guys.

She studied the bridge. It was illuminated by bright kitschy signs for the Green Door massage parlor and Tunnel Top bar. The posts that made up the bridge railing were concrete. The BMW had slammed through them like they were Lego blocks. The words *ramming speed* sprang to mind.

Beyond the bridge, Stockton Street ran uphill. For two blocks here, Stockton was a split-level road. The original street ran over the crest of the hill, and was lined with apartment buildings. Directly below it, the tunnel cut through the base of the hill, straight across to Chinatown. It looked like a throat. And it could collapse like a crushed windpipe, she knew. All it would take was a magnitude 9 quake.

The cop nodded at a woman standing near the mouth of the tunnel. 'That's Tang.'

He caught her attention. She walked over like somebody who'd been in a rush her whole life and was still scrapping to get ahead. She was tiny, sheathed in black, with hair spiked like a hedgehog. Her cheeks were red, but she looked contemptuous of the cold. She also looked chilled to the bone. She extended her hand.

'Doctor Beckett?'

They shook, and she lifted the police tape to let Jo duck under.

'What do you have for me?' Jo said.

Instead of enlightenment, Tang gave Jo the once-over, eyeing her Doc Martens, combats, jeans jacket, red scarf wound around her neck for warmth, brown hair that tumbled in random curls down her back. Tang's expression was cool. Maybe she thought Jo looked a mess, or too young. Jo didn't care. Her clothes were functional, easy to run in, though she hadn't been called here to deal with a violent psychotic. Nobody was going to grab her by the neck and try to strangle her. She wouldn't have to run, or jump out a window, or kick anybody with the good heavy toes of her boots. Not tonight.

Nobody at this scene was going anywhere.

Tang scanned Jo's face, as cops do. They gauge anxiety and truthfulness and the potential for violence, but Tang was also doing the standard California genealogy check. *What are you?*

Tang was herself San Francisco Chinese, Jo guessed from the name and the California accent. She seemed to be searching for some box to tick.

'What's your rush to get me involved?' Jo said.

Tang gave her a shrewd glance. She knew that Jo Beckett, MD, was not a first responder but a last resort.

'The driver of the BMW was Callie Harding. Know the name?'

It took a few seconds to click. 'Federal prosecutor?'

'Assistant US Attorney. She's still in there.'

Tang blew on her hands to warm them, and looked at the wreck. The forensic team was poking at the wreckage as if it was a downed alien craft that had crashed on Stockton Street.

'Why did you call me on-scene?' Jo asked again.

She didn't work for the police department. She was an independent consultant. The SFPD had given her a fair amount of work, but never in the first few minutes of an investigation, before the blood was even washed from the street. Something strange was going on here. And it wasn't just the cold street or the neon glow of strip club marquees, a seedy Dashiell Hammett glare that played counterpoint to the emergency lights. She hadn't formally agreed to take the job yet, and this scene was urging caution on her, a professional case of the heebie-jeebies.

And the dead were waiting for her, as usual.

'Even if it turns out to be a suicide, why call me out here? What's the urgency?'

'Know what Callie Harding did at the US Attorney's Office?' Tang said.

'Criminal Division.'

'She was one of their heavy hitters. A star prosecutor.'

'She put bad guys in prison. And?'

Tang lowered her voice, though the helicopter hovering above the scene made overhearing her nearly impossible. 'And she was their blue-eyed girl. Lean, mean and clean.'

Tang nodded across the street at an older man who seemed mesmerized by the wreckage. Slouched and nervous, he kept running his hand through his hair.

'That's Harding's boss, head of the Criminal Division. He's a mess. This is a mess. Which means the feds are going to go nuts over it – and they won't want to hear that maybe their prom queen just offed herself in public and took a bunch of innocent people out as well.'

Tick two boxes. Turf. Politics. Jo's reluctance to take the case increased.

She put her hands in her pockets. 'If this was a theatrical public suicide it's more than just awkward. It's appalling. But I still don't know why you want me in at the start.'

'Certain factors here would seem to call for your expertise,' Tang said.

Jo didn't know if the police lieutenant was seeking a go-between, or cover for some looming PR battle with the US Attorney's Office. She didn't know Tang. But she knew this was going to be high stakes, high profile. She should feel pleased that they'd called her. Instead she felt suspicion sliding around her like an eel through dark water.

'Please fill me in, Lieutenant.'

'Harding's death may involve elements of sexual fantasy.'

'This wreck? You're joking.'

Tang didn't smile. She looked completely humorless and lacking in irony.

'No, of course you're not,' Jo said, all at once knowing what Tang was going to say next.

'I understood that you have experience analyzing deaths of that sort. Am I misinformed?'

'No.'

'Good. Then let's talk to the ME.'

Now Tang smirked. That meant she knew the details of the Nagel investigation. She gestured to Jo, inviting her to go first.

Damn right, too. Make way for the princess of auto-erotic mortality. Wasn't that just the reason she'd gone to medical school? Mom and Dad would be so proud.

Though irked, she kept her expression mild. The Medical Examiner turned to look at her as she crossed the street. On his face she saw excitement and worry. Her annoyance evaporated.

Barry Cohen was stout, red-bearded and, in her experience, as unexcitable as a pet rock. If he was geared up, she should be too. Despite her caution, she had a feeling she was going to take this job.

Cohen nodded, grim. 'Jo. Didn't expect to see you on the graveyard shift.'

She didn't extend her hand; he was gloved and dressed in protective gear to keep from contaminating the scene. 'Looks like a full metal mess.'

'Two dead in the BMW. Two in the minivan. Bodies *in situ*.'

'What's got you cranked up, Barry?'

'We found something that set the detectives' radar pinging.'

Behind him the police photographer lit the night with his flash. Cohen called to him and the photographer sauntered over, checking his light meter. Jo felt a twinge of relief. Cohen was not going to ask her to view the carnage *in situ*. She would have put on coveralls and gloves if he'd asked, but if he didn't think she needed to view the bodies of the dead, she had no urge to disagree.

Cohen said, 'Show Doctor Beckett the shot with the writing.'

'Right.' The photographer was breathing through his mouth, as people did to shut out the smell. His eyes were watering.

His camera was slung around his neck from a strap, its heavy lens dangling. Peering at the view window, he flipped through the shots he'd taken.

'Here.'

He turned the camera so Jo could see. The small display showed a shot taken through the driver's window of the BMW. A woman's arm was visible, tanned and slim and fractured as if it were soft clay. It nestled in the flaccid white pillow of the deflated airbag. Below it, the woman's left thigh was visible. Jo saw letters, thick and red, scrawled on her skin.

They were awkward, childish almost. Shiny.

'Written in lipstick?' she said.

She glanced at Cohen and Tang. The word crawled up the dead woman's thigh to the black skirt that was hitched around her hips.

The skirt's position could well be the result of the crash. Bodies, clothing, jewelry, lives – all went horribly awry in the milliseconds of impact. The cameraman tilted the display to give her a better view.

*ir*

There were more letters but the camera's flash and the angle of the driver's leg had combined to make them unreadable. The woman's thigh was shattered so badly that it looked foreshortened. The femur had been driven backward into the pelvis by the impact, causing an acetabular fracture typical of car crashes.

'Have any clearer shots?' she said.

The photographer flipped through the shots. Various angles. Head buried in dash. Passenger equally still, face this way, unseeing eyes half open, pupils blown.

She turned to Cohen. 'Barry?'

'You should take a look,' the ME said.

She looked at the wreckage. 'Got any rubber bands?'

Cohen had them in his pocket. She put two around the front of her Doc Martens so that any footprints she left would be distinguishable from the rest. With the third she tied her hair back into a ponytail. Cohen held out a pair of latex gloves.

'I know you won't touch anything,' he said, but gave them to her anyway.

She snapped them on, waited while the cops logged her as entering the scene, and walked with the photographer to the heart of the mess. The wreckage sat astride the road. The BMW was partially embedded in the left side of the minivan.

'Gives *kiss of death* visceral meaning,' she said.

Skidmarks trailed behind the van like a giant's fingerpaint. She smelled rubber. The van driver had seen the car plunging toward him and tried to stop.

'They never had a chance,' she said.

The BMW was reaper-black. She walked toward it, felt her heart punch in her chest, and drew the cord across her mind and emotions. Slow breath in, count to five. See what's in front of you. See clearly. Take note. Clarity, not feeling, would make the difference. Slow breath out.

It was a tomb, and inside it was the proverbial Other Side. And she was here to be the bridge, the thin link between this world and that, in the shape of an explanation.

She noticed the photographer take a harsh breath. Ten meters from the mangle, he started breathing through his mouth.

The smell crept into her nose. Gasoline. Feces. Urine-soaked cloth, and a stale smell that she knew was flesh. The metallic tang of blood, faint like an aftertaste. It was the remains. What was left, organic, particulate, interacting with the living. It could have been much worse. This was recent death, a smell as insubstantial as perfume that traced the path of a woman who had left the room. The photographer's lips were retracted, his teeth clenched.

'Give it a few minutes and you won't notice it,' she said.

'Yeah.' His tone said Not.

'I know – give it a few minutes and you wouldn't notice a stake through your skull, either. But really, you'll stop smelling it. Your olfactory nerves go numb.'

'Hope I won't be around here long enough to test out that theory.'

They walked toward the car. The vehicular sarcophagus was motionless. Utterly inert – unlike death, which is final but not still. Decay is a busy organic process, almost as messy as grieving.

The photographer stopped two feet from the car. 'Stand here.' He gave Jo an analytical glance and said, 'You may have to stand on tiptoe.'

When she did, the puzzle pieces assembled themselves. The driver's tanned and pulverized arm nestling in the flaccid airbag. The woman's back. She was forward, twisted around the steering column. Blonde hair, fanned out. Jo couldn't see her face. The front of her melded into the almighty mess that was windshield, engine block, and minivan. She wasn't wearing a seatbelt.

Jo saw her leg. The letters. She stretched to see more clearly. They were written in greasy scarlet lipstick on the corpse's thigh.

'You read it the same way I do?' the photographer said.

'Without a doubt.'

Under the fizzing lights the driver's skin had a waxy sheen, and the massive acetabular fracture distorted what must have been a long, well-muscled thigh. Her leg looked bunched and flattened. The letters were unmistakable.

*dirty*

'What do you make of it?' the photographer said.

'Don't know.'

'Think she wrote it? What does it mean? Is it a suicide note?'

'I have no idea yet.'

She stepped back to get an overall impression. No blood was visible on the body from this angle. With the woman's skirt rucked up to her hips, the curve of her thigh was visible all the way to her buttocks. She was wearing a lacy black thong. Though harsh light and shadow distorted the optics, Jo could see lividity starting. With the driver's blood pooling via gravity, the top of her thigh was paling, setting off the garish letters.

'Get some more shots,' she said.

She stepped back as he raised his camera. The flash blanched the scene.

She caught a glimpse of the passenger, flung like a rag doll against the dashboard. She was paler than the driver. She too was wearing a skirt but hers was too tight to have ridden up. Her legs hadn't begun to show lividity yet. She looked crooked. Her face was turned toward Jo, eyes open. They were the frozen blue of the emergency lights.

Jo breathed out, counting to five, and walked back to Tang. The lieutenant's face was pinched.

'Is that it? That's the evidence that brought me out here tonight?' Jo said.

'No,' Tang said. 'We need to run this investigation on multiple tracks simultaneously. We're throwing everything at it.'

'Why?'

'This is not the first murder-suicide we've had this week.'

Jo gauged the woman's face and saw fatigue and strain. 'You're not sure this is murder-suicide. If you were, you wouldn't need me,' Jo said. 'These deaths are equivocal.'

'They're more than equivocal,' Tang said. 'That's why we want you.'

What did 'more than equivocal' mean? Jo's work life revolved around equivocal death. That's what the psychological autopsy examined: the ambiguous, the vague, the oblique death, the shifty cases, those that made no sense. Explaining them was her job.

Tang shot a glance in the direction of the news van outside the yellow tape. A dish antenna was unfurled on top of it. The light from the TV camera blazed around the silhouetted reporter. Tang lowered her voice.

'Then I won't call them murder-suicides. How about paired deaths? This is the third.'

The cold took on a sharper edge. The stars cut through the city lights, shining like flecks of broken glass.

'You've heard about the other cases. David Yoshida and Maki Prichingo.'

Yoshida's name rang loud in Jo's head. 'You have compelling evidence Doctor Yoshida's death wasn't from natural causes?'

'You'll get everything we have. I'm not asking you to investigate them, but you should look at the similarities. Which we'll get to.'

She nodded. 'Who's Maki Prichingo?'

'The burning boat.'

Jo looked at her, blank.

Tang's forehead furrowed. 'Maki, the fashion designer. He and his lover were found dead on his sailboat off the coast last week. You've never heard of Maki . . .?'

Her voice trailed off and she gave Jo's clothes another look. Unfamiliarity with fashion designers seemingly made sense, and she let it go.

'You knew Doctor Yoshida?' she said.

'Knew of him. He headed cardiothoracic surgery at UCSF.' And cardiac surgeons thought they were, if not God, then archangels. Their reputations soared above them. 'Word is, he had a heart attack.'

'"Word is" just means speculation. You'll get the files.'

'Lieutenant, why the urgency?' Jo said. 'What's the link between the deaths?'

'We don't know. But I think it's there, and you can help find it. We're attacking this on multiple fronts simultaneously.'

'Why?'

With a chilled hand, Tang took Jo's elbow and pulled her along as she walked across the street. 'This is the city's third bizarre high-profile death in the past week.'

That wasn't what had the cops twisted. 'Murder-suicides?'

'Sounds peculiar, I know, but this could be some kind of organized killing spree.' She nodded at the city scene. 'Something's out there.'

It was a weird time in the city. Full moon, Halloween on the way. The recent swarm of earthquakes had jarred the dishes and people's nerves. Jo looked at Tang and saw the twitchiness she'd observed on the street all week. Everybody was spooked.

So was Jo. Something seemed odd, out of place.

'We want you to figure it out,' Tang said. 'And I mean right damned now.'

'There isn't *right damned now* with psychological autopsies.'

'This time there is.'

'That's not how it works. I interview the victim's family and colleagues, review the accident report and the victim's medical history – it can take weeks. The report's credibility in court is at stake. Even more, so is the truth about the victim's life.'

'You've heard of the first forty-eight?' Tang said.

'Yeah. And I'm not FedEx. I rush, I could do even less than a half-assed job.'

Tang tightened her grip on Jo's elbow. 'That's not my point. In this case, we have forty-eight hours maximum.'

'Why?'

'That's how often people are dying.'

Jo blinked. Tang turned to look at the wreckage.

'Victim, perpetrator, we don't know who Callie Harding is. But people are going down and taking others with them. Yoshida last Thursday. Maki Saturday night. Now this.'

'You think there's going to be another one.'

'Unless we stop it.'

The Medical Examiner had finished. The fire crew was now digging into the coital vehicular mess with a skill saw.

'We need to know why Callie Harding died, and we need to know yesterday. Don't worry about protocol or court proceedings. Cut any corners you need to. You have two days.'

Jo watched the firefighter saw into the metal. Sparks hissed, white and fevered. Her spooky feeling returned. Something about the wreck was out of kilter.

'Give me everything. I'll run with it,' she said.

'Good.' Tang released her grip. 'And you won't have to start from scratch. If you move fast you can talk to our eyewitness.'

'Who?'

'The patrolman involved in the vehicle pursuit. Officer Cruz.' Tang gave her a cool glare. 'Welcome to the front line.'

# 4

'Straight up crazy, that's what I thought at the start. Then the rest of it happened and I thought – yeah, straight up crazy.'

Officer Pablo Cruz drew a breath and licked his lips as though they were dry; as though he'd been drawing a lot of sharp breaths. His eyes shone brightly. A blocky young man, he seemed both eager and anxious about telling Jo the story of his first-ever vehicle pursuit.

She spoke gently. 'So you turned onto Stockton and saw her put the BMW into reverse. What happened?'

'It got wild weird.' He looked at the hill above the tunnel. 'I hit the brakes. You can see the street up there – those vehicles parked along the curbs didn't leave me much room to maneuver. She came at me, tires spinning. I thought, she's going to ram me.' He swallowed. 'I yanked it onto the left side of the road to avoid her. But I didn't need to. She laid on the brakes. Slammed 'em, must have pulled the handbrake too. She stopped it on a dime, right next to my passenger-side window. At that point I was reaching for my weapon. But she . . .'

He looked up at the wrecked bridge railing. The muscles in his jaw bulged.

'Officer?'

He shook his head. 'It makes no sense. She drove through the railing on purpose, I have no doubt.'

'What happened when she stopped next to your patrol car?'

He continued gazing up at the railing. Jo didn't see a need to push him, not at this stage. It was okay to let everything come out – his narrative, his impressions, his emotions, even if it was all a jumble right now.

'I saw her face, clear as day. She was – I mean, she was a beautiful woman, I saw that. And she was desperate.'

She was ninety seconds from death. Desperate, yeah, that about covered it. 'What did she do?'

'She slapped her hand against her window and yelled to me. I heard it. I saw the words on her lips.' Again he looked at the bridge. 'I have no doubt she did it on purpose.' He glanced at her sharply, as though she had just disputed his assessment. 'Come on, I'll show you why.'

Cruz took her to the stairwell that led up to Bush Street. His shoulders filled the dark blue uniform shirt. The heel of his hand rode his nightstick. He seemed more than uncomfortable. Something was bothering him, and it wasn't the sleeping bags of the homeless in the stairwell.

Something was bothering her, too. She felt a scratch at the base of her brain. The feeling that the scene was askew returned.

'What's on your mind, officer?' she said.

He slid her a glance over his shoulder. 'Little late to talk the driver down off the ledge, isn't it?'

'That's not why I'm here.'

They headed up the stairs. What was scratching at her? What was aggravating Cruz?

His mouth was a taut line. 'You gonna ask me how I feel?'

Was that it? 'I'm not here to give you trauma counseling, or to evaluate your mental stability as a witness.'

His glance was sharp. 'So who are you?'

'I'm the deadshrinker.'

He slowed. 'What?'

'I don't shrink heads. I shrink souls.' Her footsteps echoed in the stairwell. 'I'm a forensic psychiatrist.'

His shoulders inched down. He looked at her with fresh curiosity. 'Exactly what is it you do?'

'I perform psychological autopsies to determine whether equivocal deaths are natural, accident, suicide or homicide,' she said. 'I figure out why the deceased got dead.'

Relief seeped across his face, and the beginnings of a smile. 'You have trouble getting DBs to pay?'

'Just zombies. I charge them up front, before they wander away moaning.'

They reached the top of the stairs. 'And you don't do your voodoo in a nice warm office?'

She saw why Cruz thought Harding had crashed deliberately. Her voice went quiet. 'Not when the juju's this bad.'

Stockton Street dead ended at the Bush Street bridge. Each end of the bridge had a staircase leading up from the street below. At the top, the staircases pointed toward the center of the bridge. They were guarded with metal railings. Jo ran her hand along one. It was cold and solid. The vertical pole that held up the end of the railing was striped with black paint and deformed from the force of the BMW striking it as it went past.

Jo estimated that there were no more than eight feet between the two sets of stairs.

Either-or. Callie Harding had either suffered unfathomably bad luck, or done a damned precise piece of driving.

Uphill on Stockton two police officers were walking the road with a pedometer, measuring. A camera flashed; somebody was photographing the pavement.

'Skidmarks?' she said.

'They're looking.'

She walked to the curb. It was heavily scored where the BMW had hit it. Across the street, under a streetlight, she saw fresh gouges in the asphalt. The BMW must have bottomed out when the angle of the road flattened. But scraping the roadway didn't look to have slowed it down much, if at all.

And she'd seen enough crash scene photos, studied the accident statistics, hell, driven the Bayshore Freeway enough, to know that when a driver wants to avoid a crash he keeps his foot hard on the brake all the way to the point of impact.

There was no evidence of that here, just a series of gashes in the road. Callie Harding: until one a.m. she had been on her way to being a celebrity prosecutor. But now the trail of gouges marked her path to a noisy death.

Jo turned back to Cruz. 'What do you recall about the moments before the crash?'

'Thinking, holy shit, she's aiming for it.'

'Did she have her lights on?'

'Yes. Headlights, tail lights, all in working order. You asking if she braked before she hit the bridge, if I saw the brake lights? I don't remember. But her brakes worked a minute earlier when she screeched up next to my patrol car. She stopped it like pulling up a horse. Sharp.'

Cruz gazed into the distance. He had an Aztec profile. It was a warrior's face, but he looked young and wound up.

'Officer?'

'She topped herself, I don't see how she didn't. Right? What else could it be?' he said. 'But why? I don't get it.'

Jo touched his elbow. 'Let's start finding out.'

'But, Christ, why'd she take all those people with her?'

The deadshrinker didn't know.

He held back a moment longer, his shoulders working their way upward. The sense that something was wrong intensified. The blue emergency lights, the flash from the photographers' cameras, the jagged shine in Cruz's eyes were giving her a sense of situational vertigo. Jo held his gaze. She was trying to take in this first burst of information, but mixed with it was concern for the young cop. He felt somehow responsible. He had been the one on the scene, and Callie Harding had died. He thought he had failed.

'Cruz. Don't even start thinking you could have stopped it.'

'Never seen anything like the look in her eyes.' His own eyes looked pained. 'Not that it shocked me. I mean . . .'

'I'm not here to evaluate you. What about the driver's eyes?'

As sharp as the flash from the photographer's camera, understanding came to her. Ice water seemed to shimmer across her skin.

*The look in her eyes.*

She turned and bolted back down the stairs. Three steps at a time, grabbed the railing and swung herself over, dropped with a thud and ran toward the wreckage, yelling at the Medical Examiner.

'Cohen, get the paramedics, *stat.*'

The ME glanced at her in alarm.

The eyes. In the photographer's digital display, the passenger's face had looked powder-white and her eyes had been half shut, dark and unseeing. But when Jo had seen her up close, her eyes were wide open and glossy blue. Blue because her pupils had contracted.

Dead people's eyes don't react to light.

'Barry, she's alive,' Jo yelled.

Heedless now of CSI protocol or preserving the scene, she leapt onto the wreckage. Cohen hustled toward her.

The passenger hadn't moved. Her eyes were still open. Blood had run into her lashes like mascara.

Jo pressed two fingers to the woman's neck to search for a carotid pulse.

'Can you hear me?' she said.

No response. No movement. She couldn't feel a pulse. But her own heart was rabbiting so hard that she couldn't feel anything else.

'Can you hear me? Blink if you can hear me.'

Cohen approached. 'What are you doing?'

Had she imagined it? Was she so spooked that it was all—

The woman blinked.

'Oh my God,' Cohen said.

Jo's whole system went into overload. She felt adrenaline dump into her veins, chills skitter along her arms, her heart jack into sixth gear, blood pressure spike so hard that her vision jumped.

'Don't move. We're going to get you out of here,' she said.

She heard Cohen calling for the paramedics. She thought she felt a pulse in the woman's neck. She was young, Jo thought, younger than her, and smashed to dust. Behind them flash photography bleached the car.

Lips moved. The woman was struggling to breathe.

Through the pounding of the blood in her ears, Jo thought she heard a sound come from the woman's mouth. She leaned in. Another flash turned the woman's face to flour. Her pupils contracted again, and pain striped her eyes. Her lips parted.

'What?' Jo said.

Her voice was nothing but a trace. 'Stop it.'

Jo turned to shout at the police photographer – but it wasn't him, it was press people beyond the yellow tape. She leaned across the passenger's face to shield her from the cameras.

'Hang on. The paramedics are coming. The firefighters are going to cut you loose.' She turned and shouted, 'Come *on*.'

'Stop it,' the passenger whispered.

She touched the woman's shoulder. 'I know it's hard. We're going to get you out of here.'

Fingers to her neck again. There, she had the pulse.

The paramedics came running with their equipment. Firefighters brought the Jaws of Life. They crowded around, ready to take over.

Jo leaned back. 'Conscious and vocal. Pulse weak and thready. Pupils equal and reactive.'

The rescue crews jostled around her. The passenger's eyes shifted. Blue, sharp as glass, they stared at her. The woman's cold fingers crawled around Jo's wrist.

'*Stop it*,' she said.

A firefighter moved Jo aside. 'Doctor, let us go to work.'

Stop *what*?

Her stomach felt hollow. She pressed a hand against it and forced herself to breathe slowly. She looked around. Cruz was near the bottom of the stairs.

She walked toward him. 'Officer,' she called. He turned. 'What did the driver say?'

Cruz frowned, seemingly uncertain. Jo kept walking.

'When the BMW stopped next to your car. What did Harding say to you?'

Cruz's guard went up at the urgency in her tone. She walked up to him.

'Tell me,' she said.

He scanned her face, and when he spoke, his voice was distressed. ' "Help me." '

Jo felt the blood drain from her face.

'She slapped her palm against the driver's window and looked straight at me. And she said *Help me*. I swear to God.' He held Jo's gaze, and the pain came out from behind his warrior's eyes. 'She was begging me to save her.'

# 5

'On three.'

The paramedics counted it off. With the firefighters they lifted the passenger just enough to fasten the cervical collar around her neck. They inched her free from the wreckage with the tenderness of someone carrying a torn butterfly. Her blonde hair fell around her head like cornsilk.

Jo tried to catch the young woman's eye but the girl looked unfocused, staring at nothing. The paramedics strapped her to a backboard and rushed her to an ambulance, one of them holding an IV bag. Intravenous drip for Raggedy Ann. Jo had rarely seen such a delicate and damaged human being. She'd seen even fewer who'd survived.

Barry Cohen stood nearby, running his fingers through his red beard. The Medical Examiner watched the paramedics load the passenger into the ambulance.

'I don't know how I missed it,' he said.

The ambulance drove away, lights casting red and blue streaks across the street. Cohen seemed to feel them as a lash.

'Did you examine her?' Jo said.

'Axial palpation. I didn't detect a pulse. And I didn't notice any reactivity to light.' He turned to her. 'That was a good catch.'

A thread of adrenaline crawled down her arm. It was a sick feeling. She fought it away, watching the lights of the ambulance wane to city-glare as it turned onto Market Street.

'Thank God I didn't take a liver temp to gauge TOD,' Cohen said.

Stabbing the equivalent of a meat thermometer into the girl's internal organs would have established Time of Death as *Oh, shit.* 'Who declared her? The paramedics?'

'Yeah. I'll get to the bottom of it.'

And if it was his fault, he wouldn't flinch from admitting it. 'I don't doubt you will, Barry.'

He offered a weary smile. 'Thanks.'

She gave him a thumbs-up as a goodbye.

At the edge of the scene, Lieutenant Tang was talking to Callie Harding's boss. Jo headed over. The chill in the air had seeped into her.

Harding's boss looked washed out. 'This is a loss to the law enforcement community, no less than if a police officer had died. I want to be kept apprised of your investigation.'

Tang's arms were crossed. 'Certainly.' She gave Jo a look that seemed full of warning. 'Jo Beckett, consulting forensic psychiatrist – Assistant US Attorney Leo Fonsecca, Head of the Criminal Division.'

Fonsecca was slight and rumpled. Under the harsh street lighting he looked sepulchral, with thinning gray hair and a Bassett hound face behind rimless glasses. He seemed disconsolate. But his voice was smooth and pointed, like a pungee stick.

'I don't understand why SFPD has called in a psychologist. I don't believe for one second that Callie killed herself,' he said.

'Psychiatrist, Mr Fonsecca,' Jo said. 'And I can help determine whether Ms Harding committed suicide or not.'

'Whatever. I want you all to find out what happened to my prosecutor. No politics, no propaganda, no bullshit.'

Tang was bristling. 'We will, sir. I imagine Doctor Beckett will want to talk to you at length. Tomorrow. Right?'

'Certainly.' Jo was getting Tang's message: *Not here, not now. Keep quiet.*

'Call my secretary,' he said.

Officer Cruz walked past. Tang collared him, possibly as an excuse to end the conversation with Fonsecca.

'Could another vehicle have been pursuing Harding's BMW besides you?' she said.

'Not that I saw,' he said. 'And the streets were empty. I would have noticed another vehicle peeling off.'

'Check with businesses near the start of the pursuit. See if you can get CCTV footage.' She pointed at the tunnel stairwells leading up to Bush Street. 'Grab the footage from the stairwell surveillance cameras, too.'

'Right.'

Jo said, 'Are you certain Harding's passenger tried to jump out during the pursuit?'

'Positive. She was frantic to escape from that car. Even at high speed.'

Again, like a tic, Cruz looked up at the bridge railing. Jo's gaze followed.

Jumpers often take their time, give it a last glance. But once they step off, they don't want to see the ground rush at them. They take off their glasses. Sometimes when they leap, they turn to see the sky and not the fatal pavement flying to meet them.

But it's almost always a leap, a determined burst into space and oblivion. They don't topple. They propel themselves away from buildings, bridges, cliffs.

And Callie Harding's exit from the world certainly looked propulsive.

'Have they identified the passenger?' Jo said.

'Driver's license lists her as Angelika Meyer,' Cruz said.

Fonsecca straightened. 'What? Are you sure?'

Cruz looked at his notes. 'That's the name.'

'No, that's – oh, dear God. She's an intern in our office. A law student at Hastings.' Fonsecca touched a hand to his forehead. 'This makes no sense. Why would Angelika . . . oh, this is horrendous.'

He pulled out his cellphone. 'Excuse me.' He walked away, punching numbers.

'What is going on?' Tang said.

Jo watched him go. 'I don't know. Why didn't you want me to talk to him?'

'He's not part of this investigation, no matter how hard he tries to butt in. He doesn't know about the writing on Harding's thigh, and he doesn't need to know. Don't reveal that information unless I authorize it.'

'I won't.'

Cruz said, 'Understood, Lieutenant.'

'Good.' Tang squinted at Jo. 'The passenger said "Stop it" to you?'

'Clear as ice.' Jo stared back. 'I know. Forty-eight hours.'

'And counting down.'

Jo nodded. She touched Cruz's arm and handed him her card. 'If you think of anything else, call me. Anything at all.'

He nodded and she walked away, heading down Stockton toward Union Square.

*That was a good catch.* For a second she seemed to hear machinery tearing itself to pieces. She seemed to hear voices speaking her name. Familiar voices, wounded and yearning. Momentarily she wanted to run. The glare of the Caltrans construction spotlight dimmed behind her. In its wake, the street lighting looked dingy. Office windows were yellow slicks on the walls of a canyon rising above her to the stars. Ahead, the street opened into Union Square. She reached the corner and inhaled as though she'd just found oxygen.

*Good catch.* Barry Cohen didn't know how his words would hit her.

For a vivid instant she saw Daniel, felt his hand take hers, heard again the words he gave her when the world turned to shit.

*No,* she thought.

She exhaled and shook off the embers that guttered in her memory, threatening to ignite. She dug her fingernails into her palms to stop her hands shivering. The shivering was nerves, just nerves. It had been a long time since she'd had to jump into a trauma situation.

She whispered to herself, 'Get over it.'

This wasn't about her. It was about the three people dead in the wreck behind her, and a young woman who was close to joining them. A young woman who seemed to be calling out a warning.

She blinked the chill from her eyes and walked on.

\*   \*   \*

The vibration from the cellphone brought his eyes open. He inhaled, staring at the dark ceiling, instantly alert.

It would be news, an automatic text update. Quietly, so as not to disturb the night, the dark, his privacy, Perry turned the phone in his hand to read the display. He was looking for confirmation, and he found it in a single word.

*Dead.*

His hand curled around the phone. The prosecutor was gone.

He didn't read the rest. The how, or the how many others. For a moment his eyes stung and his throat burned, and tears threatened to boil up. He fought them back. His gaze lengthened and he let his mind fly free. He would learn the details soon enough. Right now, he wanted to savor the moment.

Harding was dead. Gone, the dirty bitch.

His mind tried to race, but he forced it to slow down. His heart felt large in his chest, beating slowly, full of blood.

Full of joy.

He hoped she had suffered. That she had died screaming, weeping, maybe choking on her own blood, unable to breathe. Slowly he smiled. *How does it feel to be on the wrong end of the pain, Callie?* He leered at the ceiling, picturing it, until the dark ceiling above him became a movie screen. And in this private movie epic, he saw panic on Harding's face, and knowledge; watched her fighting for air through a throat that was broken and swollen, hands too smashed to move. He hated the fact that he hadn't been on the scene, at her side at that moment, to witness it live.

*You want justice? Here it is. Turnabout's a bitch, ain't it?* He bit back a laugh. His eyes were wet.

Did she give up anything? Names, knowledge, secrets? He hoped, he wished.

Wished he'd been able to walk up to the prosecutor and kiss her goodbye. The thought excited him.

In his vision he saw her. She realized death was coming. God, how he hated her. Hated them all. *I paid. Now you pay.* He saw her cry like a little child. Saw her piss herself. Saw her lips move.

She was praying. *Not this, no. Forgive me, I'm dirty, dirty, dirty. No.*

In the dark Perry Ames lay rigid, feeling as he always felt at these moments. Completely frustrated. He couldn't be with Callie Harding when she left this life, and picturing her exit relieved his rage only for a few lonely minutes.

Solitude is the best defense, because in the end you can't rely on anything but yourself.

That, and death. Dirty, dirty, dirty bitch.

# 6

The foghorn woke Jo, lowing its warning across the bay. She rolled over and opened her eyes. Sunlight needled the ceiling, gold-flecked through the leaves of the magnolia tree outside. The foghorn moaned again.

Sun and fog, together. San Francisco was a city of multiple personalities.

It was six forty-five. Jo felt the late night as a low note of fatigue echoing down to the bone. She got up, pulled a kimono around herself and raised the blinds. A vivid day greeted her. The sky was acrylic blue and the more flamboyant homes on the hilltop, blue, yellow and green with gingerbread gables, looked Easter-egg bright. In the distance, past dense rooftops and Monterey pines, the towers of the Golden Gate Bridge glowed red in the dawn. Mist clung to the water below it, but here above Fisherman's Wharf her neighborhood gleamed.

She was lucky to live here, and she knew it. Her house was a classic San Francisco Victorian, adobe-red with white gables. Tucked back from the street, it looked unassuming. And it was Plain Jane compared to the *faux* mansion next door, which had a rooftop terrace adorned with statues of Roman godlets. Cupid was covered in pigeon crap.

Curtains twitched in one of the mansion's upstairs windows. She sighed. Her neighbor was checking to see if her lights were on. She lowered the blinds and hit the shower.

If her house looked humble from the street, inside it was all air and space, and saturated with color. Big windows captured each ounce of sunlight the capricious weather offered. Her bed frame was Japanese, lacquered to a black shine, covered with a scarlet comforter and gold pillows. Hot colors were good. They helped her wake up, reminded her of heartbeats and action. The orchids on the dresser were a fiery orange.

She loathed confined spaces, and the house let her breathe. It even boasted a million-dollar view of both the Golden Gate and the Bay Bridge. To see it, she just had to shinny up the downspout to the roof. Piece of cake.

She loved this place. But it could be too quiet, now that it was just her.

Climbing out of the shower, she felt revved up. She dressed and slipped on her necklace, a silver chain on which hung a Coptic cross and a white-gold ring. Downstairs in the kitchen she booted up her laptop. Sunlight cut a wedge through the French doors. The tiny back yard was shaded by the old magnolia and overrun with sage, lilac and an unruly wall of white-flowering clematis.

Her computer sang at her. She took a look. Lieutenant Tang had sent a hunk of preliminary information.

Callie Ann Harding. Age 36. Palo Alto address. Divorced, no children. Next of kin was her ex-husband, Gregory Harding of Portola Valley. Harding had been contacted. He had identified the body.

Hell of a wake-up call for the ex. Jo pulled off the top of a pen with her teeth, opened a notebook and made a note to contact Harding ASAP.

She pulled up the next file: Callie Harding's driver's license photo.

Even under the harsh lens of the DMV camera, Harding looked strikingly attractive. Her cheekbones had the angular look common to long-distance runners. Her hair was pulled back into a serene French twist and dyed a platinum shade that hinted at a healthy ego and libido. It was a Monroe blonde, set against serious, no-nonsense, *Dragnet* eyes. Her gaze was piercing and intensely alive.

Jo pulled out her psychological autopsy checklist. Her spirits tanked.

She worked within the NASH framework – determining whether a death was natural, accidental, suicide or homicide. To do that, she gathered as much hard evidence as possible. But none of the information she usually relied on would be available here.

The police report on the crash hadn't been filed yet. Forensics hadn't analyzed the BMW to determine whether a mechanical fault had caused the wreck. Harding's family, friends and co-workers hadn't been interviewed. The autopsy was scheduled for noon, which meant Barry Cohen was clearing the decks to get it done. But toxicology screening, blood and urine tests wouldn't be back.

She was going to have to tag along with detectives and scrounge information from the Medical Examiner. And neither law enforcement nor the ME's Office was eager to share their findings with a psychiatrist.

She had a good working relationship with Barry Cohen, but some of his colleagues disdained the concept of the psychological autopsy. In their view, they did science. Jo did hoodoo.

They were half-right. The psychological autopsy wasn't science. Like all of medicine, it was an art.

She didn't split open cadavers. Nonetheless, her work dug deeply into the deceased. She investigated the victim's history – medical, psychological, educational and sexual. She looked for early warning signs of suicide. She learned about the victim's relationships. Read their writings. Excavated their online activities. Asked about their premonitions and mood swings. She gathered reactions to the victim's death from friends and relatives. She asked about old and current enemies.

People did have them. And not like her mother, who kept an enemies list of every kid who'd knocked one of her children off a playground slide.

And to evaluate the victim's mental state she uncovered their fears, phobias and fantasies. Death is a physical event but, when it comes to human beings, state of mind makes all the difference. Between murder and self-defense. Between legal insanity and manslaughter.

And in this case, between accident and murder-suicide.

Still, her conclusions were inevitably a matter of judgment. Manner of death? We have a 9.3 for suicide, 9.85 for murder. And for accident? A 2.1 from the Soviet judge. Not a winner.

In the end, the police and the Medical Examiner determined *how* people died. Jo determined *why*. Because a forensic psychiatrist doesn't cut open the victim's body, but his life.

But in this case, she didn't even have a cause of death. Welcome to the front line. Flying blind, into a fog bank.

She printed all the files, put everything in a satchel and headed out the door, locking the house behind her, a small house never intended for one person.

Jo jogged down her front steps. The air was brisk. In the small park across the street, trees swayed as though shaking themselves awake. She glanced at the mansion next door. This was generally the moment when her neighbor liked to intercept her. But today the curtains failed to twitch and the door stayed closed.

At the corner she caught the cable car. The gripman rang his bell and they tipped past the corner and angled down the steep hill. She held on while the neighborhood slid by. From a distance this hillside looked postcard neat, but up close Jo saw the crevices: narrow passageways that hid tiny courtyards, alleys that cloistered tie-dyed hippie hideaways. Halfway down the hill an old apartment building was being gutted and remodeled. Construction workers were sauntering around the site at a Monday morning pace. The guy with the hammer slung from his tool belt looked kind of hot.

Jo checked herself. It wasn't him; it was the gigantic Thermos of coffee he was carrying. She got off at the bottom of the hill and headed to Java Jones.

The coffeehouse was crowded. Behind the counter, Tina smiled.

'Johanna Renee, good morning.'

'I need an *über*-coffee, the biggest you've got, plus a blueberry muffin. And a cheese panini.'

Tina gave her a waspish look.

'I want calories and caffeine,' she said.

Tina was her younger sister. She had Jo's brown curls and athletic figure. She was wearing a black barista's apron, plus a nose stud and enough silver earrings to get reception from orbiting spy satellites. She was as bouncy as Tigger.

Jo spoke up to be heard over the stereo. 'Who's this?'

'Mahler. Quality music.'

Jo didn't comment. Tina's playlist of quality music also included Slipknot.

Tina waved to the air. 'Dark and passionate. It's the way to take things. Music, literature, men . . .'

'Coffee.'

Smirking, Tina handed over a mug the size of a Ming vase. Jo carried it to a table by the window. She took a long, greedy swallow. Sitting down, she got out her computer, and called the Central Division police station.

Lieutenant Amy Tang answered the phone sounding like a switchblade, sharp and flashy. 'What do you have for me, Doctor Beckett?'

'Nothing yet. I'm only getting started.'

Tang exhaled, with what Jo's finely calibrated psychiatric training took to be a fat breath of irritation. 'What do you need?'

'Harding's vehicle and driving records.'

Papers rustled. 'The BMW was brand new, purchased three weeks ago. Harding had a clean driving record. No DUIs, no speeding tickets.'

Jo scribbled notes. 'The Yoshida and Maki Prichingo cases. Are the files ready for my review?'

'We're swamped. It'll be this afternoon. Right now I'll send you what the press has reported.'

It would have to do. 'Any more information on Harding's passenger? How's she doing?'

'Alive. Unconscious. She hasn't talked.'

'Where is she?'

'St Francis.'

'Good.' Jo had staff privileges at St Francis. She would go by.

The lieutenant cleared her throat. 'What do you think about the sexual fantasy angle?'

'No thoughts yet. I need evidence before I draw conclusions.'

'I'd say Harding drew her own conclusion in red lipstick. She was dirty.'

'Maybe.'

Jo thought she heard the policewoman tapping a pencil against her desk. 'You need anything else before you get to drawing?'

Yes. Tang – is that your last name, favorite breakfast drink, or emblem of your biting personality? 'Not right now. Thank you, Lieutenant.'

Tang hung up without saying you're welcome. In her notebook, next to the woman's name, Jo drew a smiley face with a tongue sticking out.

She also drew a circle around Angelika Meyer's name. Harding's young passenger was key. If Meyer regained consciousness, she might be able to tell them what had happened inside the BMW. Might tell Jo what it was so damned vital to stop.

Forty-eight hours and counting down. With the information she was likely to gather in that time, she might as well ask a ouija board for help.

With a clatter, Tina set a plate with her muffin and cheese panini on the table. 'Your calories.'

'Excellent. Thanks.'

In the sun flowing through the windows, Tina's curls glowed copper, giving the impression that her head was on fire. She sat down and leaned toward Jo.

'I ran into Mike Sadowski – from your high school class? He's aching to go out with you.'

'You think everybody's aching to go out with me. Barry Bonds. The archbishop. The cable car driver on the Rice-A-Roni box.'

'Your *über*-coffee turned out extra-acidic, didn't it?' She picked at Jo's muffin. 'You busy tonight? I've got plans and it would be more fun if you came along.'

'What's his name?'

'Girls' night out. It's cultural. Aerobic. Healthy.' Tina smiled. 'It's girly. None of that nature grunge, rock-climbing shtick you do.'

Jo tapped her fingers on the table. 'Does it involve my Chi, or dancing with a pole?'

'No. Pinky swear.' Tina's eyes were wide with innocence. 'Come on.'

Jo softened. 'What time? Group's at seven.'

'After that.' Tina became pensive. 'How's it going?'

'Good.' She shrugged, and smiled. 'It gets my mind off psychological autopsies.'

'Only you would work with a bereavement group to get your mind off death.'

'Tuesdays with *Mori*.'

Tina laughed, but the pensive expression remained. It contained an ever-near, melancholy concern for her. Jo hated that look. She wanted people to stop worrying about her. She glanced away, focusing instead on her computer screen.

Lieutenant Tang had sent the list of news articles. One caught her eye.

*Boat Fire 'Deliberately Set'?*

It was an article about the dead fashion designer, Maki. His sailboat had been spotted in flames off the coast. Rescuers had found his body aboard, along with that of his lover. File photos showed them: Maki, a shaven-headed East Asian in his forties, snapped by paparazzi. Disco-ball smile, a top dog's bearing. His lover William Willets was pale, Caucasian, with a pinched mouth. The second fiddle. No cause of death had been disclosed. The article speculated that drugs were involved, or a fatal lovers' argument. Because the boat was found adrift outside city limits, federal authorities were involved in the investigation.

*Assistant US Attorney Callie Harding says no decision has been made whether to open a criminal investigation.*

Hell. Tang had said there must be a link between Harding's crash and Maki's death. And here was a link, a big fat one. Harding had been involved with investigating the burning boat.

Jo continued to scroll through the article. She stopped.

*A team from the 129th Air Rescue Wing at Moffett Field was scrambled to the scene, but found the two men aboard already dead. A spokesman for the Air National Guard declined to comment.*

Tina continued talking. 'And what would be so bad about going on a date? Friendship, that's all I'm suggesting. Jo, it's been two years. You're doing so great, but you don't have to do it all by yourself. Can you see that?'

She did. She saw who she needed to talk to. His name was there in the police department's notes: the pararescue jumper who had been on duty that night with the 129th Rescue Wing. Gabriel Quintana.

Tina tossed a sugar packet at her. 'I'll pick you up from UCSF.'

Quintana. She felt a zing in her fingertips. She looked up. 'Sorry. What?'

'You're buzzing like a bee caught in a jar. I'll pick you up tonight. Eight?'

'Unless this case I'm working on turns into a monster.'

Tina stood up. 'Monster case, ooh. Am I going to see you on television?'

'Yeah, walking through a blood-drenched crime scene with a flashlight, wearing tight jeans and a low-cut blouse.'

'And packing heat. Promise me you'll be strapped. And you'll whip off your sunglasses and vow to wreak justice. Please?'

'Absolutely. When pigs fly in formation, and battle Godzilla.' She was smiling, but felt it fade. 'I need to talk to the 129th Rescue Wing.'

'Tell 'em hey, and a big thumbs-up.' Tina stopped. 'Wait—'

'Yeah.' She shut her computer. 'Maybe I'll take a flak jacket.'

Worry creased Tina's face. Jo gathered her things, kissed her sister goodbye and headed out into the bracing sunshine. She knew a flak jacket wouldn't shield her. Kevlar only protects the heart against bullets, not grief.

# 7

Outside the coffeehouse, the sky had a silvery shine. She put on her shades. She turned and saw, lumbering along the sidewalk toward her, Ferd Bismuth.

'Shoot,' she said.

Bismuth straightened and began to strut. She had no time for a long conversation, but it was too late to turn tail and bolt. He'd seen her.

He waved. 'Greetings, neighbor.'

Ferd was he who lived behind the crap-covered cupids and twitching curtains in the *faux* mansion next door to Jo's house. He wasn't obese, but walked like he was, weight back as though to balance a stomach, hands held away from his sides as if propped on pillows of fat. He was knock-kneed and his clothes were generously sized. His hair was lustrous with Brylcreem. He looked ready for his photo at NASA Mission Control, circa 1969.

He trundled toward her, smiling. 'I must have just missed you at the cable car stop.'

She had to calibrate her response. With Ferd, pleasantries were a minefield. She hefted her satchel higher on her shoulder to give the impression that she urgently needed to get somewhere. Which she did, but need and urgency never deterred Ferd. She could have been on fire and he wouldn't be dissuaded from talking to her. For that matter, *he* could have been on fire.

Weather should be a harmless topic. 'Beautiful to see the sunshine, isn't it?'

His smile shrank. 'Should I have applied sunscreen? With it being October, I thought I was safe.' He glanced at his arms as if cancerous freckles were even now incubating.

She took a step. 'Factor Twenty, that's always good. But don't hide from the sun – it gives you Vitamin D. And it cheers you up.'

'Vitamin D? You mean – wait, no, Jo, don't go. Are you saying I could get rickets?'

She'd blown it. Never give 'em an opening – hadn't she learned anything from testifying in court? Don't ever give an open-ended answer, much less a suggestion, that a lawyer can crucify you with on cross-examination. But here she'd gone and given Ferd a bunch of nails and a *Physicians' Desk Reference* to hammer them in with.

He was the worst hypochondriac she'd ever met.

'Vitamin D? You mean with the rain and fog we don't get enough?' He looked at his knees. 'Am I at serious risk? I don't want my bones to soften.'

'You're not going to get rickets, I promise. Have a great day. I'm running behind.'

'One thing.'

She backed away. 'I have to talk to the Air National Guard. If I don't, they'll send commandos.'

'This won't take a sec.'

He inhaled and blew out a gust. Please, God, don't let him think he has High Altitude Pulmonary Edema.

'I'm – well, I'm . . .' He wiped his palms against the thighs of his chinos. 'I'm having a Halloween party tomorrow night.'

Did her face show panic? 'That's fine, the noise won't bother me. Thanks for letting me know.' She backed up another step.

'Some guys are coming – I mean, people from the firm.'

The firm was Compurama, the computer store where he worked. He wasn't a rich man. He was a housesitter for the owners of the mansion, who were away in Italy for nine months. She never saw him without his Compurama nametag on his shirt.

'I was – it's . . . well, you're invited to the party. Costume optional, but most people are coming as their *World of Warcraft* avatars.'

He glanced furtively at her chest. She presumed *World of Warcraft* contained a sexy elf in a ragged deerskin bikini. Then he seemed to realize that she didn't play the online sword 'n' sorcery game. His eyes filled with shining desperation.

He stuck out his hands in a *no worries* gesture. 'But that's totally up to you.'

'Thanks. I may have to work.'

'No problem. Just let me know.'

And he smiled so innocently, like a baby harp seal, that she felt guilty. She caved.

'I'll try. How about if I stop by? With dip?'

'Splendid.'

She began walking backward, giving him a small wave. He returned it, head tilted, and grabbed the door to go into Java Jones. She spun around.

'One question,' he said.

'I have to go . . .' But if she did, when she came home he would be watching for her from his balcony. She turned back around.

He touched his nose. 'My septum.'

'A deviated septum cannot cause tuberculosis. Really. I know for sure.'

To hear Ferd tell it, his deviated septum had variously been the culprit behind his snoring, halitosis, poor posture and recurrent anxiety.

'With planning the party, it's been acting up.' He put his fingertips to his cheeks. 'I get this pressure. What if it triggers a panic attack and my whole sinus system seizes up?'

'Ask your doctor, Ferd.'

'But—'

'You know my rule. I don't treat friends.'

'Just this once—'

'I don't prescribe for them, either.'

'This isn't about prescription decongestants.'

'Good.'

'You wouldn't be prescribing drugs. It's a whole different approach to anxiety management. Nature's way. It would be an emotional support prescription.'

Not hug therapy again. She watched for his arms to shoot toward her. Please, not that. 'Ferd, your own doctor needs to handle it. I have to jet.'

His brow creased. 'Okay.'

She waved goodbye. His face softened again into baby-seal affection. She suspected that as she walked away, his eyes were on her rear end.

Ten feet around the corner, she got out her cellphone. She found the number for Gregory Harding. She paused a moment before making the call.

Harding was Callie's ex-husband, but still close enough that he'd been the one they called to identify her body. Jo gazed at the sky and straightened her shoulders before she dialed.

It was answered on the second ring. 'Yes?'

'Mr Harding?' She introduced herself and explained that she was a forensic psychiatrist consulting for the police department. 'I'm sorry for your loss.'

'Wasn't my loss, it was hers. Why are you calling?'

Tick. There was resentment in that answer. 'I'd like to talk to you. Is there some time today we could meet?'

He paused. 'The cops want to make Callie out to be a head case – is that what this is about?'

'No, sir. It's about gathering evidence to accurately explain her death.'

There was a longer pause. 'I have an office in Palo Alto. There's a coffee place by Borders on University. I'll be there in two hours.'

She checked her watch. 'Fine.'

'Be on time.' He clicked off.

Perry Ames sat alone at a table. The sun was garish, the day breezy. Plenty of people would be outside, but he sat indoors by himself, with a Scrabble board set up, watching the television on the wall.

Three dead in the crash, the news was reporting. No names yet, but he knew Callie Harding was one of them. A passenger was injured.

He needed to know who that passenger was.

He set Scrabble tiles on the rack. Two men walked by, talking. They stared at the game board and at him. He'd take them on if they were willing. He could arrange a killer game. Take bets, run it big, like the poker game. An executive game, sure – people would be even less suspicious of Scrabble nerds than they were of high rollers playing Texas Hold 'em in a downtown hotel suite. And Scrabble players would be even easier to intimidate if they took a long line of credit, got over-extended and lost big. His bread and butter at times in his life.

Nobody offered to join the game. Nobody wanted to talk to him. He moved the tiles around.

*Doctor.* Yoshida was a proper name, so he didn't bother with that. *Son. Overdose.*

The satisfaction burned in his chest, like acid.

*Boat.* He crossed another word with it, going down. *Maki.* Screw the rules, he liked seeing their proper names. *Willets.*

The A-list fashion queen was dead and so was his shrieking weed of a boyfriend. Crankhead, skinny as a flower-stem, sadistic as all fuck. Pouted like a lily but poisonous. Like all of them.

But Perry had found a sure-fire weed killer.

The men who had walked past him sat down at a nearby table with cups of coffee. It was noisy in here. He couldn't hear what they were saying, but they were gawking at him. Fucks. They stared, hard glares. Looking at his neck, and the scar. Nobody wanted to join a game with the freak.

For a second he considered setting them straight. But this place had a guard, a fat guy loitering near the door with his thumbs hooked on his belt. A real wannabe-hard-ass lard-ass, dressed in a puke-green uniform. Where'd they get that color? Some store that made clothes for officious dicks like priests and prison guards?

The coffee drinkers stared. Perry stared back. They looked away, like submissive dogs.

Fear. Good. Blessed are the meek, for they shall inherit jack shit.

He set out another name on the game board. *Harding.*

It was a good start.

But he wasn't near the end, and time was short. He wanted answers by tomorrow. He had meetings downtown, and needed names by then.

He needed Skunk to get to work. He swept the tiles back into the box and stood up. He glanced at the coffee drinkers. He decided to set them straight after all.

He walked by their table. Pausing, he waited until they looked at him. He reached into his pocket. They went still. He took out his voice synthesizer and pressed it to his crushed larynx.

'Next time, we'll play Hangman. I never lose.'

The Intensive Care Unit at St Francis Hospital was bright and hushed. The nurse at the desk, motherly in pink scrubs, was writing on a patient's chart when Jo came up the stairs. Jo was wearing a badge around her neck that identified her as a physician with staff privileges at the hospital.

'Angelika Meyer?' she said.

The nurse pointed over her shoulder. 'Down the hall.'

'How's she doing?'

'Serious but stable. Broken ribs, punctured lung, hairline skull fracture.'

'Is she conscious?'

'Intermittently.'

'Has anybody been to see her?' Jo said.

'Just the police, and the attending kept them out of her room.'

'May I see her chart?'

The nurse found it. Jo flipped through. Though Meyer's condition had stabilized, her situation was precarious. She could still slip into the abyss.

'We found a key ring in her purse,' the nurse said. 'It has her nickname on it. Geli.'

She pronounced it the German way. *Gaily.*

'Thanks.' Taking the chart with her, Jo walked down the hall to Meyer's room.

Intensive Care never changed. Day or night, it had an atmosphere of controlled crisis. The quiet, the vigilance, the monitors and watchfulness – ICU felt to Jo like the staging ground for a Special Forces mission.

ER was a different story. From her trauma rotation at UCSF she remembered the noise, the adrenaline, the way dog bites and flu could abruptly be replaced by drownings and gunshot wounds. ER was shock and awe. ICU was a stealth campaign. But people died here in greater proportion, because you didn't come to ICU unless you were in bad shape.

And Geli Meyer looked damned bad.

Jo paused in the doorway. Propped in the hospital bed, sprouting tubes, Meyer looked like one of the aliens in the research lab in *Independence Day*. She had ECG suckers stuck to her chest and a central line IV inserted near her neck. A Foley catheter, a drain in her side, oxygen cannulas under her nose – she looked like a porcupine. Her skin was pallid gray, her blonde hair ropy. Her eyes were closed.

Quietly Jo crossed to her side.

She put her fingers to the young woman's wrist. Her pulse felt strong and regular. She stroked Meyer's hand, hoping for a response, but the girl lay motionless. Her hand was cold. Jo pulled up the thermal blanket and tucked it comfortably around Meyer's legs.

What happened to you, girl? Why were you in the car with Callie Harding? What is it you want me to stop?

She walked over and opened the small closet. Meyer's shoes and skirt were inside. No shirt or bra. They must have been cut off in the ER. Meyer's purse sat on a shelf.

Jo glanced out the door. The nurse was on the phone.

Jo wasn't a cop. She had no search warrant, and rifling a patient's belongings was far beyond frowned upon. But she wasn't a thief either, and Meyer wasn't talking. Maybe her possessions could talk in her stead. Jo glanced again at the nurse. She opened the bag and took everything out.

Pink lipstick, breath mints, lighter, grocery list. No cellphone. She opened the wallet, found a driver's license, two credit cards, eighty dollars in cash.

One photo, a snapshot of a man who had a Kansas farmer's weather-beaten face and a smile so cool he looked like he was auditioning for *Reservoir Dogs*. His thumbs were hooked over a belt with a gigantic silver buckle, rodeo-size, shaped like a casino chip. Tarantino Gothic.

Older brother? Boyfriend? No name or date, no way to contact him. Dead end. She put everything back.

She picked up Meyer's black skirt, reached in the pocket and felt a slick piece of paper. It was an album sleeve from a CD. The All American Rejects, *Move Along*. It contained the lyrics to the songs on the album. One song had been circled in black pen.

Jo blinked, and her breath snagged.

*Dirty Little Secret.*

She knew the song, could hear it in her head, the playground taunt of the melody and the singer's teasing, conspiratorial tone. The final line of the chorus had been highlighted with bright yellow marker: *Who has to know?*

A note was scrawled across the page in black ink. *Callie, this is what you were talking about, isn't it?*

And below that: *Can anybody play?*

With a smiley face drawn next to it.

Jo compared the handwriting to that on the grocery list. They matched. She returned to the bedside. Meyer lay still and silent.

'Geli, I want to help you. I wish you could help me.'

She might as well have been talking to the sky. After a minute she returned Meyer's chart to the nurses' station. She asked for a sealable plastic bag, an adhesive label and a black Sharpie. Putting on her toughest I'm-a-doc face, she held up the All American Rejects album sleeve for the nurse to see.

'This is evidence relating to the crash.' She put it in the plastic bag.

The nurse scowled. 'Where did you get that?'

'It needs to go to the police.' She sealed the bag, stuck the label across the seal, signed and dated the label. She handed the Sharpie to the nurse. 'You need to sign it as well. You're my witness that I've created a chain of custody.'

The woman looked dubious.

'Please,' Jo said.

Grudgingly, the nurse signed.

'Thanks.' Jo put the plastic bag in her satchel. It was an ad hoc solution, but it would have to do. 'Page me if Meyer regains consciousness.'

The nurse's look said that nobody expected that to happen soon.

Skunk honked the horn. Traffic on California was spastic. Loud, shiny, jerking along, slowing and pumping like blood through a clogged artery – idiots, crowding him. The sun felt like a deliberate poke in his eyes.

The Cadillac cruised east. Skunk drove with the window down, one elbow propped on the sill, right hand hanging on the top of the wheel. He felt more than saw heads turn as he motored along.

This was the way the prosecutor had run. Along California Street, blasting across the flats, blowing that big-ass BMW engine wide open over the hills, until she turned and drove into the bridge railing and died. He clenched his jaw. She was dead, absolutely stone stiff, ain't-coming-back-from-it dead. And that was good. That was a kitty treat. But he couldn't shake his nerves, this worry that felt like an itch under his skin, and that fucking sun was really annoying him, glaring off the hood of the car and the dashboard and the cherry-red leather of the big bench seat. Sports talk buzzed at him. He sank lower behind the wheel and turned up the radio. When he stopped at a red light, people in the crosswalk stared the car up and down.

The Caddy was a 1959 Eldorado, pimped out, and people gawked at it like it was a naked stripper idling in the middle of the street. It was cream-colored, with gleaming flanks that ran long and smooth all the way back to a pair of sharp fins. Real space-age, stab-your-eye-out chrome fins, which were punctuated with a pair of jet-nozzle tail lights, in titty red. This was the ultimate car, the biggest, baddest bitch on the road, power and sex on wheels, the Pamela Anderson of vehicles.

He loved it. When he sat behind the wheel, he *became* the car, because everybody in the city looked, and not one of them ever saw him.

Cross traffic spattered past. The radio was moaning about the Forty-Niners and their blowout loss to Chicago. Bad coaching, injured linemen, and the quarterback had thrown three interceptions.

'Pussy,' Skunk said.

He'd lost money on the game. The team stank, couldn't even beat a ten-point spread. The only guy putting it out there was the 'Niners', wide receiver, and Skunk didn't like the talk-jocks praising this pretty college boy white kid who grew up in luxury and got a business degree, even if he had hauled down four touchdown passes in the past two weeks.

'Rich pussy.' He leaned toward the radio. 'Scott Southern is a P-U-S-S-Y.'

Skunk was himself a white guy who hadn't grown up in luxury, hadn't gone to college, wouldn't be opening a string of sports-themed restaurants on the back of his luck and fame when he retired from the game in a few years. Skunk had been cheated. Cheated out of height and looks, cheated out of charm and the velvet tongue that lubricated a path through the world for people like Scott Southern.

Skunk believed in resentment.

Resentment was a mighty engine, a force that drove him to make things right. When the world cheats you, then getting back at the people who got the portion you deserve – that's just evening out the scales. Some folks called it sour grapes. But he loved sour things, and feasting on resentment was the sourest of all, and very, very satisfying.

The prosecutor's death was unsatisfying. Because of the passenger.

She was still alive. Three dead, the news was reporting this morning. That meant Harding plus the two crushed people in the front seat of the airport shuttle van. He'd seen them haul Harding's passenger from the wreck and put her in the ambulance. He'd been sure she was a goner, and then that dark-haired woman came running like a banshee and jumped on the wreck and hollered for the paramedics. They got Angelika Meyer out of the BMW and drove off like a house on fire.

He'd seen it from the parking garage on Stockton Street, the one overlooking the tunnel. It made his guts tighten. Because Perry was going to be furious. At *him*.

Pray, he thought. Pray, you got what you wanted. Harding, dead.

But Perry had been specific about what else he wanted: get the names of the leaders of the group from Harding. And don't blow it. But the whole thing had gone butt-ass wrong. Harding shouldn't have taken a passenger. *She* had screwed things up. Skunk was going to get the blame, but Harding was the one who blew it. And Angelika Meyer was the result. She'd become a leftover, like a trail of grease spilled on the road. Dangerous if left there, and dirty, and liable to make further mess. Grease spots were what made things spin out of control.

The light turned green. Slowly he pulled out, the Caddy crossing the intersection regally, like a great white shark. The radio kept whining at him.

Pussies. Cheaters.

Things needed cleaning up. That meant it was going to get dirty again.

# 8

Jo drove down 101 toward Palo Alto feeling pensive. Her truck was a blue Toyota Tacoma, dinged up but so rugged that it would probably still be running after she herself was buried and part of the fossil record. It had been Daniel's, which is why she'd never gotten around to hammering out the dents and scratches along the side. He put them there on their last climbing trip to Yosemite, driving stupid the night they camped in Tuolumne Meadows. He threatened to tell people she'd done it mauling him in a fit of passion. *You're a wild woman*, he said. *A crazy thing*. Then he laughed.

She knew he wasn't coming back to fix them, but they were knocks she liked living with.

She glanced at her satchel lying on the passenger seat. *Dirty Little Secret*. She'd left a message for Lieutenant Amy Tang about Geli Meyer's note. *Can anybody play?* She didn't know what to make of it. But she felt a disturbing certainty that Callie Harding had seen the note, understood Meyer's message, and acted on it.

*Play* implied a game. It implied a certain innocence, an expectation that the game might be dirty but fun. But secrets weren't always innocent. Dirty could mean dangerous.

She didn't think the note was a coincidence. She feared that Geli Meyer had badly miscalculated something. And had gone from drawing smiley faces to fighting for her life inside Callie's speeding car.

She signaled and pulled off the freeway.

Palo Alto was thirty miles south of San Francisco. Green and quietly swanky, the town buzzed with intellectual energy. It was next door to Stanford University, in the heart of Silicon Valley. In boom times, that meant careworn ranch homes sold for a million dollars. When markets went bust, it meant tow trucks prowled high-tech parking lots looking for Ferraris to repossess.

She cruised along University Avenue. Under the October sun, the street was bustling. College town vigor was overlaid with a geek-chic vibe. Old-fashioned beauty salons sat comfortably near the Apple store, that cathedral of the new millennium. She saw the downtown branch of the Stanford bookstore. She'd parsed out her meager funds there during medical school.

The coffee place was set back from the street in a shady Spanish-style arcade. She walked up at ten-twenty, propping her sunglasses on top of her head. A man with Nordic-blue eyes looked at her, down at his watch, and at her again. He tossed his *Wall Street Journal* on the table and followed her approach.

She held out her hand. 'Jo Beckett. Thank you for meeting me.'

'I thought you were going to be late.' His handshake was as brusque as his tone. Accusatory, though she was early.

Gregory Harding looked as pale and sharp as a shot of vodka. His hair was so blond it was nearly polar. His eyes were the chill blue of his dress shirt. The watch was a Rolex. Lean and tall, he bore himself like a birch switch. He had the confident detachment of the very wealthy. But his expression was ragged.

'You have a badge to show me?' he said.

She sat down. 'I'm not a police officer.'

She handed him her card. He read it, dropped it on his *WSJ* and looked her up and down. She had dressed up. She was wearing a navy-blue wraparound blouse and brown wool slacks over low-heeled boots. Silver hoop earrings. Her hair was pulled back with a barrette, wrangling her curls into submission. Harding's eyes, however, were drawn to the silver chain around her neck, with the cross and white-gold ring.

He gave her the same look Lieutenant Tang had given her the night before: what are you?

It wasn't the dusky light in the arcade. People had a hard time pinning her down. A hint of Asia here, maybe a cherry blossom.

Echo of a desert wind there, swords and sand and wailing music in a dusty ruin.

'Can we talk about your ex-wife?' she said.

'Why do the cops want a shrink to pry open Callie's head? What's the rush to judgment?'

'I'm not judging. And I'm sorry if this is painful.'

'Sure you're judging. You presume she killed herself. What if she had an aneurysm? How do you know her brakes didn't fail?'

'I don't. That's why it's important to gather all the information we can. I take it you don't think she committed suicide.'

'Not for a single second. Not Callie.'

There was a softness at the edge of his voice, and the slightest crack. And she sensed, in one burst, that he wasn't hostile. He was exhausted and jagged, barely holding it together.

He stood up. 'She lived around the corner. I'll show you her place.'

They headed out of the arcade. His stride was quick, and he walked with his hands jammed into the pockets of his chinos.

'How long were you married?' Jo said.

'Five years. Divorced seven.' He pointed a thumb toward Stanford. 'She was in law school, I was getting a JD/MBA.' He glanced at her. 'That's a four-year program, law and business school combined.'

'I know the JD/MBA program. I went to Stanford med school.'

He nodded, as if acknowledging her as part of some tribal fellowship. 'She went into law, I became a venture capitalist. We married, we broke up. No kids, no pets, no rock and roll. It was a grad school thing that wasn't built to last.' He jammed his hands deeper into his pockets. 'In the long run we managed to be decent friends.'

He glanced at her, seemingly seeking confirmation that he didn't sound weird. 'You married?'

'No.'

'Ever been?'

'Yes.'

'So you understand how things get complicated afterward.'

She looked at the trees. 'What was she like?'

'Sharp.' The edge came back to his voice. 'I mean that in a good way. Brilliant, calculating, driven. It made her a successful lawyer.'

'I understand she was on her way up in the US Attorney's Office.'

'Like a rocket. She thrived on her job. And every bad guy she put away, she regarded as a W in her own personal win column.' This time his voice discernibly fractured. 'So killing herself would only prevent her from running up the score. No way she'd do that.'

'When did you last speak to her?'

'Two days ago. She sounded fine.'

They turned the corner and headed into a residential neighborhood overhung with oaks and sycamores. Harding nodded at a row of elegant townhouses and took a key from his pocket.

'Here.'

They crossed a manicured lawn to a red-lacquered front door. He stuck the key in the lock.

'For a divorced couple, you two maintained close ties,' Jo said.

'I watered her plants when she was gone.'

'She listed you as her next of kin.'

'Neither of us have family. It seemed . . . efficient. I never thought I'd have to . . .'

He deflated. His hand went to his eyes. 'Sorry.'

Identifying her body must have been horrifying. 'I know this is difficult,' Jo said.

Shaking his head, he pushed the door open and gestured for Jo to go in. She walked through the entryway and stopped, gathering an initial impression.

The townhouse was airy, minimalist, with black leather furniture under a cathedral ceiling. An upstairs gallery overlooked the living-room. Jo could picture Callie standing there, blonde and glamorous, arms outstretched like Eva Peron. The place was elegant, simple and cold. The carpet, white as a nun's wimple, was immaculate.

*dirty*

'Have you been in here since the police notified you of her death?' she said.

'No.' He stood motionless in the entryway.

'Let me explain what I need to do.'

She led him through it. Got him to sit down in the living-room and asked the questions on her list. Had Callie ever had psychiatric treatment or diagnosis? No. Any family history of suicide or mental disorder? None. Harding answered her queries with flat resignation. Callie had no history of serious illness. She wasn't seeing anybody romantically, so far as he knew. She wasn't religious.

'She just had a Puritan work ethic. She was abstemious and judgmental. A perfect prosecutor.'

He hadn't observed any changes in her eating habits. Had seen no signs that she was cutting herself off from people. No signs that she was giving away her possessions.

'She wasn't preparing herself for death. She was working hard. Driving forward.' He stopped, realizing what he'd just said, and pinched the bridge of his nose. 'Give me a minute.'

'Take your time. If you don't mind, I'm going to look around.'

'Go ahead.'

The kitchen was a chrome emporium full of heart healthy cookbooks. One bottle of Pinot Grigio, half-full, was in the fridge. The only drugs in the cabinet were Tylenol and Advil.

A bookcase in the living-room held a smorgasbord of bestsellers. Callie's music collection stressed cheesy Nashville hits and musical theater. Jo didn't count the *Wicked* soundtrack as a red flag. Or as a serious indicator of erotic fantasies lurking under the surface.

Taking her digital camera, she went upstairs. The master bed-room was plush. The closet held expensive suits and expensive shoes. The dresser drawers held expensive underwear. Expensive, lacy, racy underwear. There were animal-print garter belts and fishnet stockings. Still, that wasn't *outré*. No sex toys, no whips or bridles. No secret S&M dominatrix closet.

She searched the bathroom. No narcotics, no pills – except contraceptives. So maybe Gregory Harding didn't know every-thing about Callie's love life.

She kept searching. Nothing else.

Harding watched her come back down the stairs. 'Find a suicide note?'

'No.'

That wasn't probative. Most suicides don't leave a note.

She went to Callie's home office, sat down at the desk and started the computer. Harding stopped in the doorway.

'How can you do this work?' he said.

She swiveled to face him. It was an important question. She gave him her full attention.

'The dead can't speak for themselves. But sometimes I can speak for them.'

'Don't you mean put words in their mouths? They're gone.'

'When somebody dies, they're not simply gone. They're an absence. And when the cause of death is unclear, it leaves a huge hole of uncertainty as well as grief. Uncovering the truth about someone's life and death brings that person more fully present to those left behind. And it helps fill that hole.'

'The truth can hurt.'

'It can put the ground back beneath survivors' feet,' she said. 'And it can help people say goodbye.'

His hawk's gaze held her. 'You lost somebody.'

She didn't need to answer. Almost imperceptibly, he nodded.

She turned back to the desk. 'I want to reconstruct Callie's final twenty-four hours. Did she keep a calendar, or a journal?'

'Beats me. Take a look.'

In the bottom drawer Jo found notebooks and a pocket calendar. She flipped through it. The month ahead was busy with appointments Callie would never keep.

It was time to dig deeper. She gauged Harding's body language: exhausted and tense. She started at the periphery.

'What was Callie's personality? Was she calm? Excitable? Violent?'

'Violent?' He laughed harshly. 'Give me a break. She put violent offenders in prison.'

'That can coarsen a person.' As part of her forensic psychiatry training, Jo had worked at San Quentin. She'd seen plenty of callous, violent prison staff.

'It made her tough, not coarse,' he said. 'She hated violence. Hated criminals. Hated men who hurt women. She punished people like that.'

She thought of Callie's final minutes, of her plea for help. 'Did she express any fears to you? Any worries about people harassing her? Had anybody threatened her?'

He shook his head. 'No. Besides, if anybody threatened her, she'd unleash a SWAT team on them. She'd have their balls for breakfast.'

'Did she have premonitions?'

'No.'

'Dreams?'

'In her dreams she was Attorney General.' A smile touched his lips. 'What Callie wanted, she went after. Relentlessly. Some people thought she held grudges. I called it tenacity.'

His smile dimmed. He turned away from Jo's gaze and wandered to a bookshelf.

'Anything else? Fantasies?' she said.

He picked up a photograph in a silver frame. He blew dust from it and brushed his fingers over the glass.

'Mr Harding? Did Callie have fantasies?'

He glanced up. His blue eyes were shining. 'What kind of fantasies?'

'Any kind.'

His voice turned wary. 'Sexual, you mean?'

She kept her own voice level. 'Any kind of fantasy.'

His mouth tightened. 'Her fantasies involved super-max sentencing for repeat offenders. She had no sexual imagination. And for your report, she liked it face-to-face, twice a week, with a shower afterward.'

He stared, waiting to see if he'd shocked her.

'Did she think sex was dirty?' Jo said.

Harding's Nordic complexion turned even whiter. 'No.'

'Did Callie think *she* was dirty?'

He seemed to recoil, as though the question had genuinely shocked him. 'No. What the hell is that supposed to mean?'

'I don't mean to upset you.'

'Callie, dirty? My God, she was beautiful. She had a face designed by Michelangelo. And now she's—'

He turned away and put a hand over his eyes.

She hesitated, trying to judge whether she could ease him back down. But things came quickly after that.

The browser history loaded. Jo saw an entire page of hits for news stories.

*Maki, Lover Dead.*

*Burning Boat Tragedy: Fashion World Mourns.*

*Noted Physician David Yoshida Dead at 52.*

*Heart Attack Fells Cardiac Surgeon.*

On and on. Nothing but Yoshida and Maki. She paused at the next headline.

*'Broken Heart' Over Son's Death Kills UCSF Doctor?*

She heard an inarticulate cry. She looked up and saw Harding punch the bookshelf with the flat of his hand. He fought a sob, mouth open. He was staring at the framed photo.

He swung an arm at the bookshelf and swept a row of books to the floor. She put her hands flat on the desk. He spun and hurled the photo across the room.

Jo ducked. It flew straight past her head and thwacked the wall like an axe-head.

'Hey,' she said.

Harding swooped across the room and pulled the keyboard away from her. 'Get out.'

'Mr Harding—'

'Now.' He was coming around the desk.

She jumped to her feet before he could grab the chair or touch her. 'Close enough.'

He brought himself up short, a foot from her. A vein was throbbing in his temple.

'Please step back,' she said.

He held still. She saw the photo on the floor. Behind the cracked glass was a picture of Callie and Harding together. She met his eyes. They were red and wet.

He backed up, giving her space, but was still standing between her and the door.

'If you don't mind,' she said.

He held still for two seconds, and three, and five. Quietly, as if extreme quiet was the only way to control his voice, he said, 'She was perfect. And now she's dust. What am I going to do?'

'I'm sorry, Mr Harding. Now I'd like to go.'

He raised his hands. 'Forget it. Just write your report, say whatever you want.' He grabbed the notebooks from the desk. 'Take it all. Read them, interpret them, x-ray them, whatever. You won't find anything.'

He shoved them into her hands and waved her out of the office. She headed straight out the front door, slamming it behind her.

Dammit.

A hundred yards from the townhouse, Jo looked back. How had that turned so nasty?

Holding your ground, that she'd learned when facing drugged-up, bipolar gang members in therapy, and angry psychotics who ranted about the prophet Elijah, and before that, shoving back against boys who said she couldn't skateboard or ride BMX. She'd learned it way back on the playground as a kid.

*Get right back in their face, and fast.* It had become muscle memory. You can talk your way out of things, but not if you're flat on the deck.

But having a venture capitalist physically intimidate her over psychological autopsy questions? She hadn't seen it coming.

Dammit.

The sidewalk was clear behind her. There was no sign of Gregory Harding, just dappled sunlight and a lawn sprinkler lazily tossing water in an arc. Her heart was thumping. She slowed her breathing. Don't get angry.

She got angry. How dare he? Jerk. Prick.

Back in the truck, she locked the doors and took two minutes to scribble notes while the encounter was still bright in her mind. Jackass. Dick. Was he aggressive, or simply grief-stricken and subject to poor impulse control? Was he hiding something? She wrote down what he'd said about Callie. Sharp. Judgmental. Punished people. *Have their balls for breakfast.*

She lifted her pen from the page. Can you say castrating woman?

Harding didn't act like he'd lost a decent friend. He acted like he'd lost a woman he still loved and loathed. And he seemed bereft.

Her fatigue, temporarily suppressed by caffeine and adrenaline, now broke again like a wave. She rubbed her eyes. She couldn't let this get to her.

Leaning her head back, she thought about the long list of articles Callie had been reading about David Yoshida and, especially, about Maki burning to death on his sailboat.

She was only ten miles from Moffett Field. She got on the phone and called the headquarters of the 129th Air Rescue Wing.

As the phone rang, she looked at Callie's notebooks on the passenger seat. She flipped one open. A bunch of papers slid out. She grabbed them before they fell to the floor.

She stopped still in the golden sunlight. Under her hand was a sheet of high-quality stationery. It was an invitation, and it had Callie's neat handwriting on it. In faultless script, at the center of the page, was a single line.

*You've been very bad. Welcome to the Dirty Secrets Club.*

# 9

Jo drove through the gate at Moffett Field. Her mind was else-where.

The Dirty Secrets Club. Was it a joke? Was it the source of the game Geli Meyer wanted to play?

Did it have anything to do with Callie Harding's death?

She thought about David Yoshida, Maki, Callie – and Geli Meyer begging *Stop it*. She felt a crawling certainty that somebody else was in line to get hurt, and soon.

The smell of aviation fuel brought her back harshly.

Moffett Field is a massive installation beside San Francisco Bay. Originally a naval air station, today the airfield hosts Onizuka Air Force Station and NASA's Ames Research Facility. It's where NASA monitors satellite and shuttle launches. It looked like a college campus, with green lawns and Spanish-style buildings cloistered around a quad. But out near the runway, on the sharp end of the business, was the 129th Air Rescue Wing.

Jo pulled up in front of the Wing's utilitarian headquarters building. A giant Hercules aircraft and a couple of Pave Hawk helicopters were parked nearby. As part of the California Air National Guard, the wing did double duty. Its peacetime mission was SAR – search and rescue, on land and at sea, often in the most dangerous circumstances. Its military mission was CSAR. Combat search and rescue. In wartime it became an arm of the Air Force's pararescue service. The people who served here were tough and dedicated. The PJs, pararescuemen, were the élite of the service, medics who would rappel, skydive or leap into boiling seas in the middle of a firefight to evacuate casualties. Its motto was painted on the doors of the hangar, six feet high: That Others May Live.

This was the unit that had been called out to the rough ocean west of the Golden Gate the night Maki Prichingo's boat caught fire.

Jo parked the truck and sat for a moment, staring at the head-quarters building. Just stay even. Walk through that door and do your job. Does this have to be hard?

'As if you didn't know,' she said, and got out.

A salt breeze was blowing off the bay. It was cold, and carried the greasy punk of jet exhaust. She slammed the door, locked the truck, and saw Gabriel Quintana walk out of the building toward her.

He was wearing civvies – jeans, hiking boots, a white thermal under a black work shirt – and his stride was relaxed. He had to be heading off duty. His eyes were hidden behind cool-dude shades, and told her nothing of what he was thinking.

He smiled. 'Doctor Beckett.'

It was an unguarded smile, welcoming and warm. He looked lean and athletic, but then PJs were supposed to be inhumanly fit. The way he walked was effortless to the point of grace. His brown hair was short but riding the outer limits of Air Force regulation.

She strolled toward him. 'Looking a little shaggy, Sergeant.'

The smile broadened. 'I'm all about rebellion. So go wild, call me Mister.'

That was a surprise. 'You mustered out?'

'Completed my tour. Staying on as a civilian.'

He stopped three feet from her, the smile lingering on his face. His tranquility was electric.

'You're looking well,' he said.

'You too.' He seemed taller than she recalled. 'I need to talk to you. It's about the burning boat.'

The smile faded. He took his time answering. 'There's a place across the freeway in Mountain View. Enchiladas verdes. I'm starved. I haven't eaten since last night.'

She looked at her watch, flustered.

'I can talk if I eat,' he said. 'My treat.'

Behind her, an aircraft started its engines. She stared at him, debating. The plane's propellers cycled up to a loud drone. It seemed to be right at her back, and felt as though a blade was spinning over her neck.

'It's on me,' she said.

He didn't move, didn't comment on how long it had been, on the circumstances under which they had last seen each other. But she sensed that he knew she hated the sound of aircraft engines, and that she felt lost standing there on that tarmac. He pulled his keys from his jeans pocket.

'I'll follow you,' she said.

His smile returned, as if he knew that was unlikely to happen.

The Mexican place was a *taquería* in an old section of Mountain View. The décor consisted of picnic tables under a corrugated metal awning. Mariachi music blared from a transistor radio. On the plus side, it boasted a view of the train tracks. The Caltrain plowed by, loud and huge. Quintana leaned on the counter, waiting for their food.

Jo raised her voice to be heard over the thunder of the locomotive. 'Maki Prichingo. Tell me about what happened that night.'

From behind his sunglasses he watched the cooks in the kitchen. 'The call came in Saturday at nineteen hundred hours. An oil tanker spotted a boat on fire west of the Golden Gate. They tried to raise it via radio. Got no joy so they alerted the authorities.'

'How'd you get the call?'

He smiled thinly. 'We didn't. The Coast Guard got the call.'

The Coast Guard and the 129th sometimes scrapped for turf. The rivalry was fed by pride, adrenaline, and the desire to help. Doctors were no different.

'But the Coasties' birds were tied up with a rescue in the bay. We sortied at nineteen-twenty. Single Pave Hawk with two PJs aboard, one of them being me.'

The cook set their food on the counter. Quintana's order could have served a family of five. He piled it onto his forearm and both hands like a waiter, and carried it to their table. Jo observed, amused. It seemed impossible that one human being could consume it, especially a man with three per cent body fat.

He unloaded it. 'What?'

'Who's all that food for, Sasquatch? And Sasquatch's rugby team?'

'Night training last night. Mountain SAR.'

Jo sat down. Her two taquitos looked like a dollhouse meal next to his banquet. Quintana dug in, downing an enchilada in four bites.

'Weather was good, and we had a fix on the sailboat's location. The pilots were flying with night vision goggles, but didn't need them. We saw the fire from miles away.'

'The boat was still burning?'

'The fire had died down, but clearly the boat had been fully involved. The pilot couldn't raise anybody aboard by radio. We descended to the water on a fast rope and swam over. Aren't you going to eat?'

Absentmindedly she nodded. 'Then what?'

'There was a fixed ladder on the port side, and we climbed aboard.'

'With the boat on fire?'

He propped his sunglasses on top of his head. 'We're not the fire department. We weren't there to extinguish the blaze.'

His eyes were darker than brown, almost black. Weather and wear had deepened the laugh lines in his bronze skin. He looked completely intense and completely calm. She imagined he had looked exactly the same as he climbed on to Maki's blazing boat. She'd known he was cool under pressure from the moment she met him.

'It was a calculated risk but, honestly, not everything explodes the way it does in Hollywood movies. It was a sailboat. And if the vessel began to sink, well, I do know how to swim.'

He spread his hands, a *think about it* gesture.

To qualify as pararescuemen, recruits had to swim 1800 meters, part of it while fighting off instructors who were trying to drown them.

In spite of herself, she smiled. 'Sorry. You were saying?'

'The fire had almost burned itself out. The heat was intense, but that was a big mother of a boat, and the ladder was barely warm to the touch.'

He drank his iced tea and ate half of another enchilada. His face clouded. 'We found the victims next to each other in the main cabin.'

For the first time, he hesitated.

'Just tell me what you saw. Anything and everything,' she said.

He took his time, as though only reluctantly moving his mind back to the scene. 'One man, his face was still recognizable. Eyes open, mouth open, soot under his nose.'

So he'd been breathing smoke before he died. 'And the other?'

He glanced at nearby tables. None of the other customers was listening, but he lowered his voice.

'Burned beyond recognition. His body was half buried under debris, still smoking.'

'Pugilistic position?' she said.

'Yes.'

Burnt corpses often curl into a boxer's pose, with arms and fists tucked under the chin. It doesn't mean the victim had retreated in pain to a fetal position. The heat of the fire dehydrates the body's muscles and causes them to contract, often after death.

Quintana looked at the train tracks, and then at her. He had stopped looking at his food.

'I've seen choppers that were downed by enemy fire. They'd burned, the crew was injured or dead from blast wounds and shrapnel—' His voice stayed steady, but he seemed to be growing ever more still. 'I know what various catastrophic wounds look like.'

PJs were trained paramedics, experienced at performing triage and minor surgery in the field. She let him talk his way to the issue. A man at the next table eyed him.

'But it didn't take a medic to see what had happened on the boat. The fire didn't kill either of them.'

'Smoke inhalation?'

'Smoke exhalation, maybe.'

She gave him a quizzical look.

'From the shotgun,' he said. 'The one that blew their heads off.'

# 10

'They were shot to death?' Jo said.

Quintana eyed her carefully, as though framing his words to protect her from them. Or to protect himself from the memory.

'Blood and brain matter was sprayed all over the cabin wall. The shotgun was propped on one guy's lap, with the barrel jammed under his chin.'

'And the other man?'

'Side of the head, close range.'

It sounded like a classic example of murder-suicide. 'You're sure?'

'The shotgun was a twelve gauge. Ever seen *Terminator Two*?'

The man at the next table stood up. 'That's it.' He grabbed his plate. 'What's wrong with you people? You have any idea about how to behave around folks who aren't body snatchers?'

He stalked off in disgust. Abashed, Jo gave Quintana an *oops* expression. He raised a hand, chagrined, and called, 'Sorry.' The man kept going.

Quintana put a hand to his chest and feigned hurt feelings. 'I don't snatch bodies. I return them, almost always. And you only excavate their brains.'

'And not even with a shovel,' she said.

He smiled, but only briefly. She set down her fork. She wasn't hungry anymore.

The burning boat: two men, two blasts to the head. Paired deaths, Lieutenant Tang had called them.

Could it be anything besides murder-suicide? Double suicide, or perhaps double murder? Could the boat have been boarded by attackers? Had somebody else killed Maki and William Willets and staged it to look like a lovers' death pact?

She took out her notebook and a pen. 'What did he look like –
the man holding the shotgun on his lap?'

Quintana raised an eyebrow.

'Aside from dead,' she said.

'Forties, East Asian. Shaved head, what was left of it.'

Maki. That suggested the fashion designer had shot Willets,
then himself.

'Did you see anything else on board – anything that could help
explain what happened?' she said.

'Saw it, smelled it, felt the heat.'

'Of what?'

'Gasoline.'

'From the fuel tank?'

'Everywhere. On the deck, in the cabin.'

'Arson?' She wondered if Maki had shot Willets, set the boat on
fire and then ended his own life. 'You think the gasoline was used
as an accelerant?'

'And more. I think somebody was playing a game.'

'What?' she said.

'We got off the boat, and fast. We couldn't help the victims, and
it was clearly a crime scene. We checked that nobody else was
aboard, then swam clear and the Pave Hawk hauled us out.'

His eyes were sharp, with the black gleam of arrowheads.
'Smoke was billowing from the boat, but the downwash from
our rotors blew it away and made the flames kick up again. I looked
down and saw it. On the deck of the boat. A word had been written
in gasoline and ignited.'

She seemed to feel a sharp finger scrape down her spine. 'What
word?'

'Pray.'

She felt clammy. *Pray*. It hit such a wrong note that she could
practically hear it, low and nauseating. And then the sound turned
real. It rolled under her thoughts and shifted the concrete beneath
her feet.

Her drink hopped. The picnic table slid sideways.

'Gabe.'

The table jerked back the other way. The corrugated roof began chattering.

She jumped to her feet. So did he. The roof flexed and bounced on the poles, keening as if in fright. She grabbed his arm and pulled him with her as she moved. Zero to outside, outside *now*, in two seconds. Into the sun, toward the parking lot, away from roofs, walls, power lines. The ground spasmed, back, forth.

'Jo. Whoa. Slow down.'

His arm was around her shoulder. He pulled her to a stop in the parking lot. She felt her fingers digging into his forearm, but couldn't get them to let go.

'Ride it out,' he said. 'We're okay.'

On the street, cars pulled to the curb. Telephone poles swayed. Phone lines and electrical cables swung back and forth as if playing a giant's game of Double Dutch.

She planted her feet wide, ground-surfing. Under the sawblade-moan of the corrugated roof, glass crashed to the concrete and shattered.

As quickly as it had started it faded away, until they were left standing tight against each other, holding their breath.

'Four pointer, max,' she said.

The quake had been nothing but a baby. At the *taquería* the other customers crawled out from under their tables. A young cook tentatively peeped over the counter.

'You don't go for duck-and-cover?' Gabe said.

Standard procedure was to dive under a table, or plant yourself in a doorway. Don't run outside, where falling masonry might kill you. But there were no bricks here, nothing to come down on top of them.

'Claustrophobia. I count on it as a self-preservation instinct,' she said. 'Experience.'

'You'll have to tell me about your experience sometime.'

Her experience was that catastrophe can happen, and to you. Reacting immediately when it hits puts you halfway to getting out alive.

'You can let go of my arm anytime you want,' he said.

'Oh.' She forced her fingers to release him.

He took out his cellphone and hit a speed dial number. Jo brushed her hair off her face. Adrenaline had flooded her system. She seemed to feel each air molecule that brushed her skin. And seemed to feel Gabe's arm around her shoulder, warm and solid, though he had stepped away.

He left a message on the phone. 'Sophie, I'm okay. Just making sure you are. Text me,' he said. 'Love you. See you at home.' He hung up. 'Listen, I should head back to Moffett in case they need me.'

'Of course.' Why didn't she like hearing that? Why did her face feel so hot?

He stilled, looking at her with concern, and put a hand on her arm. 'You all right?'

'I'm rockin'. Stick a quarter in the jukebox and let's shake, rattle and roll.' She smiled ruefully. 'I'm fine. But before you go – are you sure about the word you saw burning on the deck of the boat?'

'Sure as God made Sikorsky helicopters. P-r-a-y. I study the subject, so I'm positive.'

'Excuse me?'

'I'm in the doctoral program at USF. Theology.'

'You?'

His mouth skewed to one side. 'You mean, a killer like me? Hombre jumps out of planes with an M16 strapped to his back?'

'No. I mean—' Crap. What did she mean?

He smiled. 'My daughter's living with me. It's just the two of us, so I want to be in town and on the ground.' He got out his wallet and handed Jo a snapshot. 'Sophie.'

She was about nine years old, with hair the color of Hershey's Kisses and a smile that showed missing teeth. Her eyes were bright but shy.

'She's awesome.' She handed the photo back. 'I didn't know you had a daughter.'

He slipped it into his wallet. 'Like I didn't know you were going to go into forensic work.' He paused, and his voice quieted. 'You miss working in the ER?'

*That's not what I miss.*

The words were close enough to taste, and she bit them back. 'No. This is what I want to be doing.'

He put on his sunglasses and shoved his hands into the front pockets of his jeans. He paused another long moment.

'How are you?' he said.

In the crisp October sunlight, his black shirt seemed a hot void in front of her. She watched the rise and fall of his chest. For an overwhelming moment, she wanted to lay her head against his shoulder and whisper the truth. What did she miss? Waking up every morning next to a man she loved.

But her husband was dead, and neither prayer nor the firepower of the Air National Guard could bring him back.

'I'm good. I just miss Daniel like hell.'

She smiled and waved goodbye.

# II

*The network is busy, try again later.* The phone lines had gone schizo. Like always – shake the ground, people panic. The dial tone turns into *circuits freaking.*

Irked, Perry snapped the tiny phone shut and glanced at the walls. He saw no damage. Nothing on his desk had spilled or broken. The bay was a few yards away but he didn't hear waves lapping. Nobody was going to surf a tsunami through the building and sweep them all away.

The door was closed. Voices passed along the corridor outside. He eyed the door tensely, willing them to move out of earshot. He had only a five-minute window to contact Skunk. The voices faded and he flipped the phone open again. Redialed.

Ringing, finally.

'Boss?' Skunk said.

Perry pressed the voice synthesizer to his throat. He kept the volume low, so that the flat buzz wouldn't carry.

'The names. Did Harding give them up?'

He was owed. Harding and her playmates owed him. But he would never get what was due to him unless he discovered all their names. Harding had known, he was convinced of it, but she played things close to the vest. Prosecutors held on to information like it was gold – evidence, witnesses, everything.

'Skunk?' he said.

The line crackled. 'We got a problem. Harding took out two people in the airport shuttle van, but Angelika Meyer's alive.'

He closed his eyes and sat down. 'How did that happen?'

Skunk paused, almost like he had fumbled his voice, maybe along with his balls, into the back seat of that outrageous Cadillac.

Having Skunk frightened of him was a good thing. Having Skunk cringe like a small mammal was not. Perry needed information and he couldn't linger on the phone. Time was short.

'All I can think,' Skunk said, 'is that Harding was trying to protect the club. Hush hush, keep these people out of the limelight—'

'But we're going to find them.'

'I know we are. I tried, boss, I did. I got to the scene of the crash quick.'

Perry breathed. The robotic drone of the voice synthesizer stripped most emotion from his words. 'In the Cadillac?'

'Course not. I parked it out of sight and got down to the street on foot. I was the first one there.' Skunk's voice got stronger. 'I played Good Samaritan. Like I was the one willing to get up on that mess and check whether people were alive.'

'That was a risk.'

'Harding was no question dead. Couple guys in the airport van were moaning. Meyer was barely there.'

Perry stood up. 'Did she talk? Did you get anything from her?'

'I tried, but she just looked at me.'

He said nothing. Skunk didn't get it. 'So she saw you.'

Skunk hesitated, and then his voice had a splinter in it. 'I tried to fix that. I got the gun. I almost had time . . .' He exhaled. 'Cop came running up the street, looking freaked out and asking if anybody was alive. Man in the airport van started screaming. So I told him the women in the BMW were dead.'

'Did you think you were casting a spell? Telling him didn't make it happen.'

'The cop was right beside me, calling for doctors and backup and shit. I couldn't fucking shoot her in front of him.'

'That's good. We want Meyer alive.'

'Alive – why?'

Briefly his anger jumped up. Skunk didn't need to know everything. 'Alive for *now*. She might be useful. Leave it at that.'

'It wouldn't have worked anyway. The cop was totally freaked out, took a half-second look into the Beemer before he ran to the van. By then other people were coming. It was too late.'

Perry pinched the bridge of his nose. 'The first cop on the scene saw you?'

'It was one a.m. and pitch dark. I had on a hat. Nobody could recognize me. I melted back into the crowd.'

'Then?'

'It was a chain reaction. The paramedics showed up. The cop waved them to the van, and Meyer was still just laying there.'

'And you hoped she would simply die without attention?'

'It was bedlam, man. It almost worked, too. Then this other woman came, and out of the blue ran to the wreck going apeshit, calling the paramedics, fucking everything up.'

Perry thought about it. His gut was tight, but things might be all right. 'What's Meyer's condition?'

'I'll find out.'

'Do that. And listen to me. I don't want her to die.'

She was vital. Meyer worked in Harding's office. She was a bright spark, the do-gooder law student, all eyes and ears, eager to learn everything Callie Harding had to teach her.

'She may have the information we need,' he said.

He stopped in front of his desk. His Scrabble board was set up. He picked up a handful of tiles, thinking.

'Boss. I understand how important this is. We're going to find them. No question. We're going to make things right.'

Despite the tightness in his gut, Perry smiled. This was why he employed Skunk. The man could be stupid, but he was brutal and utterly reliable. Not just because of his greed, either. Skunk was outright loyal. He even believed in honor among thieves.

'They'll pay, boss. In full,' he said.

'Yes, they will.'

*Object lesson*. That's what they had called Perry Ames when they finished with him. They dropped the chain, threw down the crowbar, took everything and left him choking in his own blood. They laughed as they walked away. They were still laughing at him today, and they thought they were safe.

Honor? They couldn't spell the word if he shoved Scrabble tiles up their asses with a cattle prod. Yes, they were going to pay. If they all had to die. If the whole city of San Francisco had to die.

'I'll be downtown tomorrow afternoon. The Civic Center,' Perry said.

'Tomorrow's Halloween.'

His anger ignited so fast and hot that the room seemed to flare white. 'Is that a crack about me?'

'What?'

He rubbed the lumpy trail of scar tissue that ran around his neck. 'You calling me Frankenstein?'

'No, Jesus no – I just thought, Halloween, maybe it's a holiday.'

'At the courthouse? I'm dealing with the law, Levon – it never takes a holiday, you know that. It's always after your ass.'

'Fuckin' A, boss.'

His anger subsided. He thought for a moment. 'We're at a tipping point. We need to move faster. A prosecutor's death, so public – it's going to bring a huge law enforcement response.'

'What do you want me to do?'

'Talk to the wide receiver again.'

'Southern? He's a walking disaster zone. He can't cope.'

'Give him one more chance. Let him know it's now or never. He gives us the information or that's it. He'll either be our source, or be an example to the others.'

'An object lesson,' Skunk said.

'Precisely.'

'You got it, boss. What are you going to do?'

Perry placed the tiles on the board.

'Pray?' Skunk said.

'I don't do that any more. No, I'm going to work out. Then meet with the lawyers. Then I think I'll play Scrabble.'

He moved tiles around. *Carjack*, that worked. And – yeah, add letters here, triple word score. *Exsanguination*.

'Scrabble?' Skunk said.

It was time to cut off the call. Lingering on the phone any longer would be risky. Besides, this much talk was more than his throat could bear. Perry pressed the voice synthesizer one final time to his ruined larynx.

'Yes, Levon. I wish the rules let me turn *cocktail* into *Molotov cocktail,* but they don't.' He dropped the rest of the tiles on the board. 'That's up to you.'

# 12

'. . . the US Geological Survey in Menlo Park is measuring the earthquake at four point one on the Richter scale. We have reports of minor damage in the South Bay, so let's go to our traffic chopper—'

Jo punched the radio dial. She was ten miles up the freeway heading back to San Francisco, window open, hair batting in the breeze. A new station came in.

'. . . my cats sensed the quake coming, and they freaked out. If the Big One hits, I tell you, I'll know it beforehand—'

Punch.

'. . . some experts think this swarm of tremors is a sign of the coming apocalypse predicted in the ancient Mayan calendar—'

Punch to the stereo.

Music poured out, a trance-like Sahara track in an odd key. Sunlight sparkled on the bay. She stared at the road and tried to stop thinking about Gabe Quintana. His cool, his warmth, his self-assured presence. His concern for her.

Her phone beeped. It was a text message from Lieutenant Tang. *At Harding's autopsy. Important you come.*

She was forty minutes from the Medical Examiner's Office. She replied *K*, and sped up. The music was hypnotic and insistent. It was Cheb Mami, the singer who had recorded *Desert Rose* with Sting. She had started listening to this music after Daniel died. Back then, melody had become a minefield. Classical music choked her up in ten seconds flat. Rock reminded her of climbing trips and sleeping with Daniel under the stars. And country music made her want to kill herself. It made her want to buy a gun so she could blow away any radio playing a song with slide guitar.

But this music carried her off, because it carried no memories. Nothing tied it to Daniel. And yet it caught her imagination and pulled her in, but somewhere exotic and safe. Childhood memory. All she needed was a magic carpet to take her away.

She touched her necklace, rubbing her fingers over her white-gold wedding ring.

Rock music had been playing on that last morning with him. She could still hear it clearly. The Police, *Every Little Thing She Does Is Magic.* That ascending baseline in a minor key. Seven-thirty a.m. and Daniel had turned it up.

It was his day off. He worked sixty hours a week as a trauma physician at UCSF Medical Center but he had that day free, and so did she – a rarity. She was in the middle of her forensic psych residency, and moonlighting in the ER. A single day off didn't give them time to drive to Yosemite, so they planned to hit the climbing gym. She heard him on the phone from the other side of the bed, early, talking to the Air Ambulance service.

Sure, if they got any emergency calls he'd go, no problem. Page him if anything happened. Moonlighting, no better way to spend a day off.

He rolled back beneath the covers and ran his arm across her belly. He smiled at her. Morning, mutt.

Morning, dawg. She smiled back. No better way to spend a day off? If you think that, you're suffering a severe failure of imagination.

They'd been married three years. And she still felt like she'd rolled double sevens, because her husband was both a colleague and her passion. Danny was serious, capable, a climber with a head of rusty hair that only looked good when he sheared it close. He wasn't handsome; he was intense, with green eyes that always looked ready to cut through her. He not-so-secretly hoped she would switch her specialty to emergency medicine, and she had half a mind to do it. He was a shining example of everything she wanted to be. He had more enthusiasm, more curiosity about the world, than anybody she'd ever known. At work he was so calm that friends joked that he'd been doped with horse tranquilizers.

All his storms raged inside, and he let her sense them only at moments of pressure. And when he smiled, when he laughed, it transformed him.

They made love like wolves wrestling; with an energy, edged with hunger. Outside, the weather was already turning blustery.

The page came at ten a.m., when they were having breakfast at Ti Couz. Child with a ruptured appendix needed a medevac from Bodega Bay, up the coast in Sonoma County. The girl was six, and had underlying medical issues. A surgical team was being assembled at UCSF. The helicopter would go once Daniel got there, if they could round up a second medic – their nurse wasn't answering her pager.

Daniel looked at Jo.

She often wondered if things might be different now had she said something else. The wind was beginning to knock rain against the restaurant windows. She could have shaken her head and told him, *Don't go.*

But she didn't. She grabbed the car keys and said, 'I'll come with you.'

Now the sun blared off the windshield. Her memories were interrupted by her cellphone ringing. She turned down Cheb Mami and answered it.

It was Amy Tang. 'You get my message? I'm at Callie Harding's autopsy. Cohen found something. You should get over here.'

'On my way.'

Tang hung up. No goodbye.

Kisses to you too, sunshine. Jo changed lanes and accelerated.

Jo pushed through the door into the Medical Examiner's Office, hoping Tang wasn't pulling a stunt by calling her here. Cops, like the Medical Examiner's staff, occasionally goaded psychiatrists into watching autopsies. Hoping for the *Quincy* reaction – vomiting, fainting, any adverse and entertaining outcome. The front desk was decorated with jack o' lanterns. Jo checked in and was directed to the bowels of the building.

The ME's Office was no quieter than a hospital, and equally clinical. The fluorescent lighting gave everything a sterile sheen. The indelible whiff of formaldehyde lurked beneath the paint.

Autopsies were not her favorite activity. Dissecting a human cadaver in anatomy class hadn't bothered her, perhaps because people who donated their bodies to science had taken years to consider the decision. It was a gift, and their remains became a teaching tool. But autopises happened to people who weren't expecting to die. Watching a pathologist root around inside a body – with its chest prised open like Sigourney Weaver's worst nightmare – left her emotionally dumbfounded. She hated the thought of it happening to people she loved. And it had.

Rounding a corner, she found Amy Tang at a drinking fountain. Tang was wearing black clothes and black eye makeup, and her hair looked punk. She practically had to stand on tiptoe to reach the arc of water. Spiky, the Goth Gnome.

Quit it, Beckett. 'Lieutenant.'

Tang touched the back of her hand to her lips. 'This way. Cohen's about half-finished.'

'What did he find?'

'Stuff that falls on your side of the fence.'

Tang led Jo into the autopsy suite. Jazz was playing on the boom box, Coltrane from the sound of the sax, cool and melancholy. Blue – the music, the surgical drapes, the mood. Cohen's red beard stood out in contrast. He was well into the dissection.

Jo slowed her breathing and pulled her emotions back to the quiet room where sights and feelings are muffled. Behind Cohen an assistant was weighing Callie's liver. Tang loitered in the corner, arms crossed, face cross. Jo approached the table.

Callie's toes were blue. Her runner's tan was dulling to gray. The red letters scrawled on her left thigh seemed to scream. *dirty*.

The word was written with a severe slant, as if a lefthander had scribbled it without looking. Lipstick, no question.

Jo looked at Callie's face.

No wonder Gregory Harding had acted like an ass. He had seen this. It must have been like having a live electric cable jammed against the back of his head. Callie's face, a face sculpted by Michelangelo, was crushed.

'I suspect you may list cranial trauma as cause of death,' she said.

Cohen pointed with his scalpel. 'Airbag inflated when the car hit the bridge, and deflated almost instantly. It was useless when they hit the shuttle van. And she was already headed for an up-and-out by then.'

'No seatbelt.'

'No. Her injuries were unsurvivable.'

'Doctor Cohen?' Tang said.

He glanced at her. 'I'm coming to it.'

'What do I need to see?' Jo said.

'We discovered it during the external exam, when we removed her clothing.'

He pointed at Harding's left arm. It lay against the table palm up.

Jesus.

Jo said nothing, but her temples felt tight.

Cohen's assistant turned around. 'Ready for me to put these back?'

He had Callie's heart and lungs in his hands. Behind her, Jo heard a retching sound. She turned. Tang had jammed her hand over her mouth.

Cohen said, 'Not in here, Lieutenant.'

Sweat shone on Tang's forehead. Her eyes rolled back in her head.

'Crap,' Cohen said. 'Doctor Beckett, can you . . .'

Jo was already moving.

Tang keeled against the counter like a crash test dummy. Jo grabbed her under the arms and hauled her toward a chair. Her legs were like jelly. Jo plopped her down, slumped to one side.

'Put your head between your knees,' she said.

The young cop's eyes were glazed and half open. Jo leaned her forward and pushed her head down between her knees to get blood flowing to her brain.

'She seemed fine,' Cohen said.

'It happens.'

Jo kept her hand on Tang's back. After a few seconds Tang's breathing deepened. She pushed Jo's hand away and slowly sat up.

'Welcome back,' Jo said. 'Have a nice trip?'

'I'm fine.'

'Sure. Just take it easy.'

But Tang was getting unsteadily to her feet. She brushed off the hand Jo extended and held onto the counter instead.

Cohen nodded at the door. 'Doctor Beckett, you want to take the lieutenant where she can get some air?'

'It's the heat in here. I'll be all right,' Tang said.

She had paled to a shade of glue. Jo took her elbow, held tight so Tang couldn't shake it off, and guided her out the door.

'Did you see it?' Tang's tone was tough-chick, but her voice was mousey.

'I saw it.' Jo heard her own voice, grim. 'Second time today that word has shown up.'

Tang looked at her, puzzled. 'In the course of the investigation?'

'In the course of possible murder-suicide. What do you think that means?'

Four letters, on Callie's arm in black ink. On Maki's boat in gasoline. *Pray.*

# 13

Jo took Tang to the lobby. The jack o' lanterns seemed to leer at them. The detective's face looked like wet dough, but she was recovering her composure.

Self-consciously she pulled her arm away from Jo's hand. 'Somebody's writing the word *pray* on victims?'

'Or at the crime scene.' She watched Tang for a moment, making sure she was steady on her feet. 'Let me find out what Cohen can tell me about the blood work. Stay here for a minute, I'll be back.'

'I was only waiting until you showed up. I don't need to hang around to hear all the ghosts that haunt these halls laugh at me.'

'Neither of us wants to rent this place for a Halloween party. But I have information you need to know.'

Back in the autopsy suite, Cohen was bent over the table. Though he couldn't inflict pain he still moved with delicacy.

'Barry, can you give me a run-down of what you have so far?' Jo said.

'Tox doesn't have all the blood work, but there's no sign carbon monoxide affected Harding's driving, and her blood alcohol was point-zero-zero.'

'Has anybody compared the imprints on the bottom of her shoes to the pedals in the BMW?'

'Not yet.'

That meant they didn't know whether she was on the brake or the accelerator when she crashed. 'How about her clothes and effects? Anything unusual?'

He looked up. 'She liked exceptionally fine things. She was not only wearing white diamond stud earrings, but a black diamond as well.' He touched Callie's upper ear. 'Here. Several carats, I'd guess. A rare gem.'

Jo nodded. 'Anything else?'

'You'll be the fourth to know.'

'Make me the third. If we don't figure this out, I have a bad feeling somebody else might end up on your table. And I mean soon.'

She turned to go, but he called her back.

'I think I know how Angelika Meyer was declared dead.' His voice tightened. 'When I checked her pulse, I had a possible examination bias. The paramedics told me she was dead, and I didn't expect contra-indications.'

'Have you spoken to them?'

'Yes. They didn't examine her. When they arrived they were immediately called to work on the victims in the airport shuttle. The first cop on the scene said the two in the BMW were dead. Young guy, Latino. Quite upset, they say.'

Jo thought about it. 'Chain reaction?'

'Like playing Telephone.' He shook his head. 'Still, I detected no signs of life, and I should have.'

'She's alive. That's what counts,' Jo said.

He smiled bleakly. 'Thought you didn't do therapy.'

'Guess I won't bill you, then. Thanks, Barry.'

She walked back to the lobby, and with Tang headed outside. Stepping into the fresh air, they inhaled in concert.

Tang took a pack of cigarettes from her pocket. She lit up, drew hard and tilted her head up to exhale. 'Ghosts. Hate 'em. Bunch of them are my ancestors.'

'They seemed more like jinns to me. Maybe ghouls.'

'Jinns? Now you're screwing with my head.'

'Genies. Spirits. Some of them become diabolical.'

'How Old Country of you to think so.' Tang took another drag and squinted at her. 'What are you, anyway?'

'Grandma was Japanese. Grandpa was Coptic Egyptian. Couple of the Irish were horse thieves. Mom and Dad met at Disneyland.' She smiled. 'I'm pure California mutt.'

Tang smirked, pinching the cigarette between her thumb and forefinger.

'Something strange was going on with Callie Harding,' Jo said.

She found Callie's handwritten invitation, saying *Welcome to the Dirty Secrets Club*.

Tang took it. 'What the hell?'

'There's more.'

Jo handed her the sealed baggie containing the album sleeve she'd found in Angelika Meyer's purse, with the song *Dirty Little Secret* highlighted.

'What was going on?' Tang said.

'Don't know, but Callie and Meyer both worked at the US Attorney's Office. We need to talk to Leo Fonsecca.'

Tang threw the cigarette to the sidewalk. 'You drive, I'll call him. Tell me the rest on the way.'

On the way to the Federal Building, Tang sat small and prickly in the passenger seat.

'We've got *dirty* written on Harding's leg in lipstick. "You've been bad" and "Welcome to the Dirty Secrets Club" in her handwriting. "Dirty Little Secret" and a request to "play" in Meyer's. Followed by a fistfight and a swan dive off the bridge,' she said. 'They were lovers. It was a freaky game.'

'I don't think so.'

'Two women, black lace, red lipstick, self-loathing. Screaming death. Sounds like it to me.'

'Last night you thought it was part of a bizarre killing spree.'

'I still do. What do you think, they were fighting over a man? If I can't have him, neither can you – *bam*? That would be a real piece of psycho-drama. Hard-core street theater.'

Jo gave her a dark look.

Tang returned it. 'I'm working through the possibilities, and don't knock it. I've been an investigator longer than you've been playing Vulcan Mind Meld with dead people.'

Jo slowly turned her head, eyed Tang, and laughed. 'That's a new one on me. Not bad.'

Tang leaned back, a porcupine of a woman, but her shoulders dropped an inch. Traffic gleamed along in the sunshine. Ratty commercial buildings and cracked sidewalks blurred past. Then a soup kitchen, and a vacant lot where a chain-link fence guarded a profusion of weeds.

'Fine,' Tang said. 'You're the expert on cases where crazy sexual posing is part of the death scene. Tell me what you think.'

'I think the Dirty Secrets Club is more than a game Callie and Meyer were playing. I think other people are involved.'

'A real club? With a secret handshake, a refreshments committee, and a newsletter?'

'I think Maki and Yoshida were part of it. Callie's browser history was jammed with search hits for their names.' Jo stopped for a red light. 'I think all three of their deaths are part of a series. And how come nobody told me Maki and his lover were shot to death?'

'You didn't know?' Tang looked at her with suspicion. 'Then how'd you find out about the shootings? That information hasn't been released.'

'I talked to the PJ who was on-scene.'

'Did you tell him to keep it quiet?'

'He's not going to talk to the press, or even his drinking buddies.'

Tang ran a hand over her spiky hair and put up a hand. 'My oversight about the shootings. I'm snowed under.'

'Understood.'

'So these deaths are related. But . . .'

'But there's no evidence that anybody murdered Callie. Right? No bombs under the BMW, no severed brake lines?'

Tang took out a cellphone and punched a number. 'We have any results on the BMW?'

She whipped out a little notepad and scrawled. The light turned green as she hung up.

'Forensics says the BMW was in perfect condition. It was so new, when you opened the doors you could still smell the Black Forest. Brakes, drive train, engine were all fine. The gas pedal didn't jam. The car didn't cause the crash.'

'Okay. But I still can't rule out an accident. Need to look at the road, the driver, or interference from another source.'

'Road and interference, *nada*. You think Callie screwed up at the wheel?'

'Possibly. And how about the emergency brake?'

'Not engaged. And none of the tires were blown out. And no bombs.' Tang frowned out the window. 'What's the evidence for and against Harding having killed herself?'

'You want the indicators that a motor vehicle crash is suicide?'

'Knock yourself out.'

'Count five red flags. First, good weather. Second, good road conditions – dry pavement, good street lighting. Third, the road's straight – it's not like the driver lost control on a hairpin curve.'

'And Stockton Street is as straight as a ski jump.'

'Fourth, no skid marks – and the vehicle leaves a straight road headed directly to a fixed object, such as a bridge abutment.'

'Check, and check again.'

'Fifth, the driver is the lone occupant in the car.'

Tang crossed her arms. 'So there's our monkeywrench. Either that, or we're back to murder-suicide.'

'Do you have any indication that the burning boat was anything *other* than murder-suicide?'

'No. From everything so far, the evidence is conclusive. Maki shot William Willets and then himself.'

Jo was quiet a moment. 'What killed Doctor Yoshida?'

'We suspect a barbiturate overdose. It looked like a heart attack because he was found slumped at the wheel of his car at the beach. We should know later today.'

'And his son died shortly before he did?'

'An overdose, two days earlier.'

Jo glanced at her. 'Forty-eight hours?'

'I know.'

They rolled along in traffic, silent for a minute. Ahead the stately granite buildings of the Civic Center came into view.

Tang was pensive. 'Tell me what you think. Wild-ass speculation.'

'I think the Dirty Secrets Club exists, and that Callie was a ranking member. The invitation to join the club – the near formality of the note, and the stationery, strike me as significant.'

'How about the sexual angle?'

'Callie had racy lingerie and an ex who can't get her out of his head. He seems lost but also angry and emasculated.'

'She was a dominatrix?'

'This all indicates she may have been in a position of authority. If there's a club, I think she helped run it.'

'So what's it about? Guilt, you think? Expiation through suicide?'

'I don't have enough evidence to judge.'

'Is it becoming a death cult?'

'*Pray* suggests a religious aspect, but Callie apparently wasn't devout. On the other hand, it could be a message from a killer. Repent, the end is near.'

'So what's your conclusion?'

She glanced at Tang. 'I think this club is why Callie, Yoshida and Maki are dead. It's why Meyer is nearly dead. And we'd better find out if other people belong, because something bad is going on, and it's not over. That's why Meyer begged me to stop it.'

'So who's next? And how do we keep them from dying?'

Jo looked at her watch. She didn't know, but they were down to thirty-six hours.

Scott Southern listened to his cellphone ringing. Outside, the wind funneled around the car. But in the Range Rover, parked with the windows rolled up, it was hot and still. His ring tone was the USC fight song, and to his ears it sounded like a mockery.

Only three people could be calling. The offensive coach of the Forty-Niners, worried because he wasn't at practice. Kelly, hurt because he'd slammed the front door when he stalked out of the house earlier. Or the man in the Cadillac.

The parking lot at the Palace of Fine Arts was shaded by towering eucalyptus trees. Tourists strolled the grounds, wandering beneath the dome of the Roman rotunda. On the bay nearby, the water was a sparkling blue.

The phone stopped ringing.

He was in trouble and sinking like a stone. The buzz he'd been experiencing with the club, the adrenaline rush, the huge relief he'd found by being able to confess, openly – it was all dissolving. David Yoshida's death no longer seemed a sad misfortune. And Callie . . .

He ran a hand over his face. This whole adventure was going wrong.

The phone rang again. One of two people, then. Coach, getting pissed off now. Or Cadillac Man. He closed his eyes.

How did the guy get his name? Who had told him? The club promised impenetrable secrecy, but somebody had talked. And now the whole lousy story was close to coming out.

He ignored the scornful ring tone, hanging onto his last moments of quiet. Once he opened the door, all the noise in the world would howl down on him.

He was twenty-nine. He was paid four million dollars a year to catch a football for the Niners. Another six on top of that in annual endorsements for Adidas, the Outback Steakhouse and Mattel.

A week ago he was on top of everything – the NFL, his game, a skyscraper rooftop with Callie. Today he'd been supposed to meet with her, to find out if his spectacular dare had earned him entry to the top level of the club, where the big payoff was supposed to be. The breath went out of him, like he'd been punched. Callie, Christ. The thought of earning a black diamond didn't excite him anymore.

And now this.

He felt like he was sinking in tar. He had a beautiful woman at home, hurt and frightened. Cadillac Man had mailed her an anonymous note. *Your husband has a dirty secret.* He knew it was really a threat: do what the man wanted, or the rest would come out. How had the guy found out?

The trees rustled. Beyond the Roman rotunda, the surface of the lagoon shivered under the breeze. The white Cadillac pulled in, disco thumping from its speakers, and parked next to him.

Cadillac Man, the slick of grease who called himself Skunk, was behind the wheel. He got out, walked over and stood in front of the

Range Rover. He looked like a skunk, with his oily gray-streaked hair and his dumb suspicious eyes.

The tar felt thick and clinging. Scott got out. The wind was brisk, funneling through the Golden Gate headlands and across the bay.

A smile curdled on Skunk's little mouth. 'I lost two hundred bucks on your team this weekend.'

Scott felt perplexed. 'Is this about money?'

'I wish. Let's walk,' the man said.

'No. Tell me what you want.'

Skunk looked around. 'Want these people to hear it?'

The wind went further out of Scott's sails. He followed Skunk through the gate into the grounds.

Skunk looked five-foot seven, maybe a hundred forty-five pounds. Scott was six-three, two-fifteen, all speed and muscle. He could snatch a football from the air amid a tangle of defenders, cradle it like a baby, grind and spin it into the end zone. He could have straight-armed this rodent, knocked him flat with a couple of broken ribs. But that would get him nothing. Skunk wasn't the only one involved. Put him down, somebody else was behind him.

And it didn't matter how well Scott could keep from fumbling a football, how strong and nimble he was, how determined to win. This was about his failures. All at once he felt incredibly small.

'I told you, I can't give you what you want,' he said. 'I don't have the information. I don't know who does.'

'And I told you – find out.'

Ahead, through the trees, the rotunda shone in the sun. Columns were topped with gods and angels. Somebody had once called this place a beaux arts hallucination. It was like the Roman Forum had been transported to the present day and set down in a woodsy park.

Skunk leaned toward him. 'I said, *Find out.* Like I told you on the phone, the prosecutor's dead. You want to be dead, too?'

Scott didn't respond.

'How did it work?' Skunk said. 'Did she come to you, or was it the other way around? You got dirty with her, told her all those secrets you never wanted anybody to know?'

Despite the wind, the air felt suffocating. The noise of traffic was like the onrushing sense of destruction he had felt since this nightmare began.

'Here's the deal,' Skunk said. 'You get the names we need today, or your secret won't be a secret anymore.'

'I can't. There has to be some alternative. Money? I can pay you whatever you want.'

'If I wanted money I'd tell you to drop a pass or two against the Rams next weekend.'

Scott fought the constricting feeling around his chest. 'I can do that.'

Skunk slid his little hands into the pockets of his Members Only jacket. 'I bet you would. You'd throw the Super Bowl to keep this stuff secret.'

He would. And he felt the tar seeping higher, the weight pressing on his chest. The sky no longer looked blue to him, but flat gray. Jesus.

Skunk would tell. He would tell the world and he would enjoy it. He would smile at the sight of Scott Southern being torn to shreds in the media.

'It was consensual,' Scott said. 'It wasn't a crime.'

Skunk slowly turned his head. For a moment Scott thought the look on the man's face was disbelief.

'Honestly. Nobody broke the law,' Scott said.

Skunk laughed. 'Incredible.'

With dismay, Scott understood. Skunk knew he was telling the truth. But Skunk couldn't believe Scott still thought he could talk him into keeping quiet. He couldn't believe Scott thought remorse and anguish could buy him anything but destruction.

'How old was the girl?' Skunk said.

'She wasn't a minor. She was nineteen, and she never objected.' Not in so many words.

And he had been a senior at USC. How could they blame him? He'd just been a kid in college.

But he knew how, because he blamed himself. For eight years he'd suppressed it, or confessed it in secret, and tried to expunge the guilt. Last week he'd taken a whipping with a riding crop to obliterate it. And now Skunk was slapping him with it in his own way. Laughing, the bastard.

It had been crowded at the party. The frat house was always crowded at parties. A face appeared in his mind, incredibly vivid, as it did every night when he slept. Melody, with strawberry blonde hair, with a take-me smile and a tipsy giggle. Her parents were friends with his. She was a sophomore.

'You thought quick that day, I'll give you that,' Skunk said. 'What I don't get is, how come you ever told? Anybody?'

In a dark corner of the room Melody had wound her hair around her fingers, listening to him intently. The Foos were on the stereo. She was sucking on an ice cube. Her lips were cherry red.

He kissed her, sucked the ice cube from her mouth, and said, 'Let's get an ice bucket and go upstairs.'

Yeah, he was drunk, and he'd smoked a joint. Just to even out, after the coke and the tequila. Just to get his mind smooth for a while. It was a nerve-wracking time, the NFL draft only a few days away. He was going to go in the first round, his agent said. His coach and parents and teammates all said. And his future was going to be golden, all sunshine, like Melody's hot little smile.

The breath left his lungs as though he'd been tackled from behind.

These days he didn't do dope, didn't do coke, didn't even drink. He was so clean and so sober that you could scrub him against a brick wall and scrape off graffiti. He feared that if he took a drink or a toke, he'd let down his guard and spill everything. He almost had spilled things by getting the *bad* tattoo – but he could chalk that up to jock style. Still, maybe if he was drunk he wouldn't see Melody in the bed, looking at him as he put on his jeans to answer the knock on the door. As he said, 'The other guys like ice, too.'

Now he put a hand across his eyes. 'Oh, God.'

Skunk smirked. 'You never had to tell a soul. That's the thing that blows my mind. You were home free. But you told Callie Harding, didn't you?'

That night, Melody had looked at him, confused, when he let the other guys in.

He said, 'It's okay, right?' He smiled. She smiled, maybe not so brightly.

'Scott . . .' She looked at his frat brothers. 'If I – will you be back?'

'Of course I'll be back.' They weren't going to hurt her. It was a *party*. He went and sat under a tree and smoked another joint and chilled out in the quiet night.

They didn't gang bang her. She just . . . let them take turns. She was kind of like a doll. Everybody got to play.

He was still sitting under the tree when Brady found him. 'She's gone nuts,' he said.

Scott found her in the bathroom, huddled by the toilet, shaking and mumbling to herself.

Brady wanted to call 911.

'No,' Scott said. 'I'll call my agent.'

It seemed like the smart thing to do, and his agent assured him it was the right thing, too. He got her to a private clinic. Paid all her medical bills, paid her to keep quiet.

And everything had seemed okay. But even then, Scott knew it was his fault. And if he got blamed for it, his season, his career in football, would be over.

Now his chest wouldn't expand. He couldn't breathe.

Melody dropped out of school. The next year, her parents admitted her to a private psychiatric clinic. Scott's own parents told him about her folks' anguish. His agent told him to stop feeling guilty. Said, she's unstable, always has been, not your fault. But the shrinks said she had post-traumatic stress. Her mind essentially shattered. And then . . .

Skunk put a hand on his arm. 'How does the club work? Who do you contact?'

Scott shook his head. If he told this greasy little man, Skunk would just go on to torment somebody else, the next person in line.

But the truth was, even if Scott gave Skunk a name, even if he gave him the entire phone book, Skunk wouldn't go away. He'd keep coming back for another bite, because that's how blackmail worked.

Not for the first time, Scott regretted the day he ever met David Yoshida. Cardiac surgeon. 'Niners fan, friend of the team's owner, got to meet the players at a post-game party.

Now Yoshida was dead. Callie was dead. Because somebody had talked.

The club was supposed to be secret, absolutely confidential. And he knew, deep down, that it never had been. And that's why he had joined it – for the risk. Didn't they all want the risk?

He stared through the Roman rotunda at the hills of the city. What the hell had he been thinking, telling a lawyer? A *prosecutor*, for the love of God? Blonde, cool, judgmental Callie. The punisher. He had loved confessing to her. What kind of a game had he been playing?

He laughed.

'What's so funny?' Skunk said.

Games. All his life he'd been playing games. And now he was about to lose. His vision swam.

Skunk grabbed his arm. 'Hey.'

He didn't pull away. Laughter heaved from the bottom of his chest.

He had gone deep, and fumbled. Melody, oh, Melody—

Skunk shook his head. 'You're fucking nuts, man. You get the names today, or everything comes out. All of it.' He shoved Scott away. 'You'd better pray.'

Scott wiped his eyes. 'Didn't you hear what I said? I can't help you.'

'You have a pool at your house?' Skunk said.

Scott looked at him. 'No.'

'Course, pools aren't the only places accidents happen. It's a nightmare for parents, keeping their kids safe from everything that could take 'em away forever.' Skunk snapped his fingers. 'Like that.'

Sweat broke out on his forehead. 'Are you threatening—'

'That poor Doctor Yoshida, for instance. His son died of a drug overdose. Tragic.'

'You son of a bitch.'

'I saw a picture in the *Chronicle* last season, you holding your little boy after the conference final. Can he swim?'

Scott felt a ripping sensation in his chest. All the strength left his feet, his legs, his arms.

An insane thought seized him.

The lagoon was right there. Who would see? Grab Skunk. Haul him to the water by the back of his saggy-ass jeans, dunk his head and drown him.

The little smile vanished from Skunk's face. 'Don't even think about it. I'm just mentioning possibilities. But if something happened to me, those possibilities would get a lot less theoretical. You know?'

Scott could barely see. 'Touch my family, you'll die.'

'Somebody's gonna die. The prosecutor wasn't the last, bet your bottom dollar.' His small eyes were recessed and glossy. 'But it ain't gonna be me. You think hard whether you want it to be somebody you love.'

The wind stung Scott's eyes. He said nothing.

Skunk turned to go. 'The names. By four o'clock.'

# 14

Jo and Amy Tang walked across the plaza, heading for the entrance to the US Attorney's Office. It was in an architecturally dead, white concrete building, recently upgraded with steel bollards to block car bombs. Tang put away her phone.

'Leo Fonsecca's giving us fifteen minutes,' Tang said. 'Be ready to talk fast.'

Jo followed her inside. 'The city seems to be holding together after the quake.'

'We're only hearing about minor damage. Unreinforced masonry falling off a few old buildings. Car alarms going off. No injuries reported.'

Jo looked around the echoing lobby. The building seemed fine. Tang pushed the call button for the elevator.

Jo hooked a thumb at the stairs. 'We can walk up.'

Tang looked aghast. 'It's on the eleventh floor. I don't care if it's good for my heart, I'm not climbing a skyscraper.'

Jo's own heart pumped harder, and she glanced at the elevator. 'You trust that box after a tremor?'

'An elevator has never plunged to the ground after an earthquake in San Francisco. You're paranoid.'

There'd never been a bridge collapse in San Francisco either, until there had been. There'd never been a freeway collapse because of an earthquake, until it happened.

The doors pinged open. Tang walked in and held the door. 'Fonsecca has to be in court in half an hour. The timer's running. Come on.'

Jo swallowed and stepped inside. Tang pushed the button and the doors began to close. Jo leaned against the back wall; watched the doors slide shut. They reminded her of two blades closing on each other. With her back pressed against the wall, she felt, ludicrously, that if the elevator began to shrink like a trash compacter, she could brace herself and shove her feet against the doors to stop it from crushing her.

Tang looked indifferent. 'Tell me how you got your expertise with sexual fantasy.'

The car rose. Jo heard a buzz in her ears. 'You mean my experience analyzing equivocal deaths that involve sexual games gone fatally wrong.'

'Same diff. That was . . .'

'Jeffrey Nagel, found hanged in his bedroom, partially nude.'

'Accident?'

The elevator bounced to a stop on the fifth floor. She grit her teeth.

Tang regarded her analytically. 'You really hate this.'

'I'd rather stab myself in the eye with a fork.' She forced a smile. 'Luckily, all I have in my purse is a spork.'

With a smooth burst of energy, the elevator rose again. Her jaw was clenched and she couldn't get it to relax.

Tang smiled. 'A claustrophobic shrink? That seems—'

'Ironic. I know.' She watched the numbers. 'Bad quake experience.'

Tang turned thoughtful. 'Loma Prieta?'

She nodded. Her palms were sweaty. She was going to need to shake hands with people in a minute. She wiped them on her slacks.

'No fun,' Tang said.

Jo shook her head.

The air, as ever when she was in a tight space, felt electrically charged. Her skin tingled. She wanted to gulp air. She fought the temptation. Rush her breathing, try to bring in all the air she needed *right now*, to breathe while she still had the chance, before the walls and concrete and roadway collapsed, the metal creaked and pressed against her face and chest—

She exhaled. Grab for air and she'd hyperventilate. She watched the numbers. Come on, come *on*. Her face felt red hot. She knew how she must look to Tang: stupid. A mental health expert, reduced to dread, unable to handle a simple elevator ride because of an irrational fear.

She knew the terms. Anxiety disorder. Panic trigger. She didn't care. Hurry up, stupid box. Tang was watching her.

The numbers went up. Nine. Ten. 'How much have the police told the US Attorney's Office about Harding's death and the scene last night?'

'They know what's been on the news. Nothing else – not about "dirty" and certainly not this "pray" stuff. Let's keep it that way.'

'I want to ask him if he's heard of a Dirty Secrets Club.'

'That's fine.'

The elevator stopped, the doors opened, and Jo strode out into a bright hallway. Thank you, God. She resisted the urge to drop to her knees and kiss the floor.

Tang caught up. 'How old were you when the quake hit?'

'A kid. More or less.'

'You were in the city?'

She shook her head. Most of the people who died in the Loma Prieta quake had been killed in San Francisco's Marina district. But that's not where she had been.

'You weren't on the Bay Bridge, were you?'

'East Bay.'

Tang glanced at her sharply.

They walked up to the desk and showed their IDs to the receptionist. The heavy seal of the Department of Justice was on the wall behind her. She picked up the phone.

Jo reached into her satchel for her notebook and pen. She couldn't find them.

Ugh. She had left them on the table at the *taquería* after the earthquake.

The Loma Prieta quake, centered under Santa Cruz eighty miles to the southwest, had played a dirty trick on the Bay Area. When the fault cracked, incredible seismic energy had bounded down through the ground and hit a lower stratum of rock. Santa

Cruz shook, but most of the energy rebounded, like a basketball, and surfaced in San Francisco. It happened on a beautiful October evening, at the end of rush hour, when Candlestick Park was packed with people attending the World Series. It was her aunt's birthday. She was with her dad, Tina, and her brother Rafe, on the way to the party in Oakland.

Tang said, 'Don't tell me you were on the Cypress Viaduct.'

Briefly she smelled gasoline and burning tires. She offered a bitter smile. 'I seem to be a cat with eighteen lives.'

Tang arched an eyebrow. 'Who'd you take the extra nine from?'

Leo Fonsecca walked into the lobby, shaking his head. 'I hope you're here to tell me who killed my prosecutor. Because if you can't, both of you deserve to be out of a job.'

Fonsecca's office had a cramped view of the office buildings surrounding City Hall and the Federal Courthouse. He stood in front of his desk, hands clasped like a funeral director. His thinning gray hair topped a face that was sad and flushed.

On the sofa Jo and Tang sat like school kids called to the principal's office.

'Callie wasn't suicidal,' Fonsecca said.

'What was her mood in the past few weeks?' Jo said.

'Working hard, as usual.' He looked soft, but his movements seemed quick and exaggerated. His rimless glasses shone under the lights.

Fonsecca was the chief federal prosecutor for the Northern District of California, a jurisdiction that comprises eight million people. Jo knew that he was a career prosecutor, a courtroom battler rather than a political appointee. Though he looked like a mournful hamster, he was a powerful figure, respected and intense.

'Callie could not have killed herself. Period. I've known her for ten years. She didn't let courtroom losses get to her. She hated to lose, but knew we can't get every bad guy who's out there. She was not obsessed.'

'Can you tell me what she was working on?' Jo said.

His head popped around. He stared at her. 'No.'

'In general terms?'

'Absolutely not. I will not reveal details of her active cases. And I don't want you worming information out of anybody in this office.'

'I'm not your adversary, Mr Fonsecca,' she said.

His shoulders slumped. He took off his glasses and pinched the bridge of his nose. 'I'm sorry. She was aces. I consider it a privilege to have called her my friend.'

'I'm sorry.'

He put his glasses back on and attempted a weary smile. She gave him a few seconds to regain his composure.

'Have you heard of something called the Dirty Secrets Club?' she said.

He looked puzzled. 'What's that?'

'I'm trying to find out.'

He shook his head. 'How does it connect to Callie?'

'I was hoping you could tell me.'

'No. It sounds very odd. Where have you come up with this idea?'

Tang said, 'The phrase has come up in the course of our investigation.'

'It sounds like . . . a nightclub. Not Callie's type of thing at all.' Fonsecca shrugged. His face was bemused and slightly red.

'Was she investigating the deaths of Maki Prichingo and David Yoshida?' Jo said.

'No.'

He fired the answer at her like a bullet. She didn't exactly disbelieve him, but it was a shot across her bow, and she decided not to ask again.

'Can you tell us what Callie might have been doing with Angelika Meyer last night?' she said.

'Angelika was working with Callie on a couple of matters. Doing basic research, that sort of thing. She's a bright young woman. We've been happy to have her here this semester.'

'Had she and Callie become friends?'

'I couldn't say.' Wearily he ran a hand over his lank hair.

'Would you consider Callie a mentor to her?' Jo said.

'Yes. Angelika has a keen interest in criminal justice. Wants to become a prosecutor when she graduates from law school.' He thought for a moment. 'What else can I tell you? She did an undergraduate criminology internship at San Quentin – so she's not a wilting flower. She'd make a good street fighter.'

Jo nodded, but knew from her own forensic psychiatry rotation that working in the California prison system didn't prove your toughness. What the work did was remove scales from your eyes, and test your nerve.

Fonsecca's face looked drawn. 'Do you have the latest on her condition?'

Tang said, 'No change.'

He pressed his lips tight. 'She's tough. She'll pull through.'

Jo and Tang didn't respond.

After a moment, Tang said, 'Do you know of any threats against Callie? Maybe from somebody she put away?'

'We're investigating that. But so far, no.'

Jo waited a moment. 'Do you know why Geli was in Callie's car last night?'

'Maybe she was getting a ride home.'

'Did they have a personal relationship?'

His gaze was wandering, but now zeroed on her. 'Are you implying that they had a lesbian attraction to each other?'

'Asking.'

In San Francisco, the question could hardly be considered controversial or insulting. Nonetheless, Fonsecca's face was red again.

'Absolutely not.' He adjusted his glasses. 'Callie was divorced, and had dated since then. Dated *men*. Angelika – I . . .' He waved his hands, vaguely. He didn't know. 'This is groundless speculation.'

With a knock, a secretary opened the door. 'Time to head to court.'

'I'll be right out.'

Concern tightened her face. 'Sir, are you all right?'

'Fine, yes.'

She opened her mouth to say something else, but he raised a hand to forestall it. Reluctantly she departed.

'Mother hen,' he said. 'Fusses over me. Thinks I need to watch my blood pressure.'

Judging from the flush that came over Fonsecca whenever he faced a stressful question, Jo thought his secretary might be right.

She said, 'One last question. Why would Callie run from the police?'

This time his face didn't redden. He looked calm.

'There can only be one reason. She couldn't stop. Because if she stopped, something catastrophic would happen.'

His gaze panned from Jo to Tang and back. 'She was trying to keep something terrible from happening. Find out what that is, and you'll find out why she died.'

Perry waited until he was alone. People passed by in the hallway. He gave them a smile. They didn't return it. Fuck you, too.

He knew how to present a charming façade to the world. That's what the shrinks had said. He'd read his medical chart, stolen it one day from the desk, back when they were badgering him to *cope* and *adapt* and be happy speaking like a robot with the electro-larynx, the freak machine.

He turned on the cellphone, set to Silent. No calls. Goddammit. He hated to wait. He wanted an update from Skunk. He had been waiting too damn long, and Callie was already getting cold. He needed to finish this.

He longed to do it himself. He bit the inside of his cheek. His desires, he was learning, didn't get met instantaneously these days. And that made him feel like strangling the next person who told him *no*.

He wanted the names. He wanted to see them crossed off in black ink, one after another. Finally the phone lit up. *1 new message.*

The surgeons and occupational therapists and psychobabble Nazis had tried to twist him into accepting his new status as a circus freak. He had smiled and got them to believe he understood. *Shallow affect*, that's another term his medical chart had used to describe him. It meant he only pretended to feel friendly, that he faked emotion. No kidding. What was the point of feeling friendly? *Seeming* friendly, now that got you something. What else mattered?

On the other hand, *perceptual and emotional recognition deficits* – that was a helpful comment. It explained things to him. He apparently didn't recognize emotions on people's faces. Love, disgust, shame, they went right past him. That explained why he was such a lousy poker player. He couldn't read people's faces and tell what they were hiding.

The rage was spinning up again, a black mouth with sharp teeth, screaming in front of him.

He couldn't read people sometimes. That's why he hadn't seen it coming.

He calmed himself. It didn't matter. He knew he was a lousy poker player – that's why he'd gotten into promoting games. When you lose at gambling, you learn: the house always wins. So he became the house. He ran an executive game. Big time, with A-listers who could afford to gamble away tens of thousands of dollars a week. They got a buzz from the high-stakes atmosphere. And when they took the line of credit he extended to them, and lost, it didn't matter if they couldn't pay him back in cash. He busted heads, and if that didn't work he moved in on their businesses, had them buy him everything he wanted on their corporate accounts, even if it ran them into bankruptcy. He got paid.

The doctor, David Yoshida, he liked to play poker. And Perry never had to bust his head, because he was rolling in money. Maybe if he had busted the guy's head, things would be different today. But Yoshida paid up. Yoshida kept coming back. Yoshida liked rubbing elbows with Perry.

Yoshida was rotting in the ground.

And it didn't matter anymore whether Perry could spot sadness or guilt on some weakling's face. He knew how to recognize anger and fear. That was what counted.

He read the message from Skunk. *Will have it by 4 pm*. He switched off the phone.

Fear and anger. It was time to deal them out again.

The secretary opened the door to Callie's office and stepped back as if facing a portal to a frightening dimension. 'Take your time. There's no rush, not now.'

Jo lingered in the doorway. She saw the same clean order as at Callie's townhouse. Files were neatly stacked on the credenza, running shoes tucked tidily into a corner. Even Callie's iPod was lined up parallel with the edge of the desk.

She went in. 'How long did you know Callie?'

The woman fussed with a heavy turquoise necklace at her throat. 'Ten years. She never – I never – it had to be an accident. She would never hurt somebody else.'

Jo looked up. 'Geli, you mean.'

Her hand worried the necklace. 'And those people in the airport van. Never. Callie spent her life helping people who were victimized by others.'

It was the same tune Jo and Tang had been hearing for the past hour from everybody in the office. They had split up the interviews but were getting the same information. Callie was clever, driven, devoted to the Department of Justice. She worked hard but knew how to blow off steam. Once, faced with a witness whose credibility collapsed on the eve of trial, she frowned at her panicky colleagues, then with great style pulled at her perfect hair and screamed theatrically before she collapsed in her desk chair, back of her hand to her forehead. Everybody stared. Then she laughed at herself and said, 'What else ya gonna do?'

'How did she seem in the last month?' Jo said.

The secretary took her time. Jo had learned that, given the chance, most people tried to help her. The trick was to know when they were trying too hard, or shading their remembrances toward falsehood and fantasy. She analyzed all information with what the psychiatric rubrics called a 'high index of suspicion'.

'She was in a good mood, full of energy,' the woman said.

Jo looked in the only non-tidy spot in the office, the wastebasket. It was full. She tossed out half a dozen crumpled pieces of paper and found a paper bag from General Li's Chinese restaurant. It smelled distinctly of vinegar and fried dumplings.

She smoothed out the receipt on the desk. Pot stickers, Szechuan prawns – five dishes in all. Last night's date, and the time, 11:15 p.m. The food had been delivered. Callie had been working very late.

In the sack were two sets of disposable chopsticks and two crumpled paper napkins. One bore the neat imprint of pink lipstick, a *SWAK* imprint. She was willing to bet the pink kiss would match the tube of lip gloss in Angelika Meyer's purse. The other napkin had a swipe of darker lipstick, long and ragged and red, the same shade as the word scrawled on Callie's thigh.

'Were she and Geli close friends?'

'Friendly. But just around the office, as far as I know.'

Also more of the same. Nobody had known them to socialize outside of work.

Jo sat down, took the iPod and scrolled through the menu. The calendar, games, contacts – empty. The playlist was nine hundred songs and no clues.

Note pad. She spun the controls.

*DSC.*

She went still, but her heart rate bumped into third gear. 'Does *DSC* mean anything to you?'

The secretary shook her head. 'Unless it's *discovery*. You know, the parties gathering documentary evidence or taking depositions ahead of trial.'

Jo scrolled down. 'I don't think so.'

Jo flipped through Callie's desk calendar. She saw no references to DSC. But in several places she spotted the abbreviation *disc*.

She continued scrolling through the iPod. Oh, my.

*Maki.*

She scrolled further down the submenu.

*Yoshida.*

Fonsecca had instructed the office not to give her access to

Callie's case files. But Callie's active prosecutions were a matter of public record.

'Is either of these names a witness or a party in a case?' she said.

The secretary raised an eyebrow. 'Them? I would have known . . .' But to double-check, she went out to her own desk to look up court dockets and computer records. However, Jo thought this stuff was off-the-record in a big way.

She checked Callie's desktop computer. Global searches for Yoshida, Maki, and Maki's dead lover, William Willets – no hits.

They weren't in Callie's work system. Just on her iPod.

She leaned over Callie's desk calendar for a closer look. It took her twenty minutes but, four months back, she found the drawing of a heart. She could think of two possibilities: a crush, or a cardiac surgeon. She kept looking and found four other places where Callie had drawn a simple little heart. In the more recent entries, another mark was drawn beside it: a black diamond.

Next to it was a telephone number.

She picked up the phone and dialed. A recording intruded. *The number you have dialed is not in service.* She hung up. Then she looked at the number again.

The last three digits, if reversed, were a UCSF prefix. She dialed the number from back to front. It clicked straight to voicemail.

'You have reached the office of David Yoshida, MD. Please leave a message.'

Jo hung up and sat for a moment. He heart was thumping.

She returned to the calendar, looking at today's entries. Reading about appointments that would never be kept could be depressing. She blocked that impulse by looking at the calendar like a puzzle. Su Doku of the dead.

Halfway down, two sets of initials. XZ. SS. Beside them was a neatly drawn black diamond.

The Aquatic Park, on the bay near Ghirardelli Square. Four p.m.

She glanced at her watch. Crap. It was three thirty-five. Could she make it?

She jumped up and called to the secretary. 'I'm taking the iPod and calendar.'

'Okay.' The woman looked perplexed to see Jo moving fast after sitting quietly at Callie's desk for so long.

Jo rushed out and looked around. 'Where'd Lieutenant Tang go?'

'I don't know.'

Jo jogged down the hall, looked in the conference room, jogged back. Checked her watch again. Heard the elevator ping and saw Leo Fonsecca step out, back from court. He walked down the hall, frowning at her.

To the secretary Jo said, 'Tell Tang I've gone to the Aquatic Park to keep Callie's four o'clock appointment.'

Fonsecca said, 'What's going on? What do you have there?'

'I'll bring it all back.' She ran to the elevator.

# 15

It was mid-afternoon when Scott Southern got the information written down. He folded the sheets of paper in three, like a letter, and put them in the inside pocket of his letterman's jacket. He got out of the Range Rover and walked along the path through the park.

Scott had decided what to do. Skunk wanted the names of certain people in the DSC, so his boss could go after them.

Scott was going to give him more than that.

The Golden Gate Bridge visitors' center overlooked the bay from a promontory at the tip of the Presidio. Under the sun, the water was a scintillating blue. Whitecaps tore across the surface far below. In the park tourists admired the view, hunched into sweat-shirts, hair flapping in the wind. Some people put coins in the viewfinders and got a magnified look at the Sausalito ferry chug-ging through the chop on the bay. The vista took in Angel Island, Alcatraz and, to the east, San Francisco – a white and gleaming vision draped across the hills.

Kelly wouldn't forgive him. That much he'd always known. That had been the worm eating at his heartwood for the past eight years. Kelly would divorce him, out of revulsion at his part in Melody's destruction. His beautiful wife, his little boy – his family was about to go up in smoke. He'd never see them again.

He had tried to empty himself by talking to David Yoshida and to Callie. He had thought purgation would save him. That it might be cathartic. It was not.

Yoshida, a cardiac surgeon without a heart, had stirred the olive in his drink and watched Scott with cool eyes. Callie had sat stock still, face like a rock, lips ever-so-flat. Hardgirl. She might have looked as sleek as Kim Novak in *Vertigo*, but she had crazy secrets of her own. And she had judged him. Her gaze was the proof beyond all reasonable doubt that he was guilty.

But it took Skunk to pass sentence. The little man wouldn't ever know it, because Scott was going to deprive him of what he wanted. But Skunk was the one who would set Scott free.

A few yards away, the 101 ran onto the Golden Gate Bridge. The sun was sinking toward the Pacific. The traffic, the wind, all of it sounded like a river of sound, pulling him into the current. He walked along the sidewalk and onto the bridge approach. Ahead, the terrain fell away precipitously, through brambles and rock, to cold waves that crashed against the shore.

The world was going to know about his guilt, his lies, his failures. There was no way to prevent that now. And when this went public, the press would descend on him like jackals.

Headlines, blame, his wife's eyes, he couldn't bear the thought of it.

He walked. The bridge was so bright in the sunlight that it looked like a fiery hammer. Bicyclists passed him, and tourists snapping photos. One or two paused to look at him, or give a doubletake. They suspected who he was, but he was wearing a baseball cap and sunglasses, and they held back, unsure.

Cars sped past on the roadway. The bridge railing ratcheted by on his right. The guardrail was four feet high. A Highway Patrol car drove by. Nobody was watching him. Everybody was sightseeing, jogging, taking pictures. This was the edge of the continent. A gateway. Why not? Why not here?

Right under their noses.

Here was certainty. Here was all he could take. The black tar had come up over his heart. But it would never suffocate him, just leave him in torment. This bridge was a crossing, but he would use it for more than that. Here he was going to put a stop to Skunk's plan.

He was going to make sure Skunk kept his stinking hands off his family.

Jo pulled up at the Aquatic Park at three fifty-eight. She crept along the street below Ghirardelli Square hunting for a parking spot. The grass in the park was emerald green and seagulls hovered overhead in the bracing breeze. The curb was solid with parked cars.

San Francisco was the black hole of parking. Garages cost twenty bucks an hour and street parking was survival of the fittest. It caused such road rage that anger management courses refused to hold classes in the city because too many students arrived on the verge of violence.

She saw a spot, sixty yards up. Yes. She signaled. The Audi in front of her slowed and signaled too. Oh, no. Jo swung out and raced around it. She needed that spot. She swerved to the curb like a hawk diving on a mouse and stealing it from another predator.

She jumped out. The Audi pulled up and the driver put down her window.

The woman pointed at her. 'I signaled for that space.'

'No time.' Jo stuck quarters into the meter and shrugged in the cross-cultural gesture for *sorry*.

'Road thug!'

Jo waved uselessly and jogged across the park toward the water. She hoped Callie's contacts would turn up for this meeting. Though the Stockton Street crash had been all over the news, she didn't think Callie's name had been released yet. They might not know she was dead.

The grass sloped downhill toward the Aquatic Park, a sheltered cove near Fisherman's Wharf. At the pier, an old three-masted clipper ship was tied up. Down the block, tourists gaggled like geese, waiting to board a cable car. The Ghirardelli sign sat atop the old chocolate factory like a tiara.

She reached the footpath along the water and slowed to a walk, looking around. In the amphitheater overlooking the cove, a dozen people sat basking in the autumn sun. In the water, a lone swimmer braved the chill. She was wearing a straw hat and doing sidestroke at a regal pace, as if she was Cleopatra's barge rowing up the Nile.

Jo caught her breath. The bay was dolphin-blue in the afternoon light. Sailboats were out. Against the backdrop of the Golden Gate Bridge they looked like white blossoms blown across the water by the breeze.

The driver of the Audi came walking across the lawn. She was wearing a calf-length suede coat over black leather boots. The coat flared in the breeze. Beneath it she had on an ivory colored suit. Jo half-turned away and tried to look inconspicuous. The woman's skirt was short. Her hair was caramel-streaked. Her shades were bigger than Jo's windshield. She looked like she'd stepped straight from *Glamour* magazine. She had a Jack Russell terrier on a leash, bouncing in front of her like a lottery ball in the drum.

She slowed and looked around. Checked her watch. Looked some more, impatient.

Oh, brother.

Jo knew she shouldn't have hijacked the parking spot. Hello, karma. Good to see you. Go ahead, kick me in the butt.

She walked over. When the woman spotted her coming, her mouth puckered.

'Do you have an issue? You already stole the parking spot. Why don't you leave it at that? Because I am not a person you want to pick a fight with,' she said.

'I think we're here for the same meeting,' Jo said.

'You're the third person?' The woman's expression shifted from annoyance to curiosity. She raised an eyebrow. 'Well, you're certainly the eager beaver.'

'Jo Beckett, MD.'

They shook, and Jo reached into her wallet for a business card. The woman waved her off, as if shooing a fly.

'We don't do that,' she said. 'You're an MD? Are you one of David's finds?'

'David Yoshida?' Jo shook her head. Caution was jousting with curiosity. 'I'm on staff at UCSF, but no. He was cardiothoracic surgery; I'm in psychiatry.'

Behind her sunglasses, the woman was elaborately made up. She was a walking advertisement for the leather industry and the L'Oreal Group. She looked like a million bucks. She also looked familiar. Even more than that, she sounded familiar. And she acted like she expected people to notice.

They did. Joggers gave her long glances as they passed. The Jack Russell vibrated around her feet.

'A damned shame about David.' She removed the shades. Her gaze was acute. 'We don't have any psychiatrists. This could be interesting.'

She looked Jo up and down. The eagerness in her eyes was unsettling. Then she checked her watch again, and glanced around the Aquatic Park.

She was waiting for Callie, Jo was sure of it. She didn't know.

She tugged on the dog's leash. 'Let's stroll.'

Jo hesitated, ambivalent. This woman thought she was here to join the Dirty Secrets Club.

One hard and fast rule Jo played by: Don't lie. She never misrepresented herself to worm information from people. But if she explained why she was here, the meeting would be over in nothing flat. The demons and cherubs of her conscience perched on her shoulder, pitchforks and angel wings fluttering.

'Let's walk toward Fort Mason,' Jo said.

The Jack Russell ping-ponged around the woman's feet. She made a ticking sound. 'Cosette. Come.'

'David Yoshida didn't send me,' Jo said. 'I'm here because of Callie Harding.'

'She's not usually late. Maybe she's stuck in traffic.' The woman scrutinized Jo. 'You're not exactly what I was expecting. But Callie likes to play things close to the vest. And we'll find out if you have what we want soon enough.'

'What do you want?' Jo said.

'She didn't tell you?' She pulled on the dog's leash, frowning. 'Do you have a CV?'

'Not with me.'

'That's probably prudent. Before anything else, you need to understand that this isn't for everybody.'

'I'm sure.'

'Do you? Do you realize who I am?'

Her eyes were hazel. Her identity wouldn't come to Jo.

'I'm not going to lie. I should, but I don't.'

An unamused smile. 'So dishonesty isn't your sin. That's okay. We have enough members who've borne false witness. We can use a new twist.' The woman tossed her leonine hair and lifted her chin. 'Xochi Zapata.'

*So-shee*, she pronounced it. Maybe for Xochitlan, or Xochi-quetzal, though she didn't look like an Aztec princess. Didn't look like she'd ridden out of the desert to fight *yanquis*, either. She looked like a white-bread suburban Anglo. Albeit a pageant-contestant Anglo, buffed by the gleam machine.

She was XZ. And Jo realized where she'd seen her: on a billboard on a Muni bus, posing with other members of the team.

'Your News Live, right? You're the business reporter,' Jo said. 'The fast food exposé.'

' "Swimming on a Sea of Grease". That's it.'

Jo remembered now. McDonald's made you fat. She also recalled an interview conducted aboard a CEO's private jet on a flight to Aspen. Zapata reported Silicon Valley stories and attended festivals of capitalism around the globe.

'Can I tell you who I am and why I'm here?' Jo said.

'We'll get to that.' Zapata looked annoyed at the interruption. 'My point is, our club isn't simply confidential. It's exclusive. So before anything else, we need to know if you have the stuff it takes to be a member.'

'What's that?'

Jo heard the *faux* innocence in her own voice. She was going to need to wash out her conscience with soap. But she wasn't about to stop listening.

'You tell me,' Zapata said. 'What would you bring to the party?'

*My grandma left me a collection of Tokugawa era museum-quality Samurai pieces. I eat Krispy Kreme doughnuts a dozen at a go.*

'I'm a consulting forensic psychiatrist for the City of San Francisco, UCSF Medical Center and the San Francisco Police Department. I can supply you with references and a list of my publications.'

'Honey, that's great, but it's hardly sexy.'

'I solved the Jeffrey Nagel hanging. That was thought to be a case of sex.'

'Your bona fides can't relate to your patients or your caseload. The secret has to be yours. And it has to be dirty.' She scrutinized Jo again. 'Though trust is an issue. We wouldn't accept someone who divulged her patients' secrets. You might divulge ours as well.'

'I would never violate doctor-patient privilege.'

'Good. We count on our members not to speak about the club to outsiders.' She smiled knowingly. 'We're not the White House. We don't tolerate leaks.'

'I can keep quiet. I keep secrets locked up tighter than the grave.'

'Excellent.' Zapata tossed her hair again. 'To be blunt, we need to see that you've got some heat. Frankly, I don't know if you have the prestige. If Callie's nominating you, that's definitely in your favor. But you understand you'd come in at the lowest level.'

'Which is?'

'Basic membership. Fun, camaraderie, plenty of excitement.' She smirked. 'The *frisson* will be there. But rising to more exclusive levels would have to wait.'

'Understood. How will it work?' Jo said.

The wind blew back the collar of Zapata's suede coat. She was wearing a necklace on which hung a black diamond.

'You provide your résumé. Give us both halves, and girl, it had better be convincing. Your prestige and your dirt.' Zapata's hazel eyes were intense. 'We need hard evidence. Whatever secret you're keeping, you need to provide evidence that it actually occurred. And you need to provide proof that you're the one who did it. You can't claim credit for other people's shame. That's tacky.'

'I didn't know,' Jo said.

'Oh, yeah. It's far too easy to claim credit for an act. Proving your involvement – your authorship, call it – is a lot harder.'

Authorship. These people thought of bad deeds as creative acts.

'But to be frank, you might be sharp and ambitious, but I'm not convinced that you're enough of a power player for us. Not yet, anyhow.' She glanced across the park at Jo's truck. 'Generally we don't talk to folks who drive beat-up pickups, except when they come to the house with a mower in the back.'

Zapata looked again at her watch, ran her hand over the band, seemingly annoyed. 'Where is Callie?'

Jo stopped. Holding back any longer would be both untenable and cruel. 'She's not coming.'

'Excuse me?'

'She's dead.'

Zapata's head snapped back as if she'd been hit. 'Dead?'

'Last night. The wreck at the Stockton Street Bridge. I'm afraid Callie was the driver of the car that went through the railing.'

Zapata stepped back, almost physically rejecting the news. 'Jesus. Oh, no.' She put her manicured hands to her face. The Jack Russell ran around her legs, tangling her in the leash. Then her eyes sharpened.

'What are you doing here?'

'I'm a forensic psychiatrist. I—'

'I heard that. What the hell are you doing here?'

'I'm performing a psychological autopsy on Callie.'

Zapata's hand went to her forehead. 'You're from the police. Oh my God—'

'No.' Jo thought, madly. She needed to keep her from bolting. 'You're part of the black diamond group. You, Callie, David Yoshida—'

'How do you know about that?'

'You and Callie were supposed to meet here with another person. SS.'

Panic lit her hazel eyes. 'Jesus Christ.' She backed away, looking around frantically. 'You can't talk about this.'

'I'm sorry, but you can't—'

'You're a therapist – you can't talk about what people tell you.'

'That's only when—'

'Ten seconds ago you bragged you'd never violate doctor patient-privilege. Try it now and I'll take you down. I told you, you do *not* want to pick a fight with me.' She turned, took two steps, and turned back, pointing a finger. 'I can crush you under a blizzard of destructive publicity. I'll get the medical licensing board to investigate you. You'll be reduced to cleaning toilets in some dirty psych ward. You'll wish you shoveled dog shit for a living.'

Jo tried to slough off the image and the insult. Zapata was white with anger, but blinking and breathing rapidly.

'You're frightened,' Jo said.

Zapata glared, and shook her head, and ran her manicured fingernails into her hair. She couldn't have drawn more attention to herself if she'd hoisted her shirt and flashed the tourists at the cable car stop.

'You're scared to death,' Jo said.

Doe caught in the high beams. Zapata hesitated for another second, as if fearing to twitch, and then rushed forward and grabbed Jo's arm.

'I saw the raw feed, the footage from our camera crew at the crash site. It was horrible. For Christsake, what happened?' Her hand was cold. 'You performed the autopsy – did somebody kill her?'

'The Medical Examiner performed the autopsy. I'm looking at Callie's mental state.' She held Zapata's gaze. 'Do you think somebody killed her?'

She looked like she was about to cry. 'Tell me. Off the record. In confidence.'

Jo balked. 'I'm gathering information to prepare a report. I can't promise confidentiality.'

'If I were your patient you could.'

'You're not.'

'I'll hire you.'

'No.'

Zapata looked like she was crawling with bugs and wanted to tear open her own flesh with her long nails to get rid of them. She gripped Jo's arm.

'Then join us. I'll approve your application to join the club.'

'What are you talking about?'

'It's great. Lots of benefits. It's exciting. Sexy. Come on, you'd love it. You were already asking about it—'

'You're bribing me? No.'

'And later there'll be prizes – cars, trips, recognition. As long as you don't tell anybody about it.'

Jo felt torn. She was obligated to write a report for the police department. She wasn't obligated to divulge every scrap of information she obtained. And Amy Tang had given her an explicit mandate to dispense with protocol. Just get to the bottom of the psychic well.

'Why don't you tell me what's scaring you so bad?' Jo said.

Joggers were passing. On the park lawn, a kid was flying an orange kite. Jo nodded at the seats high up in the amphitheater and took Zapata's arm.

'Come on.'

She led Zapata up the stairs to the top row, well away from anybody else. The wind was cooling, the amphitheater in shade from the pine forest on the crest of the hill at Fort Mason.

'How did they find out about us?' Zapata said.

'They?'

'How did *you* find out about us?'

'Xochi, that's irrelevant now.'

'It's *secret*, don't you get it? They're killing us, aren't they?'

Jo couldn't tell what the woman wanted more – to suck up information, or to unload whatever she was holding in. Jo went quiet and, like a client in therapy, like a journalist, Zapata filled the silence.

'It's obvious. Somebody talked.' She pressed her hands to her face. 'I feel so betrayed.' She turned to Jo. 'Did Callie tell?'

'I don't know.'

Zapata was staring straight at her, but her eyes seemed far away. Her face was pale with pink patches on her neck.

'Xochi, what exactly is the Dirty Secrets Club?'

'It's . . .' She shook her head, as if deciding to hold back, and then shrugged. '. . . it's a playroom, a party, a confessional . . . You a Catholic?' Zapata glanced at the cross around Jo's neck. 'You understand the importance of confession?'

'Yes, I do.'

'But it's supposed to be foolproof. It's impossible for information to leak.'

'Why?'

'It just is. It's supposed to be fail-safe.'

'But you think it's not.'

'Either somebody's talking out of school, or—' She lowered her head. 'Or one of the members is killing us. Jesus.' She raked her nails into her hair.

'How'd you get in?' Jo said.

Zapata cut a glance at her. 'You think I'm going to tell you my secret? Right. The day that happens is the day you tell me yours, sista.'

Jo didn't respond. Zapata looked at her with disdain.

'Everybody has a dirty secret. Even you.'

Jo sat quietly. She had an intuition: the Dirty Secrets Club was absolutely secret in the same way black holes suck in everything by the force of gravity. Nothing escapes a black hole, even light.

Supposedly. But astronomers know that black holes eject x-rays in powerful bursts.

The Dirty Secrets Club had to be like that. It had to feed on negative energy. Like every clique in history, there would be a buzz around it. A sense of *I'm in*. It would reverberate at some sub-audible harmonic frequency when members were near each other. Because there's one thing about cliques: nobody can truly enjoy being *in* unless they can lord it over the people who are *out*.

Zapata ran her red fingernails over her thighs. A pelican swooped low over the cove and speared into the water, going after a fish.

'Xochi, this is important. Who's the third person who's supposed to be here?'

Zapata looked at her like *You have to be kidding.*

Jo leaned forward. 'I know David Yoshida and Maki were both members of the club. They're dead. And Callie didn't turn up here today, because she's dead too. Where's the third person?' Jo said.

'Oh, shit.'

Jo held her gaze. 'Who is it, Xochi?'

Zapata's lips parted. She seemed frozen with indecision.

'SS,' Jo said. 'For the black diamond meeting. Please.'

Zapata shook her head.

Jo felt anger flash behind her eyes. 'People are dying every forty-eight hours. Who is it?'

Slowly, quietly, Zapata closed her eyes. 'Scott Southern.'

'The wide receiver?'

Zapata nodded. She put her hands over her mouth, as though she couldn't believe she'd said it.

'Thank you,' Jo said.

Zapata pressed her hands to her lips. Her knuckles were white.

'Xochi, what was Callie's secret?' she said.

Zapata frowned at her. 'You don't know? I thought . . .'

Jo's cellphone rang. She ignored it. And heard her name being called.

She looked across the park. Shit. Amy Tang was jogging toward them.

'Who's that?' Zapata said.

'She's a police lieutenant,' Jo said.

'I thought—' Zapata got to her feet, pulling on the dog's leash. 'You set this up all along?'

'No. Please – don't go.'

Jo reached for her. But Xochi Zapata was running away.

# 16

Amy Tang jogged up. 'You shouldn't be here by yourself.'

On the street, Zapata's Audi screeched away. Jo shook her head. 'You blew it. She was a member of the Dirty Secrets Club.'

'That could have been dangerous.'

'Spare me. You gave me *carte blanche* to find out why Callie died. I don't have to clear my interviews with you.'

Tang looked at the road. 'We'll go after her.'

'She'll clam up.' Jo put her hands on her hips. 'Why are you here?'

'Fonsecca said you sprinted out of the US Attorney's Office like Lara Croft. He worried you were racing off to play cowboy, and he was right. And he wants Callie's iPod and calendar back.' Tang kept scowling, but her annoyance abated. 'Maybe he wants to download her *American Idol* playlist.' She ran her hand through her hair. 'The Dirty Secrets Club is real?'

'It's real.' Jo pulled out her phone. 'Scott Southern was supposed to be here. He's not. Can you get his number?'

'From the Forty-Niners? Jesus.' Tang frowned and began making calls. The sunlight gave a bright sting to the spray from the whitecaps on the bay.

'Thanks.' Tang hung up. 'Got it.'

She recited Southern's number. Jo borrowed Tang's pen, scribbled it on her forearm and dialed.

'The Dirty Secrets Club,' Tang said.

'It's some kind of virtual confessional. They want powerful and snotty people to give it a cachet.'

In Jo's ear, the number rang. A woman answered, sounding rushed. 'Scott?'

'No.' Jo identified herself and explained she was working with the police. 'I'm trying to reach Mr Southern. Is this—'

'Kelly. His wife.'

She got a mental picture of Kelly Southern. She'd seen the wide receiver's young wife on television, handing their little boy to Scott over the railing at the stadium after a game. She'd looked cheerleader-pretty, and fond of her man.

'I'm at a meeting he was supposed to attend,' Jo said.

Long, awkward pause. 'Oh no. I'm sorry, I don't . . .'

'Mrs Southern, is everything all right?'

'I've been trying to reach him all day. You said you're working with the police?'

'Yes.'

'Is he in trouble?'

'Not with the police. Do you think he's in trouble?'

'I don't know where he is. Something's way wrong.' Tears edged into the woman's voice. She sounded young and frightened. 'He missed practice, the Niners don't know where he is. And I got a weird note.'

'Weird how?'

'Anonymous. It said Scott has secrets he's keeping from me, and I should think twice about me and Tyler being around him.'

'Do you still have it?' Jo said.

'I gave it to Scott. It scared me. Something's awfully wrong.'

'Does Scott have a cellphone?'

Kelly gave her the number. It went on her wrist. Tang was chewing her lip.

'Mrs Southern, I'm going to try to get hold of him. And I'm going to have you speak to the police lieutenant who's here with me. She's going to call as soon as I hang up.' Jo gestured for Tang to dial the number.

'Okay,' Kelly said. 'Please try. But he's not answering.'

Jo hung up and dialed Southern's cellphone. As it rang, she heard Tang take over the conversation with his wife, drawing out more information about the letter she'd received.

Anonymous notes: the poison pill of any campaign to ruin people. *dirty . . . Stop it.*

Southern's cell number kept ringing.

Scott walked.

Skunk wanted to meet him at the vista point on the Marin side of the Golden Gate Bridge, but he was done playing by Skunk's rules. Done letting Skunk's shadowy boss manipulate him. He was ready to overturn the whole thing.

He bent forward against the wind, walking along the east sidewalk on the bridge, heading north toward the middle of the span. Far below on the water, a container ship steamed toward the Pacific. Ahead, the north tower dominated the view, massive and red, the color of iron and spirit. Scott felt as though it was judging him, that it could hammer down at any moment and crush him. On the roadway a river of traffic rushed past at sixty miles an hour. The sidewalk was bustling.

He was through with secrecy. This was as public as he could get. Up here on the bridge, Skunk couldn't do anything crazy without giving himself away. And Skunk couldn't run, either. Deadly traffic to one side. Nothing but wind and water on the other. Air below. Two hundred twenty feet of air, below the middle of the span. He'd looked it up.

At the center of the bridge he stopped and leaned against the guardrail. The view was spectacular. The bright red railing felt cold beneath his hands. The roadway vibrated with every heavy truck that passed.

Turning around, he planted his back against the rail and waited.

When his cellphone rang he let it go for a couple of seconds, the fight song marching into the third measure. Skunk would be pissed off, wondering why he wasn't at the rendezvous, wasn't on his knees begging for mercy. He made Skunk wait.

Two more bars of the fight song. He answered it.

Jo held tight to the phone. A man answered.

'I'm not at the vista point,' he said.

The voice was Scott Southern's, she would have bet money on it

– that laconic drawl with the winsome note at the edge. Her mouth was open to answer, but intuition told her to keep quiet.

'Walk south,' Southern said. 'I'm at the middle of the span, about three-quarters of a mile from you.'

On the line she heard the whine of heavy, fast-moving traffic, and the roar of the wind. The pause on Southern's end stretched too long.

'Skunk?' he said. 'Who is this?'

She had to gamble. 'Scott Southern? Doctor Jo Beckett, UCSF Medical Center. Your wife gave me your number.'

No reply. She heard the traffic and the lowing of a foghorn.

His voice came in a rush. 'Medical Center – is Tyler all right?'

'Your son?' Jo said.

'Jesus Christ, is he okay?'

'He's fine. Your wife is worried, and—'

'Kelly, God, did something happen to her? Did somebody – holy Christ, are they all right?'

'Yes, Mr Southern. Your family is fine.' With a fracturing sound, she grasped what he meant. 'Your family is *safe*.'

'You're positive? What's going on?' Another pause. 'Who is this?'

His voice was torn with anxiety. Jo smoothed her own voice and forced herself not to talk too fast. She sensed she could lose him at any second.

'I'm a forensic psychiatrist. I'm working with the police to investigate Callie Harding's death.'

'What?' A beat, then confusion. 'Why are you calling me?'

He didn't sound at all surprised to hear Callie was dead. 'I know you were scheduled to meet with Callie this afternoon. And I know your wife received an anonymous letter today. Scott – it sounds like a threat.'

'Jesus.' He could barely be heard over the noise of rushing traffic on his end. 'You're working with the police about Callie? Kelly talked to the police? Oh, Christ.'

Jo looked at Tang, who was still on the phone with Kelly. Jo had to judge how much she should reveal to Southern. If she laid her cards on the table, he might cut her off. Unless she convinced him it was too late for him to run and try to hide.

She risked it. 'I know you belong to the Dirty Secrets Club.'

Silence.

'I know something has gone wrong with the club, and that you feel threatened. I think it's connected to Callie's death. I need to talk to you, Mr Southern.'

More silence. 'Oh, Christ – are you saying this is all going to break, be news?'

'I'm saying that whatever threat came down on Callie, I'm hoping it's not coming down on you as well. Please talk to me.'

'You're a shrink?' he said.

She explained it again. 'I know about Callie, and about Doctor Yoshida and Maki Prichingo. That's too many people dead. Scott, please. Tell me what's going on. If you're in trouble, let me help you.'

Again he was silent. Where was he? She looked around, as if she might actually see him.

'There's not enough time,' he said.

'Whatever time you can give me. Even a minute. I'll listen.'

'I don't know . . .'

'I do. There's no problem that's insoluble.'

The silence stretched again. If not for the static on the line, she would have thought she'd lost him. Then he spoke. There was a note of despondency in his voice.

'I don't know how you'd protect me. The only person who could have done that was Callie. Put me in Witness Protection, make Scott Southern disappear for ever.'

'Ten minutes, Scott. Give me ten minutes to talk to you. Let me convince you that this will work. Please.'

Long wait. 'Just ten. You'd better be for real.'

'Tell me where you are. I'll come there.'

'When?'

'Now,' she said.

The foghorn cried again in the background. She waited for him to answer.

★　　★　　★

Scott closed his eyes, shutting out the dazzle from the wave tops below. He could hear the woman as if she was breathing right next to him.

She knew about the anonymous note. She knew about the club. But she claimed she could help him.

Could he let go of this weight? Could this be his chance?

He pressed the phone to his ear, hanging onto the connection. This doctor could be his lifeline. If she wasn't lying. A shrink – she could be trying to mess with his head, play with him. But if she was right, if she could help him – maybe he could end this nightmare, nail Skunk and the boss man behind him. Maybe without his secret coming out . . .

Maybe. Just maybe, nobody would have to know the truth about him.

His heart lifted. Possibility. Was what she said really possible? He opened his eyes. Even if it was just a chance, didn't he have a duty to grab it?

'Mr Southern. Please believe me,' the doctor said.

He saw the water below, and it looked bright and soothing. He nodded to himself.

A beep sounded in his ear. He had an incoming call. He looked at the number. *Unknown caller.*

His hopes crashed. That meant it was Skunk. 'There's no time. He's coming.'

'Scott, there's always something you can do. Always.'

He squeezed his eyes shut. The doctor was a long shot, and it was too late to spend time finding out if she was telling the truth.

'Yeah, but not what you want. I'm sorry, I don't have a choice.'

They *knew.* The reality rained down on him. No matter what he did, his secret was coming out. He was done.

And no matter what he did, Skunk would punish his family.

'I have to fix this. And there's only one way to do that, because I need it to be a sure thing.' The incoming call beeped. The water below looked like sharpened glass. 'Surer than a bullet.'

He hung up.

## 17

'Dammit. He hung up. I thought I had him.' Jo rubbed her fingers against her forehead. 'We have to find him. Something's extremely wrong.'

Tang snapped her phone shut. 'How wrong?'

'Death threat wrong. He's under duress, and scared shit-less.'

*Surer than a bullet.*

Where was he? She thought about what she'd heard during their conversation. Stared at the bay, focusing.

Heard the foghorn.

'The bridge.' She grabbed Tang's elbow and pulled her toward the street. 'Southern's on the Golden Gate Bridge.'

'Get up to the vista point,' Skunk said. 'You're not thinking, Scott. Think of Tyler.'

He was. Tyler and Kelly were all he was thinking of, all he could see in front of him.

'What do you think, this is hide and seek, you can play games and keep away from me? You're not from outer space. I know where you live,' Skunk said.

Tyler. Melody. Life, he could save a life. 'I'm on the bridge. East side, middle of the span.'

'Get up here, dickwad, or I'll—'

'I have the names. I'm not handing them over at the vista point. People would see my Range Rover.'

And doing it at the vista point would give Skunk a chance to pull something. Doing it here was the only way.

'You come here, Skunk, or I'll toss the list over. You can get it back when it blows to shore in San Jose.'

He hung up. Skunk would come.

Jo revved the engine and tore away from the curb.

'You think this situation is that bad?' Tang said.

'Gut feeling – it's worse than bad. Do you want to take the chance that I'm wrong?'

'No. Go.'

Jo squealed into traffic. 'Got a gumball light in your pocket to stick on the top of the truck, so we can avoid all these cars?'

'Lean on the horn. I give you dispensation.'

Jo jammed it into second, popped the clutch and swerved out to pass the line of cars ahead of her. The engine revved. She saw Tang buckle her seatbelt.

'Southern's terrified. When I said I was a doctor he immediately assumed his family was either hurt or in danger.'

'What's he doing on the bridge?' Tang said.

'Meeting the man who's threatening him.'

'Drive faster.'

She honked and swerved around a station wagon. Took the corner while downshifting.

Why would Southern want to meet his contact on the bridge? Because it was public? Did that make it safe? Was he trying somehow to pull the rug out from under his tormentor? She didn't know. But the bridge raised a dark spectre in the back of her mind.

She slowed for a stop sign. Tang waved her arm.

'Go,' Tang said. 'Run it. Run 'em all.'

She got to Marina Boulevard, slaloming around cars, and turned the corner. The road straightened, the stoplights thinned and she gunned it. Sailboat masts glinted in the sun to her right, a nautical forest. To her left, neat, expensive homes streaked by. In the distance, beyond the forested headlands of the Presidio, the bridge stretched across the mouth of the bay.

She checked the speedometer. Come on, truck, you can do better than eighty.

She poured through a light as it turned red. Tang was holding the dashboard with one hand, dialing her phone with the other.

'Calling the CHP. They patrol the bridge, maybe they can spot him.'

In a few seconds they reached the 101. The Tacoma rattled and moaned, but Jo kept her foot down. Tang got through to the Highway Patrol. Described Southern, asked them to send a car to the bridge and be on the lookout for him. Not much to go on, Jo thought.

Going ninety, on little more than her own gut feeling.

Tang kept her phone to her ear, waiting for confirmation that the Highway Patrol was on the way, and glanced at Jo. 'Will this truck hold together?'

Jo pushed it hard into a curve. 'Yeah. But I really wish I'd won the lottery and bought the Lambo.'

'You play the lottery?'

'Every time this truck breaks down.'

'Don't. You have better odds of surviving Russian Roulette.'

Or of surviving a fall from two hundred feet. 'You going to give me dispensation to stop on the bridge?'

'You think we'll need to?'

The bridge had six narrow lanes of swift traffic, no center divider, no shoulders. To stop was begging for a crash. 'Yes.'

Tang's mouth went flat. 'Then do it, and let's hope the CHP gets there to keep some Winnebago from rear-ending us.'

Trees rose on either side of the road, pines and groves of eucalyptus. Jo rounded a bend.

Tang jammed both hands against the dash. 'Damn, damn—'

Red brake lights and motionless traffic greeted them. Jo slammed on the brakes. With the ABS shaking, they squealed to a stop.

Traffic was gridlocked.

'Get on the shoulder,' Tang said. She rolled down the window, stuck out her arm and flashed her badge to the traffic.

Jo worked her way to the side of the road. She heard Tang on the phone with the CHP again. She eked her way to the shoulder of the highway and found to her dismay that it was too narrow. She gunned the right wheels of the pickup over the curb. Thinking

*Hang in there, truck,* she accelerated. They lurched forward, bouncing like a basketball.

Tang hung up. 'Car pulling a trailer jackknifed—' They hit a rock, bottomed out and kept going. 'Now I see why this thing breaks down so often. Trailer's jackknifed a hundred yards out on the bridge. Tow truck's coming, but this jam will take time to clear.'

'How long?'

'Too long.' Tang's face was tight. 'You fast on foot?'

'I'd better be.'

They neared the exit for the visitor plaza. 'Pull off here.'

Scott waited. His stomach had clenched. In the distance, the familiar figure hunched toward him.

*Moment of truth.*

That's what this was. Not a cliché, but reality – his moment of truth. How many people got one?

He was at the point of no return. Skunk was within sight, coming to get the names of the people he and his boss were after, so they could eliminate them.

Scott clutched the sheets of paper. Three slim white sheets of pulp, and here was the truth: they were about life and death. Everybody named in them was going to exit this world. They were a eulogy, the end credits. But he had no choice.

Traffic was a roar. Back by the toll plaza it was snarled, but here it was a smear, static in his head. The day looked flat. The sun was cold. The city seemed nothing but a white layer of chalk poured across the hills.

He had never felt more certain, or more frightened. He had to do this right. He wouldn't get a second chance.

That's why he'd chosen this bridge. It was a sure thing. Ninety-eight per cent accuracy rate, first time. Better than pills. Better than poison. Better than a bullet. This was the only place to do what he needed to.

He looked up at the north tower, pointing toward heaven. No hesitation, Southern. Do this thing, get it over with. This was the right decision. Tyler would be safe. Kelly would be safe. Things were going to be finished, once and for all.

*No problem is insoluble.*

He shook himself. Stop that. He couldn't let the phone call undermine his determination. Couldn't let the shrink's words eat at the edges of his certainty. He breathed out, and pushed the thought away. His stomach tightened.

Skunk walked toward him.

Skunk saw the guy in the middle of the span. Dude standing still when everybody else was walking and the traffic was a snake hissing past. The pussy was leaning against the railing.

Southern was wearing a red letterman's jacket and baseball cap. He had something in his hands, was worrying it. Skunk smiled.

Papers.

The pussy had got the names. Fucking A. He picked up his pace. Southern just stood there like the stupid side of beef he was, ready to hand them over.

Skunk's smile broadened. Southern thought once he handed over the names, this thing would be finished. Thought he was home Scott free.

'Ha.'

He stuck his hand in his pocket, feeling his lighter and the bottle. The only thing that was going to be finished was Scott Southern.

Jo jogged along the west sidewalk on the bridge. The Marin headlands were brown and sere ahead of her. Open ocean was to her left. The sun was stark in the west, the traffic a jarring roar. Though it was gridlocked on the bridge approach, out here six lanes of metal were rushing past a few feet away. Across the wide roadway, Amy Tang ran along the east sidewalk. Her spiky hair flicked back and forth. She looked grim, eyes on the hundreds of pedestrians strolling the bridge. She had spoken to the bridge control room. They had cameras on the sidewalks, but hadn't spotted Scott Southern.

Jo counted suspender cables as she ran. She and Tang were

three hundred yards past the south tower, but the bridge was almost two miles long. People on bikes cycled past her. The water, immensely far below, shivered blue with whitecaps in the wind. She squinted against the sun, breathing hard.

Her phone rang. Tang sounded winded.

'I don't know about this.'

'Let's keep going.' Jo heard the harshness in her own breath.

She tried to focus. Across the road at the center of the span, amid the moving swirl of people, a tall man in a baseball cap and letterman's jacket stood at the rail, looking at the bay. The jacket was red with gold lettering on the back.

She put her phone to her ear. 'Dead ahead. Red jacket. Is that him?'

Tang stared hard. She didn't answer, but she seemed to be drawing into herself. Growing quieter. Like a gun cocking.

'What's the name of the guy Southern thought he was talking to?' Tang said.

'Skunk.'

'Slow down,' Tang said. 'Don't spook them.'

Jo dropped to a walk, trying to catch her breath. The man in the jacket turned from the rail. Another man was walking toward him, one hand jammed in his pocket. Jo couldn't make out his face, but he was strutting like he was about to . . .

. . . win the lottery. Beat Russian Roulette. His whole attitude was a smirk.

'That's the guy,' she said. 'And something's not right.'


Skunk walked toward Southern. 'Whatever bug got up your ass, get it out. Hand over the names.'

Southern stood there, sun on his face, looking pained. The papers were in his hands. Slowly, regretfully, he folded them in half. He reached into his letterman's jacket, took out a Ziploc bag and dropped the papers in. He zipped it, checked the seal, and ran his hand over it a third time. Skunk looked at him quizzically.

'I don't need to freeze 'em like hot dogs. Just hand them over.'

Southern shook his head. 'Come and get them.'

*          *          *

Jo closed to within a hundred yards of the two men. The taller man had an athlete's bearing, that sense of supreme self-possession that arises from physical prowess. With every step she took, the lettering on the back of his jacket came into clearer focus. USC.

'It's him, Amy,' she said.

'Where? I don't have them in sight.'

Jo glanced across the road. Tang was falling behind her, fighting her way through pedestrians on a much more crowded sidewalk.

'Crest of the span,' Jo said. 'The short guy has his hand in his pocket, like he has a weapon. He looks antsy.'

She checked traffic. It was fierce and fast, six solid lanes of cars, trucks, buses slurring past, three heading south, three north, separated only by a double yellow line of paint down the center of the road. She leaned on the thin railing that separated the sidewalk from the road and looked for a break. There was none.

'Don't think about it,' Tang said. 'You're unarmed.'

And you're the size of a leprechaun, Jo thought. But you're going after them anyway. She felt a creeping admiration for Tang.

'Here's what we want to do,' Tang said. 'Number one, prevent any violence. Two, follow this guy Skunk. Three, talk to Southern.'

'Those goals may be at odds.'

Skunk stepped toward Southern. Jo clenched her hands.

Scott faced Skunk. The rodent was seven feet away from him, one hand out for the papers, the other jammed in his pocket. Scott didn't need to see a pistol to feel the threat. The man's eyes were as cruel and stupid as the hole at the end of a gun barrel.

He could take this guy.

He didn't doubt it for a second. But at this distance, if Skunk's finger was on a trigger, he could get off a shot. And there were so many people around. A family walked by, the kids eating ice cream cones.

He needed to get Skunk closer, to within arm's reach. He put the Ziploc bag in the inside pocket of his jacket, and buttoned it up.

'I'm not giving the names to you. You'll have to take them from me.'

Scott backed against the railing. It was four feet high, barely high enough for him to feel it in the small of his back.

'You washing your hands of this?' Skunk said. 'You think if I take them instead of you handing them over, then what happens won't be your fault? Like it wasn't your fault what happened to that girl in college?' He waved his fingers, *gimme*.

'No,' Scott said.

Skunk stood there, mouth half open, eyes mean. Behind him the river of traffic rushed past. Scott stretched his arms and put his hands on the cold railing. He had to hold his nerve. Stay still. Don't jump offside. Draw Skunk offside instead. His heart was racing.

Across the road, a woman was running in his direction. Her dark hair whipped in the wind. She slowed, staring straight at him.

Jo stopped at the center of the span, on the crest of the gentle arch in the roadway. Across the road Scott Southern stood facing her, backed against the rail, gripping it with both hands. The smaller man, Skunk, was six feet from him.

Tang still had seventy yards to make up. She was weaving her way along the sidewalk, dodging through the crowd. A jogger with a dog on the leash blocked her path.

The traffic on the road was ferocious. Jo couldn't run across, wouldn't get across one lane without being hit, much less six. Cars, a school bus, a big rig, vehicles going both directions. Her view of Southern and Skunk strobed in and out of sight.

Southern pressed his back against the rail and drew into himself. He looked coiled. Like he was going to launch.

She had to act. She couldn't just stand there and watch something appalling unfold. She saw Amy Tang closing from the south.

She cupped her hands around her mouth and yelled. 'Scott, the police are coming.'

At the sound of her voice, he looked across at her. Skunk stepped toward him.

'*No*,' she shouted. '*Skunk, don't do it.*'

★   ★   ★

Scott saw the woman put her hands to her mouth and shout. She acted like she knew him. Like she wanted to help. He heard her voice, swept away under the wind and the roar of traffic.

A bus passed, he lost sight of her. Skunk was inching toward him with his hand out. It was now or never.

There was no place for either of them to go. He held still. Four more steps. Come on, Skunk, do it. Then we can both let go of this thing.

Skunk's little eyes were sharp with mistrust. 'What's wrong with you? You want me to lick your boots in gratitude for this?'

Across the road, the woman yelled again. She poked herself in the chest with one hand and nodded. She was telling him who she was.

It was the doctor.

Skunk lunged at him. 'Come on.'

She was too late.

Jo saw Skunk charge at Southern. She screamed, 'Don't do it!'

Southern looked at her.

'Oh my God,' she said.

He was seventy feet away but that look might have been a kiss. His whole bearing, the way the light fell on his face, the shift of his shoulders, were like a whispered assurance in her ear.

He breathed deep, to the bottom of his lungs.

Every nerve in Jo's body seemed to fire at once. Blessed God, no.

She had to do something, do it now.

She climbed over the thin railing and stepped onto the low separation barrier between the sidewalk and the road. It was hardly bigger than a railroad tie. She heard a car slam on its brakes. She looked quickly, saw a VW close and braking like crazy. She stuck her hand out like a traffic cop and jumped down onto the roadway.

The car came shrieking toward her, honking, rubber scorching off the tires as it braked. She ran to the far edge of the lane. Directly ahead, the next lane was clear. Skunk grabbed Southern's collar. Southern leaned back.

She brought in a breath and shouted, 'Skunk, back here, asshole.'

Behind her the braking car squealed past. She dodged across the second lane. Heard more brakes, sensed another car coming from the left, kept her hand extended. She was nearly halfway across the road.

More horns honked, brakes screeched. People on the east sidewalk were turning to look at the road. A man pointed at her. Another, with a camera, pointed at Southern.

Skunk pulled Southern's jacket open. Southern raised his hands off the rail.

She was in the middle of the roadway, heading for the center line. From her right, three lanes of northbound traffic streaked past. On the sidewalk, the man with the camera gestured at Southern, looking animated. The crowd was distracted by horns and brakes. She thought she heard somebody shout, 'Crazy chick . . .' She heard an air horn split the day.

She stopped dead. An eighteen-wheeler swept past, blocking Southern from her sight. Half a second, and it sped past.

Skunk and Southern were grappling. An SUV streaked by. When it passed she saw the two men in a frenzy of movement. Skunk was tearing at Scott. A school bus roared by, horn blaring. She was stuck on the center line.

Skunk was fighting, suddenly frantic. Southern's face was focused. Their wrists were locked, as though swing dancing.

'Scott, no—'

As she shouted, she knew she was too far away. Scrabbling with Skunk's wrist, Southern launched himself into the air. His momentum was huge and assured.

More shrieking brakes, and a gasoline tanker blared across her field of vision.

It streaked clear, and she saw the railing. All the strength left her legs. Scott Southern was airborne. His red letterman's jacket looked vivid against the blue of the bay. He sailed into the empty space beyond the railing as though soaring across the goal line with a touchdown pass.

He plunged like a stone.

# 18

A high-pitched tone buzzed through Jo's head. It was a din of horror. The crowd on the sidewalk had turned toward the railing. Red iron, an empty space. She thrust out her right arm and ran across the final three lanes of the roadway through the noise of horns and squealing tires.

People clutched the rail and looked down. The buzzing sound intensified.

'Oh, my God.'

'Jesus, no—'

Amy Tang ran by her, breathless. 'Police, out of my way. Police.'

Tang grabbed the rail and stared down, chest heaving, knuckles white. Jo hurdled the barrier, pitched across the sidewalk and joined her.

She saw him in the air. She squeezed her eyes shut and put her head down on the rail.

A woman cried out in distress. Jo opened her eyes to see Tang spin away from the view.

The voices came as sharp as splinters. 'He fell?' 'Shit, did he jump?'

*He*. Tang looked at Jo and her eyes were wild, as though she'd just been poisoned. She sagged against the railing. She looked mentally unkempt, and desperate to purge herself of what she'd just seen.

Jo straightened and grabbed Tang by both arms. She blinked hard, clamped everything down, spoke through gritted teeth. 'What about Skunk?'

Tang shook her head. 'Just Southern.'

The buzzing was so loud she could barely hear herself. She could barely breathe. Her eyes were burning. 'So where's Skunk?'

They both looked around.

A woman near the rail was hugging herself. She put a hand over her mouth and began to cry.

Jo grabbed the man next to her. 'Did you see what happened?'

He waved his hand at the rail. 'The guy was fighting with this other man, a short guy.'

Tang was still sagging against the rail. 'Was he pushed? I saw them grappling. The man who fell – was he pushed?'

The man shook his head. 'No. The smaller man, he looked like – he was trying to stop the guy going over. He was pulling on him or – shit, I don't know. He was trying to save him, but the guy kept fighting. And the other one was too small.'

Jo pushed through the bubble that had formed around the spot near the rail. Looking north, she saw at least a hundred people on the sidewalk, all the way to the end of the bridge. But only one man was jogging.

'Tang. There he goes.'

He was nearly a hundred yards away. She watched him run, feeling frozen.

She heard Tang on the phone, calling in an emergency. Heard *Man has fallen from the bridge.* Heard *Second man fleeing on foot.* Saw Skunk sinking into the distance.

She ran.

Her boots felt heavy. Her mind felt numb, her thoughts blasted, like scattered buckshot. The high-pitched noise droned in her head.

Four seconds: once you fly beyond the railing of the Golden Gate Bridge, that's how long it takes to hit the water. An eternity, watching the deck of the bridge recede at terrifying speed. A few heartbeats, looking up at the people on the sidewalk, people who can't begin to scream loud enough.

Skunk was the reason Southern had sailed over the railing. He had no other reason to flee.

He was running, hands shoved into his pockets, head down. Racing flat out, she closed on him. He grew larger in front of her, bunched and furtive, scurrying for the Marin side of the bridge.

Though she was in shape, the sprint had her breathing hard. Underneath the north tower, hearing her, he turned, looked back, and stopped. His shoulders jumped. Then he accelerated.

She was in full flight, closing fast. Ahead of them, a man was leading an unruly German shepherd on a leash. Skunk charged at him and yanked the leash from his hand.

'Hey!' the owner said.

Skunk spun around and glared at Jo. His eyes were sly. His lips drew back. He looked like a trapped animal, ready to strike. She caught a whiff of sickly sweet cologne and pungent B.O. She wheeled to a stop, repulsed and abruptly frightened.

Skunk punched the dog in the head. It went wild, barking and lunging. He kicked its rump, pointed at Jo and shouted, 'Get her.'

He took off. The owner grabbed the leash. Jo tried to dodge around them but found herself entangled between the owner, the leash and the frantic dog. She tripped and went down on all fours.

The owner hauled on the leash. 'Mongo, heel.'

Jo untangled herself, got up and took off again. Skunk was sprinting into the distance like a fiend.

She pulled out her phone and hit redial, breathing hard. 'Amy, he's heading for the parking lot at the vista point. Where's the Highway Patrol?'

'Somewhere within a ten-mile loop,' Tang said.

'I'm trying to keep him in sight.'

But when she got to the vista point, she couldn't find him. She circled the parking lot, sweat trickling down her back. He was gone. She sank to the curb and put a fist over her mouth, fighting down tears and the cry that was lodged in the back of her throat. She sat staring at the glorious day, and at the shining bay that had just swallowed the city's golden boy.

Jo sat on the hood of the Tacoma, parked at the visitor plaza on the San Francisco side of the bridge. The landscaped gardens were

aglow with gold and red blooms in the late afternoon sunset.
Across the parking lot a plainclothes detective searched a gray
Range Rover, parked overlooking the bay. It was registered to
Scott Southern. Amy Tang stood next to it, talking to a CHP
officer and two uniformed SFPD patrolmen.

The plainclothes straightened, peeled off his latex gloves and
shook his head.

Tang thanked him and walked over to the Tacoma. Stepping on
the bumper, she climbed up and sat on the hood next to Jo.

'Nothing worthwhile in the Range Rover.' She nodded across
the bay. 'Coast Guard sent out a boat from Fort Baker. If he
surfaces, they'll bring him back.'

Tang had drawn into a prickly shell, like a sea urchin. Jo sensed
that, inside, she was wilting. Her black T-shirt was rimed with
dried sweat, like a salt lick.

They stared at the bridge. Burnished by the sun, it stretched like
a vast iron bow across the rough water between the headlands. It
was magnificent and frightening, a bow powerful enough to shoot
people into oblivion.

'Before he went over,' Jo said. 'When you ran toward the scene.
Tell me exactly what you saw.'

The wind riffled Tang's spiky hair. 'It was hard to see clearly with
so many people on the sidewalk. I only caught glimpses. I saw
Southern backed against the railing.' She stared at the water. 'I saw
the little guy, Skunk, advancing toward him. One hand in his pocket
like he had a weapon. I thought Skunk was going to kill him.'

Jo clasped her hands between her knees. 'Go on.'

'But Southern tackled him. I was running by then. People
blocking my view. When I got a clear line of sight, everything
looked different. Southern and Skunk were scuffling. It looked like
. . .' She paused. Wiped her nose. 'It looked like Skunk was trying
to keep Southern from going over the rail.'

Jo said nothing. The wind was taking on an edge. Across the
parking lot the SFPD uniforms climbed into their patrol car and
pulled out. Tang raised a hand as they passed.

She glanced at Jo. 'Does that make sense to you?'

'I think you're half right. Skunk wanted to prevent Southern from falling. But he also wanted Southern to give him something. He had his hand out.'

'I saw. But what?'

'Describe the scuffle. Did it look like Southern lost his balance and pitched over the rail? Like it was a freak accident?'

Tang shook her head. 'He was a big guy, but not a giant. He couldn't have just toppled over.'

'Skunk couldn't have picked him up and dumped him over.'

Tang looked at her hands. 'No. There's no way Southern fell accidentally. Skunk was trying to keep him from jumping.' She frowned. 'Or trying to grab whatever he was after before Southern fell.'

Jo's throat felt tight. 'I think Southern drew Skunk to within arm's reach and grabbed him. But a tourist distracted Southern, and Skunk managed to break free.'

'Grab Skunk? Why?' Tang said.

'Southern killed himself and tried to take Skunk with him.'

Tang stared at her hard and long. 'You think it was another attempt at murder-suicide.'

'Yes.'

'Why?'

'I saw Southern's face.'

'And?'

'He knew he was about to die.' She had seen more. But she couldn't explain. 'That's why I ran across the road. He looked at me. I saw him make the decision.'

'You're freaking. That's hindsight. You can't know that.'

Jo turned to her. 'I can. I've seen that look before. It's an absolute recognition of what's about to happen. It's the moment of truth.'

Tang didn't look away. Jo tried to suppress all her feelings but they rolled upward, through the cracks in her armor.

'He knew he was seconds from death. He understood that absolutely.'

Tang frowned and bent toward her. 'Hey. You okay?'

Nowhere close to it. 'I'm fine.'

She stood up, walked around the truck and opened the driver's door. 'You may not believe me, but I'm dead certain. Scott Southern lured Skunk to the bridge, intending to kill them both.'

She got in the truck and started the engine.

Tang climbed in and shut her door. 'What convinces you of this?'

'He told me on the phone. Said I couldn't help him, that there was only one way to fix the problem. He said his solution was a sure thing.' She put the truck in gear. 'Surer than a bullet.'

She spun the wheel. 'He was quoting the suicide statistics.'

'Oh, shit.'

'He'd done research on committing suicide, Amy. He knew that jumping from the bridge is an almost foolproof way to die.' She glanced at the bridge, with all its splendor and portent. 'Thirteen hundred people have jumped from there. Only a couple dozen have survived. You want to die, you don't take pills, you don't slit your wrists, you don't even shoot yourself. More people survive self-inflicted gunshot wounds than survive hitting the bay.' She pulled out of the parking lot. 'You want to die, you climb over that railing and you let go.'

Tang hunched into the seat. 'Two dozen have survived?'

Jo hated, more than anything, the sound of hopeless hope in someone's voice. But Tang was praying into a void. Jo knew what happened, physically, to people who hit the water.

And Tang had seen that.

'You didn't look away, Amy.'

'I saw him hit.' Her face drew tight. 'It took for ever.'

Jo was quiet for a minute. 'You saw him in the air, reaching up toward us?'

Like a stone, accelerating toward terminal velocity.

'He knew it was too late,' Tang said.

'Wishing he had Skunk.'

'Or changing his mind.'

She saw him, telescoping down through the air, already falling at seventy-five miles an hour, hand stretched toward the bridge. Roughly she shoved her hair out of her face.

'There's no fucking turning back from that. And he knew it,' she said.

She saw him surrender and spread his arms wide, as if welcoming a crucifixion.

Tang looked at her. 'You've watched people die.'

'Yes.'

Tang stared at her with wide eyes, an edgy elf. 'Was it hard to watch patients go? Too hard? Is that why you switched to psychiatry?'

A wave of compassion rolled over Jo. Tang was savvy and competent, and all thorns on the outside – but she was inexperienced at death. Even though she was a city cop, she hadn't seen people die.

'It's why I try to help survivors understand what happened to the people they loved,' Jo said. 'It's all I can do.'

She didn't say the rest. That doing what she could wasn't always enough.

They had failed today. And Tang's forty-eight hour timeline was shot to hell. She turned onto the freeway. She thought. Who's next?

# 19

Jo went home but the house felt airless.

*Was it hard to watch patients go? Too hard?*

Dust motes winked in the light falling through the bay window. The clock ticked on the mantle. Counting off yet more seconds, carrying her ever farther from her final moments with Daniel.

That last day with him, she had climbed aboard the helicopter and strapped herself in for the medevac flight. The trip to Bodega Bay was a gut-churner. The wind chucked the chopper around and rain shredded horizontally across the windows.

She held on tight while she and Daniel got the briefing on the patient. Emily Leigh, aged six, ruptured appendix on top of Crohn's disease and a constellation of other chronic conditions. She was a fragile little girl who'd just been hit with a new dose of bad luck, and she, Daniel, and the pilots knew that if they couldn't get her to the peds surgical team at UCSF she would die of peritonitis before the sun went down.

Daniel looked at Jo. 'But this weather's so bad I can't see the sun. So that's not going to happen.'

The Sonoma coast was remote. The one-hour flight took them into a near-wilderness of ragged coastline, wild waves, and mountains polished green from the constant wind and Northern California storms. Bodega Bay was an isolated bohemian fishing town. As they approached, a flock of seagulls scattered like crazy litter. Through her headset Jo heard the pilot swear. Pilots hated birds. They set down on a wet playing field and kept the rotors turning. The ambulance was waiting, lights spinning in the rain, windshield wipers struggling to keep up. Jo jumped down from the chopper and the force of the wind hit her across the side of her head.

The local docs brought little Emily across the field on a stretcher. She was bundled under a thermal blanket. A nurse held an umbrella over her as they jogged. Emily's mother ran along with them, holding her daughter's hand. They ducked and approached the chopper.

The docs loaded Emily inside, calling out vitals. Daniel wrote them down on a clipboard. Jo secured the stretcher and hung her IV bag. Emily was pale and holding very still, trying to elude the pain. She looked at Jo with huge eyes. She was biting her lower lip, trying not to cry.

Jo felt a catch in her throat, and swallowed it. Seeing Emily clear-eyed and fighting the pain was good. It showed she was lucid, and that meant infection hadn't set in. They had to keep it that way. If peritonitis got to her, the little girl wouldn't last an hour.

Her mom leaned through the doorway and shouted, 'Can I come?'

Daniel shook his head. 'No room. I'm sorry.'

The mom's face was stricken. Jo said, 'We'll take care of her.'

The door of the helicopter slid shut and the engines cycled up. They lifted off from the field, downwash splaying pale circles in the green grass. The last thing Jo saw as they turned south was the woman's face. She made the sign of the cross and blew Emily a kiss with both hands.

Was it too hard to watch people go?

No. Breathing afterward, every day, was harder. She turned away from the window.

People in the Dirty Secrets Club were dying. So were their lovers, children, and innocent bystanders. She phoned the ICU at St Francis and spoke to the charge nurse.

'Ms Meyer is still unconscious,' the nurse said.

'Has anybody come to see her?' Jo asked.

'Two interns from the US Attorney's Office. They left cards and flowers.'

'No family?'

'Nobody's been in touch.'

Jo's stomach was churning. 'The crash that injured Ms Meyer

was suspicious. Tell your staff to keep an eye out for anybody asking questions about her, or coming to the ICU wanting to see her.'

The nurse was silent for a few moments. 'You got it. Any chance we'll get police protection?'

'Not right now. I'll talk to the department, but there are no guarantees.'

'I'll tell Security.'

'Thanks.'

When she hung up, the house felt stifling. She changed into workout clothes, grabbed her backpack and headed to a little park down the hill to go bouldering.

Dusk was approaching when she pulled to the side of the road and walked through the park to a green, rock-strewn gully that was hidden from the teeming city outside. Most bouldering sites in the Bay Area were artificial walls. Actual rocks were a rarity. But past a copse of live oaks she found the jumble of boulders. She put on her bouldering slippers, tightened the Velcro, clipped her chalk bag to a belt loop and approached them.

The lights of the city, the noise of traffic, all faded into the background. The air felt crisp. Halloween air, full of the promise that good times were coming. The sky was brightening to gold in the west. She chalked her hands and approached the first boulder.

It was a good twelve feet tall, crammed with the others in the gully like rubble strewn from a giant's tantrum. The rock felt cool to her touch. It was sandstone, rough beneath her palm. The face was essentially vertical. She examined it, planning her path to the top, what climbers called a problem. Four meters – she hadn't bothered to bring a crash pad to cushion her if she fell. She knew these rocks. They were old friends, silent, uncompromising and trustworthy. There could be danger in bouldering, but that wasn't the fault of the rock. Risks would arise from her own failings.

She started the problem, putting her right foot up on a dime-edge of rock. She felt stiff. Her muscles were tight. She knew it was emotional. She pushed up, stretched overhead for a handhold, pressed herself against the rock.

Let it go, Jo. Just breathe. Give it up, stretch, turn your mind over to the problem you're in. The rocks won't lie. They won't hurt you. They won't leave. They'll still be here in a million years.

She checked her grip and footholds. Leaned out and jammed her left hand in a crack. Looked up.

The sky was shimmering, blue with a magical silver edge. Daniel had always loved this time of day, even dog-tired after twenty-four hours on call or after taking on a wall in Yosemite. He loved to empty all his stress into the stone, loved the challenge and the purity of climbing. That last time, up at Tuolumne Meadows, they had bouldered before cooking dinner over the campfire. He was wearing a faded brown T-shirt, the color of the stone beneath her hands, and he had been so tan, so rip, completely at peace with everything around him. He wasn't a quiet soul. He was a reverse cyclone, calm to the world's chaos while storms drove him inside, but that evening he had been serene. Not even hungry, except for her. It was a crystalline moment.

She wedged her fingers solidly into the crack and found two inches. Hung for a second, and pushed up hard with her legs.

She saw the look again. The whole-body acknowledgement of finality. She saw Scott Southern backed against the railing of the bridge.

She lunged, grabbed for a hold. She slapped it but missed. She peeled off and felt herself falling.

She pushed off, turned and landed on the cool dirt.

Scott Southern had killed himself and tried to take his tormentor with him. Scott Southern had been desperate, afraid that his family was in danger.

Scott Southern belonged to the Dirty Secrets Club.

What was his secret? What gave the stringy man named Skunk such power over him? What caused such desolation, and such determination to end things?

To *stop it*.

She chalked her hands and started again. Got off the ground, pressed herself to the rock, crept one arm up and secured her fingers in a seam of stone. Pulled up and dyno'd, throwing her body dynamically upward, and this time she grabbed the edge and stuck the hold.

Skunk was seemingly eating his way through the Dirty Secrets Club. First Dr David Yoshida overdosed on pills, two days after his son died. Then Maki Prichingo killed his lover and put a shotgun under his own chin. Callie Harding drove off the Stockton Street Bridge. High-flyers, every one. Linked by the freakish clique they belonged to, the glamour snake-pit called the DSC.

She hung tight to the cold face of the rock, bending herself to its shape. *Use your legs so you don't wear yourself out five feet off the ground* – she heard herself laughing as she said it to Danny, the first time they went climbing. She blew out a breath, assured herself of her foothold and pressed up. Grabbed the hammerhead of rock where the boulder began to flatten.

The Dirty Secrets Club was being wiped out one member at a time. And at an accelerating pace. But club members weren't being murdered. Somebody was twisting them into killing themselves.

With a hard lunge, she wedged herself upward and scrambled onto the top of the boulder.

She sat down. Her arms and legs were burning. Her heart was going like a racehorse. She felt pumped.

Skunk – and maybe somebody else – was convincing them to kill themselves. That meant he was confronting them with a choice so painful that they found death the lesser evil.

What was that choice? To find out, she needed to talk to the woman who had survived Callie's death plunge. Geli Meyer knew what had sent Callie over the edge. But Geli Meyer was as still and silent as these rocks. Jo sat atop the boulder and watched the evening star light up in the west.

What was worse to these people than death?

# 20

Jo parked the truck a block down the hill from her house. The sun was a blood orange in the western sky, gilding the Monterey pines in the park. The trees looked fire-lit. She hiked up the sidewalk, sorting through her keys. Hot tea, a hot shower, a bowl of udon noodles – that's what she needed, and now. She just had time to get ready before heading to UCSF to run the bereavement group session. Then Tina was picking her up, for their girls' night out. It had better be a doozy.

Lights glimmered from houses along the street. The dying sun reflected from apartment windows. She saw – late – that Ferd Bismuth's shades were up, his rent-a-mansion circus-bright. His front door swung open and he jogged outside, waving.

'Jo, come see.'

Her last nerve had been fried several hours earlier. 'Ferd, I'm sorry, I can't right now.'

He pushed the door open wide. 'I got that prescription.'

What was he talking about? Come see his prescription – was it a dancing pill dispenser? He tilted his head and smiled as though Glinda the Good Witch had just told him how to get home again.

He was practically stamping with excitement. 'You'll never guess.'

He was right, she wouldn't. He had an allergist, an acupuncturist and an anti-aging specialist, and those were just the As. Was it a dehumidifier? A mobility cart? An electric mattress that contorted to keep his deviated septum elevated while he slept?

'I hope it's helpful,' she said.

He stood in front of the doorway. Despite herself she stopped and peered past him into the dim hall. Something skittered in the shadows. She inhaled.

'Ferd, what . . .'

Grinning, he turned to the door. 'Mr Peebles? Come on out.'

The shadows spidered again. She took a step back.

In the doorway two eyes appeared. The creature was small and twitchy, black with a white face and chest, and it clung with tiny hands to the doorjamb.

Jo heard the incredulity in her voice. 'Ferd, you got a prescription monkey?'

'A capuchin.' Ferd beckoned to it. 'Mr Peebles. Come say hello.'

At the sound of his name the monkey jerked his head upward. He cringed further back in the doorway.

'Mr Peebles, that's impolite. Come here,' Ferd said.

He spoke to it as he would to a small child. A small disobedient child who was fussing with electronic gadgets at the computer store where he worked.

He gestured to Jo. 'This is my friend Johanna. She's a doctor. A *psychiatrist.*' He pronounced it slowly. 'So you'd better behave in front of her or she might send you to the booby hatch.'

'Ferd, please.' She walked up the steps to his porch. 'What's he doing here?'

'He's my service animal.'

Oh, God. 'A health-care professional prescribed him for you?'

'My hypnotherapist.'

She rubbed her forehead. 'Why?'

'He's my emotional support companion. To soothe me when I feel panicky. It's been medically proven that animals calm the nerves.'

'I know. But . . .'

'Isn't he wonderful?' He leaned over and clucked at the creature. 'Come here, fella.'

The monkey cowered, its little face screwed with suspicion.

Ferd bent and picked it up. 'Okay. Take your time.'

It grabbed the collar of his shirt and crouched on his arm, looking around frantically, as though expecting an attack from flying bats.

'This is much healthier than drugs or therapy. And a real time-saver – he can do all sorts of things for me.' Again Ferd adopted the stern parent voice. 'Mr Peebles, get me my iPod.'

The monkey crouched down and scratched its backside.

'That's okay. Mr Peebles, give me a hug.'

The monkey's eyes darted around as if the hallucinatory bats were divebombing it. Then it settled its hot stare on Jo. It pursed its tiny lips.

Her neighbor beamed. 'He's like a little Ferd.'

Jo swallowed. 'Dude, if this thing is your id, I'm seeing more than any therapist ever wants to know.'

'He'll keep me on an even keel. No more panic attacks at restaurants or on the Bay Bridge.'

Jo knew that emotional support animals could genuinely help people. But the thought of this critter flinging food in a restaurant, much less loose in Ferd's car at sixty mph, made her woozy.

'Get him a booster seat,' she said. 'With five-point restraints.'

Mr Peebles stared at her with black eyes. He bared his teeth and shrieked.

She walked along the sidewalk toward her house. Right outside, parking space *numero uno*, was taken by a black Toyota 4Runner. As she approached, the driver's door opened. Gabe Quintana got out.

She couldn't believe the way the sunset seemed to flare at the sight of him walking toward her. She put her hands in the pockets of her sweatshirt. The dome light was on in the 4Runner. She saw a little girl sitting in the front passenger seat.

'Hey,' she said.

Gabe sauntered up. 'You forgot these.'

He had the notebook and pen she had left at the *taquería*, and a paper plate covered with aluminum foil. Her lunch.

She took them. 'Thank you, Sergeant.'

'What did I tell you about that?'

'Yeah, you're a rebel. Bringing me my meals.' She smiled. 'Rebel all you want, I like it. What happens if I snap my fingers?'

'You want to find out?'

His smile was slow and knowing, and made her blink with heat. She looked down, embarrassed. His face turned wry.

'Sophie and I are on our way to grab a bite before I drop her off. It's her mom's night.'

Jo looked at the car. Sophie was singing to herself and playing with a doll.

'When did Bratz take over the world?' Jo said.

'Her mom bought her a complete set. Yasmin, Jade, Pouty and Gimme.'

'I should sell anti-Bratz accessories to irate parents. Say a small acetylene torch.'

'Naw, I don't sweat the small stuff.'

'You mean you'd go for the doll factory.'

'C-4 would do it.' He was grinning now. 'Come with us?'

In the evening light he looked flat-out handsome. Not in any Hollywood way – he wasn't pretty, not even close. His smile was crooked. His eyes were dark and watching her. Under his gaze, she felt as though she'd stepped into an electrically charged field.

It confounded her. She stepped back. When she spoke, her voice sounded distant.

'Sorry, I can't. I have a meeting at UCSF. But can I meet Sophie?'

'Sure.' If he was disappointed, he brushed it off. He waved to his daughter. 'Come here, cricket.'

Sophie Quintana hopped out of the 4Runner and came over. She held her Bratz doll like Supergirl. It flew alongside her, hair flopping, a sulky demi-heroine.

'This is Jo,' Gabe said.

'Hi, Sophie.'

Sophie had a shy smile and Gabe's brown eyes. They were deep and bright, and held more cares than Jo wanted to see in a kid. She was wearing a Disney Princess-medley T-shirt. Snow White, Ariel, Jasmine.

'Thanks for bringing me my stuff,' Jo said.

'Sure.' Sophie leaned against Gabe's side, holding the Super-Bratz close to her chest.

Jo's phone rang. She excused herself to answer it, waving goodbye to Sophie as Gabe ushered her back to the car. Her heartbeat was rushing in her ears.

Amy Tang brought her back to earth.

'Get up to Marin. They found him.'

The Coast Guard cutter was tied up alongside the pier at Fort Baker. The water on the inlet was violet in the setting sun. The Golden Gate Bridge loomed above, its towers vividly lit. Across the bay, the city sparkled with light. Jo walked toward the dock. Gabe was three feet behind her.

An investigator from the Marin County Coroner's Office was waiting. He stubbed out his cigarette and extended his hand. 'Walt Czerny.'

'Jo Beckett. This is Gabe Quintana from the 129th Rescue Wing.'

Czerny nodded toward the water. 'This way.'

His voice was heavy with resignation. Jo's spirits slid a little deeper. *Sotto voce* she said to Gabe, 'Thanks again.'

He had insisted on accompanying her. The moment she said 'Bad news', he told her she shouldn't go alone. They'd dropped Sophie at her mom's apartment. Jo had found a substitute to lead the bereavement group and canceled her girls' night with Tina. Now that they were here, she realized how grateful she felt for his presence. She'd had enough of broken bodies in the past twenty-four hours, and a fresh dose of raw death was waiting at the end of the dock.

'I've got your six,' Gabe said. He was backing her up.

She walked with the investigator toward the boat. 'ID?'

'Driver's license. Scott Grayson Southern.'

The Coast Guard had found the body floating face up in the open ocean. The Marin Coroner's office had called SFPD when they saw a San Francisco address on the license. Amy Tang had then called her.

'Have you notified next of kin?' Jo said.

'SFPD is doing it now.'

'They'd better hurry. A dozen people saw him jump. Somebody's going to call the media.' If they hadn't already.

The cutter rocked on the water. Near it, on the wooden dock in a long plastic tray, the body lay covered with a yellow tarp. Czerny crouched beside the tray, took hold of the tarp and looked up at Jo.

'Ready?'

She nodded. He pulled the tarp aside.

Though she'd prepared herself, her diaphragm still caught. *Multiple blunt force trauma.* The coroner would write it on the death certificate. *Existential despair* wouldn't be listed. But that's what had turned Scott Southern into this broken thing. His polo shirt was rucked up under his armpits. His jeans were shredded, his shoes and socks ripped off. His eyes were open and clouded.

The pain, the stupidity, the blind thoughtlessness all came to her in one sweep. What had convinced this young man that death was his way out?

She knew the lure. In the weeks after Daniel died, the truth had cascaded down on her – that she couldn't bring him back and couldn't vanquish the grief. She felt his loss like a steel spike driven clean through her, and had ached for something to *make it stop*.

Death: the instant, permanent cure.

She looked at Scott Southern with sadness. He hadn't found a way to shoulder the weight.

People who jumped off the Golden Gate Bridge would never step in front of an eighteen-wheeler on the Bayshore Freeway. They chose the bridge for its lethal beauty, for the romance and drama of the exit, and because they believed the lies peddled by suicide websites – that death off the bridge was gentle and painless.

But hitting the water at 75 mph has exactly the same effect as being smashed by a big rig. Jumpers don't slip quietly beneath the surface. The impact crushes their sternum and can tear the heart away from the aorta. It shatters their ribs, which pierce their lungs and liver. If they struggle for the surface, as most do, they find their pelvis and femurs broken, or their neck. Many are seen flailing on the water, trying too late to live. They drown in seawater or their own blood.

'Is it true you were on the bridge when he jumped?' Czerny said.

'Not close enough,' Jo said.

The cops and Coast Guardsmen were quiet. It was a down moment. When her cellphone rang, it sounded so loud as to be rude. Jo walked up the dock to answer it.

Amy Tang sounded whipped. 'Am I going to have to go tell Kelly Southern she's a widow?'

'It's him.'

'Shit. This is turning into something worse than before.'

'I think we have to assume that all members of the Dirty Secrets Club are in danger. And your forty-eight hour countdown has been jammed into fast forward.'

'Get me everything you can.'

'On it.'

She walked back down the dock. Get everything she could – what was there to get? More confusion. This was a dead, cold end. She had nothing to grab hold of – no crevice, no crack, not a single fingerhold. She stopped near Gabe. His hands were loose at his sides, his face unreadable. Silently he moved closer, like a lookout guarding her back. They watched the Marin County investigators systematically go through Southern's pockets.

Czerny pulled open the sodden letterman's jacket. A Ziploc bag protruded from the inside pocket. Jo stepped forward.

'Tell me that's what I think it is,' she said.

Czerny took it out, opened it and carefully removed three sheets of paper. They were covered with handwriting. Water had seeped in, blurring the ink in places, but it was legible enough.

Gabe leaned over Jo's shoulder. 'It's a suicide note.'

Perry ate dinner, but the meal slaked neither his hunger nor his thirst. He needed news. He needed results. He paced the cramped space in front of his desk, waiting for the call. Finally his phone vibrated.

He answered. 'Update me.'

'Southern's dead,' Skunk said.

'How? Thirty seconds.'

'Flying without wings, boss. Crash and burn. The Golden Gate Bridge.'

Horror show. A warm thrill, like the red spill of blood, flowed over him. Southern had made himself an object lesson. And as public as it got.

'Perfect. Was he trying to put out flames?'

'Only in his tortured little mind.'

'Did he give you the information?' Perry said.

'Not yet.'

Perry turned and paced back toward the cluttered desk. The voice synthesizer was turned down low. 'Stay with it. We're getting close. We press the advantage.'

'My ass is falling asleep.'

'I don't care if your arms fall off. Don't lose the trail.' He checked his watch. 'We're done. Call me back in an hour.'

Skunk put away the phone and looked down the hillside. The grass on the slope below the vista point was brown and dry. His arms were tired from holding the binoculars. Down at Fort Baker, at the edge of Horseshoe Cove, the lights at the Coast Guard pier were as white as flares in the dusk.

Skunk knew the Coast Guard brought jumpers to Fort Baker. Back in the day, he'd worked for the Contra Costa County Coroner's Office, before he got popped for helping himself to personal effects from the stiffs. As if a corpse still needed his watch, shit. But before he got arrested, he learned where dead bodies got processed. Roadkill, drug overdoses – and jumpers. When the Coasties dragged bodies out of the bay, they brought them here. So he waited and watched from the hillside until he saw the silver Coast Guard cutter go out.

It came back with the body strapped to a tray.

His arm prickled where Southern had grabbed him around the wrist. He felt a loathing like teeth, eating at the edges of his vision. The pussy had tried to kill him. If he hadn't twisted free when

Southern dived over the rail, he would have gone with him on that long ride to the water. Jesus.

The boat bobbed next to the dock. People huddled around the plastic tray like grubs around a dead beetle. They pulled back the tarp, and nobody acted surprised.

His fingers itched. He wanted to get down there and strip the corpse naked, take its clothes and rifle them.

Hold on. He put the binoculars to his eyes. All the hairs on his arms stood up.

The woman with the dark hair was down there.

Who was she? First she was at Callie Harding's BMW crash. And this afternoon when he ran from the bridge, she'd chased him, like some sort of poisonous dart. She was fast and light, like a spider, and she had a real hard-on to get him. What was her problem?

He focused the binoculars. Spider, who are you? She was white but maybe not. Maybe part Jap or Mexican. Athletic-looking, like a gymnast. Wearing a tight T-shirt and jeans. He didn't think she was a cop, but she hung out with them. And tonight she had a guy with her. Military, no question.

They stood on the dock talking to the coroner's people and looking at the body. An investigator squatted down and opened Southern's jacket. He pulled out the Ziploc bag. Skunk smiled.

You lose, pussy.

The names were right down there. All he had to do was get them.

# 21

Headlights strobed over Gabe's face as they drove back across the bridge to the city. Jo sat quietly in the passenger seat of the 4Runner. Gabe drove with one hand on the wheel, his other drumming on the gearshift. His expression was sober. Los Lobos was on the radio, *The Wreck of the Carlos Rey*.

'Adios, *querida*, I'm gone away, down in the wreck of—'

Jo punched the radio to another station. 'Anything but that. An air raid siren. George Bush. Anything.'

'Sorry.'

'Not the way you deserved to spend your evening,' she said.

'Better than being alone.'

His hand was tight around the gearshift. He resolutely watched the road.

'You're concerned about Sophie being with your ex-wife?' she said.

'We were never married. And yes. Things haven't been great. Dawn's . . . had problems.'

She waited, but he didn't say anything else. 'Sophie looks like she's thriving with you.'

'Thanks.' He glanced at her, and his eyes warmed. 'She's the daystar in my life.'

They rode along in silence for a minute. The suspension cables of the bridge picket-fenced on her right. Beyond them was the dark expanse of the ocean. It was a sweet and bracing presence. She put down her window and let the wind rush over her face.

'Got enough air?' Gabe said.

'Never enough.'

They passed beneath the south tower. Seven hundred feet of beautiful iron. 'That's why I love climbing. Get above everybody else, and it's all air. I'd climb to the top of this bridge in a heartbeat.'

'Better to drop in by parachute.'

'Says the man who HALO jumps out the back of a Herc. No way. Ropes, belt, carabiners. Chalk bag and a good pair of climbing shoes. It would be awesome.'

'You always put the window down on a cold October night?'

'Sorry.' She put the window back up. 'I hate enclosed spaces.'

'So I gather.'

She cut a glance at him. 'It's not what you're thinking.'

'I'm not thinking anything.'

'No, Gabe. The claustrophobia goes way back, to the Loma Prieta quake. I was with my dad and little brother and sister, driving to Oakland. We were on the Cypress Viaduct.'

He looked at her. 'No shit?'

'No shit.'

'What happened?'

'Boom, crack, the support columns splintered and the top level of the freeway came down like a pancake. Trapped us.'

'Damn. Everybody made it out?'

'My dad had a heart attack that night from the stress.'

'Sorry.'

'He survived, but it was scary.' She tucked her hair behind her ear. 'We were unbelievably lucky. People in the cars ahead and behind us were crushed to death.'

Gabe drove for a few seconds. 'How long?'

'Were we trapped?'

A century.

Don't go back, she told herself. Remember, but don't relive. 'Four hours.'

The smell of cement dust came to her again, and gasoline, and the stench of burning tires. The roof of the car was pressing on her chest. She had been desperate to breathe and couldn't expand her lungs. She'd kicked the car door open and tried to wriggle out, crying hysterically, before her dad bellowed, '*Stay put, Jo.*' Even then, her impulse had been to run. But her dad was right. Being trapped inside the car was dangerous. But getting out could have been fatal. If she had run, she would have been crushed by collapsing concrete.

Choking black smoke roiled through the windows. She couldn't even turn her head. Rafe was so close that Jo could feel his breath on her neck. Tina was crying, then coughing. Things got dark.

'My dad sang to us,' she said. 'TV theme tunes. He kept us from losing it.'

'Sounds like a good guy.'

'A great guy.' She gazed at the night, at the vast starlit sky spilling eternity onto the horizon. 'The 129th pulled us out.'

'I wondered. Those guys gave 'em hell that night.'

Dozens of people had died under the crushed section of the Cypress Viaduct. Cars burned, and trapped people screamed for help, for hours. The elevated roadway was unstable, and only a few rescuers had been willing to crawl into the collapsed section and pull survivors out. The 129th Rescue Wing hadn't hesitated, not even to blink or make the sign of the cross.

She turned to Gabe. 'The guys in your unit, and the docs, the firefighters, the folks from the neighborhood – everybody who risked it and came in for us – they're a big reason I became a doctor.'

'It's a good one.'

He didn't ask her why she'd decided to go into forensic psychiatry. To deal with those who couldn't be pulled out of the wreckage. But she thought he knew.

They reached the end of the bridge and curved through the Presidio toward the city. Through the forest of Monterey pines, she saw the army cemetery. White stones, row upon row, mute and eloquent.

The tires droned on the road. Gabe said, 'You think in some twisted way Southern thought he was helping his family?'

'Yes. He saw destruction as the only way stop Skunk.'

Jo turned on the dome light and took out the copy of the suicide note Czerny had made for her. The portions not washed away by seawater were disjointed and despondent.

*Kelly, Coach, everybo*
*'m sorry. It's all gone wro*
*eing blackmailed, and I'm going to put an end t*

The next paragraphs were only a blue stain. Then,

*thought the club would be a place where I could unload, and*
*people wou nderstand, because they've all done bad things.*
*lped keep me sane, but it didn't absolve me. It ruined me.*
*I've been blackmailed here. Pay up, and get us some more*
*people – that's way it works. In the end it's all pay, no play.*
*Now people are threatening me. They say I have to help them,*
*or they'll hu Tyler.*
*not going to happen. Cadillac M*
*bad. Everythi*

Gabe turned the music up. They passed the Palace of Fine Arts. Illuminated by spotlights, the *faux* Roman rotunda had a tawny glow. To their left, the bay was black satin.

*my fault Melody Cartwright drowned hersel*

Southern's note was desperately sad and, unusually, it was sane. It exhibited none of the symptoms of chronic mental illness shown by most suicides. Scott Southern had seemingly been depressed for years. But he wasn't delusional or paranoid. His mind was sound. Eviscerating guilt was the source of his pain.

She summarized the next few paragraphs for Gabe. 'He and his fraternity brothers treated a young woman like a sexual party favor. She developed psychiatric problems. Eventually, she swam into the ocean off Malibu and drowned herself. She was a friend of his family, and each time he saw her parents, he felt more and more that he'd killed her.'

She turned the page. The end of the letter was readable.

*club plays games, way out on the edge. These people have tons of dough, so prize money isn't the point. It's all about the kick. And some of them take things too far.*

*I think the club crossed the wrong guy.*

*Somebody's tracking people down. I don't know who he is, or who he's after. He wants names. I can't find out, and if I could, I'd be signing somebody's death warrant.*

*Kelly, the only way I can stop him hurting us is to stop the man he sent, who's threatening Tyler. By stopping the trail dead, here, with me.*

*There's only one way to do that. Forgive me.*

So much pain. Jo closed her eyes.

*Don't leave me.*

*We're going home.*

Before she knew it, the engine had stopped. She opened her eyes. They were parked on her street. Gabe opened his door and got out.

'It's okay,' she said. 'You don't need to walk me—'

But he had already come around to her side. He opened her door. She got out and walked with him through the cold air to her front steps. Her legs felt heavy. Her keys jingled in her hand. Gabe was a heated presence beside her. The third time she tried to stick the key in the lock and missed, he said, 'What's wrong?'

She lowered her hand. 'I wanted to kick him.'

'Who?'

'Scott Southern. I wanted to kick him, choke him, slap him smack across the face with every ounce of strength I had.'

'Why?'

'To tell him to snap out of it. Suicide solves nothing. Dying doesn't end the pain. It only shifts it onto his family.' The porch light was off, and the night hid her expression. 'I wanted to scream at him for making it impossible to turn back.'

'Why are you so angry?'

'I'm not.'

'You're about to blow.'

She looked at the street, and at the stars. 'He knew he was going to die. And he chose it, Gabe. In those final seconds. He had the choice to survive and he threw it away.'

'What do you mean, he knew it?'

'He could have lived, but he chose to trash it all.' Her voice was faltering. 'He looked at me. I saw it in the way he moved. He knew it.'

'How do you know?'

'Because I've seen that look before.'

She didn't want to tell him. She didn't want to expose herself, but she couldn't stop. It was like a scythe sweeping through her.

'I saw that look on Daniel's face.'

She was choking back tears. 'At the end, Daniel understood what was coming. He looked at me. He could barely speak, but he looked at me, and he knew.'

She pressed the heels of her hands to her eyes, horrified at her own weakness. 'And he knew he didn't have a choice. There was no hope. I hate that look, I never wanted to see it again. Dammit.'

She jammed the key at the lock but couldn't even see the door. Roughly she wiped her eyes. 'I'm not crying. Shit.'

Gabe's hand covered hers. He wrapped his arms around her and all at once she was close against his chest. She held as still as a fist, fighting it, but his fingers combed into her hair and eased her head onto his shoulder.

She pressed her face against his shirt and shut her eyes. Silently he held her, and she knew he wouldn't let her fall. He had her six.

A sob cracked from her throat. His fingers stroked her hair. She stopped shaking and let go. She let hot tears spill. Every synapse in her body felt electrified. His embrace was like oxygen, like water, like light.

She leaned against him and listened to his heartbeat. Then she lifted her head and let go of him. She ran the heels of her palms across her eyes.

'I'm being stupid. Forget this, okay?' she said.

'No. You loved him. If you didn't get angry, you wouldn't be human.'

He took the key from her hand and opened the door. His arm rested on the small of her back. She held still. She wasn't ready for this, for any of it.

In the cold night air, she touched his hand. 'Thanks, Quintana.'

He held motionless, eyes on hers, hand on hers. 'You gonna be okay?'

'Rock solid.'

'You can punch me instead, if you need to.'

Despite herself, she smiled. He held her hand for a second longer. Touching his index finger to his forehead, he saluted and left.

She closed the door and leaned against it. The house was dark and empty. Empty, and so quiet.

*Don't leave me.*

The weather had worsened fifteen minutes out of Bodega Bay. In the cockpit of the air ambulance, the pilots wrangled the controls like a couple of rodeo cowboys. Through their headsets Jo and Daniel heard the terse conversation between them. The helicopter was near the edge of its performance envelope.

The pilot was a black guy with a face like a brick wall. His expression never changed, but his voice leveled to a tight mono-tone. He had no energy or emotion to spare on inflection.

'The wind spikes any higher, we'll have to turn back,' he said.

She and Daniel shared a look. She could see the stress in his eyes – a green streak of anger, and rebellion at the idea that they would not get this child to the surgical team that was waiting for her.

But he checked Emily's IV and rested his hand on her shoulder. His voice was composed. 'You like Harry Potter, Emily?'

She nodded.

'Remember when Harry played Quidditch in the storm?' He smiled, and his face amazingly looked sunny. 'This is like that, isn't it?'

The chopper hit an air pocket and with a jolt they dropped a dozen feet. Jo threw her hand against the roof to keep from hitting her head. Out the window, she saw tattered claws of land grasping at the sea. Stands of fir trees clung to crumbling cliff sides. The ocean shuddered like a beast, gunmetal gray. Where it hit the land, white surf shattered against the rocks, booming into the air like phosphorous grenades.

Daniel kept his hand on Emily's shoulder. 'When we get to the hospital, I'll get you a toy helicopter. They don't have a Harry Potter helo. What do you play with, Barbie?'

Emily didn't answer. She looked in pain, and petrified. Jo took her hand.

'GI Joe?' Jo put a smile in her voice. 'Winnie the Pooh?'

Emily looked at her with her wide eyes. 'Tickle me Elmo.'

The chopper shuddered and swooped up on an updraft. Over the headset Jo heard the pilot say, 'We're gonna have to pack it in.'

The pilots began talking about turning around. Jo watched the landscape speed by below them. A flock of birds swooped white against the green of the hillside.

Daniel listened to the pilots' chatter and said, 'Can you make Petaluma?'

Jo knew what he meant: go back to Bodega Bay and with every hour they waited for the weather to ease, every hour that passed before they could evacuate Emily, her chances diminished.

'No,' the pilot said. 'We don't have the power to clear the mountains.'

Jo held onto Emily's hand. The girl couldn't hear the entire conversation, but could probably sense the tension in the helicopter. The co-pilot asked whether they could make it to Bolinas, at the far edge of Point Reyes National Seashore.

The pilot said, 'Bolinas doesn't have a hospital. We're turning around.'

Daniel yanked off his headset and fought his way forward to the cockpit.

Over the howl of the wind and the engine Jo heard their argument. She stroked Emily's hand with her thumb. The chopper was straining for level flight. They were thirty miles from Bolinas. Daniel was begging the pilots to try for San Francisco. They were telling him to sit down.

Daniel said, 'If you can make Bolinas you can make the city.'

'You want to bet your life on that?' the pilot said.

The cracking sound reverberated from the cockpit like a sledgehammer blow. The noise in the chopper rose to a roar and the temperature plummeted.

In her headphones Jo heard *'Bird strike.'*

Her head whipped around. She saw the windshield. It had a fat circular crack, smeared with white feathers and red bird guts.

'Seagulls, fuck,' the co-pilot said.

'Find me an LZ,' the pilot said. 'Sit down, Beckett. Right now. We can hold it and get on the ground. As long as nothing gets in the intake—'

Bad juju.

From above the roof came a horrible *whack*. It was exactly what it sounded like. The engine inhaling birds.

The engine coughed. The engine shrieked. The pilot said, 'Put it down, *now*. Open space, a hill, trees, anything but steep mountain-side.'

His voice was as labored as the engine, and Jo felt the first thread of fear.

A new sound blared: an alarm on the control panel. Jo saw a red light flashing. The engine shuddered, and the shudder rang through the fuselage and into her back. The rain pelted against them. She heard the words no pilot wants to speak.

'Mayday. Mayday.'

The Cadillac crawled up Russian Hill. Skunk chewed his lower lip, scanning the side streets. The black Toyota 4Runner had to be around here somewhere. He'd followed it from Fort Baker, across the Golden Gate Bridge, and through the marina before he dropped back so the military guy wouldn't spot him. Then it turned off Marina Boulevard and headed into this neighborhood above Fisherman's Wharf, and he had lost it.

He burrowed deeper into the red leather seat. The Spider was in the 4Runner, and she had the names.

Skunk peered through front windows along the street. This was turning into a pricy neighborhood. Apartment living-rooms had fancy track lighting and bookshelves. People in turtlenecks were drinking red wine. From real wineglasses. The Cadillac crept along. At the top of the hill a little park was dark with trees, old Monterey pines shuddering in the breeze. A big brick mansion with a balcony was dimly lit.

He drove on. This was useless.

At the bottom of the hill he parked near Ghirardelli Square. The tourists were out in force, the Ghirardelli sign lit up, cable cars clanging, everybody buying chocolate and clam chowder. He called Perry Mr Pray-and-Pay.

The phone didn't even ring before it was answered. 'Update me.'

Like always, his skin skidded at the mechanical buzz of Perry's voice synthesizer. Skunk talked fast, following the rule: thirty seconds, no more. All the big stuff – *salient points*, the boss called them – had to be told one two three, tickBOOM.

'Southern had the names. They were on his body when he got dragged out of the bay. And I know who has 'em now.'

The Spider had the names. He didn't know who she was, or why she always showed up at the scene when somebody from the DSC died, but . . .

'This spider, she always shows up,' he said.

The quiet on the other end of the line was spooky. He waited, dreading the next burst of the robotic voice.

Perry had the lights off. Darkness felt safer to him; he had superb eyesight. When people heard the electro-larynx emanate from the night, they sometimes shit themselves. Right now, however, he kept the volume low.

'Where is she?' he said.

'She slipped the tail. But I know which neighborhood she went into.'

'If you can't find her, you'll have to draw her out again.'

'I was that close to grabbing the list, boss. I can't believe Southern went over the rail with it in his pocket.'

'Regret is a useless thing, Skunk. All that matters is getting the names of the people who started all this.'

'And we're closing in on the bastards.'

'They took what didn't belong to them.'

'And we'll get it back. With interest, I know, boss.'

They had taken much more than mere money, things he could never get back. Dignity, normality, his voice; sometimes it seemed like his very independence had all been stolen by the Dirty Secrets Club, and for what – a rich people's game?

*Object lesson.* They ran off with the cash. Lying there on the floor of the warehouse, he'd heard them. *He won't talk.* They thought they'd fixed it, that he wouldn't talk because no low-life racketeer would ever go to the police, but they also thought they'd fixed it so he *couldn't* talk, ever again. Two people, a steel pipe, the chain, the pain, but even when he lay on the concrete floor, and dragged himself to the door, and heard the sirens closing in, he knew the two who hurt him were just underlings. They were playing a game, doing it for somebody in the background who had set him up. Some A-list club member thought that sending their little minions to fuck him over would insulate them.

Wrong.

Because he didn't talk. They did. They began bragging about how they robbed him and left him to die. They got away two years ago, but they'd made a mistake. They opened their mouths when they thought they were safe. And word had got out.

Now he was close to finding out who set him up.

Five hundred thousand bucks these people had stolen from him. 500K, and they had used it to make themselves even richer. Perry wanted that money back. It was part of evening the scales. Skunk, his agent, was going to get a cut. Fifteen percent, if he tracked these people down.

Before the fuckers died, of course.

'Tomorrow, Skunk. I'll be downtown at three p.m. I want the names by then.'

Skunk sounded alarmed. 'Three o'clock?'

'My attorney is a persuasive man. The other side agreed to move things forward.'

'That's less than a day.'

'Think about your seventy-five K. That should incentivize you. It's not just a target list, it's your next vintage Cadillac.'

'Right. It just gives me indigestion, that's all.'

'This woman, the spider – she always shows up?' Perry said. 'Then give her a reason to do that.'

# 22

Jo woke with an old ache. Sun and the foghorn were tangling again, and she opened her eyes to see the white ceiling, the red comforter ruched around her, orange pillows heaped by her knees, the bed warm and piled with everything except her man. *Shit.* The clock said six-forty a.m. October 31st. Halloween. She rolled over, and felt a full-on tactile memory of Gabe Quintana holding her against him.

Flustered, she threw off the covers and got up. This wasn't the right time. Thinking about Quintana this morning could only lead to grief. She jumped in the shower. When she got out she pulled on a pair of jeans and a white long-sleeved T-shirt. Opened the shutters and saw dawn creeping up the walls of the houses on the street. The day was gold and blue. Next door at Ferd's, the door to the balcony was open and the curtains were fluttering in and out. She turned away but motion on the balcony caught her eye.

Ferd's monkey was perched on the head of one of the Roman statues. He was hunched like a Notre Dame gargoyle, tearing into an orange. His little fingers peeled it with the precision of a neurosurgeon. A neurosurgeon on crystal meth.

Ferd rushed out, tying a bathrobe around himself. 'Mr Peebles, how did you open the door?' His face was covered with shaving cream and his glasses were sliding down his nose. He grabbed the monkey. 'You gave me a fright. Don't do that.'

Stepping gingerly across the cold balcony, as if hopping across hot coals, Ferd dashed back inside and closed the door.

Jo made coffee and checked her email and phone messages. Mom, Tina, her elder sister, Momo, Dad, Rafe – a full house of relatives, all her parents and siblings, were checking in one way or the other. She emailed them all back, refilled her coffee mug, and phoned Amy Tang.

'Updates?' Jo said.

'Doctor David Yoshida died of a barbiturate overdose.'

'What about his son?'

'Fentanyl. Two days earlier.'

Fentanyl was a synthetic opiate, available by prescription, more powerful than heroin. 'Was he a known user?'

'Not heroin, but other drugs. He was in rehab a couple years ago. The family thought he was clean,' she said. 'We're looking into the circumstances.'

'I presume they're suspicious. We know Skunk threatened Scott Southern's little boy.'

'If they carried out a threat against Yoshida's son – Christ, that's cold.'

'This whole thing is cold.'

Tang began tapping her pencil on a desk. 'That woman you met at the Aquatic Park yesterday—'

'Xochi Zapata. She should be warned.'

'I'm going to pay her a visit,' Tang said.

'If she sees you, she'll lawyer up or run. Let me go. She may run anyway, but it's worth a try. I'll give her your card. Fair enough?'

'Tape the interview.'

Jo turned her coffee mug on the table. 'I'll call you.'

She said goodbye, continued turning her mug, and checked the clock. Lawyers got into the office early in Santa Barbara. She needed an attorney who would tell her straight whether what she wanted to do was within bounds. And who could help her dance along the boundary line if she needed to. She picked up the phone again.

Jesse Blackburn sounded surprised to hear from her. 'Jo. What's up?'

'Calling in the favor you owe me. Got a question about disclosure and professional confidentiality.'

'Fire away.'

Jesse was a friend from her undergrad days at UCLA. He was a sharp stick, clear-headed and very smart. The previous year he had drawn on her expertise in forensic psychiatry for help with a case he was trying. Now it was turnabout time.

'I'm working on a psychological autopsy.'

She sketched the case for him. He said, 'Weird.'

'Here's the thing. When I interview people I always put it on the record. Interviews support my report, which might be used as evidence in court.'

'But this time's different?'

'I need information and I won't get it unless it stays off the record.'

'You want to withhold information from the authorities? Where do you want to draw the line?'

'I want to protect the source's identity. Don't know about the information. I'll follow *Tarasoff* guidelines, obviously.'

When a patient threatens someone's life, clinicians have a duty to warn the intended victim, even when doing so violates privilege. Although this wasn't a doctor-patient scenario, Jo would never withhold such information.

'What have you promised the police?' Jesse said.

'That I'll get to the bottom of Callie Harding's death.'

'Are you lying to anybody?'

'Not today.'

He laughed. 'You say the cops gave you the green light to scrounge any information you need. Take the whole field. Grab anything. Sounds like you're trying to stop something worse from happening.'

'You just hit the nail on the head.'

'Go for it. No qualms.'

She exhaled. 'Thanks.'

'But that's not all that's bothering you.'

'No. Could the police force me to disclose the identity of my source?'

'Yes. This doesn't fall within doctor-patient privilege, Jo.'

'You're saying I'll be climbing without a rope.'

'Bottom line, yes. That's a risk both for you and your source. Disclose it to her.'

Jesse knew a lot about risk. He'd been a world-class swimmer until the day he witnessed a crime. The people behind it tried to kill him, and he now practiced law from a wheelchair.

She rubbed her forehead. 'Knew I could count on you to splash a cold bucket of reality in my face.'

'You take reality well, Jo. You just wanted me to confirm what you already suspected. Good luck.'

She said goodbye. Finished her coffee. Called the television station and was put through.

'Xochi. I'll make you a deal.'

Jo paced along the waterfront at the Aquatic Park. The sky was as blue as a fresh bruise. She was wearing a pea coat, a red scarf and her Doc Martens to keep the wind out. She had her stainless steel Java Jones coffee mug in one hand and in the other a take-out cup, which she handed to Xochi Zapata.

Zapata shook her head. 'Scott, dead – it's crazy.' Her face soured. 'And a mega story. Jesus.'

Zapata was wearing a faded gray sweatsuit and old running shoes. A Giants baseball cap was pulled low over her forehead. Her brown hair flailed in the wind. Without makeup, her skin was blotchy. She looked like a wraith of herself.

'I know you're feeling awfully alone. You don't have to,' Jo said.

'I can't go to the cops about this – that's what you have to understand. I need you to keep this stuff quiet.'

'I promise. Unless you tell me you're going to commit murder,' Jo said.

'Truly?'

'Truly.'

Zapata's shoulders dropped. It was a gesture of surrender.

'Tell me about the Dirty Secrets Club,' Jo said.

She stared at her coffee. 'Like I said yesterday, it's a confessional. A way to come clean.'

Jo looked at Zapata's sweatshirt. It was unzipped to show her cleavage. She suspected that *making a clean breast of things* had psychological implications for this woman. She sensed in Zapata a mania for confession. It seemed part of a cycle – misbehavior, shame, confession, relief, followed by a compulsion to misbehave again. Zapata's black diamond pendant glittered in the sunlight.

'That's not the club's sole purpose,' Jo said. 'You don't sit in a circle seeking moral absolution from your friends.'

'No.' Zapata's face blotched even more. 'Some people brag about the things they've done. For them it's an ego trip. And for some people it's a game.'

'Exactly what kind of game? Do you have rules? Competitions? Prizes?'

Cupping her coffee, Zapata shrugged. 'Sure. Prizes for the best secret, dirtiest secret, biggest risk taken. Things like that. Harmless stuff.'

Jo nodded at the black diamond pendant. 'How do you get one of those?'

Zapata raised her cup to her lips but didn't drink. It looked as though she couldn't swallow. Her face crumpled like a piece of paper.

'What if I'm next?' she choked.

'Why would you think that?'

'Maki.' She wiped her bitten thumbnail against the corner of her eye. 'I tapped him into the club. What if that makes me next in line?'

'I don't know. How did you bring him into the club?' Jo said.

'I interviewed him for a package – a report – about counterfeit designer label clothing. I met both him and his lover.'

'And you invited him to join the club?'

'They were fire and ice, always either snapping or cooing at each other. Maki seemed very cool, so I sounded him out. Told him about my wild youth, and he totally dug it. Eventually I said if he wanted to meet some people I could introduce him.'

'You could tell he had something he wanted to unload?'

'Yeah.' She looked at Jo. 'How did his boat catch fire? Do you know?'

'No.'

'What a terrible way to die. Burning – I can't think of anything more hideous.' She wiped her eyes again.

Jo gave her a moment. 'Yesterday, you insisted that the club was supposed to be fail-safe. Why?'

'Because we only get together in twos or threes, ever. And there's no record of who all the members are. None of us knows the whole roster. It's like a daisy chain – you never meet more than three members of the club. That way confidentiality is supposed to be protected.'

Neither of them needed to say the obvious: the club's cell structure was shot full of holes.

Jo drank her coffee. 'Your wild youth?'

Zapata tilted her head back. 'You have to understand. Before I got into journalism I did things. On film.'

'You weren't always a revolutionary warrior queen?'

'Zapata's my ex-husband's name. And Xochi's catchier than Susan. Come on, you understand about the impression a name makes, right, *doctor*?'

'Point taken.'

'Besides, the skin flicks aren't what worries me. Big whoop, everybody does titty flicks. This was something different.' She took a breath.

'I'm listening.'

'These weren't garden-variety adult movies. They were a niche product.'

Jo raised an eyebrow, curious.

Zapata's smile seemed ironic. 'Put it this way – I was a religious extremist.'

'Excuse me?'

'It was nun-porn. We all dressed up as religious figures.'

'You're joking.'

Her expression became matter of fact. 'No, really. There's a defined market for these films. With quite a devoted fan base.'

'Really.'

'It's a fusion genre. Bondage, Catholicism, nuns and priests. We filmed at an old place in the San Fernando Valley.' The blotches reddened her neck again. As if wanting to minimize her decadence, she said, 'I wore a black rubber Catwoman mask.'

'So your face wasn't shown?'

'I wasn't known for my face.'

'Right.' Jo focused on her coffee so she wouldn't react.

'Over the mask I wore a nun's veil. And four-inch spike heels. And a rosary for a G-string.'

Jo considered herself unshockable. And she was inured to California's psychic exhibitionism. People here came with ready-to-spill emotional disclosures, like a pre-packaged Caesar salad mix. Lettuce, croutons, a corset fetish, Parmesan cheese. But Xochi Zapata's full-frontal confession to kinky-porn stardom made her blush.

'Unfortunately, some of the flicks became cult classics,' Zapata said. '*Baptism by Flier*, where the guy's a pilot. *Holy Orders*, where Our Lady of Pain disciplines the College of Cardinals, and I mean until they lick her Jimmy Choos. The big hit was *Holy Cummunion*.'

Jo snorted her coffee out her nose.

Zapata had the good grace to look embarrassed. 'Yeah, it's legendary.'

Jo wiped her face. 'Sorry.'

'There's an underground of obsessive fans who keep the films alive. They'd love to find out my true identity.'

Jo scrounged a tissue from her pocket. She'd never breached professional demeanor so ludicrously. 'The fans don't know?'

'I always wore the mask. It was my signature gimmick.'

'That's the secret that got you into the club?' Jo said.

'Now you understand why it has to stay off the record.'

Jo remembered Zapata's earlier insistence that applicants to the club had to provide evidence of the things they'd done. In her head, she heard a cheesy 1970s *wah-wah* soundtrack. The melody, horribly, was Schubert's *Ave Maria*.

'With your face covered, how did you . . .'

'I have a tattoo.'

'As one does.'

'It was always visible on screen at some point. I was very limber. So I submitted a film clip with my CV, and at the interview I showed the tat.' Her eyes were downcast. 'It's a snake. I called it Original Sin.'

She was embarrassed, yet couldn't keep from unveiling herself. Jo had never in her life met such an exhibitionist.

'At the time, it just seemed like fun. I was Sister Mary Erotica, or Mother Ignatius Rollova. I would chastise wayward altar boys with my rosary. Whip them or tie them up.' She continued staring at the ground. 'Hang them, sometimes strangle them.'

'Actual auto-erotic asphyxiation?' Jo said.

Zapata nodded and looked away. Her mouth crimped.

'Xochi?'

Jo sensed that there was more to tell, but Zapata had finally found the limits of her urge to strip.

The wind blew through Jo's hair. 'I need to know how the DSC operates.'

'I told you, it's a virtual confessional.'

'So it's just a bunch of you sittin' around jawing? Do you whittle, or quilt while you confess?'

'No. It's evolved over the years.' For another moment she looked tense, and then fear replaced caution. She dropped her defenses again. 'We've been playing truth or dare. Pulling stunts to gain points and get to the next level.'

She opened her handbag and took out a small jewelry case. She handed it to Jo. Inside was a perfect black diamond.

'It was supposed to be Scott's,' she said. 'He made the cut.'

It was beautiful. Though it refracted the sunlight, its depths were impenetrable.

'He carried out a dare last week. He and Callie . . . posed . . . on the roof of a skyscraper downtown. After the earthquake.' She looked wistful. 'Our news chopper actually got some footage. It was spectacular. It made my career in adult films look cheap.'

Well, yes.

'Xochi, why is the club being threatened?'

'I think a dare went wrong. Somebody got hurt. The wrong somebody.'

'And he's getting revenge?'

'Yeah.'

'Who is he?'

'I don't know.'

Zapata's cellphone rang. She turned away to answer it, and Jo heard, 'I'll be right in.' She hung up. 'Developing story. I have to go.'

'Will you give me the names of the other members of the club, so we can warn them?' Jo said.

'I don't know them. Like I said, it's a daisy chain.'

'Will you please talk to the police?'

'No. Send them my way, and I'll deny everything. But thanks for warning me.' She took the diamond back. 'What am I supposed to do with this? Put it on Scott's casket at the funeral? What a waste.'

Jo was walking back to the truck when her phone rang.

'Doctor Beckett, it's Gregory Harding.'

She slowed. 'How can I help you?'

'First, by accepting my apology. My behavior yesterday was inexcusable.'

He sounded strained. Gulls were wheeling over the lawn, white against the morning sky.

'The situation overwhelmed me. But there was no justification for losing control of myself.'

'Apology accepted. Thank you.'

'I need to speak to you. I found some disturbing things at Callie's place.'

'I'm all ears.'

'Can you meet me? I'm in the city for meetings at the Fairmont – there's a restaurant with a rooftop terrace. In all seriousness, you should see these things.'

She balked, but not for long. 'On my way.'

# 23

When Jo pulled up at the Fairmont in her Doc Martens and jeans and dented pickup truck, the doorman didn't bat an eye.

The Fairmont Hotel monopolized the north side of Nob Hill. A magnificent white stone building, it could have doubled for the US Mint. It had been built after the 1906 earthquake, seemingly from marble, gold leaf, and audacity. The style was Robber Baron Ornate. The vaulting lobby rang with echoes, perhaps the ghosts of railroad magnates and dance hall girls. Jo headed for the stairs. She distrusted Gregory Harding's temper, but trusted the hotel to enforce decorum, deftly and ruthlessly.

Upstairs in the restaurant, Harding was sitting at a table overlooking the city. His blond hair shone white in the sunlight. His expression was veiled. His napkin was knotted in his left hand.

He stood and offered his hand. 'I hope I haven't inconvenienced you.'

'Not at all.'

The view was astonishing. The sky was so sharp it seemed shellacked. The skyscrapers of the financial district were arrayed down the hill and the bay glimmered in the morning sun.

Harding's eyes were arctic. 'Callie was into something weird.'

'Define weird.'

He took a compact leather-bound notebook from his shirt pocket and held it up. 'The Dirty Secrets Club.'

He ran his gaze over her face, seeking a reaction. She kept her expression neutral. He slapped the spine of the notebook against his palm.

'But that's impossible, because the Dirty Secrets Club doesn't exist,' he said.

'Why do you say that?'

'Don't.' He slapped the notebook again, harder. 'Don't play games with me. It's bad enough that Callie did.'

She kept her face calm. 'Are you asking if I've heard of the Dirty Secrets Club? Yes.'

Harding slapped the notebook against his palm another time. 'That's why you asked me yesterday if Callie felt dirty.'

He was testing her, like a suspicious spouse trying to trip up an unfaithful lover. She didn't like it. 'I'm not playing games. You are. The club exists and you know it. Why don't you tell me what's going on?'

He looked away. He put his elbows on the table. After a second he rubbed his forehead. 'Callie, dammit. What was she doing?'

'Tell me from the beginning, Greg.'

He continued rubbing his forehead. 'The club was a joke. Just a joke. A law school bullshit session, that's all,' he said. 'You know what law students are like?'

'Yes.' No different from med students. Intense, intellectual, competitive. Anxious. Horny.

'They're masters of bullshit and one-upmanship. Law is taught by the Socratic method – hypotheticals, case studies, questions thrown at you by a teacher. You play "What if?" in class, going through an increasingly extreme series of fact scenarios.' He clenched the notebook. 'You argue and speculate. The temptation is to trash talk and flash your intellectual chops. Throw in late nights, this hothouse atmosphere . . . it gets crazy.'

A waiter came and poured coffee. Harding waited for him to leave.

'There was this Saturday night. The party went late. We were doing tequila shooters, and some blow. The evening had a sharp edge, you know?'

'I have an idea.'

'We got on the subject of secrets. Cover-ups, lies, the way powerful people will do anything to protect themselves.'

'Callie was part of this?'

'Yes. But not doing cocaine. She was a goody two-shoes.' He was holding himself as straight as a switch, and his face looked drawn. 'We were talking about courtroom confessions. How some people get busted and they just can't help themselves, they spill everything to the cops even though they have the right to remain silent.'

'You remember this very clearly.'

He held up the notebook. 'It's all I've been thinking about since I found this.'

'Go on.'

'In a criminal case, if you confess, you do time. Even so, some people still spill their secrets to the police. Why?' He raised his hands. 'One, they just have to get the weight off their shoulders. Or two, they want to brag.'

'Revolting but true.'

'So we started talking about secrets. People love secrets. Secrets can be horrible, fun, deadly. They can weigh on the conscience. Most of all, they can be valuable. But only as long as they *stay* secret.'

'By definition,' she said.

'Withholding information is how Silicon Valley runs – on trade secrets. Limiting information lets you gain power over the market.'

'Or over other people.'

He pointed his index finger at her. 'Exactly.'

'Blackmail and extortion wouldn't be possible otherwise.'

'You got it.' He nodded. 'But people love to tell secrets. Look at *The Jerry Springer Show*.' He fiddled with his coffee spoon. 'People who tell their secrets don't realize – talking destroys the very thing that was valuable. Tell all, and you lose all that power, all that control. It's out in the big wide world, for everybody to play with.

'When you tell a secret, you make a myth look small. Because ninety percent of the time, the things people disclose are cheap, sleazy, and eventually . . . boring.'

She shook her head. 'Revealing secrets in some societies leads to blood feuds and honor killings. In California it causes divorce, hysteria and addiction.'

'*Boring*. Check out yourdarksecret.com. "I messed around with my sister." "I love Bobby and he'll never know." "I pissed in the elevator." The word *plebeian* is the only adequate description.'

'Those people are confessing anonymously.'

'They're cowards.'

'That's an interesting judgment,' she said. 'Anonymity can provide safety. It frees people to speak their minds.'

Harding spread his hands. 'Confess online? Hide behind a screen name? Big deal. Who knows it's really you? Who knows if these supposed secrets are real? We decided that night, if you spill your secret anonymously online, you're a wanker. If you do it on Jerry Springer, you're trailer-trash, a media-whore. You ruin both the secret and your reputation. You lose power.'

'What's your point?' she said.

Briefly he looked embarrassed. 'I don't mean to sound excited. I'm trying to explain how it was. We were kids. Jackasses, full of ourselves. It was all just a joke,' he said. 'It wasn't even a real club. It was a massive bullshit session.'

'Except that it's not.'

'Here's the point. People like to confess. They do it to unburden themselves, to hurt their lovers, to show off. Even to help others.'

'Granted.'

'And yes, you can confess in private. You can talk to a psy-chiatrist – they're sworn to silence by the doctor-patient privilege. And you can confess to a lawyer – they can get tossed in jail if they spill your secret. Or you can talk to a priest, and he'll never tell, under pain of death. But priests demand something of you in return. Remorse. And they give you penance. Who wants that?'

Scott Southern.

'Plenty of people,' she said.

'You're not listening. Yeah, you can tell any of these people almost anything, without fear of exposure or reprisal. But none of these professionals will give you what you're looking for.'

'What's that?'

'Kudos.'

He let the word hang in the air.

He spread his hands. 'Praise. Recognition. Glory for one's achievement.'

'I know what the word means.'

'I'm not talking about passive secrets, like "Uncle John touched me and told me not to tell." I'm talking about actions that people have taken. Big decisions. Risks. Socially unacceptable things.'

'Crimes?'

'Of course.' His face looked taut. 'Callie took this fantasy and made it real.'

'You think she's the creator of the Dirty Secrets Club.'

He handed her the notebook.

The spine creaked when she opened it. On the first page, handwritten in black ink, was *DSC*.

She flipped through: page after page of neat, organized notes written in a narrow hand that dug hard into the paper.

*Ethos of the DSC. Secrets are valuable. Don't waste them.*

A chill spidered down her arms.

Page five. *Dirty Secrets Club: levels. (1) Entry level – white. (2) Enhanced – silver. (3) Premier – red. (4) Elite – black diamond.*

It was laid out with the banality of a frequent flyer program. She kept reading. On page six the handwriting became rushed.

*Unburdening yourself is one benefit of the club, but confession only gives you so much satisfaction. Competition gives you more. Club members get extra points for returning to the scene of a crime without getting arrested. Or for carrying on with something, brazenly, without getting caught. For lying under oath with a smile or a sad shake of the head. For risking a high-profile job or political position. For getting done what they brag that they're going to, without ever leaving their fingerprints on the disaster.*

Christ. They were treating the city like their personal game board.

'Why would she turn law school trash talk into reality?' Jo said.

'I don't know.'

'What was Callie's dirty secret?' Jo said.

'She was my wife. For five years I slept next to her while she dreamed. And I have no idea.' His chill gaze melted. 'This game killed her, didn't it?'

Jo looked at him. He seemed so thirsty.

'Can you figure it out? Can you please tell me what she was up to?' He reached down to a briefcase on the floor. He took out a baseball and set it on the table. 'Tell me where the hell she got that.'

It was old, and in good shape, a Willie Mays autographed ball. He shook his head. His face soured.

'She didn't buy baseball memorabilia. She got a hold of this under the table, as part of some absurd game. So tell me, what was she doing?'

Jo held his gaze, seeing anger and hurt. 'Are you a member of the club?'

'I wish. Maybe then I could have stopped her.'

For a moment he looked young, and almost lost. She wondered whether he felt betrayed that Callie would do this, or rejected because she hadn't included him.

'Were you two still involved?' she said.

'Fucking, you mean.'

Blank face, Beckett. Don't rise to the bait. 'Is that how you thought of it?'

'It's how she described it. It's what she liked to do to me.' His lips drew tight. 'I think she's still doing it to me. She's doing it to all of us.'

Jo had rarely seen such a heroic – and failed – effort to hide hunger, and hatred, and longing. Harding was a man on the verge.

'You wish you could have Callie right now, more than anything, don't you?' she said.

His lips went white. His eyes cooled to the temperature of sleet. He balled a fist and pressed it against his mouth.

Jo looked away, giving him a moment, and turned a page in Callie's notebook.

*Access: iPod submenu. Password: Platinum.*

# 24

Jo closed the front door and dropped her keys on the hallway table. In the kitchen she opened the patio doors and let cool air and the scent of lilac flow in. She hooked Callie's iPod into her computer and brought its menu up on her screen.

She found the prosecutor's unofficial files deep in the Extras submenu, under 'Stuff'. It was password-protected. She entered *Platinum*.

She found herself on the game board.

She was staring at records of a dozen members of the Dirty Secrets Club. Their bona fides were here. CVs had been scanned in and uploaded. All their personal information was here, all their disgusting habits, all the details and proof of authorship.

'I'll be damned,' she said.

File number one was a city councilman, confessing to bid-rigging on seismic refit construction projects. File number two was a celebrity legal pundit, previously a Las Vegas cop, bragging about taking payoffs from casinos. Call the photos supporting his résumé 'Swimming in a fountain of hookers'. File number three was a federal lobbyist, claiming he'd slept with twenty-three senators and congresswomen. And they'd *liked* it. His file was subtitled 'Deuce Bigelow'.

File number four was Scott Southern.

Jo took her laptop and the iPod outside and sat under the magnolia tree, to smell fresh air. She felt boggled by the free-for-all of smarm and chutzpah.

There was enough material on here to blackmail all these people. Was that Callie's secret? The club's cell structure supposedly ensured that only a few people would know your secrets. Nobody was supposed to have access to everything. And yet Callie was collecting as much slime as she could.

Orderly, ambitious Callie had gathered files on members of the club as if she were her own private Stasi. What was she up to?

Was she planning to win the club's *sub rosa* competitions by sabotaging the other members? Was she going to blackmail them? Or was there an élite level beyond Black Diamond, where the inner circle meted out rewards?

Did Geli Meyer find out about this super-secret stash? Was that why she ended up nearly dead?

Jo kept looking through the files. There were photos, even a video. She pushed *Play*. As if she were working a puzzle, she saw a piece turn in front of her and click into place.

'Shit,' she said.

Xochi Zapata knocked again on the door of the hotel room. Still no answer. She double-checked the number she'd written down – 1768. That was this room, high on the upper floors of the Marriott. The tipster who called the television station had given it to her.

In frustration, she went to the railing and looked down. Seventeen stories below, the hotel was bustling. The hotel was built around a huge atrium. Scenic glass-enclosed elevators ferried the swanky clientèle up and down. On the ground floor, a hundred people were eating in the restaurant. Halloween pumpkins tastefully decorated the scene.

She got on the phone. Her cameraman was downstairs, searching for the tipster. The van was parked outside in a no parking zone.

'Forget it, Bobby. Nobody's here. Some jackass jerked our chain.'

'Crap. Then let's split. The van's gonna get dinged if we don't move it.'

Down the hall, a door opened. Xochi turned. An older couple came out of their room, dressed for walking.

'I'm coming down,' she said.

She felt stupid. Such a hot tip – counterfeit pharmaceuticals, imported from Asia and sold under faked labels to drugstore chains that didn't check their provenance – it was a dream story. Men and women in the prime of life poisoned by adulterated drugs, that was better than fake Calvin Klein jeans. That was a local Emmy, maybe even a ticket to a network job. She snapped her phone shut and followed the older couple to the elevator.

But this trip was all for nothing. 'Stupid,' she said beneath her breath.

She waited behind the walkers for the elevator to arrive. They were poring over a guidebook. The woman took the man's hand, squeezed it and laughed lightly. They were sweet.

No, she decided, she hadn't been stupid to bite on the lure – to get the big stories you had to take chances. The elevator was coming down toward them. It glinted with sunlight as it descended. A maid pushed her cleaning cart past. Behind the maid another door clicked, a fire door. Xochi glanced around. A man was strolling along the hallway, hands in the pockets of his jacket.

She tried not to snort. A Members Only jacket – how long had those been out of style?

Jo paused the video. She stared at her computer screen.

A dare gone wrong, Xochi had suggested. Holy Christ, *gone wrong* didn't begin to cover it. She felt queasy. And this story had evidently leaked. Word had gotten back to Skunk, and obviously to somebody else – to the man behind him.

She called the television station. 'Jo Beckett for Xochi Zapata. It's urgent.'

Zapata was out. They couldn't put her through.

'Have her call me.'

Jo hung up and redialed Amy Tang.

The man in the Members Only jacket walked along the hallway toward the elevators. He was small and hunched, with gray-streaked hair. His eyes darted at Xochi and away.

With a *ding*, the elevator arrived. The older couple stepped in. Xochi followed. The doors started to close.

'Oh, my glasses,' the woman said. 'Henry. Hold that door.'

The man grabbed the doors before they could close. They labored open again and the couple got out.

'Sorry, sweetheart,' the woman said as they trundled back toward their room. 'Don't know where I left my mind this morning.'

Xochi watched them go. The man in the Members Only jacket was standing right outside.

'Hold that,' he said.

She pushed the Open Door button. He just stood there, staring at her. She felt a *frisson* of excitement.

'Are you the one I'm looking for?' she said.

Amy Tang's cellphone clicked straight to voicemail. Jo hung up, redialed Tang's direct line at the police station, heard nothing but ringing.

She peered at her computer screen. She had paused the video but, even frozen and silent, the image seemed to keen.

*Crossed the wrong guy*, Scott Southern had written. And now that guy was crossing off the Dirty Secrets Club in revenge. Xochi needed to know that he would be coming after her.

She ought to be aware of it already. Didn't she realize that she would be a target? Jo thought back to their meeting at the Aquatic Park. Xochi's conflicting impulses toward secrecy and exhibition-ism. Did she unconsciously want Jo to take it public? Was she deliberately exposing herself to danger?

Wait. Jo had Callie's files at her fingertips. She hung up and scrolled through them, picking her way down the menu until she found Xochi's name. Her bona fides. *Your News Live*. And yes – a cellphone number. She called.

Xochi pressed her thumb against the Open Door button. Mr Members Only glanced along the hallway first in one direction and then the other.

'I'm the one who called. Let go the button,' he said.

She did. He stood there. Her phone rang, but she left it.

'Are you getting in?' she said.

He looked at her.

As he pulled his hands from his pockets she knew this was wrong. She knew by his face and the smell that suddenly filled the air. Fear came as an instant and all-encompassing shriek inside her mind.

It was too late to run. He was blocking her exit. The elevator doors were sliding closed. She backed up against the glass wall of the car. Close, fuck it, *close* now—

The man had a lighter in his right hand. He flicked it and touched the flame to the gasoline-soaked rag that was stuffed in the mouth of the bottle. It was filled with clear liquid and she knew it wasn't water.

The flame lit orange. 'I'm the one. Sorry, sweetheart.'

He flung the bottle through the doors as they closed.

# 25

Standing near the sculpture of dancing nymphs in the lobby of the Marriott, Bobby waited impatiently for Susan to come downstairs. He refused to call her Xochi. As long as she called him Bobby the Cameraman, he would continue to call her plain Susan Daly.

He didn't know whether he looked at the elevator because he was in a hurry to move the van out of the no parking zone, or whether his eye was drawn upward by the flash. But training and a photographer's instinct led him to raise his camera and start shooting. Reflexively he focused the lens. It zoomed on the elevator and his brain stuttered. He tried to process what he was seeing, but his mind rejected it.

He felt like he was melting, heard a noise pour out of his own throat. It was an incoherent moan. He kept filming. The glass-enclosed elevator descended toward him, and with every floor the horror inside grew brighter and more ferocious. It reached the ground. He stood petrified, staring through the lens at Susan. Her face was pressed against the glass, mouth open in agony. The flames filled the elevator. It was a holocaust, red and frenzied. The door opened and he heard screams. Flames erupted into the lobby. The next thing he remembered, he was on his knees, emptying his stomach onto the marble floor.

Jo walked along Post Street toward Union Square with a sense of *déjà vu*. Police cars, a fire engine, an ambulance and a television news van surrounded the Marriott. Her hands were tingling with dread. The wind funneled down the street. The hotel's doormen looked spooked and pale. She walked into the lobby and saw

Officer Pablo Cruz ushering lookie-lous away from the elevator bank. The whole gang was here.

The hotel atrium soared all the way to the roof. She got halfway across the marble floor and saw the sooty windows of the scenic elevator. The glass had cracked. Jo smelled smoke, and the unique, ineradicable smell of burnt human flesh.

She stopped. Her throat clamped shut and she fought to keep from gagging.

Officer Cruz appeared at her elbow. 'Doc?'

She stared at the elevator. 'Zapata's dead?'

'Yes.' His voice was gentle. 'You okay?'

He was a solid blue presence. She looked at his Aztec face. 'Hardly.' Her field of vision seemed inordinately bright. 'Are you?'

He nodded. His jaw was tight.

'Nobody's going to claim this was suicide, are they?' she said.

'No.'

'Who murdered her?'

'White man. Five-seven, early forties, greasy hair with gray streaks. Red jacket.'

'His name's Skunk.'

'Two witnesses saw him.' Cruz indicated a man and woman in their seventies, sitting on a sofa in front of a large fireplace. The woman dabbed at her eyes with a handkerchief. The man rested his hand on her knee, comforting her.

'Lieutenant Tang?' Jo said.

He pointed toward the front desk. 'Talking to the victim's cameraman.'

Tang looked like a bite-size storm cloud, in a black V-neck sweater and black slacks, black hair spiked in all directions. Her arms were crossed. Jo walked over. The cameraman was talking in halting bursts.

'. . . Anonymous tipster called the station with a story about counterfeit prescription drugs,' he said. 'It was a lead on a big story.'

The man was scratching at his arms like he wanted to scrape off his top layer of skin. Maybe gouge out his eyes, too, to purge the memory of what he'd seen.

Tang said, 'Hang around a few minutes. We may have more questions.'

'I couldn't drive right now if I tried,' he said.

He headed to the bar and asked for a glass of water. Tang nodded Jo further away from the crowd. If she crossed her arms any tighter, she'd wrestle herself to the floor.

'Skunk threw a Molotov cocktail into the elevator. He would have killed that older couple too, except they got out at the last second.' She pinched the bridge of her nose. 'This is one vicious fuck.'

'I know.'

'And you thought they got people to kill themselves.'

'They did. Today they switched from one form of torture to murder.'

'Why?'

'Two possibilities. One, this was the culmination of their terror campaign.'

'How so?'

'Xochi Zapata was the leak.'

'What?' Tang said.

'I got into the files on Callie Harding's iPod. She kept records of people's qualifications for the Dirty Secrets Club.'

'They bragged about their dirt, on paper?'

'In detail, with proof. And Xochi Zapata was the key.'

'What happened?'

'The club ripped off a new applicant. Somebody in the DSC set him up. They stole five hundred thousand dollars from him.'

Tang ran a hand over her hair. 'Half a million – just flat-out robbery?'

'The deal was a double cross. The wannabe showed up, thinking he was buying his way into the club by setting up a high-stakes poker game. Big time, illegal.'

'An executive game,' Tang said.

'A-list high rollers. He was going to be their casino and their banker. He showed up with cash to fund some extravagant lines of credit.'

'But they took the money.'

'Worse. He put up a fight, and they attacked him.'

'Killed him?' Tang said.

'No. Tortured him, seemingly for sport.' Jo felt dirty even thinking about it. 'Beat him to a pulp with a crowbar. Zapata said the guy begged for his life, but they ignored him. It was like that egged them on.'

Tang seemed to shrink into herself. 'Jesus Christ, this was somebody's idea of Truth or Dare? Strong-arm robbery?'

'Not everybody in the club is like Scott Southern, seeking forgiveness for their sins. That's obvious.'

'That's psychopathic. What does this have to do with Zapata's death? It's retribution?'

'Definitely.' Jo reached into her satchel and took out Harding's iPod. She found the file. 'Zapata doesn't say what his name was. She didn't know.'

Jo scrolled through the files. 'Here.' She set it to *Play*.

Tang frowned. 'It's a music file?'

'Video.' Jo tried not to look at the elevator. 'One thing you have to know first. I talked to her this morning. I promised her I'd keep our conversation off the record, unless she told me she was going to commit murder.'

'Beckett—'

Jo put up a hand. 'She told me she'd had a career in porn, but I thought she was holding something back. When I got into her file on the iPod, I found out what it was. During filming, the sado-masochism got out of hand. An actor was accidentally strangled on set.'

'Aw, shit.' Tang looked toward the elevator. 'A snuff film. Goddammit.'

Jo worked the controls of the iPod. 'Just keep that in mind when you see what happened during the strong-arm robbery.' She scrolled down. 'Xochi was a lot of things, a bunch of them extremely troubling. But aside from anything else, she was a reporter. I found her application to join the club's highest level. Black diamond.'

She plugged in her headphones, gave one bud to Tang and stuck the other in her ear. She pushed *Play*.

They saw Xochi sitting under warm light in her apartment. Her makeup was perfect, her hair spilling over her shoulders. She was leaning forward, her dark eyes shadowed, speaking directly to the camera. Her voice was sultry, as though describing an act of base violence had excited her.

'Every time the guy begged for it to stop, he only got beaten harder. First with boots and then the crowbar.' She exhaled. 'The guy was down on his back on the floor of this empty warehouse, just a bloody mess, and he'd stopped fighting, was just trying to crawl away.'

She took a drink from a shot glass. 'I don't know who set me this dare. But it's the last one I'll ever do. You wanted me to distract this wannabe so he'd let down his guard, and I did. He wasn't really a fan, but it still worked.'

She poured another shot. Cuervo, it looked like. 'I never should have told you about the rosary thing.' She drank. 'Okay. Fade in.'

Jo paused the video. 'Xochi told me a dare had gone wrong. She didn't tell me she was there when it did.'

She pushed *Play* again. Xochi faded out and a new video began. It was a static shot of a warehouse. Crates were stacked ten feet high. The view was poor. The camera was placed in a corner, under a jacket. Clearly the filming was clandestine. The wannabe was standing in the shadows beyond the crates. He was unidentifiable.

A woman moved into the frame.

Tang leaned toward the screen, mouth open. 'You're shitting me.'

'It's Xochi,' Jo said.

She was wearing a black rubber mask, Jimmy Choos and little else. Sister Mary Erotica. Beside her a weedy man was gesticulating. He looked like a Gatsby character with cocaine nerves.

'Who's that?' Tang said.

'Can't tell.'

They watched, and Tang's face went sallow.

The beating came like an explosion. The weedy man attacked. The wannabe fought back furiously. A briefcase skidded across the floor. Poker chips spilled everywhere. Xochi ran back and forth along the edge of the scene like a caged dog.

The beating intensified. The wannable battled, but took a blow to the head and went down. And once you go down, you're done. Jo forced herself not to look away, but her eyes were aching. Here came the moment she knew she'd never forget.

The weed was beating the wannabe with a crowbar but couldn't finish him. The wannabe reached out and grabbed his ankle.

Xochi pointed. 'The chain. Get the chain.'

The weed grabbed it. He whipped it down across the wannabe's shoulders.

'No,' Xochi screamed. 'He's going to kill you. Will you— around his neck, throw it around his neck.'

'Oh, shit,' Tang said.

They garroted him.

Jo and Tang stood immobile, watching the scene on the small screen. The chain, the wannabe being dragged across the floor, legs flailing. Xochi storming back and forth, moaning like a coyote.

The video faded back to Xochi with her perfect makeup and third tequila.

'It nearly killed him. He lay there clawing at his neck, gasping for breath. We left him there.' She paused and drew herself up. 'It just went wrong. He was not a person we should ever have let apply for membership. If we hadn't protected ourselves, he would have killed us.'

She didn't look convinced.

'I don't know his name. But I know what we called him after-wards. The applicant. The Object Lesson.' She looked away, and back at the camera. 'We called him Pray. Because that's what he did when he was attacked. He prayed.'

# 26

Tang leaned toward the display screen. 'Pray?'

'It's not a directive, it's a person,' Jo said. 'It's the nickname of the man who's directing all this carnage. He's taking down the Dirty Secrets Club.'

Tang stared at the screen. 'And Zapata didn't give his name?'

'No. I've watched the entire video. She never knew it.'

'But she supplied the club with this video of the attack.' Tang ran her hand into her hair. 'What happened? Did word leak out?'

'That's my guess,' Jo said. 'Somebody talked. Word got back to him.'

'Pray. Now it makes sense. We never get a clear view of him in the video. Are we sure Pray isn't the guy we've been calling Skunk?'

'There's another segment of video, where Zapata describes him as tall and thin – almost ghoulish. Doesn't sound like Skunk to me.'

'Thanks, Beckett. This is major.'

Jo glanced at the elevator. Forensic techs were moving in. A photographer's flash caught her like a sick flashback to Callie's crash. Everything briefly looked crooked.

She blinked until the feeling passed. 'As I said, it's possible Pray was after Xochi all along. Maybe he and Skunk have been pressuring other club members into giving up her identity, and today they found her.'

'But?' Tang looked up sharply. 'Why lure her to a random public place?'

Jo felt a catch in her throat. 'Maybe they wanted to send her down in flames.'

'Or?' Tang said.

'I don't know. But I don't think we know the whole story. It feels like shifting sands underneath.'

At the bar, Xochi's cameraman put down his water glass, picked up his portable shoulder-mounted television camera and left. Jo excused herself and went after him.

Outside, the fresh air was bracing. She drew a clean breath. The cameraman had the same thought, different method. He lit a smoke. His hands were shaking as he cupped the lighter to the end of the cigarette.

Jo walked over. 'Can I ask some questions about Xochi?'

'Susan,' he said. 'She was Susan.'

'Did you see the man who called in the anonymous tip?'

'No. When we got here she went to the concierge desk – the tipster said he'd leave a message for her. All the note said was "seventeen sixty-eight". The room number. Nobody was there. I came down to look around the lobby for him, and she—' He squinted, and took a drag. 'I figure he set it up to separate us, get her alone.'

Jo agreed. Skunk was both a coward and a predator, and had wanted to hive her off from the able-bodied man who had accompanied her.

'You think he was here ahead of time, watching you?' she said.

'Obviously. He took his time. He maneuvered us right where he wanted us to be. I'm parked over here.'

He stuck the cigarette between his lips and hiked the camera under his arm. They threaded their way between fire trucks to the back of the news van. Jo hung back to avoid the smoke, though she had given up being repulsed by cigarettes. Every male in her family over forty was a dedicated smoker, so she'd trained herself to deal with it. Her doctor friends – indeed most of San Francisco – would have regarded her tolerance as shocking. It was Halloween, and tonight the city was going to explode with vampires, werewolves and drag queens, an extravagantly disrobed and preening crew that would cover the streets with good-natured decadence. But the rainbow tribe of the city would shake a finger, maybe organize a protest march, if people lit up a Winston in their midst.

'Susan was a serious reporter. Needy and obsessive, loved to see herself on camera, but she got the story. And she had a heart,' the cameraman said.

He pulled open the back doors of the van. Jo was hit with a new smell. It was coming from inside the van. The cameraman didn't react.

'I smell gasoline,' she said.

'Where?'

And she realized that he couldn't smell it. He probably couldn't smell anything – he was a smoker.

She backed up, waving him to follow. 'Get away from there.'

But it was too late. She heard a whooshing sound. A bright flare of orange light erupted from the back of the van.

The paramedics shut the doors of the ambulance. The cameraman was no longer screaming. Morphine had temporarily taken away the pain. But it couldn't undo his burns. They drove off, lights and siren wailing. Amy Tang leaned on the hood of Officer Cruz's patrol car and watched them go.

'Is he going to make it?' she said.

'Screaming's a better sign than feeling no pain. It means the fire didn't burn so deep that it destroyed his nerve endings. Maybe it's second degree rather than third.'

The ambulance jostled its way down the street. Jo's limbs felt like they weighed half a ton each.

'It was a set-up, wasn't it?' Tang said.

'Undeniably.' Her voice was shaky.

'You're lucky, Beckett. Very lucky.'

'I know.' She glanced at the van. Its interior was a scorched shell. 'Pray got burned, figuratively, by the Dirty Secrets Club. Now he's burning them, literally.'

Tang was grim. 'These guys, they're much more crafty than we gave them credit for.'

'How did he set up the bomb?'

'It was low-tech and efficient. When Zapata and the cameraman went into the hotel, he jimmied the lock on the van. Inside he cracked open the cover over the dome light, unscrewed the light bulb, and stuck an electrical wire in the socket. Stuck the other end of the wire in the gasoline bottle. Tied a string to the bottle and rigged it to fall over and shatter when somebody opened the back door. So the cameraman opens the door, the dome light goes on, the wire goes hot and ignites the gasoline . . . The bottle breaks and it's a portable inferno.'

She looked as angry as a raw scrape. 'He was covering all the bases. If he didn't get Zapata in the hotel, then when they got back in the truck – boom.'

Jo frowned at the news van. This was not fitting together in her own head as neatly as it did in Tang's. 'Why take the chance?'

'Of?'

'Being seen messing around with a television truck? It's an attention magnet. Half the people who see it are going to hang around hoping to get on camera.'

Tang's tough-elf face grew grimmer.

'It's got everybody's attention now. That makes me leery,' Jo said. The wind whistled between the buildings. 'This isn't over.'

'No, it's not. They're slick, and ruthless, and nothing's going to stop them except us.'

Jo looked at her, and felt an overwhelming sense of dread.

A block above the Marriott, parked in the Cadillac on Mason Street, Skunk watched the action downhill through his binoculars.

Just as he'd planned. The young Mexican uniform was here. The little dyke plainclothes who always wore black. Too bad they hadn't been closer when the device ignited. Toasty marshmallow cops. What a treat.

Skunk laughed. He was funny when he wanted to be.

And talking to them was the Spider. Hair writhing in the wind, all those black curls, like a web of silk flying around her head. Like a web of thoughts, all circling around one idea. *Get Skunk.*

What did you call a female spider? A bitch?

He checked the time. Close enough. He sent a text message to Pray.

★　　★　　★

Perry read the message.

*Done. 2 crispy critters.*

His entire body felt calm. Crispy? Justice was harsh sometimes. He sent a reply immediately.

*Keep checking on Meyer.*

Skunk wrote *Why?*

Stupid man. Skunk didn't need to understand why. Skunk just had to follow orders. *We can't let police question her. She's ours – got it?*

*Got it.*

Skunk wrote *Spider in sight.*

Perry replied. *Hang back and observe. Will be on co-counsel's number after noon. May have Spider's ID by then.*

Good. Skunk was sick of the Spider coming after him. She knew who had ordered the attack on Perry. All he had to do now was make her tell him.

But down the hill, the little dyke cop stepped out into the street with the Mexican uniform. She was pointing at buildings. The bank on the corner, for starters. She was telling him to get the CCTV camera footage. Fuck.

She turned and looked up Mason Street in his direction, telling the uniform to search the street.

Skunk ducked, laying himself flat on the bench seat.

After a minute he sat up. The cops were gone.

Shit. So was the Spider.

He looked around. The street was emptying, cops and firetrucks pulling away. Perry kept texting.

*Keep eye on Spider. She might have more than the names. Might know where they are. Might lead us to them.*

Too many mights, Skunk thought. *And she might come after me. Will decide how bad to do her. I will tell you soon. Pray.*

He signed off. Skunk started the engine and pulled out, driving down the hill to look for her.

# 27

Jo dropped her satchel on the hardwood floor in the hallway and headed to the kitchen. She got a pot of coffee brewing, opened the patio doors, turned on the TV to catch the news, saw flames, heard screaming and turned it off, paced the kitchen, stalked into the living-room and stood at the bay window, staring across the street at the Monterey pines in the park. They were dark green against a polished blue sky.

Why had Pray been twisting people into committing suicide, rather than murdering them?

For sport? Perhaps he was so warped that tit-for-tat revenge didn't sate him. Perhaps he couldn't be satisfied with merely torturing people the way they had tortured him. Maybe he wanted the sick satisfaction of getting them to do it to themselves. And he'd found the leverage to get them to end their own lives – a group of people with secrets they couldn't stand to see exposed. The DSC was deciding to destroy themselves rather than have their deeds become known.

She jammed her hands in the back pockets of her jeans. Outside, the street was quiet. Down at the corner a cable car clattered past. The gripman rang the bell, a jazz riff in clanging brass.

Uncertainty gnawed at her. Pray's actions didn't make sense psychologically.

The burning she could understand, in a horrible way. That was all about Pray. He was projecting his own sense of psychic immolation onto his tormentors, in the most literal way. That was need, rage, narcissism.

But his tactics didn't make sense. Why did he send Skunk to do his dirty work?

Maybe it worked strategically – keeping himself in the background, sending a confederate to threaten people. Perhaps he was protecting himself from exposure and arrest.

But he'd been tortured.

Revenge is a very personal act. And men tend to be direct about it. They want to wreak it by their own hand and to witness it unfold. However, it isn't the torturers, but the tortured who feel shame. Was Pray's shame keeping him in hiding?

Until today he'd been inciting suicides, instigated by a creepy minion. It seemed too cagy, too cool. Too removed.

She was missing something.

She needed to go back to the start. To Callie Harding, who had created the Dirty Secrets Club. Everything else flowed from that.

Glass shattered in the kitchen. She spun around.

Across the living-room, through the kitchen door, she saw the coffee pot lying broken on the floor. Coffee was running black across the stone, steam rising around shining crumbs of glass. A shadow slid across the floor and retreated out of sight.

Oh, hell.

She backed toward the bay window. Bumped against the steamer trunk that served as a coffee table. Keeping her eyes on the kitchen, she unlatched the lock on the window. She had to get out, fast, and even as her hand fumbled with the latch, her anger began outrunning her fear. How dare they? This was *her* house.

The latch was stuck. Paint had dried into the spaces between the wood and the sash. Crap.

If she broke the window with her elbow, she'd waste time knocking the glass out of the frame before she could climb out. Goddammit. Her cellphone was in her satchel, in the front hall, twenty feet away. The only downstairs landline was in the kitchen.

She couldn't see any other movement or shadows in the kitchen, but now she heard a weird chuffing sound. It set her teeth on edge.

She had to go out the window on the north side of the living-room, near the kitchen door. Fifteen feet away. This gorgeous little house suddenly felt like a stadium.

She had to get out. And she wasn't going alone.

Quietly she opened the steamer trunk. She took out her grand-mother Kyoko's legacy to her, one of the Japanese museum-quality pieces. The Tokugawa samurai sword.

It was heavy, sharp, and perfectly balanced. It was four hundred years old and hadn't sliced anything tougher than a piece of paper since wooden ships sailed the Pacific. Slowly, quietly, she gripped the hilt and slid it from the lacquered black scabbard. The metal sang quietly, like the hum of a deadly angel.

She gripped it in both hands, held it vertically and took a step toward the kitchen. The last time she'd held it this tight, Daniel's hand was on the hilt with hers. The last thing this sword had cut was the cake at their wedding.

That chuffing sound came again. The hairs on the nape of her neck jumped up. She took another step. The window was twelve feet away. She stared through the kitchen door.

With a screech, Mr Peebles sprang off the kitchen counter and skittered through the doorway toward her.

'*Shit. Jesus.*'

She shrieked loud enough to peel paint off the walls. At the sound, the monkey jerked to a stop on the floor and gaped at her. It dropped the grape it was holding. Its eyes went round as quarters.

'Stupid freaking little—'

'*Eeeeiiieee!*'

She lunged for him. Still squealing, Mr Peebles broke for the stairs. He scampered up, keening like a maniac. Jo pounded after him.

'Come here. Stop it. Oh no, you don't—'

She grabbed for him. He squirted out of reach. He hit the top of the stairs, jinked like a pro halfback and disappeared into her bedroom. She sprinted after him, the sword clanging against the wall.

'This isn't just for show. It'll turn you into pâté.'

Rounding the corner into her room, she saw him springboard onto her bed. She dived at him. 'Hold still. Idiot hairball—'

He catapulted off the comforter and pelted into the bathroom. 'Ha – small brain loses!'

She ran in after him and slammed the door behind her. Turning slowly, she saw him in the shower, perched atop the shower caddy. He was balled like a shot put, eyes blank and frenetic. She held the sword low and approached him.

Jo spun the wheel, pulled a U-turn across traffic on Geary Boulevard and screeched into the parking slot outside Compurama. She parked the truck crooked and didn't care.

She got out, stalked around to the passenger side and pulled out Mr Peebles. The door to the computer store was open. She shouted, 'Ferd.'

The monkey couldn't fight her, but she held him with his face turned away from her, just in case. She stormed toward the door.

Everybody who worked there was lined up inside the plate glass window, gaping at her.

She walked in. 'What?'

They continued staring, but shook their heads.

'Good. Get Bismuth,' she said.

A young man with meerkat eyes backed away, turned and scurried toward the stock room. 'Ferd, get out here, and I mean now.'

Mr Peebles was swaddled in a red bath towel. The towel was bound tighter than a tourniquet and wrapped in duct tape. Fitfully, wildly, completely wrapped in duct tape. The only part of him that was visible was his eyes.

One Compurama employee peered at him intently. 'You should really check your basement for pods before they get to this stage.'

Jo gave him a death stare. He blinked and retreated behind the counter.

Another young man cleared his throat and pointed vaguely in her direction. 'Did you know you have duct tape in your hair?'

'What about it?'

He withdrew his hand quickly. 'Nothing. It looks good.'

Ferd rushed out of the stock room. 'Jo. Oh, Lord.' His hand went to his forehead. 'Mr Peebles, oh my, what happened?'

Jo held her arms out straight, as though ready to dropkick the monkey. Ferd hurried, staring. At her.

She grit her teeth. 'It's shampoo. Almost an entire bottle. He's incredibly dextrous.'

'It's so foamy.'

'He turned on the shower with his feet.'

Ferd blinked, wrinkled his nose as though he was about to sneeze, and pressed his fingertips to his cheeks.

'Ferd, no. Your sinuses can't seize. I forbid it. It's physically impossible and if you try it, I'll unwrap the duct tape and set Mr Peebles loose on the new PCs.' She shoved the bundle at him. 'For godsake, take him.'

Ferd took the monkey. 'I thought he was secure in my house.'

'Wrong.'

He looked Mr Peebles in his shiny black eyes. 'Boy, we have to have a talk.'

Jo turned to go. Hearing whispers, she turned back.

'Yes?'

Meerkat Eyes blinked and swallowed. 'I just – we wondered . . . are you coming to the Halloween party?'

She stepped toward him. 'My costume tonight will not include a wet T-shirt. And it won't include one in your dreams. Any of your dreams, ever. Do you understand?' she said. 'Because if it does, the next thing to appear in your dreams will be me, wielding a gigantic pair of garden shears. So even as I speak, you are wiping the memory of this moment from your minds.'

She stared at them one by one until they shrank back, nodding. She turned to her neighbor. 'Ferd, your monkey is about to give me a personality disorder. Please restrain him.'

She was halfway home before she managed to get the bar of soap out of her bra.

★   ★   ★

She unlocked the door with hands sticky from shampoo. She tossed her keys on the table in the hall. She craved a shower. She headed straight upstairs, peeling off her sodden T-shirt on the way, squeezing out of her wet jeans and turning on the water as hot as it would go.

It was only when she came back downstairs, in a fresh white sleeveless tee and brown combats, that she saw the mail on the floor. It had come through the slot and scattered along the base-board.

She picked up a small white envelope and saw her name handwritten on the front. *Dr Jo Beckett, UCSF Medical Center.* Nothing else. Underneath was the typed label showing it had been forwarded by the Psych Department.

She slit it open with a fingernail and removed a single sheet of paper. The message was short. She stared at it, and all the blood seemed to drain from her limbs.

She saw the ink on the page. The letters looked as sharp as needles. She heard a humming in her head, white noise that swelled to a drone.

She threw open the front door and stormed down the steps. Where was he? She looked up and down the street. Where was the bastard who'd jammed the letter through her mail slot?

A jogger ran by in sweats and a watch cap, giving her a puzzled look. It was forty-eight degrees out and she was standing there in a thin T-shirt, barefoot. She felt stupid, knew the letter had been forwarded, nobody was hiding out here mocking her. Her eyes were stinging. Her face felt as hot as an iron.

*Bastard. Bastard.* She repeated it in her mind like a slap, over and over, and choked down the feeling that she was the one being slapped across the face. The words on the page spit at her.

*You killed your husband. Welcome to the Dirty Secrets Club.*

# 28

Jo stood on the sidewalk. She felt like she'd been stun-gunned. At the corner, a cable car clamored down the hill. The metallic ring of its wheels against the tracks sounded to her like an aircraft engine spinning higher and higher, before the metal screams and tears itself apart. She crushed the letter in her fist.

She ran back inside and slammed the door. She smoothed out the letter and stared at the message as if possessed by it. She couldn't look away, even when tears obscured the words.

What kind of joke was this? Who had sent it?

'Sons of bitches.'

How did they know about Daniel's death?

She stalked into the kitchen and grabbed the phone. Her hand was shaking. Barely able to see, she stabbed the number. Amy Tang's cellphone clicked to voicemail. She hung up, wiped away tears and called the police station. Tang was out.

'Have her call Jo Beckett. It's urgent.'

She hung up. She squeezed the phone in her hand, and flung it across the kitchen like a fastball pitch. It hit the stove and sprang into pieces.

Who the hell had been talking about Daniel's death? Who had given some sick son-of-a-bitch an emotional knife that would cut through her heart like this? She stood in the kitchen, wanting to scream, feeling the swell of memory like a rising wave, about to break and hit her full force.

'No. No you don't.' She wasn't going to let this happen to her. Not now.

She found her cellphone and dialed a new number. When it was answered she didn't even give him time to say hello.

'Quintana. Where are you?'

'Jo.' His voice had a smile in it. She killed that.

'I have to see you, and I mean right now.'

Gabe was waiting for her outside St Ignatius Church at the University of San Francisco. He had his hands in his jeans pockets and a backpack slung over one shoulder. With his shades on, he looked watchful. He didn't look like a graduate student. He looked like a Special Forces killer masquerading as a graduate student. She marched across the plaza.

He crossed the lawn to meet her. 'What's wrong?'

She held up a baggie with the letter sealed inside it. 'Somebody's toying with me. They sent this . . .' She waved at it. 'This . . .'

'You're shaking.' He took the baggie from her. He read the note and his mouth tautened.

'How did they find out about Daniel?' she said.

He glanced up sharply. 'You think I told them?'

She stood rigid, staring at him. He took off his sunglasses. His gaze was as still as a sheet of black ice.

'It wasn't me.'

She didn't move. He touched her arm and she didn't respond. He let his hand fall back to his side.

'I've never talked to anybody outside the unit about Daniel's death.' He looked at the note again. 'And I would never tell a lie like this.'

She held his gaze, and the day, cold and sunny, felt blindingly hot.

He was telling the truth. And she didn't believe him.

When she spoke, her voice seemed to emanate from the far end of a tunnel. 'I know you're not lying. But it's true.'

'What are you talking about?' he said.

'The note, Gabe. It's the truth. I killed him.'

'Are you delusional?' Gabe said.

'The Dirty Secrets Club wants people who've done the big bad thing. They found me,' she said.

He took her hand and led her to a bench at the edge of the lawn. When they sat down, he held on. His face was solemn, framed by palm trees and the white spires of the church.

He leaned toward her and lowered his voice. 'Why do you believe this lie?'

His hand held hers tightly. She tried to let go and couldn't make herself. She gripped him as though he was her last remaining handhold against a vertical drop into a chasm.

'*Mayday. Mayday.*'

The co-pilot had shouted it into his headset. Jo's vision turned bright with adrenaline. The engine hacked, fighting against the bird it had ingested. Feathers and seagull remains had blurred across the windshield in the rain.

The pilot swiveled his head, looking urgently for a stretch of open ground where they could set down on the rugged headlands. No matter how hard they banged the ground, hitting dirt would be better than ditching in the water.

The co-pilot repeated, 'Mayday, mayday,' giving their coordinates, hanging onto the control stick, and urging every last second of power out of the chopper. Below them Jo saw fir trees and crumbling hillside.

Daniel groped his way back to Jo's side. He looked at Emily and his face was still calm. But Jo sensed tension pouring off him.

He took the little girl's hand. 'We have to land. A bird flew into the engine and we need to get another helicopter to take us the rest of the way. Think you can hang on while we switch rides?'

'Okay,' she said.

'Good.'

The co-pilot said, 'Open space, two hundred meters ahead. Hang on.'

Jo couldn't see anything past the two-foot circular crack in the windshield. That meant the pilot couldn't either. She saw him hauling on the controls, fighting for altitude. The treetops racing past below them looked almost black in the sunless day. The trees seemed only a few feet below the skids.

She and Daniel got on either side of Emily's stretcher, ready to hold her steady if the landing was rough. Painkillers were running via her IV, but if they hit hard nothing would deaden the little girl's pain. And now she was going to have to wait extra hours for medevac, when every minute counted. Jo felt a cramp in her chest.

The engine coughed and over-revved. The wind was howling, the rain actually running uphill on the windows. Treetops swept past beneath them. *Come on, come on,* she thought, willing the wounded chopper to clear the forest and find open ground.

Out of nothing, a grassy hillside appeared. Her heart rose. Desperately the pilots slowed the helicopter to a hover. Painfully, battling the wind, they began descending.

The co-pilot called out their altitude. He sounded like he was trying to talk while sprinting flat out.

'Seventy feet.'

Jo looked out and cold sweat bloomed on her forehead. The hillside was steeply sloped. They were going to have to land on a thin slice of crumbling land between fifty-foot Douglas firs and an eroding cliff that dropped away to rocks and surf.

'Fifty feet.'

The engine juddered. The wind caught them and shoved the chopper sideways. Jo pressed one arm tight across Emily's chest and reached for Daniel with the other. He took her hand. His palm was hot.

She squeezed. 'Glad I'm spending the day moonlighting with you.'

'Nothing better, mutt.'

'Thirty feet.'

A gust of wind drove the chopper sideways. The uphill skid hit the grass. Emily cried in pain. The engine shrieked. Jo let out a breath, knew she was about to break Daniel's hand, thought *Come on, come on, just shut down the engine and let us stop moving.*

The chopper tilted.

'Fuck,' the co-pilot said.

They slammed the power as hard as they could.

Daniel said, 'It's too steep.'

Jo looked. The ground was slick, hard, and too precipitous to hold the chopper. If they shut off the engines, the helicopter would tilt and skid down the hill.

The pilot made a snap decision. 'Out. We have to keep the rotors turning while you unload the patient. Otherwise we'll slide.'

'What about you?' Jo yelled.

'We'll ditch. We can swim. The girl can't. We'll shut down the engines and auto-rotate down. Go, go, go.'

Jo was already hauling back the door. The cold and wind slammed her in the face. The noise of the sick engine was terrifying. They were six feet off the ground.

They weren't going to be able to do this.

They had to do this.

She had to move fast. She needed to get the stretcher out the door before the wind slapped the chopper into the hillside and the rotor blades caught the dirt.

Daniel had the IV drip off the stand and lying on Emily's chest. He released the stretcher from its locked position. Jo maneuvered into the doorway. He pointed outside.

'Get out,' he said.

'No, let's pull her from either side.'

'No, Jo. Get out and I'll slide her out to you.'

'*Now*,' the pilot said. 'Go.'

The chopper was swaying in the wind, the skid brushing the ground. Jo eked her feet out onto the skid and stood on it. Holy hell. She waited and unbelievably, miraculously, the pilots steadied the chopper. They held it, poised against the wind and engine damage, steady on the hillside. She stepped down onto the blessed ground.

Daniel swung the stretcher around. 'Hang on, Emily.'

It all happened in a few seconds. The co-pilot said, 'I can't hold it.'

'Power,' the pilot shouted.

Jo reached for the stretcher, and it wasn't there.

Her hands grabbed empty air. The engine hacked. The chopper lurched and began sliding away from her. She saw Daniel haul on the stretcher, hanging on to it with every ounce of strength to keep Emily from plummeting out the door. And horribly, the chopper sank away from her, one skid scraping the hillside. It fought for power, for altitude.

The engine abruptly went silent.

She lunged for the door. Daniel shouted, '*Jo, down.*' She threw herself to the wet ground and felt the whir of the main rotor blade spinning past her head. She scrambled to her knees, to her feet, falling downhill in the rain, hand out, desperate, knowing in the base of her heart that she couldn't possibly stop the chopper from sliding down the hill, that Daniel was throwing himself across little Emily, and that she wasn't going to reach him, nothing was going to stop the helicopter from skimming faster and faster down the steep slope, the blades still shrieking around and why the hell wouldn't they grab the ground and stop the fucking thing and, oh, Jesus—

The blades caught the earth. The chopper spun like an animal. Turf flew into the air in huge green clods. She stumbled after it, sliding downhill on the slick grass. She couldn't even scream as it corkscrewed, reached the edge of the cliff and dropped out of sight toward the ocean.

The wind whipped the rain across her face, so hard she could hardly see. The cliffside was eroded and crumbling. Rocks fell away beneath her feet, roots tried to tangle her, her hands slipped in the mud. But she knew she could descend it. She forced herself to go slowly, not to leap or risk anything in the mud and slick. She was the only chance they had left.

The chopper was at the bottom of the cliff, upside down on the rocks. She could smell aviation fuel. There was debris all over the rocks, bolts and screws and metal fragments, medical equipment, bandages, syringes, everything she needed to help the people inside. She fought down the panic and felt her way down the cliff.

She reached the bottom and picked her way toward the chopper. Breakers exploded on the rocks. The spray was freezing.

'Danny,' she shouted.

She felt her way around the mangled wreckage. The fuselage, so gleamingly smooth when she'd climbed aboard at UCSF, was crumpled, dirty, streaked with mud, gouged by the rocks. One of the main rotor blades was twisted along the rocks like a broken scythe. A pure white fear wheeled up and hit her. She grit her teeth, but a sob jerked from her lungs.

In the cockpit, the co-pilot lay crushed against the windshield, dead.

The pilot was alive. He had managed to undo his safety harness and crawl out the cockpit door. He was slumped against the fuselage, bloody but conscious.

She slid across wet rocks and scrambled to his side. 'Are you all right?'

His face was wrenched with pain. 'Busted leg. I can't get to the others.'

Jo worked her way across slick rocks to the bay of the chopper. Her hair was stuck to her neck in long strings. Her hands were red with cold, and her fingers wouldn't work properly. The open door was facing the ocean. It was flattened to a width of two feet, and the waves were running inside.

'Daniel.'

She held onto the fuselage, crouched down and peered in. She saw nothing but debris.

She heard a whimper. In the dim interior she saw Emily Leigh, thrown like a discarded toy against the back wall of the chopper. Water rushed over Jo's feet, so bitingly cold that her breath caught.

The wave retreated, bringing the stench of jet fuel and a tide of medical supplies. The door was a mouth, the interior dark, and her brain hissed *Small spaces collapse.*

She stared in, breathing hard, looking for her husband.

*Small spaces will eat you.*

'Daniel.'

She got down on her hands and knees and crawled in. The roof gave her only eighteen inches of space. She dropped to her stomach and crawled on her elbows. Blood rushed in her ears.

Her skin was goosebumped, her breath racing. She knew she had to slow it down or she'd hyperventilate.

Emily whimpered again. It wasn't a cry of discomfort or fear. It was a base, animal moan. It was the sound of dying.

'I'm coming.' She crawled through the mess and wet and cold and stink. 'Daniel. Where are you?'

And she saw his hand. The stretcher and half the chopper's medical supplies were dumped on top of him. She began throwing debris aside, digging for him.

'Danny.' She couldn't make her voice say anything else.

She dug out his arm, tossed aside some wrecked equipment, looked back and saw Emily. The girl's eyes were barely open.

'Jo.'

His voice was little more than a whisper, and the most thrilling sound she'd ever heard.

'I'm here,' she said. 'Can you move?'

'Banged up, but yeah.'

He was face down, smashed against the side of the chopper, covered with junk. He turned his head, looked at her, and squeezed her hand.

'The girl,' he said.

'She's bad. I'm going.'

Triage is a system that helps medics decide who to treat first in multiple casualty situations. When the injured outnumber the doctors, triage rates patients to give medics the best chance of saving the most lives.

Jo crawled through the mess toward little Emily, repeating the triage criteria in her head.

Sort patients into three groups: immediate care, delayed care, and unsalvageable. Red tag for immediate care, those who will die if not treated now. Yellow tag for delayed care, those who will survive even without treatment – the walking wounded, those with stable vital signs, people who are conscious and aware of their surroundings. Black tag for the unsalvageable, those who will die no matter what the medics do.

Daniel was talking and moving, conscious and coherent, had no obvious head or spinal injuries. But from five feet away, Jo knew Emily was a red tag. Hell if she was going to let that become black.

'Emily, I'm coming.' Her hands were throbbing from the cold. She shoved aside more debris. The stink of aviation fuel was almost enough to make her gag. 'Danny, you still with me?'

'Babe. The radio.'

'I got through to 911 on my cell before I came down the cliff. Rescue's on its way.'

Not fast enough for the co-pilot. But it had now been twenty-five minutes, and somebody was outbound to help them.

Belly-crawling through the crumpled chopper, Jo edged the last couple of feet to Emily. She grabbed her hand. The girl's skin was cold, her soft hair tossed over her face. Jo found her pulse. It was weak and thready.

She saw blood in the child's mouth and cuts on her pale little legs. When a kid loses blood, it's easy for them to get into trouble because they have less volume than an adult. Emily was freezing. She was undoubtedly in hypovolemic shock. She may have been bleeding internally. Jo had to stabilize her long enough for rescue to arrive.

Jo heard that awful wounded moan again.

'Hang on, honey,' she said. 'Hang on, Emily.'

The waves rushed in again. Freezing water ran up her legs like a molesting hand. The fuselage seemed to shrink. She tried to breathe deep and felt her chest constrict.

She scrambled to grab the thermal blanket to warm Emily up. She looked for anything with which to brace her head and neck.

She heard, behind the crash of the waves, the rhythmic thud of helicopter rotors. Tears sprang back into her eyes.

'Daniel, they're coming,' she said. 'Can you see them?'

The jet fuel and cold briny water sloshed around her legs. She checked Emily's eyes. Her pupils were unreactive.

She wasn't breathing. Shit.

*We'll take care of her*, she had promised Emily's mother. She had pledged it.

This is not going to happen, she thought. I will not let you slip away. She put two fingers against the child's neck and checked for a carotid pulse.

The sound of the helicopter outside grew louder. It was close and it was big. She pulled Emily away from the wall and fought to get her into a position where she could administer CPR. In the smashed interior, she didn't have room to kneel above the girl and extend her arms to give chest compressions.

Jesus, girl, don't die. Do not die. The child's face was the color of paper, with blue veins showing underneath. Her eyes were glassy.

No. 'Stay with me, Emily.'

She turned her flat on her back, checked that her airway was clear, and began CPR. Breathed into her mouth. Gave chest compressions, struggling with the angle. Heard a big chopper hovering outside, its engines a drone, a brilliance, deliverance.

Another two breaths into her soft little mouth. Thirty compressions. Two more breaths.

Again.

Come on, Emily.

Outside, the air ambulance pilot shouted, 'Here.'

Jo breathed for Emily. Again, and again. No response. She heard men outside. She turned her head and hollered, 'In here.'

Back to chest compressions. Come on, baby, come on. She could do this for as long as it took. Stay with us, Emily.

'I'll get you a Tickle Me Elmo helicopter, Emily. Come on, honey.'

Twenty-five compressions, thirty. She breathed into Emily's cold mouth. Footsteps clattered outside, somebody pounded on the fuselage, a man called, 'Are you all right?'

'Get in here.' She kept up compressions. 'Two injured survivors. Child in cardiac arrest. Help me.'

Behind her, men shouted instructions back and forth. The chopper rocked as one of the rescue crew crawled inside. She heard him sloshing his way through the debris. He appeared at her side.

'How long have you been going?' he said.

'Two minutes.'

He had on a green flight suit. He reached out and took Emily's pulse while Jo continued compressions.

'Are you injured?' he asked.

'No.'

'Let me take over.'

Jo scooted aside. The man crawled forward to take her place. He had an Air Force insignia and chevrons on his sleeve.

'You a PJ?' she said.

He nodded and went to work on Emily. Jo's heart soared. This was the child's one, only, best chance. The man was serious, looked seriously competent, unperturbed and focused.

For a moment, tears of relief obscured her vision. She crabbed her way backward, trying not to break down, to hold her cool a while longer. The 129th being here meant they had trained professionals, medical supplies, equipment to extricate all of them from this hell, and what was undoubtedly a beautiful motherfucking Pave Hawk helicopter holding on station above them.

She turned and crawled back to Daniel. 'PJs. We're getting out of here.'

She took his hand and looked out the crushed door of the chopper. The surf seemed at eye level. A second pararescueman appeared, sliding down a rope from the sky.

'Jo,' Daniel said.

His hand was icy. She pressed herself against him to warm him with her body heat. 'We're going, ASAP. Just hang on.'

He looked at her. He was wheezing. A trickle of adrenaline ran down her chest. He hadn't been wheezing before.

'Daniel, can you breathe?' she said.

He whispered something. She leaned closer. All her fear returned, black and huge, like the big bad wolf.

His lips moved. No sound. He mouthed, 'Jo. Love.'

'Danny.'

He grabbed for breath. She saw his chest catch. Saw his nails. Blue in the nailbeds. Shit. She leaned away and yelled out the door at the second PJ.

'Patient in respiratory distress.'

Daniel squeezed her hand.

'Come on, Danny,' she said. 'Hold on.'

He gulped with pain. She squeezed his hand. 'Damn it, Beckett, we're almost out of here.'

He touched her face and looked at her with green eyes.

'We're going home, Beckett. You and me,' she said.

He squeezed her hand. His eyes told her he was going, but not home.

She went frozen with understanding. With the clarity that absolute zero bestows. His eyes were clear, and for a second he fought the pain, to tell her he knew the truth, and she needed to know it too. He was a doctor. He knew he was already gone. His spirit was just holding on for a few final seconds, looking out at her from the wreckage of his body, telling her goodbye.

And then he was across the border.

Everything after that was swallowed in the unbridgeable gulf that had just torn open. All noise, all light. The waves, the turbines of the Pave Hawk, her grief. She lost it. Not crying, but shouting at him, and then she was being pulled out of the chopper, wet and trembling, fighting every inch of the way, and who the *fuck* was the man dragging her away from Danny?

'Doctor, the surf's swamping the chopper. You'll drown,' he said.

'Let go. Let me go. That's my husband in there. Let me go. We have to get him out.'

Strong arms went around her, clutched her tight. She smelled his flight suit, saw a nametag reading *Quintana*, refused to hear what he was saying.

He held her hard and wouldn't let go. When he put his lips against her ear, his voice was gentle.

'I'm sorry. They're dead.'

# 29

The blue October sky hurt her eyes. Church bells were ringing. They seemed to reverberate in her chest.

Gabe leaned forward, hands clasped between his knees. 'Jo, you didn't kill Daniel.'

'Don't humor me. I know what people said behind my back.'

He looked perplexed. 'What are you talking about?'

She felt a catch in her throat. 'That day. Back at Moffett.'

The 129th had flown her back in the Pave Hawk to Moffett Field. On the flight, pitching through the sky, Quintana sat beside her. Nobody spoke. When they landed, she climbed out in a daze. She wanted never to approach another aircraft again. Not a helicopter, a jetliner, a paper airplane. She shucked off the Pave Hawk like a snake shedding its skin and walked away from it.

She now knew that she was already in shock, which hits the grieving and turns the world dim and glassy when a spouse dies. She learned that in the bereavement group, when Tina finally dragged her there, physically, and sat with her through the first meeting.

She walked with the rescue crew to their HQ building. They wrapped her in a blanket, got her coffee, sat her down on a plastic chair under fluorescent lighting. They walked down the corridor and talked to the unit's commanding officer. She stared at the wall. She heard subdued voices. *Survivor*, she heard. *The guy's wife.*

*Triage*, she heard. And, under his breath, the second PJ talking about Daniel.

Now, under the shimmering Halloween sunshine, she looked Gabe Quintana in the eye. 'He said, "Even a paramedic should have caught it."'

Gabe gazed at her for a long, breathless moment. She kept herself from looking away. She felt like she was going to splinter.

'I made a mistake. And it killed him,' she said.

Gabe looked at her for another second. Still grasping her hand, he stood up and led her across the plaza. 'You had nothing to do with Daniel dying.'

'Where are you taking me?'

'I don't know. Someplace where you can get this outrageous notion out of your head.'

Her face felt hot. 'I heard him, Gabe. The other PJ talking to your CO. He said that Emily was a black tag.'

Unsalvageable. And that was the verdict of the Medical Examiner. Emily Leigh had been critically ill, physically frail, and the injuries sustained in the crash of the air ambulance were too severe to treat. Jo could not have saved her.

But Daniel had not been a black tag. He was desperately injured, but quick action could have saved him. He had internal bleeding, a collapsed lung, and cardiac tamponade. The pericardium, the sac surrounding the heart, was damaged during the crash. It filled with blood, which prevented his heart from beating. That killed him.

Gabe led her away from the plaza. 'The letter was delivered to your house?'

'Via UCSF. They sent it to my office, and the med center forwarded it. So maybe they don't know where I live.'

'Good.' His hand was hot. 'Who do you need to talk to?'

'About the note?' She tried to think, but her mind remained stuck on the moment that her life, her plans, her understanding of herself and her role in the world had screeched to a stop in the face of staggering failure.

'Mother of God.' Gabe stared straight ahead. 'You've been carrying this for two years?'

She didn't answer. She didn't think she could speak. She had thought she was out of the woods. She'd fought her way back to daylight thanks to her family and friends, and with the support of the bereavement group. That's why she had taken over as facilitator – to give back. She thought she was out of the dark.

Now this.

'Is this why you got out of emergency medicine completely? Why you went into forensic work?' Gabe said.

'Yes.' She felt angry that he didn't seem to understand. 'First, do no harm.'

His eyes had become remote. He pulled her across the plaza, holding her hand.

'You've retreated behind the Hippocratic Oath?' he said.

'Not retreated. It's the pledge every doctor takes, the foremost duty of every physician. Help, but don't put lives in danger. It's what I live by.'

'So you've sealed yourself off from the living?'

'Cheap shot, Quintana.'

She couldn't tell whether he felt furious, or pained. She couldn't tell what she felt *more*, furious or pained.

Sealed herself off from the living? He didn't understand. Every time she looked at him, she heard an echo. She heard him tell her that Daniel was with the dead.

'You don't deserve this.' He pulled her to a stop. His eyes were flat with anger. He put his hands on either side of her face. 'Do you hear me?'

She heard her pulse rushing in her ears. She heard *Hey, mutt*. She could almost hear the smile in Daniel's voice.

Get it together, Beckett. This was no time to subside into self-pity.

Time to be a junkyard dog.

She looked up at Gabe. 'I hear you.'

'Good.'

He lowered his hands. She looked at the note, telling her she was being initiated into the Dirty Secrets Club.

'No more secrets. It's time to drag all this shit into the light,' she said.

'I'm with you. What do you want to do?'

She stared into the sunlight. The wind lifted her hair from her face. 'Dig.'

'Where?'

'Into the person who's at the center of my investigation. Callie Harding.'

The key to the note, the key to all the deaths, the key to finding Pray, lay with the dead prosecutor. And Pray's identity lay not just in Harding's psyche but her criminal work.

'Let's talk to the US Attorney's Office. I'm taking this to Harding's boss, and this time I'm going to get some real answers.'

# 30

Jo's truck streamed along in traffic on Van Ness, heading down-town to the Civic Center. Leo Fonsecca was at the Federal Courthouse. Gabe was a silent, fuming presence in the passenger seat.

He snapped his cellphone shut. 'Nobody in the unit has been contacted about the air ambulance crash. It wasn't us who leaked the story.'

'Thanks. I'm relieved.' She guessed she was. She guessed Gabe regarded this as a matter of honor. 'Frankly, it wouldn't be hard to find out what happened that day. It was in the papers. Anybody with enough determination could dig up plenty of information.'

'Anybody with an agenda, you mean. And money.' He looked at the anonymous letter.

On the street, people were already dressed in Halloween cos-tumes. Two glam rockers swanned along the sidewalk on roller skates, covered in enough gold lamé to gild the dome of Saint Peter's.

The light ahead turned red. She stopped amid a pack of cars. 'Thanks, Gabe. For coming with me.'

'This is something we have to stop.'

He made another call and got a fellow grad student to cover for the seminar he was scheduled to teach that afternoon. The light turned green.

He glared at traffic. 'This isn't just about you. It's about lies somebody's telling about you. And they're doing it to maneuver you into a position where they can hurt you.'

They passed the War Memorial Opera House. Long red ban-ners flew from the façade, swirling in the breeze.

Jo shifted gears. 'This will sound strange, but Callie Harding's death has parallels to another case where I performed a psychological autopsy. The Nagel case.'

'What happened?' Gabe said.

'It was an apparent instance of a sexual fantasy going fatally awry. But nothing was the way it first seemed, and that gave me the professional creeps.' She changed lanes. 'I have the same feeling with this case.'

'Why?'

'Jeffrey Nagel was twenty-nine, single, lonely, a computer programmer who lived in a garage apartment. When he didn't show up for work one Monday, his boss came knocking. He and the landlady found him.'

'Bound and gagged?'

'Hanged.'

She checked her mirror. 'Nagel was found suspended from a metal bookshelf that was bolted to the wall. The noose around his neck was padded with a chamois cloth. He was nude from the waist down. There was Swedish bikini pornography on his computer monitor, and copies of *Hustler* scattered across the floor. A stool was kicked over near his feet, just out of reach. It looked like a case of auto-erotic asphyxia.'

'But the police thought it was suicide?'

'The police thought it was an accident. They were wrong. It was murder.'

Gabe looked at her, curious. 'How did you find out?'

'I re-traced Nagel's last week. He had gotten involved in a gay fling with a man he met at a computer convention. I went back into his emails and online activity. The hook-up turned out to be pathologically jealous of Nagel's online friends. He wanted Nagel all to himself. When Nagel balked, he killed him.' She looked at Gabe. 'Nothing was as it seems. It seemed like a solitary death, but somebody was lurking in the background. I get the feeling something similar is going on with this case. There's something in the shadows. We have to shine a light on it.'

'Before Pray, or the Dirty Secrets Club, gets to you,' he said. 'That's the plan.'

Jo and Gabe crossed the plaza in front of the Federal Courthouse. The building was blue glass and stone. Trees shivered in the wind. Leo Fonsecca was pacing back and forth in front of the Courthouse steps. He looked small and rumpled, staring at the checkerboard paving squares of the plaza as though figuring out where to place himself on a life-sized chess board. When Jo waved to him, he ran his palm over his thinning gray hair and shot a look at his watch.

'I have *voir dire* starting in ten minutes,' he said.

He looked so inoffensive, with wide blue eyes, a harmless fringe of hair the color of marshmallows, sunken cheeks, rimless glasses. Like a squirrel elder. But she knew he was an *über*-prosecutor, that his milquetoast façade hid a masterful tactician.

Jo stuck her hands in her back pockets. 'I won't waste your time, Mr Fonsecca. I just need you to tell me what you know about the Dirty Secrets Club.'

'I have nothing to tell.'

'But you've spoken to the police about the club?'

'I'm in the loop. Why are you here?'

'Callie Harding was a high-powered prosecutor in your office, but she was neck-deep in a club that revels in dubious and even criminal activities. And you have no comment? No reaction?'

'Do you need my moral opprobrium in order to complete your psychological autopsy?'

He was annoyed, but Jo sensed no disgust at Callie, and no fear that she had compromised his office or any prosecutions. Either he was a tremendous poker player, or he had nothing to worry about.

'The Dirty Secrets Club runs on the principle that no single member should keep information about everybody who belongs. They meet in small groups. They almost run it along a cell structure.' She turned to Gabe. 'Wouldn't you say?'

'Typical of subversive groups,' he said.

Fonsecca frowned up at Gabe. 'Who are you?'

Jo said, 'Pararescueman, retired sergeant in the Air National Guard, and a guy who used to chopper into Afghanistan to rescue his buddies from the Taliban under heavy fire. He knows about subversion.'

Fonsecca's lips pursed.

'What she said,' Gabe said.

Jo brushed her hair out of her face. 'The club is supposed to run on trust. Members don't have an internal email system, or send each other memos in triplicate.'

'So?'

'Callie kept records of everything her playmates did. She was quite methodical about it. I found most of the records on her iPod.'

'If you're trying to needle me into beginning an investigation, or thinking to scapegoat my office for Callie's deeds, don't.'

Okay, she thought. Let's see if he's holding any cards close to his vest. 'In that case, I'm going to go public with the existence of the club. I'll call the *Chronicle*.'

'I can't believe the police department wants you to do that.'

'Five members of the club have died in the past five days. Some of them took others with them. I'll shout from the rooftops to warn people they and their families might be in danger.'

'Don't.'

'Why not? I'll call Your News Live. One of their reporters was murdered this morning. I'm sure they'll put me on camera.'

Fonsecca's eyes were wide and watery. His lips pinched white.

Jo turned away. 'Come on, Quintana. This is fruitless.'

He put on his sunglasses. 'Okay, doc.'

They walked away and didn't look back. Jo took her phone from her back pocket and began punching in the television station's number.

'Miss Beckett, wait.'

She looked back. Fonsecca walked toward them, smoothing down his hair. She flipped her phone shut and waited for him to cross the chessboard plaza.

'Don't call the press.' He looked at Gabe. 'Excuse us, please.'

Gabe glanced at Jo. She nodded, and he strolled out of earshot. Fonsecca lowered his voice.

'You mustn't go public with the existence of the Dirty Secrets Club. You'll only jeopardize more people.'

'Why?' she said.

He scanned her face as if looking for cracks in her resolve. He took off his rimless glasses, cleaned the lenses with a silk handkerchief, and put them back on. He straightened his shoulders and lifted his chin.

'Because the Dirty Secrets Club isn't a playhouse for rich crooks. It's a sting operation.'

# 31

For a moment, Jo thought she had heard him wrong. The wind was gusting and traffic was slurring along behind them. But Fonsecca's blue eyes were sharp and resentful.

'The Dirty Secrets Club is a sting?' she said.

'You seem dubious. The DSC is an operation Callie set up to elicit criminal confessions. It's run in concert with federal, state and local law enforcement agencies. And it's doing its job brilliantly.'

'This whole thing is a scam?'

'Calm down, Miss Beckett.'

'It's Mrs Beckett, or Doctor Beckett. What the hell is going on?'

A red flush climbed his neck. His voice remained bland. 'It's a sophisticated undercover operation, and it's taken several years to set up. Revealing its existence could compromise important investigations.'

'Talk, and fast, Mr Fonsecca.'

'The club is a subterfuge, designed to draw people out. It's like the "you've won a free car" ruse that convinces criminals to turn up at auto dealerships, where the police are waiting to arrest them.'

A sting. Holy stinking shit. 'And Callie had the perfect scam in her back pocket, because in law school she and her friends had trash-talked about inventing a Dirty Secrets Club.'

'She was a brilliant strategist, Doctor Beckett,' Fonsecca said.

'And she set it up with herself at the center. She went undercover.'

'Brilliant and dedicated. Hasn't everybody been telling you that?'

'Yes.' Damn, this was what had seemed so creepy about Callie's involvement in the club. She thought about it. 'This was Callie's secret.'

He nodded.

'She wasn't a confessor. She was a trapper. She was setting out bait and waiting for high-flying suckers to step up and take it.'

'Don't feel sorry for the members of this club,' he said.

'What instigated it?' She recalled the words of Callie's ex-husband. *Some people say she held grudges.* 'Was it tenacity, or vindictiveness? Was she after somebody in particular?'

'I can't reveal operational information. That could jeopardize ongoing investigations.'

'How big is the club?' she said.

Fonsecca looked away. Gabe was standing on the far side of the plaza, arms crossed, looking relaxed and utterly ferocious. Jo would have smiled, but her stomach was about to cramp.

'Do you know?' she said.

'That information, I believe, is far beyond your remit.'

'Oh my God. You don't know, do you?' Her head felt hot. 'Who else knows what the club really is? Does Lieutenant Tang?'

'No.'

He didn't ask her to keep her mouth shut with Tang. He knew he was losing his grip on the information. But he'd already lost hold of a lot more.

'It's out of control, isn't it?' she said.

He no longer looked harmless. He looked cornered. 'Let's call it a victim of its own success.'

She felt a knot of anger rise in her throat. The club wasn't a victim. Members were victims. Their families and lovers were victims.

She thought about how undercover operations worked. 'Did the police hold off arresting members so they could net as many confessions as possible?'

He didn't exactly nod, but his gaze skipped in her direction.

'But they waited too long, didn't they?' she said. 'You don't know who's in the club anymore, or what they're doing, do you?'

'I thought Callie had it under control.'

Buckpasser, she thought.

'Unfortunately, it's like a mutating virus,' he said.

'I know how it works. Whoever tells the dirtiest secret gets to set the dare for the other players. The winner sends them out to commit acts that will become new dirty secrets.' She felt queasy. 'The club has become a chain reaction. A generator instead of a trap.'

'It's the age. An age of unremitting public exposure of the self, the body, the mind, everybody's entrails, virtually.'

'Spare me the sociology op-ed. These people are thrillseekers. And nothing fuels thrillseekers like competition, except for danger. It encourages them to take increasing risks.'

'That worked naturally to our advantage. These are big egos, and that blinded them. They failed to realize that eventually somebody was bound to talk, or sell them out.'

She put a hand on her forehead to keep her skull from exploding. 'Yeah, but word didn't just get back to the US Attorney's Office. It got back to the criminals they injured. Callie lit a fire that got out of control.'

He raised a hand. 'I know. I know.'

She glanced at the courthouse building, and took out her phone. 'Amy Tang needs to know this.'

He grabbed her arm. 'No.'

Peripherally, she saw Gabe straighten and begin walking in their direction. She removed Fonsecca's hand from her wrist.

'I don't care about how much extra dirt you can scoop on these people. You're going to keep risking the lives of the public so you can get bulletproof, slam-dunk evidence for your showcase prosecutions? Forget it.'

'We need to wind it down in an orderly fashion. A big investigation is close to fruition.'

She took the anonymous note out of her satchel and handed it to him. 'Orderly is impossible. This thing is exploding, and somebody's decided to turn the tables on those of us who are looking into it.'

Fonsecca stared gravely at the note. 'I don't understand.'

*Snap*, it came to her. Callie Harding didn't have a dirty secret. The sting was her secret. So why did she have the word *dirty* written on her leg in lipstick?

Fonsecca didn't know about the writing. Jo dialed Amy Tang's cell. 'There's something you need to know about Callie's body. Let me clear it.'

She was getting a new picture in the back of her mind. It was shadowy, still fractured, but beginning to come into focus in a new way. Everything she'd assumed about the crash needed to be turned inside out.

Gabe had drawn close enough to project a physical presence. Jo beckoned to him.

Amy picked up. 'Tang.'

'I'm with Leo Fonsecca. You two need to swap information.'

'Wait – first, the good news. The witnesses to the Marriott firebombing, that older couple, did an Identi-Kit drawing of the man who threw the Molotov cocktail.'

'And?'

'And I searched databases for criminals and associates with the nickname or aka "Skunk". Guess what?'

'You found him?'

'Don't get excited yet. We've got an ID. An ex-con, name of Levon Skutlek. Two-time loser, a petty fraudster with a last known address in the Avenues. We've issued a BOLO.'

'But you don't have him.'

'No. But DMV records say he drives a white 1959 Cadillac Eldorado.'

'Scott Southern's suicide note mentioned a Cadillac.'

'You keep your eyes open for that whale. See it, call 911.'

'Before I can whistle.' Almost reflexively, she looked around the plaza, at the busy avenues that ringed the Civic Center area, looking for the car. 'I'm putting Fonsecca on the phone. Tell him the details of Callie's death. He's going to tell you about the Dirty Secrets Club.'

'Fine, but you need to come down to St Francis Hospital.'

Acid burned in her stomach. 'Geli Meyer?'

Hearing the intern's name, Fonsecca turned his head, alarmed.

'Bad news?' Jo said.

'She's conscious.'

Jo drove toward St Francis, snarled in thought. She pried apart her previous theories about what had happened in Callie's BMW in the last five minutes of her life, and tried to layer the facts together again in a new way. But it still felt as if she was seeing it underwater, a strange view through slanting light and shifting shadows.

Why did Callie have a word written on her leg in messy red lipstick?

*dirty*. It wasn't an accusation written by a tormentor. It wasn't a confession, or a declaration of self-loathing. It was a signal. It was a message she wanted to send, because—

The light turned red. She braked and downshifted sharply. 'Sorry.'

Gabe didn't react. She glanced at him. 'You're awfully quiet.'

'Remind me never to cross you,' he said.

'Say what?'

'You just ran one of the state's biggest prosecutors through a wringer and left him dripping on the pavement. It was startling.'

She stared at him, taken aback. His face was unreadable. 'Usually I put them through the CIA psy ops interrogation regimen. I thought today I'd mix it up.'

He put up his hands. 'I didn't mean—'

'Maybe tomorrow I'll give him a multiple choice quiz. "Where did you get this information? A – Yellow Pages. B – Billboard. C – The voices inside your head."'

'I wasn't complaining about your methods.'

'You thought I should go easy on him?'

'I thought you were spectacular.'

Her face heated. The light turned green.

Gabe smiled. 'Jo Beckett, Samurai Shrink.'

She revved the truck across the intersection, feeling touched and somehow embarrassed. 'Fonsecca was nothing. You should see what I can do to a four-pound monkey.'

Gabe watched the street rumble by. Outside a Mediterranean trattoria, a man in rags sat against the wall, holding a cardboard sign. *Will take verbal abuse for small change.*

His smile faded. 'That remark you overheard at HQ after the air ambulance crash. You have it all wrong.'

'Gabe, I know what I heard.' Clear as glass, never gonna fade.

She pulled up in front of St Francis. She turned off the engine and handed Gabe the keys.

'Take the truck. I'll be here a while. You go teach your class.'

She climbed out. He caught her heading toward the hospital's automatic doors.

'Wait.' He put a hand on her arm. He seemed off-kilter, his face strained.

'Don't try to sugarcoat things,' she said quietly. 'What happened to Daniel happened. I have to carry it.'

'No.'

'You saying I heard the guy wrong?'

'You heard him right.'

A dark blade of pain cut through her. She looked away from his eyes, focused instead on his chest.

His hand went to her shoulder. 'The guy's an asshole. Just to begin with.'

'Gabe—'

'Listen to me. Maybe even a paramedic would have caught the cardiac tamponade. But Jo.' His hand tightened on her shoulder. 'You weren't even a paramedic.'

The blade seemed to cut back again, bright this time. She looked up.

'Paramedics are trained to handle trauma life-support in the field. They arrive with a full complement of drugs and equipment, and radio communications with base. Their job is emergency care on the scene.' He held onto her shoulder. 'You were a forensic psych resident moonlighting on an angel flight.'

He lowered his voice. 'You were Daniel's wife. You'd just survived a near-crash yourself. You weren't a paramedic.'

Light seemed to cascade over her, a jolt like being caught in an electric current. Tears spun up behind her eyes. She put a hand against his heart.

His chest rose and fell beneath her hand. His brown eyes were unfathomably full of pain.

'I was the paramedic,' he said.

She seemed to see the invisible blade swing around one hundred eighty degrees and ring out a blow. Oh, God.

'Gabe, no, don't even start to think that you're responsible—'

'Please don't.' He put his fingers to her lips. 'Not now.' He put the keys back in her hand. 'I'll make my own way home.'

# 32

Perry shrugged into the jacket of the suit, straightened his collar, and neatened the knot in his tie. The tie was blue, cheap polyester, but it covered the gnarled scar tissue that ringed his neck. He brushed lint from his shoulder and checked himself in the mirror. His haircut looked cheap. He seemed a little down on his luck. He looked inoffensive, well-meaning, a hopeful citizen. With the garroting scar hidden beneath his collar, he didn't look like a man who had survived a lynching. He looked normal.

With a knock, the door opened. 'Five minutes.'

He put the voice synthesizer to his throat. 'Almost ready.'

The man nodded and smiled. That saccharine, *Look at me. I'm pretending you're not a freak. Ain't I wonderful?* smile. Then he shut the door.

Pray stared at it. The condescending bastard wasn't afraid of him. With the suit on, he didn't look scary. Appearing normal neutralized a powerful weapon in his emotional armory. For a moment he felt castrated, and the anger gyrated through him, rising red. Then he stopped himself.

He looked again in the mirror, finger-combed his hair and worked his face into an approximation of an earnest country bumpkin. He looked innocuous. He sounded injured. That would lull people into a false sense of pity.

Mental disarmament – it might be an even more powerful weapon today.

He went to the door, pressed his ear to the wood, heard nothing. In the pocket of the suit jacket he found the cellphone. He had taken it from one of the lawyers who would shortly be joining him in court. He removed the cover of his voice synthesizer and slid out the SIM card. He stuck the SIM in the phone and waited for it to power up.

He was dealing with the law. That meant nothing was out of bounds. He would lie, he would bribe, he would cheat, he would bolt if he had to. He would do anything except pray.

He sent a text. *Where r u? Do we need to get Meyer? Call.*

It was almost time.

Jo slipped her hospital ID over her head and jogged up the stairs to the St Francis ICU. Her footsteps echoed on the concrete. The stairway seemed to be crooked, a strange corkscrew. Her heart felt the same way.

For the first time in two years, she seemed to taste pure oxygen on her tongue, to breathe without constraint. A weight was easing from her back, and she felt like she was breaking to the surface after an age in the deep. But only because somebody else was taking the weight.

A deep stream of melancholy flowed through her. But for once, she didn't see Daniel, his brilliant smile, the fading light in his eyes as he reached for her in the air ambulance.

She saw Gabriel Quintana.

Fierce, proud, watchful and self-assured, trained to kill an enemy before he'd let a patient die. That laid-back smile, which hid the edge. The soldier studying with priests, searching for God.

Why had she never considered how deeply the men of the 129th cared about each rescue – how much they pinned on bringing people out alive?

'Shit, Beckett. And you call yourself a shrink?'

She reached the landing, shoved on the fire door and headed into ICU. With effort she shut the lid on her own mental turmoil and walked to the nurses' station. The motherly nurse in pink scrubs was on duty.

'Angelika Meyer. May I see her chart?'

The nurse found it for her. 'A policewoman's in there. I told her she had five minutes. Chase the gal out, would you?'

Jo found Amy Tang at Meyer's bedside. Meyer looked small and pale in the bed, a collection of elbows and knees under the blankets. Her blonde hair was browned and mussy. She had black circles beneath her eyes. But they were bright blue and alert. They immediately focused on Jo. Her mouth opened, maybe in surprise.

Jo smiled. 'Hi. I'll be with you in a second.'

She signaled Tang, and they stepped into the corridor.

'She doesn't remember much,' Tang said.

'Could be short-term memory loss. Typical of trauma with a head injury.'

'Says she worked late at the office, helping Harding organize trial exhibits for a case. That jibes with the Chinese takeout receipt.'

'Anything about the car chase? The crash?'

'Very fuzzy. Remembers being terrified. Remembers opening the door of the BMW. Doesn't remember the crash.' Tang smiled tartly. 'She does remember you.'

'Let me speak to her alone.' When Tang's face pinched, Jo added, 'It'll make the nurses happy, and give me a chance to get her to open up.'

Tang's cellphone beeped. She turned away to read the text message and Jo went back into the room.

Meyer's eyes followed Jo as she approached the bed. With IVs and monitors surrounding her, the girl looked spindly. But a can of Seven-Up sat on the bedside tray. If Meyer was able to take liquids by mouth it was an impressive indicator of recovery.

Jo rested her hand on Meyer's and said softly, 'It's good to see you awake.'

'You're the one. From the wreck.' Her voice was surprisingly clear. 'You found me.'

Out in the hall, Tang said, 'I'm at St Francis Hospital. Do you have the information?' Jo caught her eye, put a finger to her lips and shooed her away. Bristling like a cactus, Tang headed for the nurses' station.

Jo rubbed Meyer's hand with her thumb. 'I'd like to talk for a minute.'

'I can't remember the crash.'

'Then let's talk about what you said to me.'

'I don't remember saying anything to you.'

The light in her eyes was hot. Jo bet that, upright and healthy, she had the eager-beaver, clean-cut energy of so many law students. Pretty in pink, with a hungry ambition beneath the twin-set. Maybe it had helped her survive.

'That night, you worked late at the office with Callie. You ordered dumplings from General Li's.'

'Yeah.'

Keeping her voice light, Jo led her through it. Meyer and Callie had worked until nearly one a.m. That wasn't unusual before trial, Geli said. Then Callie offered to drive her home. It was far too late for her to catch the bus.

'So you got in her BMW,' Jo said.

Geli blinked. Fear flashed in her eyes. 'I don't know what happened after that. All I remember is being really, really scared.' She bit her lip. 'I don't want to talk about it.' She slid down in the blankets. 'I'm really tired.'

'Okay.' Jo rubbed her hand. 'But I'll come back and check on you. All right?'

Pale smile. 'Sure.'

Jo turned to go, and stopped. 'One thing, Geli. I found the CD album sleeve. The All American Rejects.'

The girl went completely still.

Jo kept her voice on the friendly side of neutral. '*Dirty Little Secret.* I know you gave it to Callie as a message about the Dirty Secrets Club.'

Meyer's face looked like plastic. 'I don't know what you're talking about.'

'Callie gave it back to you. She was upset, I imagine.'

'Oh, that?' She licked her lips. 'That was a joke.'

'You weren't going to get in the club. It never would have happened.'

Meyer began blinking rapidly. 'I don't feel well. Please go.'

'You'll find it a lot easier to talk to me than to the police,' Jo said.

She turned her head. 'Stop. Just stop it.'

'That's exactly why I'm here. What do you want me to stop?'

Meyer grabbed the call button and pressed it. She pushed her cheek into the pillow and closed her eyes.

Jo said quietly, 'Think about it. We'll talk again.'

Vehemently, Meyer said, 'Leave me alone.'

A young nurse bustled in. She hooked a thumb over her shoulder, ordering Jo out. In the hallway Tang was pacing, her face inquisitive. Jo walked out and gestured her toward the nurses' station.

'How'd it go?' Tang said.

'Compared to what? Compared to an intervention, that was a home run. She knows a whole hell of a lot about the Dirty Secrets Club. I just have to figure out how to pitch to her.'

'Bean ball?'

Jo set Meyer's chart on the desk at the nurses' station. Tang urged her toward the lobby.

'Come on.'

Jo expected Tang to head for the elevator, but instead she pushed through the fire door into the stairwell. When the door clicked shut behind them, Tang held up her PDA.

'That text message I got? It was about Pray.'

'Information?' Jo said.

Tang stared at her. 'You could call it that.'

The elevator stopped with a quiet *ping* and the doors opened. Skunk waited for a moment, scanning the scene. A sign said Intensive Care Unit. The place was quiet and felt anxious. He pushed his mop and bucket out of the elevator. There was nobody at the nurses' desk. A big whiteboard on the wall listed patients' names and what room they were in. He stopped and read it.

Angelika Meyer. His heart rate rabbited.

He peered around. Nobody had noticed him. They would, in a minute. He was wearing an orderly's uniform, and an ID badge around his neck. He'd paid the guy a hundred bucks to let him have it. Janitorial was outsourced, and an unfamiliar face wouldn't set folks off here, not right away anyhow. Cleaners came and went all the time.

If he played this right, it was a twofer. Get Meyer, and find the Spider. Yesterday at the Marriott he had lost track of her after the TV van barbecued the cameraman. He had to draw her here. She had the names.

He pushed the mop and bucket down the hall toward Meyer's room.

Tang checked up and down the stairwell, ensuring she and Jo were alone. They started walking down the stairs. Her voice echoed off the concrete walls.

'I sent search requests for information on anybody nicknamed "Pray". Database searches for arrests, known associates, that kind of thing.'

She was looking at the PDA. In the harsh light of the stairwell, she seemed like a fist of a woman.

'I got thinking about what we saw on Xochi Zapata's video – this guy getting garroted with a chain. That leaves a scar. I set search parameters to look for a nasty neck scar as a distinguishing characteristic.'

'Smart. Any luck?'

'One possible. Right here. The photo just came through from the FBI.' Tang handed her the PDA. 'Take a look.'

On the small color screen Jo saw a photo taken with a telephoto lens. Three men in a hot dusty climate, aloha shirts rimed with sweat. They were close enough to talk *sotto voce*, but standoffish. It seemed clear they were doing business, but without much trust. Two men looked unfamiliar. The third, weathered and grim, with sunken cheeks and sunken eyes, had a gruesome scar that ran completely around his neck. Red lumpy tissue fading to gristle. Grisly souvenir of a lynching.

Sweat pricked her pores. Still staring at the photo, she dodged around Tang and ran up the stairs.

'Hey!' The lieutenant charged after her.

'Come on.' Jo pumped her way up the stairs. 'I've seen that face before.'

'Where?'

She shouted her answer, but her words were lost beneath the howl of the fire alarm.

Jo shoved the fire door open. She and Tang ran into the ICU. The alarm was shrilling. Red emergency lights throbbed on the wall. Nurses were massed in the hallway near Geli Meyer's room.

The motherly nurse was spraying a fire extinguisher through a doorway. White clouds of carbon dioxide filled the air. Jo sprinted toward her, smelling smoke and gasoline.

'Jesus—'

'What's going on?' Tang called.

The young nurse put out her hands. 'Get back.'

Jo held up her lanyard with her hospital ID. Tang pulled out her badge. Seeing it, the nurse pointed down the hall. 'That way. He ran that way.'

'Who?' Tang said.

'The janitor. Who threw the Molotov cocktail.'

'Shit.' Tang drew her weapon. 'Exits?'

'All kinds. Corridor leads to other departments, and there's stairs . . .'

Tang took off. 'Get Security. I'm calling for backup.'

Jo pushed through the crowd. The nurse with the fire extinguisher inched forward into the burning hospital room. In the corridor Jo saw an abandoned janitorial mop and bucket.

'The patient?' she said.

'Nobody's hurt. It's an empty room.'

The smoke, she saw, was seeping from the room next to Meyer's. Head thumping with relief, she ran to Meyer's door. The bed was empty.

'Where's Geli?'

'Waiting area. We grabbed her and moved her out of harm's way.'

The nurse with the extinguisher called, 'It's out.' She came out coughing, fire extinguisher hanging from her hand. 'How the hell did he get in here?'

The young nurse turned to Jo. 'The guy was loitering outside Geli's room. I didn't recognize him, so I asked for his ID. He grabbed this bottle, lit it and threw it into the empty room, then took off.'

Jo went into Meyer's room, to the closet, and got the girl's purse. She walked back past the elevators and around the corner to the waiting area. Geli was huddled on a sofa, with her IV hanging on a stand beside her. She was wrapped in a blanket, clutching her knees with whitened knuckles. She saw Jo and looked simultaneously relieved and horrified.

Jo sat down, opened Meyer's purse and dumped it on the sofa.

'Hey,' the girl said.

'You need to talk. Now.' Tossing aside Meyer's lipstick, lighter and junk, she found the wallet and rifled through it.

Jo pulled out the snapshot. The Kansas farmer with the *Reservoir Dogs* smile and the silver poker-chip belt buckle. Mr Tarantino Gothic.

She compared it to the long-range photo on Tang's PDA. They were before and after shots.

It was Pray.

The fire alarm continued ringing, like a hammer. Jo held up the snapshot. 'What's his name, Geli?'

'Him?'

'Please don't tell me the photo came with the wallet.' She showed Meyer Tang's PDA. 'This shot was taken after he was garroted. It isn't from *GQ*.'

Meyer pulled the blanket up toward her chin. 'I don't have to talk to you.'

'Nope. I'm not a cop. I'm not even your mom. I'm just a shrink. And I'm the one you begged to help *Stop it*.'

Meyer tried to hold her gaze, and couldn't.

'Geli, Skunk killed another woman today. With a Molotov cocktail. It was horrifying.'

Meyer stared at her knees. She didn't react to hearing Skunk's name, but her eyes were skittish.

'I know Skunk works for Pray. So guess what, honey? One plus one equals your buddy wants you dead.'

The girl's face was growing pale. Jo had seen this look before, on people who were deep in denial – on alcoholics who insisted they could stop drinking anytime they wanted.

'Or do I have it wrong?' Jo said.

She'd seen the look on people who loved danger – on the faces of climbers who thought they could handle a big wall solo. And she'd seen it on the faces of women who lived with batterers. It frequently came with *But you don't understand* or *It's not that way; he really loves me.*

'You're way off base,' Meyer said.

Jo turned the PDA so Meyer could see. 'The police have Pray's photo. You have his photo. You have his buddy Skunk trying to turn the ICU into Dante's Inferno. What part of this don't you get?'

Meyer clutched her knees. Her dirty hair was falling over her face. She looked sullen and cornered.

Two hospital security guards appeared in the corridor. Behind the din of the fire alarm, Jo heard them talking urgently to the nurses.

'Pray sent Skunk here to burn down the ICU. How does that not add up to wanting you killed?' Jo said.

'Stop talking about him like that. You have no idea.'

'Then give me an idea.'

Meyer stole a glance at the PDA photo. She seemed to drink it in. Hot patches of color appeared on her cheeks.

'He would never hurt me. He couldn't. He can't harm anybody.'

'Sure.' And here's a lump of polonium for your tea. It tastes just like sugar. 'What's his name?'

'You're the genius, you figure it out.'

'If you want to make me wait until Lieutenant Tang tells me, fine. I'll call him Pray, or the Object Lesson.'

'Don't.' The sudden anger in Meyer's voice carried above the alarm.

'How have you been contacting him? Is he phoning you here? You know we'll find that out as well, right?'

Meyer finally looked at Jo. Her expression said *I've outsmarted you*. 'Not if he doesn't have a phone number.'

Jo tried not to look surprised. 'Really? How about an address?'

A strange look entered Meyer's eyes. It was both sly and sad. 'He's physically incapable of harming anybody.'

Jo stared at the young woman. Why was Pray incapable of harm?

'You don't understand anything,' Meyer said. 'He was abandoned twice. First when he was attacked. They robbed him and left him to die. They took everything and left him maimed.'

No phone, no address. Why was Pray inaccessible?

Meyer's pale face was livid. 'Then he was abandoned by the system. Nobody's willing to help him get justice. Nobody cares that he was robbed and mangled, because he wasn't some rich asshole from the city. He's just dirt to them.'

And with a little *click*, Jo remembered Leo Fonsecca telling her Angelika Meyer was a streetfighter, not a wilting flower. She had worked in the criminal justice system during college. She was tough.

Jo felt herself turning cool. 'He's in prison.'

Meyer's eyes looked feverish.

'Pray's in prison, isn't he? He's a convict,' Jo said.

Meyer's lips drew back. She looked wounded and savage. 'Now you understand. How could he hurt anybody when he's locked in San Quentin?'

# 33

The stench of gasoline was wafting down the hall. The alarm was still ringing. Jo stared at Geli Meyer. Her palms felt hot.

Meyer's eyes heated. 'Pray couldn't attack anybody. He's been in Quentin the entire time. He has no contact with the outside world except for his lawyers and . . .' She stopped.

'And Skunk. And you,' Jo said.

A convict. It began to make sense.

'He can't even find out who it was that injured him. Who'd help him do that? The cops? The District Attorney? He's nothing but a con. Nobody cares about injustices inflicted on a con.'

'Why's he in prison?' Jo said.

'Ask your precious Dirty Secrets Club. Those A-list dickheads screwed him over. Playing their games, like he was just a video game character to them.' Meyer straightened under the blanket. 'But he's working it through. He's doing righteous time. All he cares about is finding the people who tore up his life.'

Jo heard what Meyer was saying, but her mind was racing. It made sense to her now. This was why Pray was using Skunk as his sock puppet. He couldn't reach people personally. He had to send a messenger. A stinking rodent to pour out the message.

'He's completely alone, in an awful situation. Can you imagine what prison is like?' Meyer said.

It was like a Hieronymus Bosch painting. Depravity, despair, far more danger than outside the walls.

'I worked at San Quentin. I know what it's like,' Jo said.

The elevator dinged and a fire crew arrived. Their blue uniforms and yellow turnout coats looked like a walking wall of reassurance.

'What's his name?' Jo said.

Meyer resisted for a few more seconds. Quietly, she said, 'Perry Ames.'

'Did you meet him when you volunteered at San Quentin?'

Meyer shook her head, smirking, as if to say *You still don't get it.*

A fierce anger spiraled through Jo. Stupid, stupid girl. Meyer kept Pray's photo in her wallet. Jo bet she looked at it every night before she went to bed. Thumbed it lovingly and lay down to dream of him.

'How would you describe your relationship with him?' Jo said.

'I'm his advocate.'

Jo exhaled. Did Meyer have any idea how damning that description could prove against her in court?

Things began falling into place in Jo's mind. Not only the reason Pray sent Skunk – and maybe Meyer – to be his troops in the field, but the reason he had been manipulating the Dirty Secrets Club into committing suicide. It was a hands-off method because he couldn't physically lay hands on them.

She suspected it was more than that. She suspected that Pray didn't want his goons to kill people – that he got satisfaction from threatening people with such utter ruin that they chose instead to violently destroy themselves.

Meyer looked feverish. She was sunk in the blanket, as though she'd heated herself up to defend Perry Ames and would burn herself out to protect him. She was undoubtedly trying to protect herself now, but all her emotional capital was invested in the man they called Pray.

The fire alarm shut off. Silence filled the ICU. Jo heard footsteps and hard breathing. Amy Tang appeared, looking whipped. She shook her head. They hadn't caught Skunk.

Jo stood up, crossed the room and handed her Meyer's snapshot of Pray. 'Catch your breath. You've got some phone calls to make.'

Tang held onto it. 'Holy—'

Jo pulled her around the corner, out of Meyer's earshot, and gave her a thirty-second rundown.

'A convict. This is fucked,' Tang said.

'This is good. He's directing Skunk. We can contact San Quentin and sever his lines of communication. We can shut him down.'

Tang nodded, eyes darting, thinking. 'But Skunk's still out there.'

'Maybe we can use Pray to trace him. Amy, find out how Pray's contacting him, and send a message telling Skunk to be somewhere at five p.m. You can trap him.'

Tang's eyes brightened. Briefly, Jo saw her smile.

They headed back around the corner to the waiting area and saw the motherly nurse wheeling Meyer back through the door to her room. Jo followed. From the wheelchair, Meyer glared sullenly at Jo.

'You still don't understand. Perry depends on me. I *have* to help him.'

'Get some rest. You'll need your strength when the police question you,' Jo said.

'That's not going to happen.'

'Geli, it's over. Perry's going to be shut down. And you're not getting away. The photo connects you to him. It connects him to all the deaths of the Dirty Secrets Club. It's all over. You're cooked.'

'They can't make me testify.'

'Groupies don't get immunity, hon.'

Meyer's face crinkled with disgust. It was an unconscious, visceral reaction, and Jo realized she'd got it completely wrong. Meyer wasn't Pray's groupie. She wasn't his lover.

Jo pushed her hair off her face. Something still wasn't making sense. Why did Skunk firebomb the room next to Meyer's? She looked around the room. Monitors, bedpan, messy bed. There was a second, empty wheelchair near the door. Where had that come from?

A sharp realization cut through her. Skunk hadn't come here to kill Geli. He had come to snatch her. Not to rescue her – to keep the police from finding out what she knew.

Fear spilled over her. She turned. 'Geli, who is he?'

Geli was playing with something under the blanket. The nurse was setting up her oxygen cannulas again, adjusting the flow, getting ready to settle her back in bed.

'Oh, shit,' Jo said.

Geli looked at her. 'I'll never testify against him. He's my father.'

Geli took hold of the oxygen line. Her other hand came out from under the blanket. She was holding a lighter.

With a rattle of keys, the bailiff opened the door to the holding cell. The bailiff, a bulky black man in Sheriff's Department green, gestured to Pray.

'You're up. Let's go.'

Perry Ames stood, smoothed his cheap blue tie, and put the voice synthesizer to his throat. 'Please don't shackle my hands to my feet. If you do, I won't be able to raise the voice-synth to my neck. I won't be able to talk.'

He saw the usual reaction to the robotic buzz of the electro-larynx. The bailiff fought a shiver of aversion.

'Hands front,' the man said.

Pray put the synthesizer in his pocket. The SIM card was safely back inside the little device. He held out his hands.

The bailiff cuffed him. 'It's okay. Word from the prosecutor, we'll uncuff you before you enter the courtroom.' He led him out. 'Testifying against a bunch of lowlife fraudsters, you have to look reputable.'

Lowlife fraudsters, yes, but they'd ripped people off by using stolen credit cards and had shipped goods across state lines. That made it a federal beef. Perry nodded dutifully and let the bailiff lead him down the hall. Testifying, oh my, yes. In exchange for a reduction in his sentence and early parole. He kept his face blank and walked toward the courtroom, here at the US Federal Court-house, at the San Francisco Civic Center.

Jo sat in the St Francis hospital cafeteria, nursing a cup of coffee the size of a 55-gallon drum. The cafeteria decor was Halloween *in excelsis*, strewn with pumpkins and fake cobwebs. Behind the counter, Dracula and Marge Simpson were serving meatloaf.

Amy Tang walked in, looking like a gnome who'd spent a hard day in a salt mine. She walked over, plopped down at the table and nodded at the coffee.

'Any good?'

'You like forty weight?'

Tang smirked, excused herself and came back with an even bigger cup. 'They've transferred Angelika Meyer to the psych ward. She's under suicide watch and under guard.' She took a long swallow of the coffee, eyeing Jo. 'You're fast on your feet.'

Jo shrugged.

'Any slower, Meyer would have toasted herself, the nurse and you. That oxygen line would have burned like a bastard.'

'Fight or flight,' Jo said. 'When you have to jump, do it.'

'Yeah, but you hit her in the skull with a bedpan.'

'It was close at hand.' She took another swallow of her coffee. 'Learn anything more?'

Tang took out her tiny notebook. 'Perry Ames, serving eight years for fraud and extortion. He ran an illegal gambling racket. High stakes. Gave the high-rollers a line of credit and when they couldn't pay up, took repayment by having them run his expenses through their businesses. We're talking cars, airline tickets, everything. The victims defaulted on their debts, of course, and went out of business.' She closed the notebook. 'His sentence has six years to run.'

'What about the earlier crime?'

'The attack on him? There's no legal record on that. Just rumor. Or as Geli Meyer would have it, legend.'

'How has he been contacting her? Convicts have to make collect phone calls.'

'And we've contacted the prison. They'll be sure to search Ames's cell for a contraband phone. It's possible he's been borrowing one from somebody on staff. A cook, a janitor. Or from his lawyer. Did Meyer tell you her theory that Pray can't be hurting people because he's locked up?'

'Cognitive dissonance. It may get to her in the end. Maybe she'll tell us more.'

'She's still pretty weak.' Tang looked up. 'What do you think happened the night Callie Harding died?'

'Not sure. Trying to get my thoughts to make some kind of sense.'

Jo reached into her satchel for the anonymous note welcoming her to the Dirty Secrets Club. She handed it to Tang. The policewoman stared at it, and stared some more, surprise turning to concern. She glanced up sharply.

'This wasn't sent to your house, was it?'

'UCSF. My home phone and address are unlisted.'

Tang nodded. 'That's good. You think Pray sent it?'

'Or the Dirty Secrets Club, playing one of their games with me.'

Tang held onto the baggie, and framed her words with care. 'I take it they don't have incriminating evidence of this allegation.'

'My husband died—' blank, swarming heat surrounded her '—in the crash of an air ambulance. The note is meant to break me down.'

'Assholes.'

'Let's hope that's all it is.'

'I'll check the note for fingerprints and the envelope for DNA.' She glanced at Jo, and her face seemed drawn. Her eyes filled with compassion. 'I'm sorry. I didn't know.'

She set the baggie down. It slid across the table. As it came toward Jo, the light seemed to twist, the tabletop shiver. She put her hands flat against the wood. The building creaked. Tang looked at the ceiling.

'What was that?' she said.

Jo looked around. Everybody else in the cafeteria was looking around. She and Tang glanced at the lunch line. The heat lamps were swaying.

'Aftershock,' Tang said.

'Or precursor.'

It was done. Conversation started again. People went back to their food.

Tang stood up. 'Let's book. These jack o' lanterns give me the willies.'

The jack o' lanterns all had perky smiling faces. 'It was just a three pointer.'

'No, it's these freakin' gourds. Stringy guts and those giant seeds. Make my skin crawl.'

'Happy Halloween.'

'And later tonight all the little hoodlums start throwing eggs.'

Jo cast her a sideways glance. 'Eggs scare you?'

'Revolting things. All that viscous yellow ooze . . . and they have no holes, you notice? They're unnatural.' She mock-shuddered. 'Worst holiday of the year.'

Jo tried not to smile.

Tang picked up the anonymous note. 'Don't let this get to you. These dickheads are finished. Meyer's going to be arrested as soon as she's strong enough. There's an arrest warrant out on Levon Skutlek, our friend Skunk. And Pray's safely behind bars.' She put the note in her pocket. 'As for the Dirty Secrets Club, they're a bunch of posers. The District Attorney's going to move on any prosecutions they can. And if they don't, I will. Go home, Jo. Write up your report. We've broken this.'

'Thanks, Amy.'

Outside the hospital, Jo slung her satchel over her shoulder. The sun was brilliant, the breeze fresh. So why did she feel as though a heavy shadow was trailing her?

# 34

Jo headed for home through the late afternoon sunlight. People on the street seemed to bustle, as if they were hurrying to finish their business and get to the serious work of trick-or-treating, dressing up, maybe hitting the street parties in the Castro. A gigantic drag queen, tall as an Ent, came out of a drycleaner wearing white platform go-go boots and a Borat-style mankini. Jo didn't know whether he was in costume or daywear.

The electric wires that crisscrossed the streets, like neural connectors for the city, swung in the breeze. She didn't want to go home and didn't want to examine the reasons why not. She felt exhausted and on edge.

She stopped at Java Jones. Tina was behind the counter. *Bang a Gong* was thumping on the stereo. Her sister gave her a big smile.

'Jo. Want to try a pumpkin-cinnamon latte?'

'Coffee, black.' She sorted change in her palm. 'I like the costume. The hatchet through your skull suits you.'

Tina curtsied, and got her coffee. 'You going to any parties tonight?'

She put her money on the counter. 'I am a party. I'm a one-man band. Thanks.'

She saw Tina raise an eyebrow.

'Smile. It's about a man,' she said.

By the time she stepped outside, she was dialing Gabe's number. She heard it ring and wondered if he had call recognition, was staring at her name on his display, deciding whether to pick up. Her chest felt tight.

Just as she was about to give up, he answered. 'Quintana.'

'Can we talk?'

There was a drawn silence. 'I'm picking up Sophie.'

She stared at a mother pushing a stroller up the hill. She wondered if she should press. 'Gabe . . .'

No, don't overthink. And don't let it slide.

'I'll make soup. And my neighbor's having a Halloween party later. I'm taking dip, and I bet if I brought cheese whiz he'd be happy for you and Sophie to join in. I can ask him.'

More quiet.

'I'll go two rounds with his new monkey. Blindfolded.'

Gabe laughed. The sound eased her into a smile and set her pulse pinging.

'Half an hour, okay?' he said. 'We'll head home to trick or treat later, but if you don't mind—'

'See you at my place.'

'Jo . . . we don't have to talk. But I'll be there anyway.'

'We do. And thanks.'


Dusk comes early to San Francisco at the end of October, before the end of the working day. Its blue shadow brings out a million lights, turns the air crisp, softens the crusty edges of the city. Streets twinkle. Downtown shimmers. The Bay Area looks like a bowl of light, the water a smooth soul at the center of it, rimmed with gold. Sunset streaks the horizon, blue fading to red, a gleaming and saturated light that demands attention and tells people *this* is beauty.

Jo parked down the street from her house. Her shopping bags rustled as she hoisted them and locked the truck. Jack o' lanterns were already glowing in front windows. Ferd's balcony sported a pair of them, really sterling creepy efforts, flickering orange through twisted mouths.

She unlocked her front door, turned on the lights and kick-started some music – The Gipsy Kings. She also dug out an old album Danny had bought, Spooky Favorites. Moaning ghosts, rattling chains, 'Monster Mash' – she hoped Sophie Quintana would like it. She went into the kitchen and unloaded her groceries. She was still feeling uneasy.

A wolf was hiding in one of the back rooms of her psyche, and she wanted to keep it caged. Wanted to dodge all the riotous feelings the anonymous note, and Gabe Quintana, had riled up this afternoon.

She slammed the fridge. Avoidance, that's an excellent strategy, she told herself. Almost as good as denial. Works like a charm, till your life implodes.

She got a big wooden bowl and poured the Halloween candy into it. She looked out the patio doors at the garden. The lilacs were almost indigo in the dusk. Disquiet snaked through the base of her mind. She didn't know whether it related to Pray, the anonymous note, or the falling night.

She shook the feeling off. It was Halloween. She didn't need to feel morbid, she needed to look ghoulish. She went upstairs to find a costume.

The doorbell rang. Jo jogged down the stairs, glanced at the hallway mirror, pulled her hair again, and opened the door.

'Trick or treat . . .' Gabe's voice dribbled off.

Jo swung an arm. 'Come in, Quintanas.'

Sophie gazed up at her. 'Are you a zombie?'

Her head was hanging to one side. 'Zombie doctor.'

'Awesome.'

Jo pulled her tongue back into her mouth. 'Thank you.'

They came in. Sophie's brown eyes were wide with curiosity. 'How'd you get that fake arm to look like it's just hanging in the middle of your back?'

'I got an old doctor's coat and stuffed the sleeve with socks. Then I pinned a surgical glove on the end.'

Gabe smiled. 'Hence the three-and-a-half fingers. The makeup suits you.'

'It's Gangrene by Dior.'

He took the picket sign. 'I can has brayn?'

'What else does a shrink want, but to get inside people's heads?'

His smile widened.

Sophie said, 'Can I be a zombie too?'

'Of course.' Jo pointed her toward the kitchen. 'Soup's on the stove.'

Sophie skipped ahead, suddenly a sprite.

'Thanks,' Gabe said. 'Her mom got her a "non-consumerist" costume. An eggplant or something. This will save the day.'

They walked into the kitchen. Jo tried to read his displeasure, but he murmured, 'Never mind. At least she chose a legal plant.'

Jo poured a bowl of noodle soup. When Sophie was settled at the table, she said, 'Will you excuse me and your dad for a few minutes?'

Her throat was dry. Behind the ghoul makeup and kohl, she knew her face was flushed. They went out back and stood under the magnolia.

The branches shrugged in the night wind. Jo crossed her arms against the chill.

'I don't know how to start, so I'll just dive in,' she said. 'You threw all my assumptions overboard this afternoon.'

'I didn't mean to upset you.'

'Quintana. You picked me up, you slammed me down, you held onto me.' She looked at him, knowing she needed to speak the truth. 'Some nails hurt when you hit them on the head. What you said about the Hippocratic oath, it was like a slap.'

'Jo, I shouldn't have said that.'

'No, you were right. I have been hiding. After the helicopter crash, I felt guilty and ashamed.'

'Why did you add that hurt to everything else that was hurting you?' he said. 'Nobody blamed you for Daniel dying. Jo, if you'd stayed up on top of the cliff and never climbed down, nobody would have blamed you. You risked your own life to try. You gave every last ounce of courage to keep them with us.'

Her throat caught. She looked down and told herself not to let tears get a foothold.

'I started disbelieving everything I'd always imagined about myself. I tried to look at myself clearly, without illusions.' Which can be excruciating. 'First, do no harm. I draw on that now, as my source of duty.'

'I didn't mean to hurt you, when I said you were hiding from the living.'

'Psychological autopsies are an invaluable service. To learn about the dead, to help those left behind find out the truth about what happened to the people they loved – it's a privilege and a responsibility.'

'So how come you feel like you're hiding from life? If you didn't, you wouldn't be emphasizing this to me.'

When she didn't speak, he said it. 'Because in forensic psychiatry there are no life and death decisions. There's only history.'

*You're part of my history,* she thought. They stood close. She felt a pulse of heat between them. She felt pain, deep, and wanted a way to let it go, say it was all right, to give up this resistance she felt.

'Gabe, you're trying to ease my pain. But that's not why I wanted to talk to you. I have to apologize to you. Deeply.'

'That's the last thing you have to do, Mrs Beckett.'

Shit. Don't think of me as Daniel's wife, not tonight, please don't complicate it that badly. She opened her mouth to say something, anything, and the phone rang.

'I'd better get that.' She went in and picked up.

Amy Tang sounded feisty. 'Just thought you should know. Meyer is out of danger, so we're going to be interrogating her in the morning. Join us.'

'I'll be there.'

'I think she applied for the internship at the US Attorney's Office because Pray already knew Callie Harding was in the Dirty Secrets Club. Meyer was hoping to get close to Callie and worm information out of her.'

'I wouldn't be surprised. It's no coincidence that Meyer went to work there.'

'One other thing. Pray – Perry Ames. He never rests. He's turning state's witness on a federal case, hoping to get his sentence reduced, maybe make parole.'

'What?'

'He's testifying in Federal Court.'

'Here?'

Gabe glanced her way.

'The US courthouse, yeah.'

'Are you going to go down and inform the judge that Pray isn't such a model prisoner?' Jo said.

'Hell, yes.'

'Call Leo Fonsecca. I saw him at that courthouse two hours ago.'

'Even better. He can watch me and my officers double-shackle the son of a bitch.'

'What about Skunk?'

Tang went quiet. 'You think he'd be stupid enough to show up in the courtroom to see his mentor?'

'He showed up at the hospital to break out his mentor's daughter.'

'Holy shit.'

Jo thought about it. 'I don't know if Pray would ever attempt an escape, but—'

'But if he tries it, we'll be there. Damn, just let him try.'

'Amy. When Skunk went to St Francis he brought—' She peeked at Sophie. 'Gasoline.'

'We'll form a posse. Armed bailiffs, US marshals, metal detectors, shackles – Skunk doesn't worry me.' Tang's voice sprouted thorns. 'I need to get on this.'

'Okay, Amy.'

'Beckett, we know who they are. We know where Pray is, and where Skunk wants to be. This is over.'

Jo leaned against the counter. About ten thousand volts of tension began running out her fingertips and dissipating.

'I'll let you get to it.' She hung up and leaned back, smiling to herself. 'Go get 'em, Spiky.'

Gabe stood by the kitchen table, arms crossed, watching her. 'You look like you just won the Undead Big Brain Sweepstakes.'

'Even better.'

A feeling of cool excitement flowed through her. They had Pray in a box – the hurting was finished. Feeling thankful, and lighter by the moment, she drew a breath. Maybe now she could set this worry down and instead look ahead.

She gestured to Sophie. 'Come on, kiddo. Let's get you ghouly.'

Halfway up the stairs, the earth cracked beneath their feet.

# 35

The noise rolled underneath them like a freight train. The house jerked sideways. The wall knocked Jo in the face. And *bam*, it slammed back the other way, as if a giant had jerked it with a chain. She lost her balance, grasped at the rail and slid to her knees on the stairs.

'Daddy—' Sophie said.

'Cricket.' Gabe grabbed her around the waist and charged back down the stairs.

The roar deepened to ferocity. Jo fought to her feet and pitched down behind them, pressing her hands against the stairway walls to keep from falling. Upstairs a hallway table crashed over. A brass vase clanged to the floor and bounced down the stairs after her, caroming off the walls.

The shaking intensified.

Sophie cried, '*Daddy . . .*'

Gabe swept her into his arms and ran down the hall, threw open the front door and pulled Sophie under the frame.

He turned and extended his arm. 'Jo.'

She staggered to the bottom of the stairs. Ahead in the hall, a glass-fronted cabinet keeled forward, hit the opposite wall and vomited china onto the hardwood floor. Glass chimed into shards. She clawed her way over the back of the cabinet. She ran to the doorway and jammed herself in with Gabe and Sophie. She pressed her back against one side and lodged her feet against the other. The ground thundered beneath her.

Sophie was clawing Gabe's shirt. 'Daddy, let's get out. Please, I want to get out.'

*I do too.* Jo could see the street. Parked cars were bouncing arrhythmically. The towering Monterey pines in the park raked back and forth. Streetlight poles heaved with them. It looked like old film footage from nuclear bomb tests – buildings, vehicles, trees, the ground hooking sideways and hauling back. The sound mowed through her bones.

She pushed her head back against the doorframe. Sophie buried her face in Gabe's chest. He reached out. Jo took his hand.

Car alarms lit off all over the street. Burglar alarms joined the shrieking. In her kitchen, glass shattered. A bookshelf hammered to the floor. The wood frame of the house creaked. Then squealed. Above the roof someplace, she heard a tree branch crack. Wood and leaves racketed, and she heard one of her upstairs windows splinter as the branch speared through it.

The roar died away.

The ground stopped moving. The neighborhood kept shrieking, a bell choir of panic in dissonant keys. Jo could hear the chorus echo across the city.

'We're okay,' she said.

Sophie's shoulders hupped. She let a single loud sob fall against Gabe's shirt. He stroked her hair.

'Ssh, Cricket, we're safe.' He glanced at Jo. 'You all right?'

She nodded, but clung to the doorframe. 'Thank you for flying Air Beckett. Please ensure your seatbacks are upright and tray tables are stowed for landing.'

He flashed her a grin. She was still squeezing his hand when the lights flickered and went out.

At the US Federal Courthouse, Leo Fonsecca ventured out from the doorway of the men's room and looked up and down the hallway for damage, ready to duck if plaster came down on him. The hall looked undamaged. The dark paneling gleamed. The marble floor had returned to polished stillness. Above his head the lights swayed back and forth like incense holders at a Catholic mass, sending light and shadow swaying around in the dusk. He pressed his cellphone to his ear.

'Lieutenant, are you still there?' he said.

'Yeah.' Amy Tang sounded terse. 'But I'm gonna have to get off the line here in a second. Listen, Mr Fonsecca, what I called to tell you is – aww, crap.'

'Lieutenant?'

'We just lost power.' Her voice veered away for a second, and he heard her calling to colleagues. 'Sorry. This is about the guy who's directing the hunt for the Dirty Secrets Club. Pray. His real name is Perry Ames. He's serving a sentence at San Quentin but he's in the courthouse there with you, testifying in a case.'

'What?' Fonsecca looked around. A couple of people peeped out of a courtroom down the hall, and a security guard came running up the stairs, checking for damage. Fonsecca waved an all-clear. 'Which judge?'

'I don't know. I just wanted to alert you. Ames's accomplice is at large, and I don't know what he's got in mind.'

'Okay, Lieutenant, I'll inform the marshals.'

The swinging light fixtures blinked as if having a seizure, and the power cut out. The hallway dropped into darkness.

Tang kept talking. 'Good. Let me know once Ames is securely back in the custody of—'

The call was cut off. Fonsecca tried to reconnect and got a *network busy* signal. He looked around the hallway. The window at the far end was dribbling with dim outside light. The normally well-lit Civic Center was a gray shadow with dark windows, as if it had been abandoned. He heard voices down the stairway. In the long hallway he could barely see his own hands.

He went in search of a US marshal.

The courtroom hollowed into complete darkness. It was windowless, and the light simply vanished, sucked away, and turned them all blind. There was a commotion, all the lemmings in the room going skittish.

The judge whacked her gavel, a stupid sound in the dark, but it cut through the fussing. 'Just stay calm. The emergency lights will come on in a few seconds.'

Perry was on the witness stand. The prosecutor had been questioning him. Now he put his hands on the wooden rail.

His nerves spitfired. He could sit here, wait for the lights to come on, keep testifying, hope the prosecutor had the juice to influence the parole board about his release date. He could play nice, and go back to his six-foot wide cell in North Block at Quentin, and wait to find out if the law played nice with him.

Or not. He shut his eyes and visualized the courtroom. The bench, the court reporter's chair. Jury box. Prosecution and defense tables, with the gate and aisle through the gallery straight behind them.

Then the door.

Perry opened his eyes. He slid sideways out of the witness box and cut like a snake through the courtroom.

The judge cracked her gavel again. 'Everybody stay where you are. Bailiff, secure the prisoner.'

Everybody ignored her. He went out right behind a bunch of lawyers.

'On three.'

Jo and Gabe counted it off and shoved the wrecked cabinet upright in the hall. Sophie held the flashlight so they could see. Jo ripped long strips of strapping tape, bit them off the roll with her teeth and bound the doors shut. The coyote howl of car and burglar alarms outside was nervewracking. Looking out the bay window, Jo saw a neighborhood returned to an earlier time. Candles flickered in windows, an anachronistic amber glow.

She got the broom and began sweeping up broken glass and china. Gabe pressed his cellphone to his ear and walked around lighting candles, trying again to reach the 129th. He gave up.

'Circuits are going nuts.'

Jo pointed at her landline. 'Give it a try.'

Sophie was standing in the kitchen doorway, gripping the flashlight, looking lost. Jo put down the broom.

'Weren't we going to get your costume?' she said.

Sophie raised her shoulders in a tense shrug. Her brown eyes were wide and dark, flowing with candlelight. Her face had a look of deep tension, like a steel cable drawn too taut and asked to secure the world in a stiff wind. Jo felt a moment of sadness. She hated seeing anxiety so overt and constricting in a little kid.

She tossed her shoulder so that her zombie arm swung around. 'This way. Do you want to be an old-school slow zombie, or a new-style fast one?'

'I don't know.'

Jo headed up the stairs. Reluctantly Sophie followed her.

Upstairs, a hall window was blasted apart. The grasping branch of her neighbor's oak tree filled the far end of the hallway. The house smelled like dust and oak. Glass crunched beneath their feet. Sophie shrank from it when they went past into Jo's room.

'How about a SpongeBob zombie?' What was it Sophie played with? 'A Bratz zombie?'

'Maybe.' That earned a tiny smile. 'Daddy hates Bratz.'

'Then you'll be exceptionally terrifying, won't you?'

When they came downstairs ten minutes later, Gabe had the kettle going on the gas stove. He was bent over the kitchen counter talking on the landline, writing on a notepad under candlelight.

Jo moaned. 'Sergeant Quintana.'

He looked up. Sophie stuck her arms out straight, like a doll, and tilted her head sideways. 'Daddy, take me shopping.'

Her voice was an eerie high-pitched zombie squeak. He suppressed a smile and raised his hands, as though cowering.

'No, please – not that. Keep away from me.'

Sophie staggered stiff-legged across the kitchen toward him. She was dressed in bits and pieces of fashion disasters Jo had exhumed from her closet, including a sparkly spandex top that she'd ripped all along the bottom. She had teased Sophie's hair to a Helena Bonham Carter full-throttle-insanity level, and rubbed black kohl all around her eyes.

The blue glitter eye shadow, left at the house by Tina years ago, she had dribbled from the corner of Sophie's mouth to her chin. It looked as though she'd been gnawing on Miss Teenage America's ball gown.

'Buy me makeup, Daddy.' She careened toward him. '*Now.*'

He backed against the counter and threw his hands over his face. 'No – it burns, it burns!'

Sophie laughed. Gabe hugged her and smiled at Jo. But he sounded serious.

'I have to go. The unit's short-handed.'

'Damage?' Jo said.

'Still getting a clear picture, but they need me.' He knelt down beside Sophie. 'Sorry, Cricket. I won't be able to take you trick-or-treating.' To Jo he said, 'Preliminary reports of some road closures.'

Jo's transistor radio was reporting fires and buildings collapsed south of Market. Streets were blocked by toppled telephone poles. Electrical wires were down in a number of neighborhoods.

He looked momentarily fraught. 'I can't get through to Mrs Montero. The babysitter.'

'Sophie can stay with me,' Jo said. 'If that's okay.'

Gabe nodded. He took his daughter's hand and sat down at the kitchen table.

'You scare the neighbors here, okay?'

'Okay,' she said half-heartedly.

'Sorry, cricket. This is my job.'

She nodded, eyes down. He kissed the top of her head and stood up.

Jo walked to the door with him. 'We'll be fine.'

'Thank you. For this, and for cheering her up.' He reached out and stroked her hair off her forehead with his index finger. 'Jo, I—'

She put her fingers against his lips. 'We'll talk. But right now, you go to work.'

He held her gaze for a moment in the candlelight. He took her hand in his and kissed her palm. Then he was out the door and running down the steps.

The courthouse was a dim warren in the autumn twilight. Perry rushed down the corridor, cut through a fire door and ran down two flights of stairs. He came out on another hallway. Everything was still dark. How long till the emergency generators kicked in?

People were wandering the halls. He had to get out. Get outside with this blackout, and he was gone. Gone for long and hard and good.

He ran to the far end of the hall, looking for an exit. He wasn't going back to prison. With every step he ran, his lungs filled with fresh air and his mind with more certainty. He wasn't going back to the locked cell by the bay, to the noise and mayhem, where he was voiceless and caged and surrounded by the constant roar of other men's rage.

If he could get out of the building Skunk would pick him up. Then they would track down the people who robbed him, tortured him and ruined his body. He could finally mete out justice. All he had to do was get away from this fucking courthouse.

He found a set of back stairs and shoved open the fire door. The stairwell was coal black. He heard footsteps below in the dark, tentative, feeling their way. He grabbed the rail and ran down.

Half a flight down the emergency lights blared on. Harsh halogen ghost-lighting, it turned everything black and white.

Below him the footsteps picked up pace, sounding assured now. A man was coming up the stairs. Pray put on a severe face and kept jogging down. The man coming up was small and gray and wearing a funereal suit. He looked like an apprehensive chipmunk. He glanced up at Perry and continued climbing.

'Excuse me,' he said.

Perry kept going past him. After a moment, he heard footsteps again, this time descending the stairs. Gray Man was coming back down.

'Excuse me. Sir, if you don't mind,' the man called.

Perry couldn't answer without using his voice synthesizer. He ignored him.

'Excuse me.' The footsteps came faster. 'Have you seen any marshals?'

Marshals? He stopped and turned to look at Gray Man. The guy was red in the face and out of breath. He descended the stairs, puffing.

'Did you come from Judge Wilmer's courtroom?' the man said.

Run, or not?

Perry was a good five inches taller than this guy, and had ten years on him. The guy was a mouse, but something in his eyes was mean. He looked Perry up and down. Even though all the man could see was a citizen in a cheap suit, Perry still didn't like it.

Out in the hallway an alarm began ringing. Gray Man's eyes got agitated. He looked at Perry. He looked at Perry's collar, at his neck. His whole face changed.

He turned blood red. He knew.

Gray Man turned to run, but Pray was faster. Perry caught the man around the legs, clipped him, and watched him go down.

Gray Man hit the concrete stairs face first. When Perry leapt down the stairs toward the fallen figure, he already had his cheap blue tie in his hands.

He knew exactly how a garrote worked.

## 36

Jo and Sophie came into the house with cold cheeks and fingers. Sophie reached into her trick-or-treat bag and pulled out a prickly fruit.

'Who gives kiwis for Halloween?' she said.

'Don't eat it. We'll turn it into Mister Kiwi Head.'

'What's that?'

'Like Mister Potato Head.'

Sophie stared at her, perplexed. Jo felt old and square.

Halloween was a bust. Neighbors wanted to know what Jo had heard. Did her phone work? Did she have a radio? How bad was it? they wanted to know. Were there fatalities, were the bridges okay, how about the Marina, anybody know if it held up this time? The neighborhood was veering between depression and mania, trying to carry on like London in the Blitz but having a nervous breakdown.

Alarms were still ringing. A few parked cars were still flashing their lights, coloring the street like some post-seizure aura.

The wires were down. The city was cut off from itself.

Jo locked the front door and looked out the bay window. 'Hang on a minute. I'm going upstairs.'

She jogged up the stairs in the dark. The enormous tree branch in the hallway looked like a dragon's exploded tongue. In her bedroom Jo opened the window. The city seemed to keen at her. It was a nervous sound, too scattered, abnormal. She heard sirens down near Fisherman's Wharf.

Sophie appeared in the bedroom door. 'Is something wrong?'

'Wait here,' Jo said.

She took off her zombie doctor coat. Pushing open the sash as far as it would go, she swung a leg over the sill and grabbed hold of the downspout.

'Where are you going?' Sophie said.

'On the roof. To see what's going on.'

She pressed her hand against the recessed frame of the window, stood up on the sill, balanced carefully and reached up for the edge of the roof.

She counted to three, wedged her foot against the top sash of the window and boosted herself up. She swung a leg over the eaves and pushed her way onto the roof.

The view up here was the best on the street. She could see over rooftops and all the way from the Golden Gate to the Bay Bridge.

'Oh, man.'

The entire bay was dark.

Pray pushed open the doors of the courthouse and headed down the steps into the darkened plaza. The Civic Center was as lightless as post-war Berlin. The city looked eerie, with dark blue dusk suspended in the western sky, all the streetlights off, trams stopped randomly in intersections, powerless without the electric grid. Only the streets were lit – by car headlights. Traffic was snarled. All the traffic lights were out, and drivers were inching their way into a jumble. Pedestrians were ghostly black silhouettes.

He walked away from the courthouse. Half a block up the street he turned the corner, headed up Van Ness and knew he was away. He shot a look back. The city streets were full of people, all of them worried about themselves. Nobody was charging after him.

He picked up his pace, striding confidently along the avenue. He inhaled the cold air. Gasoline exhaust, city grime, dog shit. What a wondrous perfume. He lifted his face. It was the smell of freedom.

This was an unbelievable opportunity. O Fortuna, smiling on him. He didn't know how long the blackout would last, but every minute the city remained cut off was a minute he could use to get what he needed – and to get away.

He took his voice synthesizer and slid the phone SIM card from inside it. Then he took the cellphone from his pocket. Finally, he had a phone he could keep, not one he had to borrow and return to lawyers or kitchen staff at the prison. He had taken the phone off Gray Man before he dumped his body at the bottom of the stairwell. He loved modern technology.

He looked around. It had been more than a year since he'd walked free along a city street. He felt elated, euphoric, and ready to eat the world.

He had to hurry. The lights would be coming back on again. Unless the state was a colossal disaster zone, unless the governor called out the National Guard to impose a curfew. Unless thousands were dead – in which case he could steal an ID. But this didn't look like a mass-graves disaster. He didn't think he'd get quite that lucky. But he knew there was going to be so much confusion tonight he could become almost anybody, do almost anything.

He had to contact Skunk.

Skunk had the names. It was beyond vital that he get them. First, because he was going to torture these people. Of course he was. Justice *would* be served. Second, he needed the names because his attackers knew what had become of his money.

It had been a bad idea from the beginning, doing business with them. He should have known he couldn't trust the Dirty Secrets Club. The rich and infamous, selfish bastards interested only in playing games. Setting up an executive poker game. Sure. Ha ha. They sent dishonorable people to the meet. He could tell it in their jumpiness and paranoia, especially the porn chick in the rubber mask.

He should have seen the robbery coming.

That's what he told himself now, but it was too late to go back. Too late to tell himself he should have gotten their names back then, so he wouldn't have to track them down now.

The goons who attacked him, of course, weren't the ones running the show. Those people hid behind the veneer of fancy businesses and shell corporations. They were the type who passed for normal society.

They were the type who invested money, even stolen gambling

money – in businesses, start-ups, the stock market, real estate. They weren't the type who would keep briefcases full of cash lying around. They'd put it into bonds or money market funds or a cash account. But they'd be concerned about liquidity. That meant they would have instant access to the money he was owed.

And they would definitely have the funds, and the ability to make an overnight electronic funds transfer to an account Perry designated. Especially if he took their families hostage and started injecting them with Fentanyl, or holding a kid's face underwater in a bathtub.

They had no idea how much time he had spent thinking of ways to even the scales. Turnabout? Not even close. They had taken his money, his voice, his freedom. He would make them pay everything.

Then he would fly away.

He powered up Gray Man's phone. He knew there was almost no chance of a voice call getting through in the wake of a big earthquake, but a text might make it. He squeezed the phone in his hand and waited.

He kept walking along a street full of honking cars and rushing people. Only those going by foot were getting anywhere. Geli would never make it out under these conditions. A shame, in a way. She was so devoted, she would do anything for him. Luckily, that meant she knew what to do if she was compromised. She'd take care of herself, to protect him.

The phone vibrated.

He looked, and smiled. It was a name and an address.

Very, very good.

So that's who she was. *Johanna Beckett, MD.*

He strode up the dark and disorganized street, sending a text message as he went. *Johanna.* Come out, come out, wherever you are.

The entire Bay Area was blacked out.

Jo's chest tightened. The Bay Bridge was invisible. Coit Tower, usually brightly lit at the top of Telegraph Hill, was a dark shadow, like a burned-out flare. Headlights marked San Francisco's streets, thin streams of light that ran like ribbons on the roads down the hill, but there were no houselights, no streetlights. The city looked as if a shroud had fallen over it.

And beyond, all around the vast shores of the bay, everything was simply black. Lights usually ringed the bay like a bowl of gold, but the enormous harbor was an empty sink of darkness. Dark water, dark land, dark sky, all blending into one. The Berkeley hills had winked out. A few pockets of light were giving off a glow far to the south, toward San Jose, but they were like a faint promise, a pocket of the twenty-first century amid a land plunged back to pre-Columbian days. A hundred miles of shoreline, how many megawatts, now black. This was the closest she'd ever get to seeing this land the way Francis Drake did when he sailed into the bay in 1579.

She heard horns carried on the night air. She didn't hear the ringing of the cable car tracks, a constant companion, she realized, until it was gone. It was as if the city had snapped, sinews torn.

More sirens. Several miles to the west, in a dense low-rise neighborhood of what were inevitably wooden Victorian apartment buildings, she saw the roiling orange light of a fire.

They were down but not out. The area had taken a solid blow, but at least for now they were holding together. But in medical terms, it was going to be like they'd suffered a stroke. Synapses were disrupted. Wires literally down. Communication, movement, all that would be fouled up. She didn't know for how long, but the fact that everyplace from Sausalito to Oakland was also dark told her the lights weren't going to flip back on in the next few minutes.

From her bedroom, Sophie called, 'Jo? What do you see?'

'The lights are out but California's still standing. We're going to be okay.'

She should have felt reassured. Instead she felt uneasy.

She climbed back down and shut the window. Sophie looked at her with a strange admiration.

'How'd you do that?' she said.

'Lots of practice, from rock climbing.'

'Can I go up too?'

'Not to the roof. Maybe to my climbing gym.'

'Really?'

Jo took her hand and headed back downstairs. 'Really. But I should tell you, some people think I'm crazy.'

'All zombies are crazy, right?'

Jo smiled. 'Kid, I think we're going to get along great.'

They headed into the kitchen. The radio was buzzing. 'We have reports of several buildings down in the marina. No confirmation, but listeners are calling in a twelve-car pileup on the approach to the Bay Bridge.' Papers rustled. 'And we've just received a press release from the SFPD, urging people to stay off the streets. Please don't travel unless absolutely necessary, folks. The city needs to keep the roads clear for emergency vehicles.'

She felt a draft. She turned the flashlight around the room. The French doors to the patio were open. She pulled them shut. They wouldn't close.

The doorframe was – damn, it had shifted in the quake. She pulled harder. The wood stuck. She braced one foot against the wall and hauled. The wood squeaked, and she managed to close the doors enough to stop the draft.

. But not enough to lock them. The frame was only a couple of millimeters off, but the lock wouldn't line up.

She was going to need to take them off the hinges and plane them to fit. And she didn't have a carpenter's plane.

'Come on, we're going to my neighbor's,' she said.

Skunk sat behind the wheel of the Cadillac at a strip mall on Van Ness. The lights were out, the stores were dark, and people were still going in and out – through the doors. He couldn't believe it. Nobody had smashed any windows. Nothing had been set fire to. Nobody was running out of Circuit City with television sets. What was wrong with these people?

A fire engine roared past on the street, lights and siren screaming.

He looked at the video store. His fingertips itched. He could use the Season 3 *Sopranos* box set. And some microwave popcorn.

His phone beeped.

He looked at the message. Forgot everything else.

*Your gal Johanna Beckett, MD.*

'Got you, Spider.'

It was about time. He scrolled through the rest of the message.

*No firearms. Must appear accidental.*

Huh? Perry, what the fuck?

*Need time to get what they owe me. And to get away. City is crazy –
'accident' means cops won't look for us.*

Skunk read the rest, dropped the phone on the bench seat and
started the engine. The Caddy purred heavily to life. He pulled out
onto the dark lunatic street. Another fire engine went roaring by.
His mind was roaring too. Accident, fine, he could handle that. He
screeched up the road, turning over the final phrase from the
message in his mouth. It was a new one, high-powered even for
Perry. Equivocal death.

Didn't matter. It meant the Spider was going down.


When Jo stepped outside the air felt colder. In the beam from her
flashlight she could see Sophie's breath frosting the air.

'We'll get my neighbor and his buddies to come over and help
me muscle the doors into shape,' she said.

Or maybe Ferd and his World of Warcraft crew could bring a
lock and chain to secure it. Or they could guard her house. She
took Sophie's small hand and led her next door.

At Ferd's, jack o' lanterns provided ruddy light. The front door
was open. Jo knocked, called hello and went in. She heard conversation in the back of the house.

'This is spooky,' Sophie said.

Jo had never been inside Ferd's home. The front hall was
hardwood, varnished and creaky. Lit only by low-burning candles,
the light faded and the ceiling was lost in darkness. It did feel
spooky. She held tight to the little girl's hand. Sophie's palm, so
chilly when they were trick or treating, now felt clammy.

'Ferd?' she called.

At the end of the hall he appeared in the doorway. 'Jo!'

He clapped his hands and trundled down the hall toward them. 'You're here. This is wonderful.'

He was wearing improvised medieval gear and carrying a plastic sword. He seemed to have antlers.

He touched his chest. 'I'm a Blood Elf. And look at you two. You came as the Undead. Thank you.'

'This is Sophie Quintana,' Jo said.

'I'm a Bratz zombie.'

Jo handed him her bowl of artichoke dip. He pulled the cling wrap off the top and scooped a glop onto his index finger.

He made a *yum* sound. 'This way. Oh, thank God. Hardly anybody's able to make it. The city's had a system crash. They're going to have to do a hard restart to get it back up and running.'

In the kitchen they found three people standing around a cauldron of popcorn. Candles and a hurricane lantern provided the light. The costumes gradually came into focus. There were fewer Klingons than she had expected, and more women. In fact, now that she was here, there were twice as many women as she had expected.

Mr Peebles was perched on the kitchen table. He was wearing a harness, like a human toddler. Or a small prisoner. He was also wearing a tiny Blood Elf outfit. Even from across the room he still smelled like a bottle of Forest Fresh shampoo.

He turned his head sharply to stare at Jo. His eyes were shiny black buttons. Disturbingly, she couldn't tell whether he was thinking *Run, it's the duct tape lady* or *Drain cleaner in her coffee*.

Ferd rubbed a hand over his chest. 'I filled the bathtub with water, and sealed all my food in freezer-proof bags. I just don't know what kind of disaster we might be facing. How long will it be before there's a risk of cholera?'

'You're safe for at least a week. And in a minute I need you and some of your friends to help me get my kitchen doors shut and locked.'

'Sure.' He looked around. 'B'Etor can help us.'

The Klingon lurched forward. 'Qastah nuq!'

Soprano battle cry. Make that three times as many women as she'd expected.

'Thanks,' Jo said.

She looked back down the hall. Through the open door she thought she saw a man standing on the porch, silhouetted by the faint light coming from the street. She stopped. Sounds and images ran through her head.

*Help me.*

*Stop it.*

She felt a cold breath of fear pass through her. She looked closer down the long hall. The jack o' lantern light threw weightless shapes against the walls. In the night beyond the front door, everything was shadow.

A car passed on the street. Headlights swelled, illuminated the porch like a scrimshaw carving, and faded. Nobody was there.

'I'm nearly out of Maalox,' Ferd was saying. 'If the pharmacies can't get supplies, what'll I do? Or if there's looting . . .'

'If there's looting, they'll go for the narcotics before the antacids,' Jo said. 'Kiddo, don't hyperventilate.'

'Right. Right.' He pressed the back of his palm to his forehead.

'Use your emotional support mechanism,' she said.

'Of course.' He hurried to the kitchen table, unhooked the harness and picked up Mr Peebles. The monkey gripped his shirt with his feet and reached up to hang on Ferd's Blood Elf antlers.

Jo's phone beeped. Mr Peebles leapt from Ferd's chest to the stove, aiming for the cauldron of popcorn. She had a text message.

*From: Leo Fonsecca.*

Concerned, she took a look.

*Urgent. Felon at large. May have your address. Vital you go Central Station immediately.*

She stared for a hard moment, and called Fonsecca's number. Circuits busy.

She tried the Central Station. Same. Amy Tang – third strike. Only texts were getting through. She replied to Fonsecca's number. *Going now.*

'Sophie, come with me, honey.'

Ferd rubbed his chest. 'Is something happening? You sound alarmed. Do we need to seal the house?'

'I need you to walk me to my truck.'

He inhaled and seemed to stand five inches taller. 'I would regard it as my honor.'

Eyes shining behind his glasses, he strode beside her, plastic sword at the ready.

Sophie hopped into the Tacoma beside Jo.

'Lock your door and buckle up.' Jo started the engine.

Ferd stood outside, her knight in shining antlers. 'Call me when you get there.'

'If I can get a call through.'

She shut the door. Ferd backed up and saluted with the sword. Then he looked at his house.

'Oh, the door. I left it open—' He hurried away. 'Mr Peebles . . .'

Jo's heart was thumping. 'As soon as we get to the police station, we'll call your mom.'

'She's at a party. I don't know where. She doesn't have a cellphone.'

The flatness in Sophie's voice told Jo all she needed to know about her mom's reliability. 'In that case, you get to be my zombie apprentice tonight.'

'Okay.' The anxiety was back in her voice.

Jo pulled out. 'If you're real good, I'll let you pry open a brain.'

Sophie looked small in the seat. 'Do you think my dad's okay?'

'Yes.' Jo didn't need to put conviction in her voice. She had no doubts. 'Sophie, this earthquake isn't a disaster; it's a hassle. Ferd's a nervous guy. Don't worry about the stuff he was saying. Your dad is fine. He's just making sure everybody else is fine, too. That's his job.'

'I know.'

'And he's extremely good at his job.'

Sophie looked at her, like, *Really?* Jo had a sad feeling she didn't hear that very often from her mom.

Jo turned the corner and drove down the steep hill toward the police station. Up here traffic was spotty, the streets empty. The station was only a mile away, on Vallejo near Columbus Avenue, but to get there she'd have to navigate dense downtown streets where the traffic was likely to be messy. She checked her phone again. No messages. No signal.

At a corner she stopped and checked all ways, looking for wraiths, ghouls or ex-cons. A block to her left, a car tore through the intersection parallel to hers. She went straight. The road angled sharply downhill and she kept it in low gear. Everybody had been warned to stay indoors, but she didn't want to hit any intrepid trick-or-treaters. Or even a looter making off with Ferd's Maalox. She turned the radio to a news channel. Chatter streamed out, words keeping pace with the city's incipient panic.

She signaled left, turned, and braked sharply to a stop. A Volvo had crashed into a PG&E truck. They sat in the middle of the street in a spray of broken glass, abandoned. She swerved back and kept going. In her rearview mirror, headlights rose, bright and harsh. She adjusted the mirror, making sure the car didn't get too close. Nervous, she turned left at the next corner. Glanced again in the mirror.

The car behind her kept heading straight, down the hill out of sight. She breathed out and accelerated.

She only heard the revving engine for a single second. It came at her from the left, a gigantic whale of a car with its lights off. She was in the middle of the intersection when it slid around the corner and slammed her broadside.

# 37

The noise and the blow swallowed everything. It was a huge heavy sound. Two tons of momentum snapped the truck sideways. Jo's head hit the frame of the cab. Sophie shrieked.

The pain flicked her hard, but she held onto the wheel. Jesus.

She braked, head pounding, and held her hands steady on the wheel. She'd been knocked to the right like a hockey puck slapshot into the boards. She realized the car hadn't T-boned her, but had swung around the corner like a scythe and sideswiped the truck.

He was still sideswiping the truck. He was pushing her toward the curb.

What the hell was the guy doing?

'Sophie, you okay?'

'I'm scared.' Tears were in the girl's voice.

Jo looked out her window. The car was squealing against her, forcing her toward the sidewalk. Adrenaline jacked into her system like a flood, so hard that her vision lit white.

It was a vintage white Cadillac.

There were cars parked along the curb. She felt her truck getting pushed toward them. The Cadillac outweighed the Tacoma by a ton.

It was a gleaming shark of a car, beautifully restored; she could see that by the shine of the roof under the moonlight. If the driver was willing to wreck it, that could only mean he wanted to do something worse to her. He wanted it bad.

'Sophie, hold on.'

She couldn't let him force her to a stop. She floored the truck.

The Cadillac accelerated with her. Shit. She held the wheel with all her strength. Sophie wheezed and sobbed, a high-pitched sound of terror. Come on, truck, come on, you tough son of a bitch. She felt tears sting her eyes.

The screech of metal against metal grated on her ears. In the corner of her eye she saw sparks jumping between the vehicles. Come on . . .

The Cadillac was muscling the truck toward the curb. Foot by foot.

'Come *on*,' Jo shouted.

Too late. The telephone pole was twenty feet ahead of her. She braked but momentum carried her forward. The Cadillac shoved her at the curb. The truck hit the pole straight on.

They smashed to an instant stop. Seatbelts, airbag punched her in the chest, gray gas from the airbag everywhere, she and Sophie whipped forward, hard, and snapped back.

The shock of it was like a slap across the face. She bounced back against the headrest.

Her headlights were still shining. The engine was still running. The Cadillac had stopped ten feet ahead of her.

*Don't just sit here.* She threw the truck in reverse. The gears ground. She popped the clutch, floored it and heard the tires spin. The truck shrieked and limped backward. A foot, two feet, bumping hard. Something major was broken in the front end. She saw steam blowing from the radiator.

She pressed the horn. Nothing happened.

The Cadillac idled in the street. In her headlights, she could see exhaust pouring from its tailpipe.

The driver's door opened. A shudder ran through her.

Sophie was keening uncontrollably.

'Don't touch your door. Don't unlock it. Hang on. We're getting out of here.'

The man called Skunk got out of the Cadillac and walked toward them.

From the far end of the street, another car's headlights came toward them. Thank God. Thank God. The car approached the wreck, slowed for a look and drove on by. Jo tried not to cry.

She kept the pedal to the floor. The engine revved like a maniac. Rubber burned off the back tires. They only moved a foot.

Skunk walked toward them, stepping without concern into the glare of her headlights. He was a hunched thing, with no neck. His eyes shone in the headlights.

'Hold on, Sophie.'

Jo wrestled the gearshift, put it in first and popped the clutch. The truck jerked forward. Skunk stared at her.

She saw him swell in the windshield, and her heart constricted. He just stood there, right in front of her. He wasn't scared. She wasn't going fast enough to kill him.

He raised his right arm. Oh, Christ—

She grabbed Sophie roughly by the shoulder and shoved her down. But it wasn't a gun in Skunk's hand. It was a tire iron from the Cadillac. He leaped out of her way and swung it against the windshield.

She heard a crack, and a hole appeared in the windshield. She bit on her lip to keep from bursting into tears.

This wasn't going to work. The Cadillac was blocking her path. The telephone pole blocked the sidewalk, bent and tottering at an angle. Steam was shrieking from her radiator. She had nowhere to go.

She fumbled her phone from her pocket and shoved it into Sophie's hand. 'Call 911.'

Skunk stepped around to the driver's window of the truck. This time when he swung the crowbar, the glass pebbled.

He swung again and the window broke.

The glass fell like a sheet of rocks, spilling on Jo's lap.

'Sophie, get out. Run. Scream.'

Sophie was looking past Jo's shoulder at Skunk. She was frozen.

'Now!' Jo started screaming herself, as loud as she could. 'Go!'

Sophie fumbled for the door handle. Her seatbelt was still buckled. Jo hit it. She kept on screaming.

Sophie jumped out and ran up the sidewalk. She was screaming now, too.

Skunk reached through the shattered driver's window, grabbed Jo's hair and hauled her head back.

'Shut up,' he said.

She screamed. He slapped her across the side of the head. She fumbled for her own seatbelt.

'Shut up. Where are the names? Give me the fucking names.'

What the hell? 'Names?'

He hit her again. Her vision shot fireworks white. Oh, God. She saw the phone on the passenger seat. Christ . . . She stretched for it, fighting him, and grabbed it.

911. Even when the entire phone system was locked solid with panic, that single number should still be available. And Sophie had dialed it.

She yelled, 'Police. Help. I'm being attacked.'

Skunk heard what she was shouting and reached in to grab the phone. She stretched, trying to keep the phone from his reach.

She was so scared that it took her a moment to grasp that he was panicking too. He was reaching through the broken driver's window. Sophie was shrieking. The truck itself seemed to be shrieking.

She fumbled behind her back for her door handle.

'Give me the fucking names. You have them. I saw you take them off Scott Southern's body.'

She scrambled for the handle. What names? Southern's body?

She got the driver's door handle in her fingers. She jammed her feet against the gearshift – and saw the cup holder. She pulled the door handle. With her weight pressing back against it, the door popped open. As soon as she felt it give, she shoved hard with both feet.

The door swung, she fell backward, and Skunk was knocked off balance. He let go of her hair.

She scrambled upright. He was already coming back at her. She grabbed the Java Jones stainless steel coffee mug and swung her arm as hard as she could. It hit him in the face.

Into the phone she shouted, 'I'm being attacked. I have a child with me.' She yelled the street name and fought her way across the handbrake and gearshift toward the passenger seat. Skunk looked at her through the doorframe. His face was murderous.

She'd never known what that phrase meant. Oh, God. With a clarity like ice, she understood. It was up to her. There was now, or it would be never.

Skunk yanked the driver's door open wide. Jo pulled her knees up and kicked him with both feet, hard, in the face.

She heard his jaw crack closed, teeth hitting teeth. His head snapped back and he staggered away from the truck.

Oh, shit, now he was really going to be mad. She stumbled crazily out of the passenger door. Sophie was about ten yards up the street. Jo ran toward her.

'*Help*,' Jo yelled. 'Help us!'

Nobody else was on the street. All she could hear was Sophie crying, and an eerie echo of the little girl's voice against the walls of the unresponsive buildings around them. In an apartment window, a curtain shivered aside and Jo saw a silhouette. The curtain dropped back into place.

She turned back around. 'The names are in the glove compartment. Take them, I don't care.'

She ran and grabbed Sophie. Skunk was gathering himself up, rubbing his jaw. Had the police gotten her message? Did they hear her?

If they did, how long would it be before they came?

She hauled Sophie to the nearest apartment building. The front door was locked. She pushed the doorbell.

Nothing. The power was out. Nobody could buzz her in.

She looked back at the truck. Skunk was digging through the junk in her glove box. He stopped, straightened, looked around. He knew what he was after wasn't there.

A quick black blur pounced from the Tacoma's cargo bed onto the roof of the cab. Skunk looked up.

'What the fuck?'

He was staring straight at Mr Peebles.

The monkey shrieked. Jo saw it fling something at him. Skunk jumped back, yelling, 'Shit!'

The monkey skittered across the roof, pounced down onto the hood, leapt from the truck and ran toward the open door of the Cadillac. Skunk spun in the street, howling and wiping his hands over his face.

Jo grabbed Sophie's hand.

It was dark; they were by themselves. They were in a broken city.

They were half a mile from the police station.

They were on her turf.

This was her neighborhood. A house of cards, perhaps, but it hadn't yet come down around their ears. Victorian apartments, cable car tracks, weird alleys where tie-dyed flower children hung Age of Aquarius banners from their fire escapes. Where they could slip away into the dark.

It was a big boulder problem, a series of cracks and holds, and a woman on foot might make it through the fissures, where a man in a Cadillac never would.

She held Sophie tight. 'Now. Run.'

Gripping Sophie's hand, Jo sprinted along the street. Behind them the Cadillac made a wallowing U-turn and came after them.

Fifty yards up the sidewalk, Jo found a narrow footpath between two buildings. She cut through it. She pulled Sophie along in the dark. It was difficult to see their footing, to know whether anybody or anything was around.

How had Mr Peebles turned up? The monkey must have followed them out Ferd's front door and scampered into the bed of the truck before they left.

She heard a dog bark. They came out the footpath onto another street. A cable car was stuck dead in the middle of the road, derelict. She led Sophie around it.

At the corner, the Cadillac appeared.

Shit. He'd seen them cut through the alley. She reached the far sidewalk and hurried along it. Lights rose in the night: the Cadillac's headlights were trailing them. She saw a path between two houses. She pulled Sophie toward it and stopped, hearing growling. The Cadillac's headlights illuminated the eyes of four dogs on the path, tearing into food scavenged from a garbage can.

Jo spun around. There. In the middle of the block, a flight of stairs. She dashed to it, grabbed the railing and started down. Behind her she heard the Cadillac roar away.

'Sophie, you just have to hold on for a few minutes. The police station is—' How many blocks? Ten? A light year? 'It's this way.'

'That man's coming after us.'

'We're going to hide from him. He can't come down these paths.'

They ran down fifty steps. When they got to the bottom Jo's legs were shaking. They lurched out to the street. The Cadillac was idling directly ahead of them.

Skunk knew they were headed for the police station. Jo looked around. In the dark, momentarily, she felt disoriented. The darkened buildings looked eerie and unfamiliar. Then she realized she was only two blocks from Java Jones. She was half a block from the reconstruction project, the old apartment building that was being gutted and rebuilt. If they cut around the back of it, they might be able to slip past Skunk and make it to the next block.

'Come on. This way.'

She pulled the girl with her into the shadows and backtracked. Her legs were burning, her lungs aching. Sophie was game, but running ragged. They came out near a corner.

Her heart leapt. Across the street, she saw a bonfire in a trash can. Men were standing around it warming their hands.

'Hey.' She ran into the street. 'I need help.'

The men ignored her. She got close enough to see them. Oh no.

They were homeless men, they were drinking, they were close to fighting among themselves over who got priority heat from the burning garbage in the trashcan. They were people who brandished their schizophrenia and a two-by-four. One of them looked at her. In the firelight, his eyes said that if she came close they'd surround her, but not to help. She veered away again.

Sophie was hanging onto her. 'I can't keep running.'

'Then walk fast.'

All they could do was keep going toward the police station. She found another alley and led Sophie down it. When they came out on the next block, Jo looked both ways. She saw no sign of Skunk. She did see the alley continuing on the other side of the road. She dashed into the street.

Down the block, the Cadillac's headlights flashed on. They caught Jo in the middle of the road. The Caddy roared at her. Fighting a scream, she hauled Sophie across the road, aiming for the alley.

Behind her tires squealed to a stop. She looked back and saw Skunk jump out of the car. He was close. Oh, God, he was going to see them. She ducked into the alley, aimed for a group of trash cans and pulled Sophie down behind them. Crouching low, she peered between them at the street. Skunk was standing in the road looking for her.

The alley was dark. He couldn't see where they'd gone. He inched away from the car, peering into the night.

A new idea jumped in her mind. She leaned close to Sophie's ear and whispered, 'Ssh.'

Feeling on the ground in the dark, she found a rock. Please, Lord, grant me one major league pitch. She picked it up, twisted and hurled it down the alley. It hit. Glass rang to the ground.

Skunk spun and ran after the sound. Crouching behind the trash cans, Jo saw his legs go past at eye level.

She pulled Sophie to her feet. 'Come on. Fast.'

The Cadillac was idling in the center of the road.

The Cadillac was facing downhill on a steep grade, with the driver's door open. Jo shoved Sophie inside and jumped in after her.

The car was as big as a 747. The interior was like a 1950s travesty – a malt shop, underwire bra, shiny chrome nightmare. Scarlet leather glowed under the dashboard lights. Jo felt as though she was sitting in a wet red mouth. She grabbed the gearshift on the steering column.

Christ, how did you put this whale in gear?

She pulled, she twisted, yanked, felt the gearshift move. She stomped on the gas. The car leapt forward.

Straight at the curb. She spun the wheel and straightened it out. Behind her, she heard Skunk shouting. Then she heard the back door open. Sophie started sobbing.

Skunk was in the car. Or half in the car. She drove, veering down the street, heard him grunt with effort, heard his hand smack hold of the bench seat right behind her shoulder. Beneath the growl of the engine she thought she heard his boots scraping on the asphalt as his legs dragged out the door. She jammed the pedal down.

Like an oil tanker, the car gained speed. With a hard groan Skunk pulled himself all the way in. Then he started to climb over the front seat. Sophie sobbed wildly.

Jo shouted, 'Sophie, on three, jump out and run.'

She heard shrieking again. A little outbreak of the collective unconscious, the id rising to scream its will. In the rearview mirror Jo saw the monkey spring at Skunk. Its tiny hands clawed into his hair.

'One, two—' She braked, screaming to a halt. '*Three.*'

The car slewed to a stop. Skunk slammed against the back of the bench seat and bounced around. Sophie jumped out. Jo hit the gas again. In the rearview mirror she saw Skunk right himself and rise up to lunge for her.

Mr Peebles was clinging to Skunk's head. He had one small hand on an eye, the other in Skunk's nostrils. Skunk was clawing at the creature. Jo floored the car, opened the driver's door and thought, *If I break something I'm cooked . . .*

She rolled out.

Hitting asphalt even at thirty miles an hour, even rolling, hurt like a mother. The breath clapped out of her like she'd been hit broadside with a door. She rolled to a stop face down and lay there stunned. Then she breathed.

Junkyard dog, mutt. This was no worse than losing your grip on a boulder problem and hitting the dirt. Get the hell up.

She pushed up. Her hip killed. Her knees killed. Her entire left arm was abraded raw, and she knew gravel was embedded in it. She struggled to her feet.

The Cadillac sailed down the street. The dome light was on and she saw Skunk, still trying to get over the seat.

The car reached the lip of a steep hill and flew past it, an out-of-control white whale. The hot-nozzle tail lights dropped out of sight.

Chest heaving, Jo staggered down the road to the cusp of the hill. The Cadillac was racing toward an intersection at the bottom. Its headlights caught the scene that awaited it. Power lines were down at the corner. A telephone pole had fallen and was hanging by the wires. The top of it was aimed this direction, about four feet off the ground, like the barrel of a cannon.

God. She knew what was coming, and couldn't look away.

She heard Skunk scream.

Full speed, carrying two tons of momentum, the Cadillac speared the telephone pole. It skewered the windshield of the car like a roasting spit. With a cacophonous crash, the Caddy slammed to a halt. The tail humped into the air and slammed down again.

Silence.

Jo stood motionless for a moment, staring. Through the open driver's door, Skunk's arm flopped limply. It hung like his neck and head were maybe pinned someplace in the back seat. She was too far away to see clearly, but something dark began dripping onto the street.

She backed away. Turning, she saw Sophie standing near the curb, hands balled and pressed to her mouth. Her zombie costume glittered in the moonlight. She was shivering. Jo limped to the curb and put her arm around the little girl.

'We're all right.'

Sophie was rigid under her embrace. Jo hugged her, hoping to warm her and to thaw her terror enough to get her to move.

In a tremulous voice, Sophie said, 'The monkey.'

Jo looked at the lip of the hill. 'I know.'

'Is he okay?'

'Hope so.'

Sophie's fists shuddered against her mouth. 'Poor little guy.'

Jo rubbed her hand up and down Sophie's back. 'Yeah. Come on. We need to get to the police station.'

Gently she turned Sophie and got her walking back along the sidewalk. Jo's entire left side was throbbing. This might be a little worse than hitting the dirt without a crash pad. In the morning she was going to look like a raw steak.

But right now she could still move. 'Let's go.'

She held tight to Sophie and limped along the sidewalk. The buildings around them remained bleakly dark. They neared the construction site, and for once Jo wished for hooting carpenters with heavy tools, and a big F-150 pickup to ferry her and Sophie down the hill. She saw that much of the building's scaffolding had collapsed in the quake. The site was a mess.

'It's only about six blocks from here,' she said. 'And when we get to Columbus Avenue, there'll be people. Maybe even a cab.'

Sophie said nothing. This Halloween was no treat. Just a dirty trick to play on a kid.

'The police will be able to contact your dad on the radio. We'll talk to him.'

A freakish noise set all her nerve endings alight. Sophie jumped. The noise came again, from the dark behind them. Jo's hair was standing on end. It was an electronic buzzing. High-pitched, inarticulate, simian. An artificial robotic voice.

She turned around.

From a doorway behind them, Mr Peebles teetered into view, walking upright. He had a device in his hands. He shook it, turned it around and put it to his mouth. When he shrieked, so did the device.

It was an electro-larynx. A voice synthesizer.

They stared at the monkey, petrified. Slowly Jo looked over her shoulder. Pray was standing on the sidewalk fifty feet behind them.

# 38

Jo pushed Sophie behind her and began backing up. Pray stared at them.

She knew it was Pray even though he was little more than a darkened form on the sidewalk ahead. The height, the gaunt figure, the slack angle of his shoulders. How had he found her? He had to have been riding with Skunk. They had followed her from her house. He must have gotten out of the Cadillac before Skunk sideswiped her. He'd been trailing them, silently and on foot, ever since.

He walked toward them.

Behind her, the voice synthesizer screeched. It sounded like Mr Peebles was contacting some egregious monkey mother ship. Jo walked backwards.

She whispered, 'We have to get out of sight. Have to hide. Lose him.'

Sophie walked raggedly. Jo had the feeling that if she let go, the little girl might just drop to the concrete. She estimated their chances.

If she let go of Sophie and ran out into the street, would Pray follow her? Or would he go after Sophie instead?

They backed past the corner of a Victorian building. She saw a pathway, running between it and the construction site. It dimmed into a collapsing darkness only five feet from her.

She whispered, 'Fast.'

Shoving Sophie ahead of her, she darted into the pathway. It was narrow and overgrown with weeds. Her hip and knee were throbbing. Sophie ran, bless her heart, what a kid. Jo pummeled behind her, hands out, feeling blind. She heard feet running behind her. She looked back and saw a shadow on the street.

She heard a scuffle, and the monkey squealing.

She kept running.

Sophie said, in a terrified little whisper, 'We can hide in there. Please.'

Barely able to see, Jo said, 'Where?'

Without explaining, Sophie ducked through a break in the chain link fence that guarded the construction site.

'Come on, hide. Jo we should hide. Come in here.'

'Sophie, no—'

The girl disappeared into the dark.

Pray appeared at the head of the path. There was the slightest edge of light behind him, blue-gray rather than black, and she could see him silhouetted. He was feeling his way, hands outstretched, searching for them.

For a moment Jo watched him come. He was about fifty yards away. She didn't think he had seen Sophie duck through the fence. She didn't think he could have seen it, that he even suspected it, or that he would be able to spot her in the tar darkness beyond the chain link.

Jo could duck in as well, but at this point even if Pray didn't see her do it, he would hear her, and he'd follow. She could turn and keep running down the weed-strewn path to the street at the far end. But doing that would mean leaving Sophie alone in a hazardous area. Dammit. Damn everything to hell.

Her breath was coming faster and faster.

She could draw Pray away from the little girl. And maybe she could stop him. But if he caught her, Sophie would be completely on her own. She didn't know where the police station was. The streets were dangerous. The building site was dangerous.

She felt like she couldn't breathe.

Pray kept coming.

She couldn't duck through the fence without him seeing it. And she couldn't let him know that's where Sophie was. She tried to fold herself into the shadows as she backed toward the far end of the path.

She saw him come past the opening in the fence.

He was waiting for her to run out the far end of the path onto the street. He couldn't see her right now. But if she stayed where she was, he would run right the hell into her.

There was a clatter from the other side of the fence, inside the construction site. Metal rods crashing, wood splintering, a whole cascade of noise. It sounded as though something had collapsed. It sounded like an avalanche.

And mixed up in the noise was a little girl, crying out.

Her heart seized. Pray spun toward the noise. He was between her and the hole in the fence.

Shadowy movement was all she could see on the path in front of her. From the construction site, someplace deep in the half-torn building, she heard a fearful moaning.

The electronic voice spoke. 'Give me the information and I'll let you go find her.'

He'd grabbed the voice synthesizer back from Mr Peebles. Could he see her? Was he only guessing that she was still on the path?

'The names. Give them to me. If you don't, I'll take them from you, kill you, and leave her to die.'

She didn't move.

'Fine.'

He ran at her.

Jo went up.

She grabbed the fence and climbed. Six feet off the ground, she spun and grabbed the rain gutter of the apartment building on the other side of the skinny sidewalk. Please God, let it hold.

The gutter was cold and covered with rusting paint. She stuck to it like tape and inched up it. Her leg hurt like hell.

Pray stopped beneath her, breathing heavily. Jo climbed another three feet, feeling the gutter creak on old brackets. She looked over the top of the fence. *Dynamic*, she told herself.

With a huge breath, she pushed off and sailed over the top of the fence into the construction site.

★   ★   ★

She landed hard on the dirt, crashing to all fours. The pain in her leg fired off like a Roman candle, so sharp she almost heard it hiss into the sky. Spots flashed in her eyes. She grit her teeth and clambered to her feet.

The building loomed in front of her like an empty skull, windows dark, doorway a gaping mouth. Inside it, the front hall was a throat. Her skin constricted. She couldn't see a thing inside it.

But she could hear Sophie crying. The sound was coming from deep in the building.

Outside the chain link fence, Pray's mechanical voice rang out. '*Bitch.*'

Jo ran up the front steps and through the door of the building. The darkness was like a velvet curtain. There was sawdust and debris beneath her feet. She kicked something, a nail or bolt, and it bounced into the wall with a bright *ting*.

Outside she heard the fence rattle. Pray was coming.

*The names, the names* . . . He and Skunk were fixated on the idea that she'd obtained the names of the people he was hunting. They thought she had them.

The bridge. Skunk with his hand out—

The suicide note.

Was that what they wanted? Did they think Southern's note contained Pray's hit list?

She felt her way along the wall. She had the smothering feeling that Pray thought she was the final target in their hunt.

Sophie's crying was closer now. Jo knew she had to feel trapped, completely cut off – and she couldn't call out to her without drawing Pray's attention. Her jaw ached from clenching.

Her hands were sweating. She wiped them on her jeans. With every heartbeat, her vision spiked. In the dark, it created the optical illusion that the hallway was throbbing. That it was undulating, getting ready to swallow her. She looked up. The ceiling was solid. But this building was half torn down, and the scaffolding along the side had collapsed in the quake.

*Sophie, what have you done?*

She reached a doorway and ran her hand along the edge. The crying was stronger on the other side of the wall. She slipped around the corner and slid her feet along the baseboards. Saw shadows, faint moonlight from a dust-ridden window.

The crying was coming from below her.

She inched herself forward in the dark. Her foot found a broken floorboard.

Sophie was in a cellar. Jo saw that the floor was just gone. There was a hole in the room – had the girl fallen through it?

She heard footsteps in the front hallway. Pray was in the building. She stepped back against the wall, heard him pass by on the other side.

Her vision continued pulsing. It made the building seem to breathe. And a breathing thing could swallow you.

She clenched her hands. No, don't do this, Beckett. Not now.

She dropped to her knees and inched forward to the edge of the hole.

'Sophie,' she whispered. 'Don't say anything. I'm here.'

There was a sharp break in the crying. Please, don't shout my name, don't give me away . . .

'Don't talk,' Jo said. 'You can keep crying. Don't let him know I'm here.' She wiped sweat from her eyes. 'I'm going to get you out.'

She stared down into empty space with no idea how she was going to do that.

She focused her eyes, tried to focus her mind on the darkness below, and could only see a maw, ready to swallow her. She was not going to find a ladder. She wasn't going to levitate Sophie out of the depths.

If Sophie was in a basement, that meant there were stairs. If she went down, she should be able to get back up.

She hoped.

Slowly, as silently as she could, she lay flat, scooted parallel to the hole in the floor and edged herself over. She swung her legs down into open space, then hung from her hands. She couldn't tell how far down the floor was, or whether anything was down there that she might land on.

'Sophie,' she hissed, 'can you see me? Just cry.'

Sophie cried.

'Can I drop okay?'

Sophie cried.

Jo figured three to five feet – she hoped. This was the leap of faith. She let go.

The fall carried her down, and she hit the floor. She crumpled and rolled. Held still for a second, trying to restore silence. Her leg was screaming. Slowly she got to her feet.

'Sophie?'

She followed the sounds of crying, crouching low, hands out. She found a doorway with boards nailed over it in an X. The crying was coming from the other side. She crawled under and found herself in a stone-floored room that felt cold and smelled damp.

'Jo . . .'

Jo felt her way forward. She heard snuffling, and saw a faint shadow. She found her. Sophie buried her head in Jo's chest, grabbed her shirt and gulped a loud, hard sob.

Jo held on, put her mouth close to Sophie's ear, and whispered, 'You're very brave. You're doing great.'

In tiny jerking bursts, Sophie whispered, 'I fell down a slide. I didn't mean to come in. I know a building like this is dangerous.'

Yeah, Jo bet Gabe would have lectured his kid on safety. But a slide? She looked around the inky room. The light, what few tendrils there were, was coming from above her, high on the wall.

This was a coal hold. It was an old Victorian building. Sophie had fallen down the coal chute.

'I went around the building to hide, and there was all this stuff, a big board, and I wanted to stay close to the wall, and I walked on the board and it wasn't where it was supposed to be and I fell down the slide and . . .'

'Bad luck. I'm not mad. Your dad won't be mad.'

She felt Sophie hold on for a second longer, and exhale, shoulders softening.

'Are you okay? Are you hurt?' Jo said.

'I got cut. It really really hurts.'

'Where?'

'My arm.'

Jo felt Sophie's sleeve. The fabric was torn, but it had been torn when they made her costume. However, it was wet, and it hadn't been wet before. When Jo touched it, Sophie recoiled.

Feeling as gently as she could, Jo parsed out the dimensions of the cut. It was about five inches long, a ragged slice in Sophie's arm. It was bleeding profusely. It could have been sliced open by a shard of metal or a rusty nail.

She kept her breathing even. She needed to see it. She was going to have to take a chance.

The phone system was locked in a spasm, but her cell wasn't useless. She could use the display as a light. It might alert Pray to their location as well, but so would fumbling blindly around the basement. And with the light, she could see what they might use for weapons, or tools. And she could see how badly Sophie was cut.

She got the phone and lit the display.

She saw Sophie huddled on the floor in a pile of debris, covered in dust, biting her lip, looking very pale. Her eyes were liquid in the blue light of the display.

She looked at Sophie's arm and didn't like what she saw. The cut was long, deep, and dirty. Behind Sophie she saw a broken two-by-four with a bloody nail protruding from it.

Cupping her hand to control the glow from the display, she swung the phone around the room. They were in a coal cellar, all right, one that had seen a lot of construction debris come down the coal chute just like Sophie did. She shut off the light.

She pulled off her shirt, bit into the hem and tore a strip off. As quietly as she could, she made a pressure bandage. She had no idea whether it was all Sophie needed, or just a patch on a threatening injury.

Holding still, she listened. She couldn't hear Pray but she didn't think he had left the building. She listened harder. She heard creaking upstairs.

'Be right back.'

She scooted back to the doorway, leaned over the crossed boards and into the next room. She looked up at the hole in the floor. There were only shades of black and gray, and an indistinct patch of starlight filtering through the first-floor windows.

In the other room there was also a long plank propped against one side of the hole in the ceiling. It reached to the floor above. It had been there all along – might have been used as a bridge across the hole, and been knocked down by the quake.

Maybe she could use it to climb up. She could boost Sophie ahead of her, or piggyback her. She looked again at the little girl.

'Can you make a fist?' she said.

Sophie looked at her hand. She worked to squeeze her fingers closed, and her face crumbled. She couldn't do it.

Jo needed to find another way out.

She crawled under the crossed boards and tiptoed across the room to a doorway leading to the basement hallway. The door was missing and there was debris blocking the doorframe. Jo leaned out the doorway and shot a burst of light down the hall. She saw a staircase at the front of the building. She saw wood framing and insulation, ripped-out wiring, and drywall half torn down. She saw . . . Oh, shit.

Above her in the hall, the ceiling was about to collapse. There was a single four-by-four support beam holding up a precarious piece of the kitchen above. She had a feeling that the glint she saw was a corner of a refrigerator.

She ducked back.

Closed her eyes, turned off the display, slunk back into the coal cellar.

From someplace above came Pray's mechanical voice. 'I know you're in the basement. I suggest you tell me what I want to know now. Then maybe I won't burn down this building with you inside it.'

Jo didn't answer. Sophie gasped.

'My late acquaintance Skunk, his Cadillac was an amazing

vehicle. It had everything, even a wet bar. With gasoline, bottles and rags, so he could whip up Molotov cocktails. And what do you know, here's one in my pocket.'

Jo tried to swallow but her throat refused. The darkness seemed to compress around her. The whole building seemed to be exhaling like a constrictor. The panic began to vibrate inside her. Heat, smoke, choking darkness, the building collapsing to pin her and Sophie motionless under a burning pyre – all it would take was a match.

*Run. Scream, punch, climb the hell out of here, right now.* Every synapse in her nervous system was trembling.

'Johanna,' Pray said.

The sound of her name in that flat buzz nearly made her pee her pants.

She lifted Sophie by the armpits. 'Come on.'

They crawled out of the coal hold under the crossed boards and scurried across the next room to the door. Sophie was unsteady. At the doorway Jo lifted her over the debris into the hallway and climbed out after her.

Wood creaked at the top of the staircase. *Buzz.* 'Johanna Beckett.'

Jo tried to breathe and her chest wouldn't expand. She felt like she was encased in wet cement. The sweat on her arms was freezing cold.

Pray was blocking the stairs. The coal chute was impossible for Sophie to climb. She glanced down the hallway behind them. It was a dead end.

She knew Pray didn't intend to leave her alive. He had the rage of the maimed. He had the shame of the tortured. He had a blind lust for revenge. She had nothing to give him, no names, no information that could slake his thirst to inflict pain.

She looked up and down the hallway. She looked at the wall.

Her breath came faster. Briefly she lit the cellphone, saw the hole in the drywall. There was a space on the other side of it.

A small space. A crawlspace, maybe where central heating ducts were going to be installed. A tunnel, coffin-wide. Tears stung her eyes.

The stairs creaked. 'You keep flashing me. I can flash you, permanently. It'll be very hot.' Another creak. 'Give me the names.'

'Pray.' Her voice was a whisper.

No. It was time to shoot with everything she had, everything she could conjure from the cobwebs and crumbling plaster around her. She couldn't slake his thirst for pain.

But she could incite it.

She cleared her throat and hoped her voice stayed level. 'Pray. If you burn down the building you'll never find out who ordered the attack on you.'

'Why?'

'Because the trail stops with me. I'm the last one who knows.' She bent down to Sophie's ear. 'While I'm talking, go through that hole in the drywall. Get on the other side of the wall. Get as far from it as you can.'

Sophie was shaking. So was she.

'Pray, if you kill me the names go up in flames.'

Trembling, Sophie scrambled through the hole in the framing and disappeared into the dark crawlspace on the other side. Jo picked up a sawn-off two-by-four, about three feet long.

The stairs creaked. Jo felt pressure on her chest, and the tears broke from the corners of her eyes.

'Let us go. I'll give you the names. Just let us out,' she said.

She crouched down and put her back against the half-ripped drywall along the wall next to the hole. The hole, a passage, so dark, the size of a sarcophagus. Oh, God. Her head throbbed. She bit back the urge to scream.

'Shall we make a deal?' Pray said.

He was coming down the stairs now. One slow step at a time. He thought he knew where they were. He'd been listening to their voices, and probably figured that they had nowhere to go.

'Yes, a deal. You back off, I'll leave the names right here,' she said.

'And I'll cover my eyes and count to ten?'

Meg Gardiner

Fucking joker. 'Don't play games.'

She heard the quaver in her voice. She pressed her back against the wall. She was going to have to move hellaciously fast, and she had to keep her head out of the way. She could live without her legs. She couldn't live without her brain.

And she had to get him close. So close that he couldn't throw the Molotov cocktail without immolating himself along with her. He didn't want to die. She had to draw him right up beside her, close enough to grab.

And she had seen what happened to Scott Southern when he tried the same thing.

'You want to know who ordered us to rob you?' she said.

His footsteps stopped. ' "Us?" '

'God. You really haven't figured it out, have you?' She laughed. She heard the edge of hysteria in her voice. 'I was the one in the mask that day.'

No sound. Would she hear him if he was gliding along like a rumor? Like a curse? Like—

'Prayers. You prayed. You cried and *begged*.'

Creaking. He was coming down the stairs slowly. He couldn't see her and didn't trust her. He wasn't close enough. She had to get him close enough to breathe on.

'Did you actually think we'd let a scuzzy low-level gangster in the club? You think because David Yoshida played in your executive poker game, you were accepted?'

'You did it as a dare. You robbed me for fun.'

'It was your fault. You shouldn't have resisted.'

'That weedy faggot tried to kill me. And you told him to get the chain.' Another step. 'For what? For money to fuel your lifestyles and businesses? Your yachts and IPOs? For blackmail?'

The creaking stopped. She forced her breathing to slow. Her heart was pounding in her ears. She braced the two-by-four in one hand. She was going to get one chance, and she had to time it right. She took out the phone. She heard Pray sliding his feet along the floor, feeling his way toward her.

She listened. How close? She counted to ten, aimed her cell-phone at the stairway and lit the display.

In the dark, it was like a flashbulb. Pray manifested like a monster, black and gray and gaunt, standing right above her.

She took the two-by-four and pushed one end against the cracked support beam that was supporting the kitchen floor above. Screaming her lungs out, she shoved with everything she had left. The support beam keened. She heard it splinter. She dropped the two-by-four and crab-crawled backward through the hole in the drywall, into the dank dirt of the hole behind it.

Everything came down in a horrible crash. The support beam disintegrated. The kitchen floor collapsed. Floorboards, bricks, a chimney, and the refrigerator pounded down like a hammer on a blacksmith's anvil. Choking dust blew through the wall. It filled her world.

# 39

Firefly lights. Jo had an inkling the blackness was being bombarded with firefly light. It wasn't merely spots in her eyes, not this time. A man's voice, muffled, called out.

'Sophie.'

The voice was distant, and cut with an edge of desperation. Jo lifted her head.

'Gabe,' she said.

Her throat was dry to dust. Her legs had cramped. Her left hand was stiff from dialing 911, over and over. Her right arm was numb from holding pressure on Sophie's arm.

The little girl was curled under Jo's shoulder, asleep. Please, Lord, let her be asleep. In the tiny crawlspace Jo inched her fingers across Sophie's cheek.

'It's your dad,' she whispered.

Gabe shouted, closer now. 'Jo, are you there?'

'Here.' She rasped it. Stroked Sophie's cheek. 'Sophie?'

The fireflies clarified into flashlights, and men's voices rose on the air. Footsteps charged down the stairs.

She heard an older man caution, 'Wait. We haven't cleared the basement – dammit.'

There was more noise. 'Jo. Sophie.'

Jo inched her hand through the debris field and clawed her fingers out of the crawlspace.

'Mother of God. Jo.'

'We're here.'

Frantic digging on the other side, the debris from the ceiling collapse being scooped out brick by brick. She held onto Sophie. The girl was silent, and so cold.

Gabe and the fire crew dug through the collapsed pile of kitchen debris that was blocking the exit. Then Jo heard the drywall being physically ripped off the wall, saw hands rip through the insulation.

'Sophie.'

She drew a breath. 'Daddy?'

Jo looked up and saw Gabe literally pull the wall apart. He leaned in, a shadow under the harsh flashlights in the hallway. She breathed. She had never in her life felt so certain she could let go, could release everything, and have somebody else catch it all.

'Sophie needs attention,' she said. 'Here, take her.'

Her voice was only a scratch. Gabe leaned in and reached for his daughter. She was limp in his arms when he lifted her out.

Jo reached up, for the light, for air, and couldn't pull herself up. The firefighters helped her out.

'Time is it?' she said.

'Midnight.'

Hours with that cut untreated. In the cold basement hallway, Gabe set Sophie down next to the wall. Jo saw the ugly debris field where she'd brought down the ceiling. It smelled of gasoline.

A firefighter took her arm. 'Come on. This structure's unstable.'

She pointed at the debris. 'There's a man under there.'

Their heads swiveled and they leveled their flashlights at the pile. She saw Gabe bent over Sophie, checking the field dressing on her arm. She looked at her own hands. They were stiff with blood.

'Sophie, baby. Look at me.' Gabe's voice was harsh. 'Cricket, come on, honey.'

The firefighters circled the kitchen debris, flashlights swinging. 'Here he is,' one called out. 'Why's there a gasoline smell?'

Jo walked over to him. 'He had a Molotov cocktail.'

The firefighters glanced at her with alarm. They took a step back.

She looked at Perry Ames. He was looking back at her. The firefighters swung their flashlights over the scene.

'Broken bottle, right there, with a rag,' one said.

'All right, let's get everybody out of here,' said another.

Pray held Jo's eyes. She climbed onto the debris field and leaned down next to him.

'What are you doing?' a firefighter said.

She put her fingers against his neck and found his pulse. She looked at his pupils. She saw that he was lucid, tracking her, that he had a clear airway.

She said to the firefighters, 'He has a pre-existing laryngeal injury. He speaks with a voice synthesizer.'

His eyes were spinning with pain and an almost feral anger. He formed his lips into words and spoke silently, staring at her.

The firefighters hollered up the stairs for an ambulance. They lifted debris from Pray's torso. He reeked of gasoline. Jo saw him take a deep breath. The refrigerator was across his lower legs. He was pinned, but not on the verge of death.

They lifted a splintered piece of a floorboard and he was able to move his arm.

Like daughter, like father. He had a lighter in his fist. He stared straight at her, and he began to flick it. His thumb was shaky. He couldn't get it to catch.

He mouthed words at Jo again, and kept flicking the lighter. She watched his lips. She wasn't a lip reader, but there was no mistaking what he was trying to tell her.

*Unequivocal death.*

'You want me to black tag you?' she said.

He flicked the lighter.

She reached down and took it from him. She flicked it, saw the flame brighten into a clean hot spire of light. She saw it reflected yellow in Pray's eyes.

She held it over his chest. 'Pray, you son of a bitch.'

She clicked it off and put it in her pocket. 'Pray for the people who are dead because of you.' She turned to go. 'And I don't have the names. I never did. The only person who might have known is dead. Skunk burned her to death. You can think about that on death row.'

The firefighters gaped at her. Jo walked past them.

'Leave him,' she said. 'He's a yellow tag. The little girl needs us.'

Down the hall, Gabe was bent over Sophie. Jo walked over to him, knelt at his side and put a hand on his arm. His muscles were rigid. She saw him blink away tears and grit his teeth.

'Gabe, let's get her out of here.'

He scooped Sophie into his arms and charged up the stairs, with Jo right behind him. He hit the ground floor and kept going, out the door and through the gate in the chain link fence where the lock had been cut open. She walked out into a night of blue spinning lights and biting air. She called to the firefighters.

'Do you have medical equipment in your truck?'

'Yeah.'

Jo put her hand on Gabe's arm and guided him to the curb. 'Set her on the grass.'

He lay Sophie down and knelt beside her, but his hands were shaking. He pressed his fingers against her wounds and looked at the night with empty desperation.

Jo leaned close. 'Stand down, sergeant.'

The firefighters hustled over with a first aid kit. They brought blankets and an IV. Jo pulled Gabe's hand off Sophie's wound and set it tight against Sophie's good hand.

'Hold onto her,' she said.

He held on while Jo and the firefighters went to work. He held on until Jo told him, 'She's a red tag, Gabe. She needs treatment, but she's going to make it.'

He looked at her, and bent over to kiss his daughter's face, over and over.

Jo stood up. She breathed, looked at the stars, listened to the night and the broken city struggling to awaken.

# 40

Jo stood at the cash register in the hospital cafeteria. The coffee cup in her hand was hot. She was thirsty. The power was back on, and the cashier wanted money.

'I don't have money,' she said.

The cashier chewed gum, staring her up and down.

'Not because I'm a zombie.' She reached into her pocket. 'I need this coffee. I'll give you my cellphone if you let me take this coffee.'

'A dollar fifty,' the cashier said.

A hand reached around her and put down a dollar bill and two quarters. 'That coffee's strong, but not strong enough to reanimate you.'

Amy Tang gave Jo a tart look that Jo guessed was her version of a grin. Behind it, Tang's eyes looked sleepless. And bright.

'How's your city, Amy?'

'Needs patching, but it's alive.'

'Rough night?'

'Not nearly as rough as it could have been. Things held.' They walked out of the cafeteria. 'How about you?'

'Had rougher. But not many.'

Tang took a cigarette from a pack and tapped it into her hand. 'Leo Fonsecca's dead. They found his body at the bottom of a stairwell in the courthouse. Garroted.'

'Oh no.' The news seemed to empty her out. 'I was afraid of something like that. Pray took Fonsecca's phone and used it to send me a text message. He lured me out into the streets.'

'Yeah. He was in Skunk's Cadillac by then. He waited for you to leave and go to the police station.'

They walked along the first-floor corridor toward the doors. The hospital had a buzz, the feeling of teeth set on edge, nerves revving in the red zone on the tachometer. But everybody was on the downslope of an adrenaline jag. Things had held. November 1st was a sunny day.

'I don't understand why they didn't—' Tang stopped herself. 'Sorry.'

'Why they didn't murder me in my house? I think they wanted to make it look like an accident. Give themselves more time to get away before suspicion fell on them.'

Jo pulled the lid off her coffee and took a long swallow. It was horrible. It had been brewing since the Nixon administration. She drank the whole thing greedily.

They reached the lobby. The sun shone through the doors.

'My forty-eight hours were up last night,' Jo said.

'I didn't actually expect you to collar the perp, but thanks. Though police apprehension techniques don't generally involve dropping a refrigerator on suspects. Paperwork's a bitch.'

The automatic doors opened. They strolled outside. The sun was gold between the skyscrapers of the financial district.

Jo took a deep breath. The city smelled like it always did. Dust, exhaust, salt water, energy. Tang lit her cigarette and inhaled.

'Before the quake hit I was going through Callie's files. I found Maki's secret,' she said. 'A few years ago, he had a stable of runway models. One of them developed bulimia and a serious meth habit. She died.' She exhaled. 'Her brother was William Willets. He met Maki at her funeral and they became lovers. Willets always credited Maki with helping him through his grief.'

'But?' Jo said.

'Maki admitted to the Dirty Secrets Club that he was the one who introduced the girl to meth. To keep her weight down. He drove her to her death.'

'And he rode that secret to a membership in the club? Callous.'

'That information must have got leaked, and Skunk revealed it to Willets.'

'That's why the murder-suicide on the boat. They must have fought about it, to the death.'

'Yeah.'

Jo tossed her empty coffee cup in a trash can. 'That's not all. I think Willets was a member of the club too. He was the one who garroted Pray.'

'No way.'

'Take another look at the video of the attack. The guy who looked like the cokehead Gatsby character. At one point Xochi says, "Will you." I thought it was a request, but now I think she was calling his name.'

'Jesus.'

'Last night, Pray was ranting about Xochi and the "weedy faggot" who attacked him. I think he learned who it was. He could have seen Willets's face in a hundred paparazzi photos with Maki.'

'I'll look at the video.'

'Do you think Skunk went out with them on the boat the night they died? Or met them via a motor boat?'

'And poured gasoline on the deck saying "Pray"? That's my guess. The burning boat became a flare, a signal to others in the club what would happen to them if they didn't turn over the names of the people who attacked his boss.'

Morning traffic was light. Life was rolling forward, as it always did.

'Some club,' Jo said. 'All fun and games until somebody loses an eye.'

'That line going in your report?'

'I haven't submitted my psychological autopsy report. I haven't determined the manner of Callie Harding's death yet.'

Tang was squinting like she had sand in her eyes. Her black T-shirt was tired. Her black boots were dirty. She would have looked like she'd lost Fight Night at the biker bar, if she hadn't had the face of a cuddly toy.

She took out her PDA. 'We got the CCTV footage from the camera in the stairwell at the Stockton Street Tunnel.'

She found the video. It was only fifty-five seconds of footage, but it was enough. Jo watched with increasing surprise and under-standing.

She gave back the PDA. 'Can you make me a copy?'

'Of course. There's more, too. Forensic techs recovered a cellphone from Stockton Street. And a weapon from Skunk's Cadillac.'

'Fingerprints?'

'And phone records. What do you think?'

'That we need to go upstairs and talk to Angelika Meyer.'

'My thoughts exactly.'

Halfway to the elevator, they saw Gabe coming down the hall. Sophie was walking at his side. She was wearing a pair of scrubs sized xxx-Small, rolled up so she didn't step on them. Her bandaged arm was in a sling. She looked pale even though her zombie makeup had been washed off, Jo guessed by a brusque and relieved father. She was holding a brand new Bratz.

Jo smiled. 'Don't scare your dad with that.'

'Dad got it for me.'

'She can have anything she wants,' Gabe said. 'For the next week. Don't start pricing cars.' He looked at Jo. 'And you should get yourself some coffee. Your throat's hoarse.'

Sophie said, 'That's because she sang for so long.'

'What?'

'In the crawlspace. Jo sang the whole time. TV songs. It kept us awake.'

Gabe gazed at Jo. His eyes were dark, the storms veiled. 'It's what the best people do when they need to keep your spirits up. It's a classic.'

He was trying to maintain his composure. Jo put her hand around his wrist. He pulled her close, laid his cheek against hers, opened his mouth to speak and closed it again.

Jo whispered in his ear. 'Soon.'

He nodded, put his hand to the corners of his eyes and walked with Sophie toward the morning.

Geli Meyer was sitting up in bed drinking orange juice. She put down her glass when Jo and Amy came through the door.

Tang approached the bed. 'Good to see you looking well, Geli. Listen closely. Your father is in custody, and he's never getting out of prison again. He's going to be charged with capital murder for killing Leo Fonsecca.'

Meyer went as still as a stone.

'We found your cellphone in a storm drain on Stockton Street near the crash site. It was ejected from Callie's BMW in the wreck. And we got your call records.'

Meyer reached for the phone. 'I want a lawyer.'

'Go ahead. Call the entire law faculty at Hastings. We also found a handgun in Levon Skutlek's Cadillac. A .32 caliber HK semi-automatic pistol. It's registered to the late David Yoshida, Junior. It has your fingerprints on it.'

Meyer had one hand on the phone, but she didn't dial.

'Skunk got it from Callie's BMW after the wreck, didn't he? He took it out of your hand.'

Meyer held onto the phone.

'Here's the lowdown,' Tang said. 'You can go to prison for conspiracy, for murder, for felony murder for your part in further-ing Perry Ames's escape plan and vendetta. Or you can talk.' She smiled. 'You can talk to Doctor Beckett. She'd love to shrink your head.'

Meyer let go of the phone.

'You don't understand. You couldn't.' Meyer was sunk in the bed, arms crossed. The yellow sunlight coming through the window striped her face with bars.

Jo sat quietly by the bedside. 'He's your father. I understand your loyalty to him. I don't understand why you got involved with Doctor Yoshida's son.'

'The Dirty Secrets Club hurt us. They broke up our family. After they attacked Perry, one of them called the police. Perry was arrested for illegal gambling and that fraud and extortion garbage. As if the DSC didn't extort more money from all its members than he ever did.'

Jo glanced at Tang. Tang gave the look back.

'What about David Yoshida, Junior?' Jo said.

'He didn't do anything he didn't want to. He was a rich boy with an addictive personality. He took the Fentanyl willingly.'

'The first dose? Or the next two?'

Meyer looked at her with fierce eyes. 'They took my dad away from me. From *me*. They ruined Perry's life. Why should I feel sorry for Doctor Yoshida? His son was a skel.' She wiped her nose. 'NHI. No Humans Involved. David Junior was a drug addict who didn't care if he lived or died. He'd been hurting his father for years. He *wanted* to hurt his father. I just helped him get his wish.'

Tang leaned against the door, saying nothing.

Jo wove her fingers together. 'The night of the wreck.'

'What about it?'

'Callie offered you a ride home?'

'I asked her for a ride. It was almost one a.m.' She seemed to relax. Her eyes were intense.

She wanted to confess. She wanted to enjoy telling the secret. She was lording it over Jo and Amy, as if dispensing power and favors.

'Callie never suspected. She was such a hard case, so clever, and she never once suspected. Not even up to the second I showed her the HK.'

'So you pulled the gun and demanded information about Pray's attackers.'

'Their names. I told Callie to drive and not to stop. I took her phone. Held the gun on her. She didn't want to talk. But I knew I could make her.'

'While she was driving, you made some phone calls yourself,' Jo said.

Meyer didn't disagree. They had her phone records. Jo didn't reveal what she knew must have happened: while Meyer was dialing, Callie was able to write *Pray* on her wrist, and later get her lipstick and write *dirty* on her thigh.

'Callie wasn't running from anybody that night, was she? Nobody was chasing her,' Jo said.

'I got her to run,' Meyer said.

Jo wanted her to say it. She knew what the video footage from the bridge showed, but wanted Meyer to explain it.

'What did you tell her in the car?'

'I told her about Perry. I made her understand. About the extortion, the robbery, how the Dirty Secrets Club destroyed his life. I told her about the injustice.' Her eyes were agitated. 'If he has to stay in prison he'll kill himself. That's what I told her, how bad it is for him. He begged me to help him, because nobody else will. And without justice, he'll kill himself.'

'Is that what he told you? If you didn't help him, he'd kill himself?'

'Yes. Jesus Christ. Aren't you listening? That's how bad it is.'

Jo leaned on her knees. Pray had manipulated her into helping him by threatening suicide. The man was a sociopath.

'Callie wasn't running *from* something when she passed Officer Cruz's patrol car, was she? She was running *toward* the Stockton Street Bridge. Because time was running out,' Jo said.

Meyer's face turned sly.

'We saw the CCTV footage from the bridge,' Jo said. 'We know Skunk was there.'

That's what the stairwell cameras showed. Skunk on the bridge, pacing back and forth immediately before the crash.

'Callie went nuts,' Meyer said.

'Why?'

'Because she thought she needed to get there in a hurry.'

'Why was that?'

'Because she was too stubborn to tell me what I needed to know.'

'What did you threaten her with?' Jo said.

'Nothing real. I told her Skunk was there with some other members of the club, and was going to do something.'

'What kind of something?'

'Get one of the DSC members to kill somebody.'

'Who?'

'Toss Scott Southern's kid off the bridge.'

Jo's heart shrank, but she kept her voice even. 'But you made all that up.'

'It was easy. She panicked. She totally freaked. I found her notes on the Dirty Secrets Club. I found out about Xochi Zapata and Scott Southern. And I knew Callie was all twisted up over this dare thing. She was obsessed. She liked to punish people.' Meyer shook her head and laughed. 'She believed every bit of it.'

'And Callie couldn't disprove anything you were saying, because you'd isolated her in the car and taken her phone.'

Tang said, 'So Callie floored it, hell for leather, thinking that this grand plan of hers, the Dirty Secrets Club, which was supposed to bring people to justice, was instead going to get innocent people killed?'

Meyer nodded.

'And it backfired,' Jo said. 'You got nothing.'

'Not nothing. I got Southern's and Zapata's names, and gave them to Skunk.'

'But you wanted the name of the person who ordered Xochi and William Willets to attack your father, and you didn't get that.'

The passion in Meyer's eyes began to dim.

'Instead Callie drove straight down Stockton Street. Do you remember the rest?'

'She begged the cop for help. But it was too late. I was on the phone with Skunk. I told her he was gonna have the club people carry out the dare and throw the kid over.'

'And she floored it.'

'Like a maniac.'

'*Stop it.* That's what you said to me, Geli. You wanted me to stop the Dirty Secrets Club. But you're the one who's been stopped.' Jo leaned back. 'And now three innocent people are dead. You're going to go to prison. And you'll never see your father again.'

Meyer looked at her for a moment. When she started screaming, Jo didn't think she'd ever stop.

## 41

The sun stayed out for the rest of the week. When Jo walked into Java Jones Friday morning, the city was running at ninety percent. There were still pockets without electricity and gas, dozens of buildings condemned or uninhabitable. But things were going ahead. The Forty-Niners were playing a home game on Sunday. They'd already passed out black armbands in memory of Scott Southern.

Tina looked particularly puckish behind the counter. When Jo walked in she smiled. 'Americano for my lovely sister.' The music was lush and sweeping, a piano concerto to break the heart, apparently, because halfway through pouring Jo's coffee Tina had to stop, listen and regain her composure.

She put Jo's mug on the counter. 'Rachmaninoff. You should be crying too.'

'Not today, sis.'

Jo carried her coffee to the table by the window where Amy Tang was having her breakfast. She sat down and handed her a copy of her preliminary report.

'You can check for corrections, but the gist is there,' she said.

'Bottom line?'

'The crash of Callie Harding's BMW was deliberate.'

Tang leaned back. 'What convinces you?'

'That during the race across town in the BMW, Callie wrote "Pray" on her wrist and "dirty" on her thigh, as clues.'

'Clues about?' Tang said.

'About what was behind her death.'

'She knew she was going to die? She killed herself?'

'She became willing to sacrifice herself,' Jo said. 'Callie wrote clues on her own body, to let the police know what was going on. That meant she didn't think she would be alive to tell the police. She had to get the information to them somehow. She may have hoped to live, but she was willing to die to stop what she thought was a murder at the bridge.'

And maybe she thought it was the only way she could redeem herself for the mess she had unleashed.

Tang said, 'And on the race to the bridge, Callie caught a lucky break. She drove past a cop.'

'She ran the red light because she wanted Officer Cruz to join the chase. At that point Meyer knew she'd blown it. She thought she'd set things up to keep Callie under her control, to isolate her and spring all this on her as a trap. But she let her keep control of the one thing that ended up being a deadly weapon.'

'The BMW.'

'Right. Once Cruz joined the chase, Meyer desperately wanted to stop the whole thing and get away. That's when she fought with Callie and tried to jump from the BMW.' Jo sat back. 'And then the whole thing went even more wildly wrong.'

Callie saw Officer Cruz in her rearview mirror, gaining on her. She thought she had time to ask him for assistance. She stopped, backed up, and shouted to him.

' "Help me." She even stuck her left hand up to the driver's window, with the word *Pray* written on it.' Jo shook her head. 'But that's when Meyer got through to Skunk and told him to go ahead with killing the kid. It wasn't for real, but there was no time for Callie to explain to Officer Cruz. She knew Cruz would continue following her. She accelerated toward the bridge.'

Tang fiddled with a coffee stirrer. 'On the bridge, Skunk ran out of the way. Why didn't Callie chase him?'

'No time. Panic. Miscalculation,' Jo said. 'She went racing down Stockton toward the bridge. She saw Skunk standing there. She saw he didn't have the kid.'

'Didn't that tell her it was a hoax?' Tang said.

'She thought they'd already thrown the boy off. She kept going headlong, straight into the wall.'

They sat for a minute. Tang finished her coffee. 'They?'

'It's not over,' Jo said.

'Don't tell me that. I'd rather eat a raw egg than hear that.'

'There's one piece missing.' And it was like a piece of broken glass. Hard to see and liable to cut without warning. 'Somebody tried to initiate me into the Dirty Secrets Club with that anonymous note about Daniel's death.'

'Pray?'

'No.'

'Is somebody still threatening you . . .?' Tang said.

'The threat's there. And I want to stop it.'

'What do you have in mind?'

'Meyer said something. That she got Callie to think Dirty Secrets Club *members* were conducting a dare that night on the bridge, messing around to win points by threatening to toss Scott Southern's little boy off the bridge. I think I know who Callie thought it was, and why it got her so hysterical. And I think the same somebody took a dare to see if they could bring me down.'

The door opened and Ferd Bismuth trundled in. When he saw Jo he pushed his glasses up his nose, glanced around furtively and came over. He slumped down at the table. The aroma of Brylcreem filled the air.

'Can we speak in confidence?' he said.

'Ferd, this is Amy Tang.' Jo gestured at the lieutenant. He gave Tang a salute. Jo said, 'I can give you ninety seconds.'

'It's about Mr Peebles.' His brow crenellated. 'Can monkeys develop psychological problems? Neuroses? Unhealthy obsessions?'

She sighed. 'I'm not a simian therapist, but yes.'

'Oh, dear. That's what I was afraid of. I think the trauma of his near-death experience has caused him to snap.' He hunched lower, eyes darting. 'He's become a kleptomaniac.'

Jo felt herself heating. 'He'd better not have lifted my wallet.'

Ferd reached into his pocket and pulled out a baseball. He set it on the table. He gestured at it and spread his hands, frantically, like *Help!*

Jo and Tang gaped at it. It was an old Willie Mays autographed ball.

'I've seen this before,' Jo said.

Tang nudged it with a clean coffee stirrer. 'I think I know where this came from.'

Ferd wrung his hands. 'Can he be treated?'

'Don't worry,' Tang said, 'we'll take care of this.'

'And Mr Peebles won't even have to testify. I'll get him immunity,' Jo said.

Ferd balled his fists with relief. 'Thank you. Thank you.' He shook Jo's hand, stood up and shook Tang's. 'Thank you.'

When he dashed out the door, they looked at each other.

'Does this relate to what you were saying, about people in the club daring each other to do crazy things?'

'Yeah. And to them trying to toy with me. The monkey could only have gotten that ball from Skunk's Cadillac. And if Skunk or Pray had it, there's only one person who could have given it to them.'

'What do you want to do?'

Jo parked the rental car and got out into bracing autumn sunshine. Cypress trees and Monterey pines stood like sentinels all along the roadway at Lands' End. The hills of Lincoln Park were verdant. People sat on the benches, watching the tide flow in. The Pacific was a booming blue, pricked with whitecaps. She walked to the overlook. Below, the ocean frothed white around the rocks. To her right she could see the Golden Gate Bridge. Straight ahead, the brown hills of Marin County rolled north to Point Reyes, Bodega Bay, the rocks where Daniel had died, to San Rafael and the cemetery where he was buried. Jo leaned on a fence post. The wind lifted her hair. She waited.

It was half an hour before the silver Maserati thrummed into the parking lot. The driver's door opened and the sounds of Nirvana tumbled out. Jo gazed out to sea and waited for Gregory Harding to join her.

Callie's ex-husband was wearing a banker's slick suit with an open-collared shirt and his Rolex. He propped his sunglasses on top of his arctic blond head.

'What's this about, Doctor Beckett?'

'A courtesy. You were Callie's next of kin. I thought you should know what my psychological autopsy report is going to say.'

'Shall we cut the crap? What nasty news do you have to break to me?'

'I got an anonymous letter this week. It was an invitation to join the Dirty Secrets Club.' She turned to face him. 'It set my hair on fire. But when I calmed down, I wondered, why send it? And it came down to this. I got the note because somebody was trying to wreck my investigation and expose me to danger.'

'And?' Harding glanced at his watch. 'I'm sorry, but what does this have to do with Callie? I have a busy day. Can you get to the point?'

'You sent the note, Greg.'

He put a foot on the anchor chains that made up the fence. He stared at his hands, checked his cuticles, smoothed down a hangnail.

She took hold of his wrist and looked at his Rolex. 'Custom detailing, very nice. How much did it cost to get the black diamond inserted on the face?'

He withdrew his wrist and put his right hand over the watch.

'You're a member of the Dirty Secrets Club. And you're playing truth or dare. With my life.'

His expression didn't change. He reached into his inside pocket and took out a portable radio frequency scanner. He turned it on.

'Hold out your arms.'

'You think I'm wired?' she said.

'You're a police consultant. Of course you're wired.'

He waved the scanner over Jo's shirt. It squelched. Harding looked at her as he would at a toad he was about to step on, and moved toward her.

She put out a hand. Reluctantly, feeling the wind on her neck, she unbuttoned her pea coat, reached around beneath her shirt and unstrapped the digital microrecorder she had taped to the small of her back. Harding held out his hand. She gave it to him.

He dropped it and ground it under his heel. 'Now your phone.'

She held it out. 'Just wand it. Don't squash it.'

He held it under the scanner. The signal squeaked. He took out the battery and hurled it over the rail into the riptides below.

'Satisfied?' Jo said.

He put the scanner away. 'You think you're a genius, don't you? The puzzle mistress, mind-fucker extraordinaire. You're an amateur.'

'You had me going, I'll admit,' Jo said. 'The grieving ex. Confused about why Callie turned a law school bullshit session into the real deal. In fact, you and she were the first two members of the club, weren't you?'

'Are we going to have a pissing contest to see who's got the other's number? I can piss a whole lot farther than you. Even if you are a black widow.' He leaned on the fence. 'You'll never prove it. There's no mention of my name in Callie's files. She certainly didn't have my résumé in her desk. You're guessing.'

'You know that for sure, do you?'

He turned and smiled, like a lizard. 'She never put my name in the files. Because she loved me. She loved fucking me too much.'

'Did she know you were blackmailing the other members?'

His smile stayed icy, but his eyes withdrew.

'I noticed something,' she said. 'In Scott Southern's suicide note, in Xochi Zapata's video, in the rant Perry Ames shouted at me the other night – and in what Geli Meyer talked about in her confession. At some point, they all talked about blackmail.'

He stared out over the headlands.

'Pray even talked about extortion being used to fund club members' businesses and IPOs,' she said.

His smile was diminishing. He looked as cold as an icepick.

'You forced Xochi Zapata and William Willets to rob Perry Ames. That was not only a dare, but the price of keeping their secrets,' she said.

'This is bullshit.'

'Members gain status by pulling stunts and getting away with them. That's what you decided to do to me, the first day we met. You decided to play Truth or Dare with me. Now that I look back, it was obvious. You practically shoved information about the DSC at me. You faked a tantrum at Callie's and handed me the "welcome to the club" note in a way that made it look totally innocent. Then at the Fairmont, you flat-out handed over her notebook with all the rules in it.'

He tried ignoring her. She tilted her head. 'How much did it cost you to find out how my husband died – some Google research and a few bribes?'

He refused to look at her. 'You'd be surprised how cheaply people will sell information. Gossip. Secrets. They love it. They'll practically give it away.'

'How much for the claim I killed my husband?'

'Forty bucks, plus a Maserati polo shirt. Guy was a former civilian dispatcher for the Air National Guard.'

She felt a sour taste in her mouth. Hurting people was a cheap commodity. 'Originally I thought by sending the note, you were trying to scare me into stopping my investigation. It was getting too close to you. But that was exactly backwards. You tried to tell me as much about the Dirty Secrets Club as possible, from the very start. You were dancing in the fire, giving me Callie's notebooks. You wanted to see if you could slide by right in plain view. But then you went farther. You gave my name to Pray.'

He stared at his shoes. He seemed inordinately pleased by how shiny they were.

'How did you do that?' Jo said. 'Just tell me that.'

He slid a glance her way. 'You know you'll never prove a thing, don't you? I'm golden. Nobody's going to touch me.'

'So tell me. I'm dying to know.'

'Insatiable curiosity, is it?'

'Professional hazard. Nature of the people who become shrinks.'

He smiled. 'I'm the one who tapped Susan – I mean Xochi Zapata – into the club. Why do you think that is?'

'You tell me.'

'Venture capital is the grease that drives business in Silicon Valley.' He swept an arm out, showing Jo the glorious panorama. 'From San Francisco down to San Jose, the entire tech industry slides on money. And I'm the one who provides it. No matter what. If we need bucks to get a deal going, I get it.'

'Raising money isn't always clean, is that what you're saying?'

'You actually look at the dank underside of people's minds, and it doesn't occur to you that money is dirty too?'

She kept her face neutral. 'You wanted funds for your business, didn't you? You raised it by blackmailing other members of the club.'

'Imagination is my strong suit.'

'Do tell.'

'It was a perfect set-up. Get all these rich thrill-seekers to join the club by telling us their secrets. Then blackmail them. I recruited them, bilked them, and then moved them on up to a higher level where they got a cut of the proceeds by blackmailing the next round of new members.'

'A pyramid scheme.'

'I like the classics.'

The wind twisted her hair. 'And when Perry Ames applied to join, you tried to blackmail him. And he was the wrong guy.'

'Yeah, that one didn't go as well as it could. A lowlife gambling promoter, I should have known he was trouble. Though I did get the money.'

'Were you there, Greg? When William Willets nearly killed Ames?'

'Of course not. He never knew I was involved in that. I'd had Xochi and Will set up the meeting. My name was never mentioned to him.'

'You're the one Pray's been after all along.'

He smiled. 'He wants the name of the man who ordered the robbery. He never knew he killed the people who could have given it to him. He killed Willets and Xochi, and burned the trail to me.'

'Perfect.'

'It is, isn't it?'

'Did you ever feel bad about stealing his money and letting him be garroted?'

'Feel bad about exterminating a cockroach? Why should I?'

'And then poor Xochi couldn't keep quiet, could she? She was a compulsive babbler. Once she was in the club, she leaked information to people she shouldn't have. Word got out on the street, didn't it?'

'So we didn't bat a thousand with our membership drive. That problem's solved.'

'You actually think the DSC is going to keep going? You're planning your next membership drive to replenish the ranks?'

'Why not? Nobody's going to believe you. You're a weak woman who killed two people through medical incompetence. You have no proof of anything you're hearing today. And if for some reason anybody does believe your incredible tale, I'll explain that I came to you in confidence, for therapy, and you're breaching your professional obligations. No reputable psychiatrist reveals what their patients tell them. You'd lose your license.'

The wind shook the Monterey pines. 'Why did you pass my name around to the members of the club? Did you really want to egg me into joining?'

'No. You don't have the juice. You couldn't cut it.'

'So by giving my name to Pray, you thought you might even lure Pray into killing me, solving your problem for good. Of course, you were also exposing yourself to the risk that I or the cops would trace things back to you.'

'But that was my challenge. It was all part of the fun.' He smiled. 'Just like meeting Pray before he went after you was part of the fun. David Yoshida was the one who had lured him into applying to join the club – so he just thought I was Callie's ex, nothing more.'

'You wanted me to die an equivocal death. That's why you told Pray and Skunk not to shoot me. You wanted it to look like an accident.'

'I figured suicide would be too much trouble to arrange.' The smile was chilly. 'Equivocal death. Irony is a big thing with me. We don't have enough irony in America.'

He laughed. 'Don't you see? You have no proof. You have nothing.'

'Having fun bragging to me?'

'It ain't bragging if you really done it.'

'You really took the club and ran with it, didn't you?'

'Callie had a good idea. It took me to fine-tune it. She was judgmental and straightforward. I can see around corners.'

'How entertaining for you.'

His smile was becoming broader. 'This is really getting your goat. There's no chance I'll ever be prosecuted. No evidence to link me to Perry Ames. Xochi might eventually have told, but she's dead. It's a foolproof setup.'

'Maybe this is a good time to tell you, Greg. You're so shit-hot on secrets. I know something you don't.'

'Yippee-kay-fucking-yay.'

'You and Callie spent all the years you were divorced trying to destroy each other, didn't you? It's not that hard to figure out. Everything you've said tells me you had a destructive obsession with each other. Sexual and emotional.'

He said nothing.

'You said she punished people. You meant she punished you. And you punished her. Did she know you'd turned the DSC into your own private blackmail operation?'

'She must have realized it the night she died.'

He was so self-satisfied, so angry, so full of hubris, that she wanted to retch. She kept her face calm. 'That was how you were secretly punishing her.'

He smiled. Jo let him enjoy the moment.

'Callie had a secret too. Something that's going to punish you permanently. The Dirty Secrets Club is a sting operation.'

His head tilted, just slightly.

'That's right,' she said.

Jo watched his mouth curl, his diaphragm catch, as though he'd just choked on a lump of meat. He backed up and caught his breath, trying to right himself.

His lips drew back. 'I'll come after you anyway. I'll get you. So you won't talk. The only way to stop me would be to kill me, and you don't have the guts.'

The sun glinted from the ocean. She didn't move. 'You're right, I won't. I took an oath. It's a bitch on days like today, but I abide by it. First, do no harm.'

He sneered. 'Jesus Christ. Quilt it on a sampler and sing God Bless the USA. Fuck you. I took no oath.'

Twenty yards down the path, Gabe Quintana stood up from the park bench where he was sitting. He strolled toward them, removing an earpiece from his iPod.

'Excuse me,' he said.

Harding didn't look at him. 'Get lost.'

Gabe stopped two feet from Harding. 'I'm sorry, sir, but I couldn't help hearing what you said to the lady.'

'Fuck off.'

'No.'

Harding looked at Gabe and did a doubletake, sensing an undercurrent of violence.

'I said, I heard everything. And I'm not barred from backing Doctor Beckett up.'

Harding's mouth pinched.

'And I happened to be recording dictation on my iPod. My mike may have picked up what you were saying.'

'Listen, pal, you don't—'

'And nothing, repeat, nothing bad is going to happen to this woman. Because I also took an oath. That Others May Live. That means Jo. And I'll kill you to make sure I keep that oath.'

Gabe stepped closer and lowered his voice. 'Pray went after my daughter with a Molotov cocktail. But you're leaving here alive. Think about how lucky that makes you.'

Harding looked down.

Jo turned to go, and turned back. 'One last thing. I think you lost this.' From the pocket of her pea coat she took out a baseball. 'I don't know how it got in Skunk's Cadillac, but you had to have had a part in it.' She tossed and caught it, and turned it over in her hand. 'Willie Mays. My expert says it's the ball from the

1954 Series. Worth over a hundred thousand dollars. I don't know how you'll fence it on eBay to fund your next deal, but good luck.'

She turned toward the cliff and threw it over the fence, a high arcing fastball that sailed into the blue and down toward the rocks.

'Jesus Christ. You bitch—'

He vaulted over the fence, ran to the drop off and began scrambling down the cliffside.

Jo called after him. 'I'll see you in court, Mr Harding.'

She saw his manicured hands and shining Rolex claw at the dirt as he bumbled his way down. She and Gabe watched until he disappeared. They turned and walked away.

A hundred yards down the path, she said, 'May I borrow your phone?'

He handed it to her. She called Amy Tang, who was down the street having coffee at the Seal Rock Inn.

'All yours,' Jo said.

She handed the phone back to Gabe. 'What were you recording on your iPod, the Beatitudes? Blessed are the peacemakers?'

'John Wayne. Grab 'em by the balls, and their hearts and minds will follow.'

They walked farther. He said, 'When do you think he'll figure out you bought that baseball at Manny's Sporting Goods this morning and signed it yourself?'

They kept walking.

'You're smiling,' he said.

She was. She felt the sun on her face, the breeze caressing her hair, the day spreading before her. A weight was gone from her shoulders.

'Tell me?' Gabe said.

She heard the roar of the sea behind her.

'Is it a secret?' Gabe said.

'Hell, no.'

She knew the Marin headlands would always be behind her, reminding her where Daniel lay. She didn't know what lay ahead, but she could risk that.

'When am I going to find out?' he said.

She pulled him to a stop. She turned him to face her and put her hands on either side of his face. She felt his arms curve around her back and draw her close to him. She gave him a smile, and stood on tiptoe.

'Now,' she said.